Civil and Uncivil Violence in Lebanon

History and Society of the Modern Middle East
Leila Fawaz, General Editor

The History and Society of the Modern Middle East
Leila Fawaz, General Editor

Janet Afary. *The Iranian Constitution, 1906–1911: Grassroots Democracy, Social Democracy, and the Origins of Feminism*

Andrea B. Rugh. *Within the Circle: Parents and Children in an Arab Village*

Juan Cole. *Modernity and the Millennium: The Genesis of the Baha'i Faith in the Nineteenth-Century Middle East*

Selma Botman. *Engendering Citizenship in Egypt*

Thomas Philipp. *Acre: The Rise and Fall of a Palestinian City, 1730–1831*

Elizabeth Thompson. *Colonial Citizens: Republican Rights, Paternal Privilege, and Gender in French Syria and Lebanon*

Civil and Uncivil Violence in Lebanon

*A History of the Internationalization
of Communal Conflict*

Samir Khalaf

COLUMBIA   UNIVERSITY   PRESS   NEW   YORK

COLUMBIA UNIVERSITY PRESS
Publishers Since 1893
New York   Chichester, West Sussex
Copyright © 2002 Columbia University Press

Library of Congress Cataloging-in-Publication Data
Khalaf, Samir.
    Civil and uncivil violence in Lebanon : a history of the internationalization of
human contact / Samir Khalaf.
        p. cm. — (The history and society of the modern Middle East)
    Includes bibliographical references and index.
    ISBN 0–231–12476–7 (cl. : alk. paper)
    1. Lebanon — History — 20th century. 2. Violence — Lebanon — History —
20th century. I. Title. II. History and society of the modern Middle East series.
DS87.K393 2002
956.9204 — dc21   2001058253

Columbia University Press books
are printed on permanent and durable acid-free paper.
Printed in the United States of America

c   10   9   8   7   6   5   4   3   2   1

To My Family

Roseanne, George and Ramzi
A tender heaven in a heartless world

Contents

Preface

"Bloody encounters have been the most visible molders of peoples' collective destinies."
—A. B. Schmookler, *Out of Weakness* (1988)

Lebanon's national image has been, for much of its checkered political history, associated with three seemingly intractable aberrations: protracted and displaced hostility, reawakened communal solidarities and obsessive dependence on, often subservience to, external patronage or foreign intervention. To a considerable extent, in fact, these are also the country's defining elements which, off and on, have informed much of the country's sanguinary history with collective strife.

The overriding thrust of the study is predicated by the view that by probing into the persisting character of those three basic elements one can better understand the destabilizing consequences of the interplay between internal divisions and external dislocations and, consequently, the changing form and magnitude of collective strife.

The internal disparities are generally a byproduct of deep cultural cleavages inherent in sharp communal, confessional, and other primordial and segmental loyalties. Juxtaposed to these are the uneven socioeconomic and cultural transformations that have always had a differential impact on the relative standing of the various communities.

The external sources are discordant and divisive in at least three respects. First, in earlier and more recent episodes of collective strife, as the country became increasingly embroiled in superpower rivalries, it could not be sheltered from the destabilizing consequences of such struggles. As this occurred, the original issues provoking the conflict receded. Threatened and marginalized groups, victims of internal socioeconomic disparities or political neglect, sought external protection and patronage. Foreign powers, keen on gaining inroads into the region, have always been too eager to rush into the fray. Such intervention, solicited or otherwise, almost always served to polarize the factions and deepen sources of hostility. In short, Lebanon again and again became an object and victim of these "inside-outside" dialectics.

Second, unresolved regional conflicts, incited by ideological rifts and personal rivalries, also managed to find receptive grounds among the disenfranchised and neglected groups. Much like the insidious character of super-power intervention, regional rivalries were also used as wedges or sources of political patronage. Hence, ideological shifts in adjacent regimes — be they Pan-Arabist, Ba'thist, Socialist, Islamist, or the resurgence of Palestinian resistance — managed likewise to reinforce communal and sectarian cleavages. They also served as proxy platforms for the radicalization of discontent and social unrest.

Finally and, perhaps, more penetrable are the recent global transformations engendered by the transnational information highway, media technologies, and the diffusion of mass culture, life styles, migrant labor, marketing, and consumerism. Here, as well, local groups markedly differ in their resistance or adaptation to such threatening incursions.

For purposes of analysis, three different layers or magnitudes of violence are identified. First, there is social strife, the byproduct of forces such as economic disparities, asymmetrical development, relative deprivation, and ideological rivalries. Normally, these are not militant in character and express themselves in contentious but fairly nonbelligerent forms of collective protest and political mobilization. Second, if the disparities persist and the resulting hostilities are not redressed, conflict and discord could readily become more militant and bellicose. More so when such disparities are accompanied by feelings of threatened communal heritage and confessional loyalties. It is here that social discord is transformed (or deformed) into communal violence. It is also at this point that *civil strife* passes the threshold of no return into *civil war*. Finally, civil violence is not, or does not always remain "civil." When incited by the atavism of reawakened tribalism, enmity, and deep-seated suspicion of the "other," internecine feuds and unresolved regional or global rivalries, collective violence easily slips into the incivility of proxy wars and surrogate victimization. Willfully or otherwise, regional and foreign powers are drawn into the conflict. Invariably, such intervention heightens the intensity of internal conflict. It is here that violence acquires its own self-destructive logic and spirals into that atrocious cycle of unrelenting cruelties.

Given the anomalous ethos of "no victor and no vanquished," which has

long characterized Lebanon's political history, it is understandable how violence can find the recurrent circumstances to reproduce itself. Or, more
likely, when the cruelties of protracted strife become a sanitized or ordinary
routine, they also become more tolerable than the intolerable psychic
wounds of defeat. Indeed, even bloody decisive confrontations never ended
or were never permitted to end, by the unequivocal defeat or victory of one
group over the other. It is in this sense that virtually all the wars that beleaguered Lebanon were for naught. Despite the intensity, massiveness, and
depth of damage and injury, the fighting went on. More disheartening, the
resort to violence neither redressed the internal gaps and imbalances nor
ushered the country into a more civil and peaceful form of pluralism or
guarded co-existence.

Violence was not only relentless, protracted, and futile. It also assumed,
particularly during the last interludes of civil strife, even more pathological
forms: it became random, diffused, and displaced. Unlike other comparable
encounters with civil strife, which are often swift and localized and where
much of the population could remain sheltered from its cruelties, the Lebanese experience has been much more overwhelming and homogenizing.
The savagery of violence was also compounded by its indiscriminate, random and reckless character. Hence there is hardly a Lebanese today who
could be exempt from some of its atrocities, either directly or vicariously as
a mediated experience. Virtually no area of the country has been spared the
ravages of war.

Equally unsettling, the rounds of fighting had no predictable or coherent
logic to them. They were everywhere and nowhere. Everywhere, because
they could not be confined to one specific area or a few combatants. Nowhere, because they were unidentified or linked to one explicit or overt
cause. Repeated cycles or episodes of violence erupted, faded, and resurfaced
for no recognized or coherent reason.

Most menacing, perhaps, was the displaced and surrogate character of
violence and victimization. As the hostility degenerated into internecine
fighting between fractious groups, combatants were often entrapped in localized turf wars where they ended up avenging almost anyone, including
their own kinsmen. This is, doubtless, the most perfidious feature of the
incivility of violence. Fighters were killing not those they wanted to kill but
those they could kill. In repeated episodes of such in-group hostility wanton
killing was the bloodiest in terms of its victimization of innocent bystanders.

Within this context it is instructive, both empirically and conceptually,
to identify and account for those critical watersheds during which commu-

nalism, foreign intervention and the magnitude of violence converge and reinforce each other. Indeed, an exploration of the future prospects of any society caught up with such indelible realities necessitates a comprehensive and probing analysis of their manifestations and consequences. It is bizarre after all to journey into a future without having some notion about where a society is going, how it is going to get there and what one will find upon arrival? No one today can plot such a journey in Lebanon without first considering the probable outcomes of this fateful interplay.

By way of preamble the first three chapters sketch out some of the conceptual and analytical considerations deemed relevant for elucidating and accounting for the unsettling consequences of this interplay. Attempts are also made to advance a few premises and/or propositions to render the presumed relationships more plausible and cogent.

Chapter 1 explores the meanings and manifestations of proxy wars and surrogate victimization. Under what circumstances and why, it is asked, are ordinary forms of socioeconomic and political protests deflected into more militant violence? More graphically, how and why was Lebanon transformed into a killing field for other people's wars?

I focus, in answering this query, on how the protracted and displaced features of collective strife feed on each other and how, by doing so, they compound the pathologies of each. The insightful views of René Girard (1977) on the release of unappeased hostility are invoked here. When grievances and feelings of anger are not pacified, Girard tells us, they are prone to be released on proxy targets unrelated to the sources that originally provoked the hostility. Such targets, or alibis of displaced enmity, are often chosen, as was to happen repeatedly in Lebanon, on the basis of how vulnerable and accessible such groups happen to be at the time.

An attempt is also made to provide a more balanced and realistic view of the inside-outside dialectics. Rather than assigning blame exclusively either on the internal disparities or on the unresolved regional rivalries or divisive foreign incursions, the study will argue for and substantiate the mutually reinforcing character of the inside-outside dynamics.

Chapter 2 shifts the analysis to the circumstances in Lebanon's socioeconomic cultural history that heighten and mobilize the radical consciousness of communal identities. How and why are communal loyalties, which conventionally serve as vital sources of sociopsychological support and venues of welfare, benefits, and privileging networks, transformed into belligerent vectors for radical mobilization? More concretely, how are feelings of communal solidarity undermined and under what conditions do the undefined fears and threats become sharper? It is during such moments that communal identities are heightened to reinforce the intensity of enmity toward other groups perceived as different and hostile. Special focus is based on elucidating those particular features of Lebanon's "retribalization" exacerbated by the inside-outside dialectics.

The prosaic distinction between "horizontal" and "vertical" divisions is introduced here to shed further light on the circumstances that radicalize communal identities. "Horizontal" socioeconomic disputes, though aroused by embittered feelings of injustice, loss of status, material advantage and privilege, are likely to remain less militant unless deflected into confessional or communal hostility. "Vertical" divisions, on the other hand, particularly when engendered by communal and sectarian loyalties, are threatened by more compelling and existential issues such as the loss of freedom, identity, autonomy and heritage. In the language of Theodor Hanf (1995) it is then that the conflict shifts from a struggle over "divisible goods" to "indivisible principles". As this happens, the intensity of violence is bound to become more savaging and, hence, the prospects for resolving the conflict peacefully all the more remote.

Chapter 3 extends the analysis to the third layer of violence; namely a consideration of the circumstances under which collective civil strife degenerates into the incivility of reckless, indiscriminate and random killing and destruction. Stated more poignantly, how can a fairly peaceful and resourceful society exhibiting a rather impressive history of viable pluralism, and coexistence, be mobilized into so much barbarism and incivility? Rather than seeking the answer in symptoms of reawakened communalism and the macro geopolitical forces of unresolved regional and global rivalries, I focus here on the unfolding and escalating character of violence itself.

Two distinctive features, which are generally overlooked by both conceptual and empirical explorations of collective strife, are exposed here. First, that the circumstances which *initiate* or impel marginalized and oppressed groups to resort to political violence are not necessary those which *sustain* their mobilization or inform the direction, character, and outcome of conflict. Second, once violence is unleashed it becomes difficult to quell. Its self-destructive dynamics acquires a life of their own and begins to generate their own belligerent momentum. In conceptual terms, violence in this sense is no longer a dependent variable but is transformed into an independent variable reproducing its own ferocious cycles of violence.

Here, as well, the chapter is guided by a few conceptual and analytical premises extracted from the seminal works of scholars like Paul Ricoeur

(1967), Randall Collins (1974), Natali Davis (1975), Robin Williams (1981), J. Bowyer Bell (1987) John Keane (1996), Sudhir Kakar (1996) among others to highlight these and other features which can account for the descent of violence into incivility. Special efforts are made to disclose the sociocultural and psychological circumstances associated with the normalization and sanctification of cruelty, particularly conditions closely aligned with the manufacturing of enmity and the sanctioning of violence. Or, in the words of Collins (1974), how violence becomes both morally indifferent and morally motivated?

With the first three chapters serving as a conceptual backdrop, the study moves on to re-examine in Chapter 4 the recurrent episodes of peasant and sectarian uprisings (1820–1860) in Mount Lebanon. Since the uprisings were largely a reaction to some of the abusive institutions and loyalties of feudal society, part of the exploration is concerned with those features which could have initiated and sustained collective protest. A set of direct and cogent queries frame the discussion: What inspired and motivated the insurgents to collective action? When and why did the protest begin to assume more belligerent manifestations? Were peasants acting on their own, or were they instruments and/or surrogate victims of other sources of conflict? What, if anything, did these episodes accomplish?

We find much here in support of our proposed conceptual premises. For example, all three uprisings were originally incited by a sense of collective consciousness and a concern for public welfare. Yet, at one point or another, they were all deflected into confessional hostility. Likewise, episodes of communal conflict, initially sparked off by legitimate socioeconomic grievances, were transformed into factional or sectarian rivalries. Expressed more conceptually, struggles over "divisible goods," i.e., contests of distributive justice as to who gets what and how much, are deflected into primordial struggles over "indivisible principles," those loged in the ingrained sentiments of kinship, community, faith, and creed.

The forms and consequences of the nineteenth century uprisings also provide persuasive evidence in support of the two broad perspectives on civil strife advanced by James Rule (1988). In one respect there is much to substantiate the "consumatory" or expressive type of collective strife, the kind impelled and sustained by group solidarity, in which the sharing of emancipatory excitement and the frenzy of agitated gatherings and mass collective mobilization, the sheer ardor and devotion to collective struggle become the glue that cements the groups together. In other respects one also encounters evidence to support what Rule labels "instrumental" violence. Here the insurgents were not only incited by the impulse to correct injustices and seek some respite from feudal abuse or to wreak vengeance for its own sake. They were also driven by a utilitarian desire to secure basic amenities and material rewards.

Finally, the peasants rarely acted alone. Several groups were more than eager to step in and appropriate or manipulate the uprisings for purposes unrelated to the original grievances of the peasantry as a genuine protest movement: The Maronite clerics, Ottoman authorities, and foreign powers each had their own motives for meddling in the conflict. In the process, a genuine local uprising was deflected into a global crisis. Irate peasants, already violated by the adverse effects of Ottoman repression and European economic transformations, were victimized further.

The comparative insights of Gabriel Baer (1982), Charles Tilly (1978), Ernest Gellner (1997), among others, are invoked here to render these and other relevant features of collective strife more cogent and plausible.

The crisis of 1958, explored in chapter 5, stands out as a striking watershed in Lebanon's political history. For nearly a century, despite the disruptive burdens of the inside-outside dialectic, the country managed to evolve into a fairly prosperous, peaceful, and vibrant republic. This was all the more remarkable since this interlude is normally marked by turmoil in the lives of new nations.

In 1958 a succession of fairly benign political events — presidential succession, mounting political grievances and disputes over constitutional amendments and foreign policy — started to change the non-strident tone of public discourse. Bargaining, compromise, guarded contact, consent, avoidance, even "mutual lies," until then the hallmarks of the political system, started to be displaced by more contentious forms of political confrontations.

As in earlier episodes of collective strife, the generally non-sectarian disputes degenerated into confessional hostility and, thereby, reawakened communal solidarities and heightened the magnitude of violence. Here as well Lebanon became increasingly drawn into the regional and global conflicts of the period and became once again an object and victim of Cold War rivalries.

The questions we pose here are a variant on those we addressed in the preceding chapter. Why did the tone of public debate become more belligerent? How and why did the contentious groups resort to, or drift into, insurgency? What forms did the violence assume and how did they rationalize their participation in it?

There is much in our conceptual propositions that can be fruitfully applied to elucidate those features of political violence which were to become more pronounced in the protracted strife of the 70's and 80's namely, that the sources often associated with the origins or initiation of violence are not necessary those which sustain and heighten its intensity. By doing so, we can better understand how violence acquires a more perilous life of its own and how it crosses over into incivility.

The brief interlude — between 1958 and 1975 — has invited a relentless stream of polemical writing. Those who see this rather perplexing period as a prelude to the protracted cruelties of 1975 tend to exaggerate the country's internal contradictions and hold them responsible for much of the havoc, violence, and destruction. Others, with a more optimistic frame of mind, are more predisposed to see this period as a privileged interlude, a testimony of the ingenuity and resourcefulness of the Lebanese. Chapter 6, Lebanon's Global/Gilded Age, tries to offer a more balanced and realistic appraisal of the overall legacy of this interlude by reassessing some of its salient socio-cultural, economic, and political attributes; both those which reinforce its salutary image as a "success Story" and those which render it more vulnerable to the inside-outside dialectic.

Chapters 7 and 8 deal with the protracted hostilities of 1975–90. The discussion departs from much of the prodigious volume of writing on Lebanon in at least two distinct ways. First, it does not provide yet another blow by blow account or a chronology of the war. Nor is it exclusively concerned with the inception or origins of collective strife.

We know too much already about the preconditions, changing political settings (both regional and global), economic disparities, psychological, and sociocultural circumstances that predisposed groups to resort to collective protest. Instructive as these are, they tell us little about the forces which sustained violence and heightened its cruelties. More grievous, perhaps, they do not help us in understanding how seemingly ordinary and pacific groups became entrapped in relentless cycles of chronic hostility and how they came to cope with its gruesome realities. Similarly, this almost obdurate obsession with the origins of violence is of little relevance in elucidating the impact of the war on collective memory, on changes in group loyalties, collective psychology, perceptions, and changing attitudes towards the "other."

Chapter 9 shifts the analysis to a reconsideration of all the five major covenants, pacts, and attempts at reconciliation: from the partition scheme of 1843 to the Ta'if Accord of 1989. Virtually all these schemes came either in the wake of bitter communal or collective strife (1843, 1861, and 1989) or after critical watersheds in the country's political history like the collapse of the Ottoman Empire in 1819 or national independence from the French in 1943. All five dealt with the contested issues of national identity, sectarian balance, foreign policy in a changing regional and global setting. More relevant for our purposes they were all brokered by foreign governments.

The thesis I propose here is that the pacts that where comparatively more successful (i.e. the Règlement Organique of 1861 and the *Mithaq* of 1943), had recognized the realities of confessional loyalties but sought to secularize them in such a manner as to encourage harmonious coexistence between the various communities. In essence, they made efforts to transform some of their divisive features into a more constructive and enabling system.

The final chapter on "Prospects for Civility" is predominantly concerned with exploring measures to reduce or contain the country's vulnerability to the destabilizing consequences of the inside-outside dynamics while en-hancing opportunities for self-determination and empowerment of lethargic and excluded groups. The discussion skirts issues of national sovereignty, political reform, and economic development and focuses instead on matters more accessible to viable modes of voluntarism and participation in public life.

The chapter considers programs and measures, proved effective in other comparable settings, which can provide venues for participation in public space and nurtures some of the attributes of civility and collective conscious-ness. A largely self-evident proposition is advanced, namely that offering more accessible opportunities to participate in civic and welfare associations, rehabilitative ecological, environmental, public health and heritage pro-grams, even competitive sports and popular culture can be invaluable as strategies for healing symptoms of fear and paranoia. More important they can also serve as venues for transcending parochialism and allaying the in-difference to others still salient in post-war Lebanon. I also consider, by way of conclusion, pertinent views and measures for the articulation of new cul-tural identities more germane for a political culture of tolerance and civility.

I wish to end this preface by a personal caveat. There is more to my interest in exploring the changing character of collective strife than a pure, dispassionate, and conceptual analysis of the circumstances associated with their transformation into the more barbarous incivility of protracted and displaced hostility.

Except for the comparatively benign civil unrest of 1958 (and I was pur-suing my graduate studies in the U.S. at the time), my generation has been spared the menacing encounters with collective violence. This is why the almost two decades of free-floating hostility and treacherous bloodletting served as a crude awakening, often received with shock and disbelief. What compounded the shock was not only the magnitude and futility of violence, but also how, in the process, Lebanon was unduly maligned and defiled. At times, in fact, the country was reduced to an ugly metaphor, often no more than an allegoric figure of speech used to conjure up grotesque images by way of evoking the anguish of others.

More grievous, perhaps, is the fact that much of Lebanon's felicitous history, or at least interludes when the country managed to sustain more than just a modicum of peaceful co-existence, economic prosperity and sociocultural mobilization, was either overlooked or dismissed as fortuitous byproducts of external circumstances. Lebanon, as it were, was only acknowledged when it was being held accountable for the havoc and collective violence it was beleaguered with. Here, as well, much of the violence was seen as a mode of self-destruction as if the Lebanese were collective victims of national suicide. No sooner had the fighting erupted in 1975 than the pundits, self-appointed and otherwise, rushed to vilify and pillory Lebanon as a flawed, artificial entity, doomed for self-destruction since its wavering birth.

Within this context, the laborious research and writing demanded by this undertaking were made more palpable, even redemptive. Writing was more than just an effort to validate the "social facts" associated with the changing forms of collective strife. I found myself groping to exonerate Lebanon from such faulty perceptions and allegations. It became an effort to demystify its abiding and defining elements, both enabling and disabling.

Cathartic as writing might be in such instances it served, at least in my case, to only add insight to injury. The more lucid and insightful the analysis (and I have been enriched by borrowing so liberally from the seminal work of other scholars), the more grievous the injury.

By then the work started to acquire an existential tinge. It became an anguishing quest to grapple with the disheartening realities of witnessing the pathologies of human bestiality at such a close range. When collective strife descends into random and reckless killing without mercy and without guilt, and when it is transformed into a sanitized ordinary routine, one can no longer free oneself entirely from the realities that people have natures or impulses that are often vile and offensive to human sensibilities. But by accepting the fact that people have natures that are often so repugnant, one begins to harbor the hope for ameliorative action. Indeed, this study is also buoyed by the hope that rehabilitative strategies can be designed to mitigate the effects of man's baser instincts.

It is in this existential sense that any encounter with collective violence, like most other encounters with the darker and more foreboding foibles of humanity, will serve as the most visible molders of people's collective destinies. We are indelibly marked by them. For better or worse, we are never the same again.

Samir Khalaf
July 2001

Acknowledgment

This book has been a long time coming. By nature of its multiple perspectives, let alone its extended time frame, my debts to others are innumerable. It is virtually impossible to thank all those who helped in developing the sensibilities which informed the study. The extensive bibliography is a testimony of how liberally I borrowed from others. I do want, though, at the risk if the inevitable sins of omissions, to recognize a few.

Foremost I must acknowledge the continuous and generous foundation support I have been privileged to enjoy. Initially, the study was launched in 1982 as part of an empirical survey, funded by the Ford Foundation, to explore the impact of collective strife on three communities in Beirut. The escalation of unrest compelled me and my associates on the project (Salim Nasr and Samir Nassif) to suspend the survey. While on leave at Princeton University, I was the beneficiary of a MacArthur Research and Writing Award (1987) that enabled me to review the extensive literature on comparative political unrest, civil violence, and third-world insurgency. The graduate seminars I offered at Princeton, New York University, and MIT (1988–92) allowed me to deepen and extend the scope of the study and formulate specific queries which merit further exploration.

In 1990 work on the study witnessed yet another unexpected suspension. A long-term Lilly Endowment research grant — to study the impact of New England Puritanism as a cultural transplant on sociocultural change in the Arab world — required my full-time commitment for more than three years. I must express here my gratitude to Sister Jeanne Knoerly of the Endowment for permitting me to return from time to time to address a few of the suspended issues, particularly when political events in the region became more compelling, conceptually and otherwise.

Upon my return to Lebanon in the spring of 1995 to resume my appointment at the American University of Beirut and to reactivate the Center for Behavioral Research (CBR), my writing and research suffered yet another inevitable setback. The travails of reviving the Center in a postwar setting were much too distracting. My research interests also shifted, understandably, to problems of reconstruction and rehabilitation. I must acknowledge here the initial and renewed support of the Andrew W. Mellon Foundation, without which the CBR would not have evolved during the past six years into an animated research site for local and visiting scholars. Nor would I have been able to benefit from the much-needed summer respites for uninterrupted research and writing. It is my hope that the credible standing of the CBR and the Research output it is generating are a testimony of well-earned support. I am grateful to President William Bowen, Vice President Harriet Zuckerman, and Martha Sullivan of the Foundation for their sustained encouragement and understanding of the needs of the Center.

Colleagues, students, friends, and relatives have all sustained me over the years in ways too numerous to count. Some, by merely asking about progress on the book(s) as years swiftly ticked by, helped to goad me on. Others, in perhaps more substantive ways, have been immensely generous in offering enlightened and critical advice. Richard Yorkey, ever since he taught me English in High School, until his passing two years ago, retained that same tutoring intensity for uplifting the quality of my prose. I hope I have inched closer to his exacting demands and regret he is not around to bear witness to whatever modest improvements I have made in this regard.

Philip Khoury, once a recalcitrant but spirited student of mine, has evolved into an accomplished scholar, writer, and university administrator. We have had stints of joint teaching and authorship. In these, and as Dean of Humanities and Social Sciences at MIT, as Trustee of the American University of Beirut, and in his leadership of the Middle East Studies Association, he has been an constant source of stimulation and enlightened concern for upgrading the creative potential of students, colleagues, and friends. He is an endearing colleague and friend, but a hard act to follow.

Some colleagues, particularly Michel El-Khoury, Farid El Khazin, Ghassan Tueni, Fawaz Gerges, Walter Wallace, Ghassan Hage, Mohammad Ali Khalidi, Peter Johnson, and Chibli Mallat were generous in returning solicited comments on earlier drafts. Others, like Suzanne Keller, Edward Said, Richard Norton, Joseph O'Neil, Ali Banuazizi, Shibley Telhami, and Micheal Centano suggested useful premises, readings, and perspectives.

Leading the life of a displaced scholar at a time one's country was being savaged by senseless violence is not a very felicitous state of being. Likewise, reentry into postwar Lebanon, beleaguered by unresolved hostility, political uncertainty, lethargy, mediocrity, and creeping indifference, has been even more disheartening. Thanks are due to a growing circle of caring friends and colleagues in Lebanon, Princeton, and elsewhere who rendered the anguish of exile and return salutary, even beneficent. In ways I cannot fully enumerate, the following offered the coveted intellectual companionship and other genial venues of self-renewal and well-being: Fadlou and Alison Shehadi, David and the late Doris Dodge, Woody and Elizabeth Littlefield, Jane deLong, Charles Westoff, Henry Beinen, Serane Boocock, Carl Brown, Marvin Bressler, John and Marianne Waterbury, Ted and Mary Cross, the late Charles and Yanina Issawi, Touma and Layla Arida, George and Alexandra Assiely, Ghassan and Chadia Tueni, Myrna Boustani, Nasser Chamaa, Khalil Bitar, Fadi Tueni, Hashim Sarkis, Nadim Shehadi, Oussama Kabbani, Asaad Khairallah, Maher Jarrar, Chibli and Nayla Mallat, Riad Tabbarah, Fawaz Traboulsi, and Fadi Tueni.

Kate Wittenberg, formerly Senior Executive Editor at Columbia University Press, was initially very supportive of the project. Her successors at the Press, particularly Anne Routon, have been equally forthcoming. I am grateful to Leslie Bialler, who copyedited the manuscript with such scrupulous and professional care.

Mrs. Leila Jbara, my administrative assistant, has become now fully adept at the cumbersome task of typing numerous drafts and preparing the final version for publication. She is also disarmingly genial and accommodating.

In paying tribute to the boundless gratitude I owe my family, one and all, I am reminded of the advice Leo Tolstoy gave his son's fiancée as they were about to commence their matrimonial life together: "One can live magnificently in this world," he told her, "if one knows how to work and how to love." At the risk of sounding self-indulgent, I have been privileged to enjoy generous doses of both and, always, in tandem. Indeed, I owe so much of my well-being and inspiration to my family that three of my earlier books were dedicated to each individually. At different interludes of our blissful life together, and in different ways, each managed to nurture this enabling symbiosis between love and work.

George was barely a toddler, still unaware of the raging war outside the serenity of our home in West Beirut, when I started to probe the character of communal unrest in nineteenth-century Lebanon. The joys of parenting a first child were a soothing antidote to the savaging world outside. Hence, *Persistence and Change in 19th-Century Lebanon* (1979) was dedicated to him. *Lebanon's Predicament* (1986) was Rosanne's book. We suffered the travails of war and exile together. She suspended her career to the be the tender and nurturing mother to all her "three boys" as she was keen on refraining from work at the time. Ramzi was not yet ten when we made our first trip back to Lebanon in the summer of 1992. It was then, buoyed by the intuitive sensibilities of a precocious child, that he came face-to-face with all the nagging disharmonies between the country's captivating landscape and rich history and its treacherous political culture. *Reclaiming Beirut* (1993) was his book. It was inspired by him and, thereby, addresses issues of concern to his own generation in the hope that they will be able to reconnect with, and reclaim, their country's disinherited legacy.

A book like this one, which chronicles the magnitude and futility of violence while bearing witness to some of the pathologies of human bestiality, is hardly a fitting tribute or gift to a loving and peaceful family. Yet the entire life-cycle of our family for almost three decades has been enveloped in the trials and tribulations of relentless collective strife and political uncertainty. By virtue of the abiding love and filial devotion we felt for each other, our family became more than just a haven in a heartless world. Perilous as it was at times, the pathos out there was transformed into an indelible, often redemptive, reality to be probed and lived. In the process all four of us became not only more compassionate and caring, but also more appreciative and jealous of our life together. The exigent tasks exacted by arduous research and writing, like all the other pressing demands of public life, were transformed, thanks to Roseanne, George, and Ramzi, into a labor of love. This book is lovingly dedicated to them.

Civil and Uncivil Violence in Lebanon

1   On Proxy Wars and Surrogate Victims

"When unappeased, violence seeks and always finds a surrogate
victim. The creature that excited its fury is abruptly replaced by
another, chosen only because it is vulnerable and close at hand."
— René Girard, *Violence and the Sacred* (1977)

"The practice of violence changes the world, but the most
probable change is a more violent world."
— Hannah Arendt, *The Human Condition* (1958)

"When in doubt, just bomb Lebanon."
— Charles Glass, *The Daily Star* (2000)

The social and political history of Lebanon — despite occa-
sional manifestations of consensus, balance and harmony — has always been
characterized by successive outbursts of civil strife and political violence.
The brutality and duration of almost two decades of senseless bloodletting
might have obscured some of the earlier episodes. Consequently, observers
are often unaware that much of Lebanon's history is essentially a history of
intermittent violence. Dramatic episodes such as the peasant uprisings of
1820, 1840, and 1857 and the repeated outbreaks of sectarian hostilities in
1841, 1845, 1860, 1958, and the protracted civil war of 1975–92, reveal, if
anything, the fragility of Lebanon's confessional democracy, its deficient
civility and perpetual grievances of dominant groups within society. Because
of such inherent deficiencies and contradictions, Lebanon has always been
vulnerable to inter-Arab and superpower rivalries. Quite often a purely internal or local grievance is magnified or deflected to become the source of
international conflict. Conversely, such foreign intervention has always exacerbated internal cleavages.

Typical of small, communal and highly factionalized societies, much of
the violence in the early nineteenth century took the form of internal strife
between factions and feuding families. Little of it assumed an open confessional conflict. At least until 1840, the bulk of violence was more in the

nature of feuds, personal and factional rivalry between bickering feudal chieftains, and rival families vying for a greater share of power and privilege in society. Nineteenth-century travelers and local chroniclers all uniformly commented on the spirit of amity that had characterized confessional relations at the time (for further details, see Hitti 1957; Salibi 1965; Khalaf 1979; Abraham 1981; Akarli 1993; Fawaz 1994).

Throughout the nineteenth century, Lebanon witnessed various forms of social change which began to dislocate feudal relations and disturb the balance of forces between the various sects and religious communities. The interplay of both external and internal transformations opened up the society to new ideological and cultural encounters, various forms of secular reforms, and generated further socioeconomic mobilization. Such swift transformations, however, also produced pronounced shifts in the relative socioeconomic and political positions of the various religious communities. These dislocations almost always touched off renewed outbreaks of civil unrest and political violence.

In some obvious respects, Lebanon has all the features of a fragmented political culture. In fact, it has been fashionable in the relentless outpouring of literature to depict the country as an "improbable," "precarious," "fragmented," "dismembered," "torn" society; a house so "divided" and riven by ethnic, religious, and communal schisms that it has become extremely difficult to "piece it together again." Indeed, given this inherent "deficiency in its civility," some go as far as to doubt whether Lebanon has ever existed as a viable political entity.[1]

Such conceptions, particularly those propounded by Lebanon's detractors, and they are legion, are often exaggerated. They bear nonetheless some measure of truth. Even those who continue to entertain a more flattering and felicitous image of Lebanon and speak — often in highly evocative, idyllic and romanticized tones — of this "valiant little democracy," as a "privileged creation" and a "bold cultural experiment," a "miraculous" pluralistic society sustained by resourcefulness, resilience, and *unfuwan* cannot entirely dismiss or mystify the inherently problematic nature of Lebanon's pluralism.[2]

Lebanon's predicament, given the resurgence of what is termed "Low Intensity Conflict" (LIC) by experts on global warfare and Third World insurgency, is far from unique. Its sanguinary history with protracted strife epitomizes the predicaments other small, plural, fragmented political cultures caught up in turbulent regional and global rivalries are also facing. More, perhaps, than other comparable entities, this interplay between internal dislocations and external destabilizing pressures has been much more acute and problematic in Lebanon. It is also a long-standing and persisting feature. Neither the internal divisions, nor the external unsettling forces are of recent vintage. Nor should they be attributed, as claimed recently, to the divisive presence of "borrowed ideologies" and other disheartening derivatives or fallouts of the new world order, post-modernity or the "clash of civilization."

Long before the state of Lebanon came into being in 1920, it had been a puzzling and enigmatic entity: extremely difficult to manage politically, or to cement together into a viable and integrative social fabric. To a large extent, its fragmented political culture is a byproduct of two general features. First, it reflects some of the traditional forces and sharp cleavages, sustained by striking differences in religious beliefs, communal and sectarian loyalties, kinship and fealty sentiments, and other primordial attachments which continue to split the society vertically and reinforce its factional and parochial character. Second, and superimposed on these, are some of the new forms of socioeconomic and cultural differentiation generated by the asymmetrical growth Lebanon has been undergoing with the advent of modernity. These differences manifest themselves in virtually all the common indicators of socioeconomic mobilization, demographic variables, literacy, quality of life, exposure to westernization, professionalization and the like.

Hence, there have always been both vertical and horizontal divisions which on occasion pulled the society apart and threatened the delicate balance of forces. With the exception of the massacres of 1860, all earlier episodes of conflict were however comparatively limited in scope, clearly not as belligerent or devastating in their destructive consequences. For better or worse, prompt foreign intervention always managed to bring about a cessation of hostilities, if not a firm or just resolution of the issues underlying the conflict.

Disruptive as they might have been by standards of the day, all earlier episodes of collective strife pale when compared to the ruthless atrocities the country has been afflicted with recently. For almost two decades, Lebanon was besieged and beleaguered by every possible form of brutality and collective terror known to human history: from the cruelties of factional and religious bigotry to the massive devastations wrought by private militias and state-sponsored armies. They have all generated an endless carnage of innocent victims and immeasurable toll of human suffering.

Even by the most moderate of estimates, the magnitude of such damage to human life and property is staggering. About 170,000 have perished, twice as many have been wounded or disabled, close to two-thirds of the popula-

tion experienced some form of dislocation or uprootedness from their homes and communities. By the fall of 1982, UN experts estimated that the country had sustained $12–15 billion in damages, i.e. $2 billion per year. Today more than one-third of the population is estimated to live below the poverty line on a subsistence budget of $600 a month as a result of war and displacement (Corm 1998: 9).

For a small, dense and closely knit society with a population of about 3.5 million and an area of 10,452 km^2, such devastations are, understandably, very menacing. More damaging, perhaps, are some of the socio-psychological and moral concomitants of protracted hostility. The scars and scares of war have left a heavy psychic toll which displays itself in pervasive post-stress symptoms and nagging feelings of despair and hopelessness. In a culture generally averse to psychoanalytic counseling and therapy, these and other psychic disorders are more debilitating. They are bound to remain masked and unrecognized and, hence, unattended to.

The demoralizing consequences of the war are also visible in symptoms of vulgarization and impoverishment of public life and erosion of civility. The routinization of violence, chaos, and fear only compounded the frayed fabrics of the social order. It drew groups into the vortex of bellicose conflict and sowed a legacy of hate and bitterness. It is in this fundamental sense that Lebanon's pluralism, radicalization of its communities, and consequent collective violence have become pathological and uncivil.

Rather than being a source of enrichment, variety, and cultural diversity, the modicum of pluralism the country once enjoyed is now generating large residues of paranoia, hostility, and differential bonding. This pervasive "geography of fear," and the predisposition of threatened and displaced groups to relocate in cloistered and homogeneous communities, only serves to accentuate distance from and indifference to the "other." This is not to be dismissed as a transient, benign feature. Given the resistance of displaced groups to return and reclaim their original homes and property, this drastic redrawing of Lebanon's social geography might turn out to be more ominous and fateful. At the least it is bound to complicate prospects for rehabilitation and national integration.

Impressive as they may seem, one need not be deceived by the public mood of optimism and symptoms of national well-being generated by the massive, often exuberant, schemes for reconstruction and physical rehabilitation of the country's devastated infrastructure. Nor does the outward political stability rest on firm foundations or consensus over substantive issues of national sovereignty and ultimate political destiny. The sociocultural polarization-visible in striking differences in values, normative expectations, life-style, public display of wealth and privilege, cultural artifacts, popular entertainment, consumerism, the reassertion of spatial and communal identities and, more recently, in the polemics over public issues such as civil marriage, electoral reforms, and foreign policy-are much too apparent to be masked by the fickle manifestations of national solidarity and collective consciousness. Sentiments, and avowed claims on behalf of the transcending entities of national unity and secular allegiances, pale when pitted against symptoms of social division, sharp cultural differentiation, and distance between communities.

The precepts of history in this regard are not on Lebanon's side. At least if modernity and progressive change stand for diversity, mix, hybridity, and openness, then what has been happening in Lebanon, in a majority of areas, is a movement away from such enabling encounters. Social and intellectual historians are keen on reminding us that a fascinating transformation in the historical evolution of most societies involves their passage from a relatively "closed" to a more "open" system: membership, exit or entry, access to privileges and benefits are no longer denied by virtue of limitations of religion, kinship, or race. Such openness accounts for much of the spectacular growth in the philosophical, artistic, and political emancipation of contemporary societies. It is in this sense that Lebanon is now at that critical threshold, since it is about to invert and reverse this natural course of history. Indeed, what we might be witnessing is the substitution of one form of pluralism, imperfect as it has been, for a more regressive and pathological kind. We are destroying a society that permitted, on and off, groups with divergent backgrounds and expectations to live side by side. What is emerging is a monolithic archetype that is hostile to any such coexistence or free experimentation.

While such reawakened communal solidarities provide shelter, the needed socio-psychological support and access to welfare, benefits, and privileging networks, they also heighten and reinforce the intensity of enmity toward groups perceived as different. Though open fighting and warfare have been momentarily suspended, the country remains riven with suspicious, unrelenting, and unforgiving recriminations.

Altogether then, the resort to violence — willful or otherwise, generated from within or without, byproduct of fortuitous circumstances or conspiracy and design — has been wasteful and futile. It has had little effect on redressing the gaps and imbalances in society or in transforming Lebanon's communal and confessional loyalties into more secular and civic entities. Indeed the very persistence of such enmity means that something is not changing.

Inferences of this sort prompt me to carry the argument even further and suggest that insofar as violence has served to widen rifts and cleavages in society, it has already become counter-productive and self-defeating. The process of "breaking eggs and making omelets," to borrow a trite metaphor, need not in other words always prove judicious. I take my hint here from Hannah Arendt, who has suggested that "the practice of violence, like all action, changes the world, but the most probable change is a more violent world." (Arendt 1958: 182) It is also in this sense, as will be elaborated shortly, that civil violence slips into incivility.

Who is to rescue Lebanon from the savagery and scourge of violence unleashed upon it for so long? In all earlier episodes of collective strife, though foreign powers and regional brokers had a role in inciting and escalating hostilities, they also stepped in to contain the conflict when it began to undermine their strategic interests. Both, for example, in 1860 and 1958, conflict ended largely because the interests of the superpowers were better served by stabilizing Lebanon. As will be seen, it took 32 weeks and about 50 meetings of intensive diplomatic negotiations between the concerned foreign actors at the time (i.e. France, Great Britain, Austria, Russia, Prussia, and Turkey) to arrive at the *Règlement Organique* which reconstituted Lebanon as an Ottoman province under the guarantee of the six signatory powers. Through French initiative, the international commission was set up to fix responsibility, determine guilt, estimate indemnity, and suggest reforms for the reorganization of Mount Lebanon.

Likewise, in 1958 the strategic stature and significance of Lebanon was at its height. The region was seething with political ferment and ideological disputes. The Cold War had transformed the region into a proxy battlefield for superpower rivalry. The Baghdad Pact of 1955, the Suez Crisis of 1956, unrest in Jordan in 1957, the formation of the United Arab Republic (the abortive union between Egypt and Syria), the military coup in Iraq in 1958, all had unsettling implications. Since Lebanon at the time was identified with the Western camp, by virtue of its support of the Eisenhower Doctrine, the events had, naturally, direct bearings on the political standing of Lebanon. Indeed, the peace accord which ended the war was brokered by the U.S. and Egypt.

It should be noted, however, that before the Iraqi coup Eisenhower was reluctant to intervene directly despite the repeated requests made at the time by President Chamoun and foreign minister Charles Malik. Even when the US finally decided to commit its Marines, as Secretary of State John Foster

Dulles put it, "Lebanon was not very important in itself" (For this and other details, see Gerges 1997: 88–89). Hence, the intervention should not be taken as evidence of Western commitment to the security of Lebanon as such. Rather, Lebanon served as a proxy for other broader regional interests. The ultimate concern of the Eisenhower administration at the time was, of course, to curtail the spread of communism and radical Arab Nationalism which were perceived as threats to America's vital interests in the region, mainly oil supplies.

The deployment of American troops was also intended to demonstrate America's military clout and its determination to protect its regional and global interests. The US was also beginning to realize that with Nasser's charisma and growing influence in the region, Egypt was fast becoming the epicenter of Arab politics. This must account for its inclination to abandon Chamoun and work jointly with Cairo to arrive at a resolution of Lebanon's crisis. This, as in earlier and subsequent crises, served to reconfirm what was to become a recurrent modality in the resolution of conflict in Lebanon: the state is so enfeebled and divided that foreign and regional brokers take on this responsibility. Lebanon's impotence, or at least the failure of the state to immunize or protect itself against regional destabilizing forces, was of course translated into that ironical political doctrine, namely that the "country's strength lies in its weakness"! In effect this meant that the state was to surrender or relinquish its national security responsibility to other regional and global actors.[3]

Lebanon in the early and mid-seventies was not even in that mildly privileged a diplomatic or bargaining position. The détente between Russia and the U.S. defused much of the Cold War tension. Egypt under Sadat shifted toward the U.S. American inroads into the Arab Gulf and Iran became more substantive. Hence the major powers, in the wake of the first round of the war of 1975–76, had no immediate or vital interests at stake to interfere in the conflict. France was in no position to mobilize international initiative on behalf of Lebanon as it did in 1860. Unlike 1958, the U.S. also found little justification (at least initially) to dispatch their Marines or to engage in sustained diplomatic effort in settling the conflict.

Little wonder that when the war broke out in 1975, neither Washington nor Moscow felt the need to be involved in any direct diplomatic engagement as long as the conflict did not affect their vital interests. Henry Kissinger's disengagement diplomacy toward Lebanon, as Fawaz Gerges has persuasively argued, was "informed not only by his perception of the inherent precariousness of the country but also by the strategic need for a safety valve where Arab-Israeli tensions could be released without the threat of a major Arab-Israeli confrontation" (Gerges 1997: 78). Theodor Hanf (1993) was even more explicit in arguing how by abandoning the search for a comprehensive peace settlement in the Middle East, Kissinger's step-by-step diplomacy had actually increased the risk of proxy war in Lebanon. Indeed, Lebanon's suffering seemed of little or no concern as long as the internal hemorrhaging did not spill over, contaminate, or destabilize other vital spots in the region.

There is no evidence that the USA ever had a 'plan', as Palestinians and Christian Lebanese believe. As early as 1969 the USA took the view that the Lebanese state could not effectively control the Palestinians. By abandoning the search for a comprehensive peace settlement in the Middle East in favour of a policy of step-by-step diplomacy or bilateral agreements between Israel and the Arab states, Kissinger *de facto* brought peace to Syria and Egypt, but greatly increased the risk of war in Lebanon. Kissinger's objective was gradually to reduce the risk of another conventional war in the Middle East. He regretted the fates of the Palestinians and of Lebanon, but regarded them as of secondary importance. Kissinger had suggested a policy of benign neglect toward Latin America; his policy toward Lebanon was in word benign, and in practice neglect. This attitude persisted in US foreign policy in the post-Kissinger era. Lebanon was to play a role only when, and in so far as, conflict there threatened to spill over into other states: Lebanon per se counted for little in American foreign policy (Hanf 1993: 176–77).

The "quick-fix" diplomacy the Reagan administration resorted to was ill-conceived, ill-timed, and mismanaged. There was, of course, more than just a civil war raging in Lebanon at the time. The country was already a proxy battlefield for other peoples' wars and a succession of unresolved regional/global rivalries. Reagan's rash adventure (or misadventure) undermined completely the balance of power equation between the regional and superpowers and placed the U.S. in an illusionary superior standing.

Agnes Korbani (1991) in her evaluative study of the two American interventions in Lebanon (1958 and 1982), concludes that Eisenhower's "move was effective, it brought peace without the use of force. As a result, the marines withdrew peacefully and proudly and were welcomed back home as heroes. Reagan's move however was defective. It left Lebanon in shambles.

And the victim marines were carried away to their last rest" (Korbani 1991: 124). More devastating, Lebanon's victimization from then on was compounded.

It must also be kept in mind that both in 1860 and 1958 the fighting was summarily ended with a political settlement, backed by major powers and reinforced by internal public opinion. The settlements also brought auspicious times. During the second half of the nineteenth century, Mount Lebanon was wallowing in an enviable "silver lining" (Hitti 1957) and enjoyed a blissful interlude of "long peace" (Akarli 1993). In the wake of the 1958 crisis the country was also privileged to enjoy another felicitous interlude of political stability, state building, and cultural enlightenment.

While Lebanon was released from the specter of global rivalry, it was caught instead in the more foreboding web of regional conflict. As long as the Arab-Israeli conflict was unresolved, Lebanon became once again an expedient and surrogate killing field. Indeed, all the fierce battles which inaugurated the prolonged hostilities in 1975 (PLO-Lebanese war, the PLO-Syrian war and the PLO-Israeli war) had little to do with the internal dislocations and political tensions.

More perhaps than other political observers, Ghassan Tueni has been propounding this persuasive thesis (i.e. Lebanon as a proxy killing field for other people's wars) with relentless tenacity; first as head of Lebanon's UN delegation and subsequently in many of his trenchant weekly columns in an-Nahar (Tueni 1985). Charles Issawi, another astute observer of Lebanon's unsettled history, was equally poignant in contemplating Lebanon's victimization in the wake of 1958 crisis. He had this to say by way of accounting for the moral indifference of the regional and international community:

Lebanon is too conspicuous and successful an example of political democracy and economic liberalism to be tolerated in a region that has turned its back on both systems. . . . It may be answered that such fears are unfounded, that the conscience of the world would not allow any harm to befall such a harmless country as Lebanon, that the neighboring world would not want to have a recalcitrant minority on their hands, and that it is their interests to preserve Lebanon as "a window on the West." But to anyone who has followed the course of national and international politics in the last fifty years, such arguments are sheer nonsense. Minorities have been very effectively liquidated, windows have been violently slammed and hardly a ripple has stirred in the conscience of the world (Issawi 1966: 80–81).

Lebanon as an Ugly Metaphor

The moral indifference to Lebanon's suffering Issawi was bemoaning three decades ago has slid further into hardened denial or rebuke. The conscience of the world did not get softer, more charitable, or apprehensive of Lebanon's continued abuse as a surrogate victim of inveterate regional rivalries. Ironically, it turned a callous blind eye and started to blame and malign the victim instead. It is also odd that this should continue to happen at a time the country is beginning to display some reassuring signs in concerted efforts of reconstruction and rehabilitation and in containing the level of open hostility. Such disheartening indifference is most visible at the diplomatic level. Even consequential issues, which have direct bearing on Lebanon's national security and sovereignty as an independent nation-state, are being debated, Lebanon is usually the last country to be involved.

Not only are events in Lebanon overlooked and mystified, but also "Lebanization" has been reduced to an ugly metaphor indiscriminately employed by sensational journalistic accounts and media soundbites. At times it is no more than an allegoric figure of speech; a sobriquet, a mere byword to conjure up images of the grotesque and unspoken.

These, and other hidden abominations, are pardonable. The most injurious, however, is when the label is reduced to a fiendish prop without emotion; a mere foil to evoke the anguish of others. When cataloguing the horrors of Lebanon at a time when it was still newsworthy on American TV, I kept a ledger of the times this indignant label popped up compulsively in an incredulous set of random but dreaded circumstances: a fireman fighting a blaze in Philadelphia, the anguish of an AIDS victim, a jogger facing the fearful prospects of Manhattan's Central Park, survivors of a train crash, dejected Vietnamese "boat people," evacuees from China, the frenzy of delirious masses mourning Khomeini's death, looting and the chaos in the wake of the Los Angeles earthquake, a shooting rampage of a crazed spree-killer, even the anguish and perplexing bewilderment on the face and demeanor of a psychopath was described by a noted American psychiatrist as if his subject was deranged by the cruelties of war in Lebanon!!

At times the pejorative codeword spilled over to include natural catastrophes: fires, earthquakes, hurricanes and the like, and the damage they inflict on vulnerable and braceless people. Even wanton acts of bestiality, the hapless victims of anomie, entropy and other symptoms of collective terror and fear are also epitomized as analogues to life in Lebanon.

Tabloids and sensational image-makers may be forgiven these epithets. As of late scholars, sadly, have begun to appropriate the label. Indeed, considering the growing number of scholarly writing which readily invokes "Lebanization" or "Lebanonization," it has now entered part of the regular lexicon of social science terminology. *Larousse*, the prominent French dictionary, might have well been the first when, in 1991, it introduced "Libanisation" formally into the French language to mean "proces de fragmentation d'un État, résultant de l'affrontement entre diverses communautés" (process of fragmentation of a state, as a result of confrontation between diverse communities). *Larousse* goes further to suggest that the term might be considered as an alternate to "balkanization," to capture more graphically the collapse and dismemberment of the "Eastern Bloc" in the wake of the Cold War.[4]

James Gillian, in his recent wide-ranging work on violence, singles out Lebanon (Beirut in particular)-along with the atrocities committed by Hitler, Stalin, Idi Amin, Saddam Hussein, Kamikaze pilots, the Baader-Meinhof Gang, the Red Brigades, and the victimization of innocents in Belfast, Bosnia, and Bogata-as illustrative "of the most horrendously destructive of human life around the world in this century" (Gillian 1996: 95). Rupesinghe does not remain at this broad narrative level. He goes further to accord "Lebanization" the attribute of a concept to refer to "situations where the state has lost control of law and order and where many armed groups are contending to power" (Rupesinghe 1992: 26). Nor does Helene d'Encausse, in an otherwise excellent study, where she talks about the "Lebanization of the Caucasus" to explore the clash of Christian Armenians with Shi'i Muslim Azeris for control of the Armenian Nagorno-Karabakh in Azerbajian (d'Encausse 1993).

Even serious scholars could not resist the allure of the metaphor. The most revealing, perhaps, is the way William Harris has chosen to use the label in his most recent book on sectarian conflict and globalization in Lebanon (Harris 1997). In fact, the distinction he makes between the "Lebanization" of the 1980's and that of the 1990's informs the guiding thesis of his work. The former referred to "sectarian strife and temporary cantonization at a time of global transition." Lebanon then attracted attention as an "extreme case of regime multiplied across Eurasia" (Harris 1997: 6). Lebanonization of the 1990 ushered in a new threat. Extreme and militant Shi'is, by becoming the most potent political force, "represented the principal extension of the Iranian revolution in the Arab world." Hizballah quickly acquires its international bogeyman image and "Lebanonization" begins to signify "a black hole of destruction, extremism and terror" (Harris 1997: 7).

It is also in this context, incidentally, that militant Shi'ism becomes the harbinger of the sort of collision between Islam and the West-a most likely preamble of the next world war-as hypothesized in Samuel Huntington's celebrated "Clash of Civilizations" (Huntington 1993 and 1996). Harris, to his credit, is critical of Huntington's rough divisions of "cultural zones" and "fault lines" through the entire Mediterranean region and he, accordingly, cautions against such "superficial generalizations." Yet, surprisingly, he turns around to assert, in view of General Aoun's "ill-fated bid to break the constraints of sectarianism and external pressures" in Lebanon's wars of 1989–90, that "Lebanonization by then has eclipsed Lebanon" (Harris 1997: 16).

These and other such characterizations — particularly those which either exaggerate the fratricious innate character of Lebanon's internal divisions and dislocations or those which view it as a victim of predominantly external sources of instability — are naturally too generic and misleading. They do not capture or elucidate the rich diversity and complexities of the country's encounters with collective unrest. Nor do they do justice to some of the peculiar pathologies and circumstances associated with Lebanon's entrapment in that ravaging spiral of protracted and unappeased hostility which has beleaguered its strife-torn history for so long.

These two features — *displaced* and *protracted* hostility — remain the most defining elements in the country's encounters with collective strife. They also feed on each other and compound the pathological consequences of each. This is understandable when grievances or feelings of anger are not allayed or pacified. Agitated groups are prone to release their unappeased hostility, as Girard (1977) reminds us, on any accessible and vulnerable alibi. Episodes of protracted strife in Lebanon, as will be demonstrated, are replete with such instances of displaced enmity.

The character of communal strife and peasant uprising, in the early and middle decades of the nineteenth century, displayed many of these symptoms. Aroused peasants, aggrieved by the oppressive exactions of distant pashas or *amirs*, turned against the relatively weaker and more accessible feudal lords. Likewise, an *amir* or *hakim*, unable to resist the demands of an Ottoman sultan or *wali*, would vent his outrage on his defenseless feudal lords, often by playing one faction against another. Feuding cousins, sometimes brothers, vying to win the patronage of a *wali*, would end up in a fractious and bloody tribal rivalry. More decisive, in all these and related instances, the original character of the conflict was transformed in the process. A gen-

uine social protest was deflected into confessional rivalry; a sedition of oppressed peasants was muted and derailed into factional belligerency.

Foreign intervention in the 1958 crisis, by regional and global powers,
also generated its odd coalitions and proxy and divisive turf wars. Here again
an internal crisis over political succession and the intractable issues of socioeconomic disparities, grievances of neglected groups and regions, and
Lebanon's contested national identity and foreign policy orientation, degenerated into sectarian and communal strife. It was then that the largely nonbelligerent forms of collective protest started to slip into vengeful cycles of
reprisals with all the atavistic and free-floating violence begotten by it. It was
also then that innocent citizens became proxy victims of unprovoked hostility. They just happened to be there; "vulnerable and close at hand" (Girard
1977). With the absence of public order, unanchored masses were released
from the arbiters of conventional restraints. Acts of hooliganism, banditry,
pillage, looting, and disdain for law and order became rampant.

The grievous consequences of displaced hostility were naturally far more
barbarous during the protracted strife of the past two decades. Indeed, when
one reexamines some of the most ominous episodes, particularly those
which were fateful in redirecting the pattern of collective violence and
escalating its intensity, they were all byproducts of such surrogate victimization. For example, when Syrian forces were alternating their targets of
hostility-by shelling Christian militias' strongholds or, contrarily, when ward-
ing off the logistical gains of Palestinian fighters-they would rather have been
attacking their more ostensible enemies, namely, Israeli or Iraqi forces. Yet
neither of these regional superpowers were defenseless or at hand. Displaying their military powers over lesser and more compliant groups also allowed
them to extend or reinforce their patronage over alternate client groups.
This, as we shall see, accounted for much of the protraction of hostility and
miscarried cruelties.

The war raging in South Lebanon is a glaring instance of such proxy
violence. It has had little to do with the internal disparities or contradictions
within Lebanon. The war began when the ousted Palestinians from Jordan
relocated their bases and resumed their guerrilla operations from South Lebanon. From then on the South became an embattled war zone with grievous
repercussions for escalating the levels of hostility elsewhere in the country.
It is the war in the South that unleashed throngs of uprooted Shi'ites who
ultimately congested and radicalized the suburbs of destitution encircling
Beirut and other urban fringes. It is out of such slums of squalor and dereliction that Hizbullah emerged during the Israeli invasion of 1982. Ironi-

cally, when Israel expelled the PLO from Beirut it had in effect created a more ferocious and recalcitrant enemy. Hizbullah, like the PLO before it, is now embroiled in the same interlocking web of regional and global rivalries. Hence much of its activities are profoundly shaped by its two principal backers, namely Iran and Syria. Iran is, after all, the fount of Hizbullah's brand of Shi'ite fundamentalism and a source of an estimated $2 billion in support since the early 1980s (Norton 1999). Syria remains the sole vector through which the arms supplied by Iran have flowed.

The slightest shift in the balance of such exogenous forces, or the conduct of the intermittent Arab-Israeli peace talks, is bound to reactivate the cycle of belligerency. Not only the defenseless and innocent villagers in the South stand to suffer the outcome of such assaults. Both the magnitude and targets of Israeli reprisals for Hizbullah's Katyusha rockets on their settlements have recently witnessed some momentous changes. First, they are rarely directed against those ultimately responsible for them, namely Syria, Iran, or the military bases of the Shi'ite resistance forces. The reprisals are massive and disproportionate when compared to the benign damage generated by Hizbullah's rocket lobs or forays into the 9–mile "security zone" Israel has occupied in South Lebanon since 1978. Also the targets of such attacks always devastate civilian installations, power plants, villages, towns, families very far removed from Shi'ite guerrilla bases. In the latest bouts of Israeli belligerency (June 1999 and early February 2000) three power stations were destroyed, thereby leaving 80 percent of the country in utter darkness.

In fact, it does not really matter who provokes Israel's wrath. Nor does it need to fabricate alibis by way of justifying its reprisals. Over the years its government has not been able to restrain its compulsion to take out its wrath and pent-up hostility on Lebanon. In a recent editorial, aptly titled "when in doubt, just bomb Lebanon," Charles Glass expressed no surprise, in this context, if Israeli war planes were to be dispatched over Lebanon because "the Orthodox vigilantes in Jerusalem's Mea Shearim throw rocks at people driving on the Sabbath"! Such an affront may be far-fetched. Still the thirty years of relentless war in South Lebanon is one of the saddest tales of modern times, precisely because it is the one prime proxy war that does not seem to go away. The recent round of bellicosity attests to this. If anything, Hizbullah's stepped-up military offensives against Israel were most certainly encouraged by Syria by way of wresting concessions that Israel has refused to agree upon in the suspended talks.

Much of the internecine fighting, because it often involved spilling the blood of one's own kinsman, has been clearly more perfidious. Unlike its analogue in biblical mythology, Cain and his many facsimiles, were never banished by avenging God for killing Abel. Rather than wandering fearfully, they were instead entrapped in a relentless carnage of renewed blood baths. In such settings of heightened emotional contagion, belligerent groups find themselves avenging almost anyone. *Instead of killing those they wanted to kill, they end up victimizing those they could.*

Another defining element needs to be noted. The blurring of boundaries between internal and external sources of conflict is not of recent vintage; a portent, as some claim, of the new world order or a precursor of what is to become the dominant unfolding pattern of political violence. Virtually all episodes of collective strife during the first half of the nineteenth century — recurrent peasant uprisings, sectarian rivalries, even petty factional feuds — were all predisposed to being manipulated by external circumstances. Such internationalization of the conflict almost always contributed to the protraction of hostility. In earlier and more recent conflict, as the country became increasingly embroiled in regional and superpower rivalries, it could not be sheltered from the destabilizing consequences of such struggles. As this occurred, the original issues provoking the conflict receded. Threatened and marginalized groups, victims of internal socioeconomic disparities or political neglect, sought external protection and patronage. Foreign powers, keen on gaining inroads into the region, have always been too eager to rush into the fray. Such intervention, solicited or otherwise, almost always served to polarize the factions and deepen sources of hostility. In short, Lebanon again and again became an object and victim of this "inside-outside" dialectics.

Inside-Outside Dialectics

To assert that Lebanon's entrapment in protracted strife is largely a by-product of the interplay between internal dislocations and external pressures is, in many respects, an affirmation of the obvious. Yet, it is an affirmation worth belaboring given some of its persisting complexities and disruptive consequences. The catalogue of the recent horrors of nearly two decades of bloody strife makes it abundantly clear that unless we consider alternative strategies for neutralizing external sources of instability and pacifying internal conflict, Lebanon's precarious polity will always be made more vulnerable to such pressures.

There is nothing novel about this kind of polemics. Long before the state of Lebanon came into being it was a subject of much speculation and won-

der. Early in the nineteenth century, foreign travelers, missionaries, chroniclers, and historians were already intrigued by how this tiny republic, perhaps one of the smallest sovereign nations in the world, could have survived
as the only liberal and relatively orderly and prosperous democracy amidst
a host of authoritarian and turbulent political regimes. From Volney's ad-
miring remarks-the celebrated French traveler who visited Lebanon in the
1780s-and was so impressed by that "ray of liberty and genuine republican
spirit," (Volney 1788: 73–74) to the more recent critical studies of dispassionate social scientists, observers almost always disagreed in their assessment
of Lebanon's nature and prospects.

Until the outbreak of hostilities in 1975, the tone of much of the literature, both favorable and unfavorable, remained on the whole fairly guarded
and cautious. Even those who were writing off Lebanon as a "precarious,"
"improbable," or problematic republic, were not oblivious to some of its
distinctive accomplishments — particularly its survival as a parliamentary democracy and liberal economy in a region that had turned its back on both.
Indeed, to many of its critics, this is precisely the one attribute of Lebanon's
"success story" which they did not disparage. Avowed Marxist and left-
leaning thinkers, normally eager to attribute Lebanon's pitfalls to internal
disparities, did not overlook or exempt the disruptive impact of external
forces. The war was hardly a year old when Fuad Faris, an activist in the
Organization of Communist Action and part of the left alliance of the Lebanese Nationalist Movement (LMN), was already asserting that the Palestinian issue "explained much of what has happened in Lebanon. This is not
so much because the Palestinian Liberation Organization (PLO) has been
one of the main protagonists during the actual fighting, but more because
the Palestinian issue remains one of the linchpins that lock the internal
Lebanese situation into its external context"(Faris 1976: 174). The same year
Frank Stoakes had also pronounced the Palestinian dimension as the most
powerful irritant among the wide range of other disruptive extraneous elements already visible at the time (Stoakes 1976: 10–11).

Lebanon's bloody encounters with almost two decades of relentless cruelties, unleashed a less charitable, at times pernicious, genre of writing. The
cautious, balanced assessments of the country's shortcomings and prospects,
so common in the 1960s and 1970s, have given way recently to a barrage of
endless diatribes. It has become so fashionable, much too facile in fact, to
malign and defile Lebanon, that the country's origin, legacy, and future seem
bereft now of any redeeming virtues. Typical of "obituary" writers nothing
is spared. Even the undisputed accomplishments the country enjoyed, par-

ticularly during the post World War II era, are dismissed either as byproducts of external fortuitous circumstances or as anomalies or an illusive silver lining disguising the gathering darkening clouds.

A recurrent, almost stereotypical version of this now popularized image, maintains that Lebanon's economic prosperity and political stability are rooted in factors beyond its borders. Invariably, most observers single out, in this context, events like the partition of Palestine in 1946. Displaced Palestinians, the oil boom, the inflow of Arab capital, and protracted political turmoil in adjacent regimes were seen as the prime catalysts underlying Lebanon's enviable stature at the time.

These and other such external factors are not, clearly, all that neutral. Nor are they entirely positive in their impact. Yet in much of the literature, most of the ruinous byproducts of such considerations are often overlooked. Only their presumed benefits are highlighted. For example, rather than considering how the establishment of the state of Israel in 1948 had a devastating impact by disrupting the vital economic, commercial and social bonds that for centuries had linked Lebanon (via the Beirut-Haifa-Cairo railroad) with Arab Africa, Northern Palestine, and Southern Syria and accounted for the economic unity and prosperity of the entire region (Petran 1987: 65–66), the literature instead dwells almost exclusively on their presumed regenerative consequences. Hence, we are repeatedly reminded how Beirut's position as an entrepôt, or a transit port, is largely a byproduct of circumstances associated with the 1948 war in Palestine. The imposition of economic boycott by the Arab states against Israel redirected traffic and capital toward Beirut. The Trans-Arabian Pipeline (Tapline), which was originally slated to terminate in British-held Northern Palestine, was rerouted by Saudi Arabia to Sidon. Similarly, Iraq's pipeline, originally destined to Haifa, ended up instead in Tripoli. To David Waines (1976) it was primarily these external factors which ensured Beirut's position as the key transit port to and from the entire Eastern Arab World. Mackey is much more triumphant in heralding the instant transforming impact of such forces. "Almost overnight, Lebanon found itself the major way station of the oil route between the Persian Gulf and Europe" (Mackey 1989: 6).

Likewise, the literature dwells all too often on how Palestinian resources, including highly skilled professionals, bankers, speculators, and that large pool of cheap labor, were instrumental in propping up the Lebanese economy. Without the aggressive and competitive skills Palestinians and other displaced groups brought with them, sparked by the ethos of exile and marginality, Beirut would not have become, it is argued, the appealing haven for Arab and Western capital. Here as well Waines, among many others, attributes Beirut's emergence as an "intellectual emporium" for a wide range of radical groupings and novel cultural and artistic expressions to such exogenous incursions.

Until very recently there was little or no methodical documentation of the impact of Palestinian militarism on the destabilization and radicalization of Lebanese society. If and when Palestinian military presence was recognized as a protagonist in the war, it was largely depicted as though the Palestinians were trapped or drawn unwillingly into Lebanon's sectarian quagmire. Their own meddling in the internal affairs of Lebanon was dismissed as *tawrit*, a conspiratorial design to tame or liquidate the PLO. Its deepening involvement in heavy fighting was seen as an act of self-defense to protect its own defenseless civilians in hapless refugee camps or to provide support to the progressive forces of their endangered Lebanese allies. Others go further to suggest how an otherwise pure and emancipating revolutionary movement was corrupted and demoralized by Lebanon's tribalism and confessional politics.[5] Two noted and recent exceptions are Winslow (1996) and el-Khazin (2000) who provide persuasive evidence of the role of Palestinian militarism in undermining the consensual character of Lebanese politics and in escalating the magnitude of violence.

Similar claims are also made regarding the massive infusion of oil revenues. So much, in fact, is made of the pervasive impact of the ubiquitous petrodollar, that Lebanon is often reduced to a disparate medley of languishing mountainous fiefdoms, desolate and impoverished rural enclaves, and sparsely settled urban centers until resurrected by the gush of Arab oil!

Finally, and perhaps most intriguing, is the view that the boom Lebanon enjoyed was largely accidental and momentary, more the outcome of what its surrounding regimes were beleaguered with at the time rather than the result of indigenous sources. While much of the Middle East was embroiled in the Arab-Israeli struggle or convulsed by factional and/or ideological rivalries, Lebanon stood aloof, reaping the benefits from the disorders of others. Even Lebanon's lush topography and scenic beauty became appealing only when juxtaposed against the overwhelmingly arid and desert landscape of the region.

There is a painful irony in all this. When Lebanon is not being maligned as a flawed, artificial creation, its accomplishments—little as they may seem—are linked to external and fortuitous circumstances. Its blemishes, however, are always attributed to endemic forces and internal contradictions. The Lebanese, in other words, are only made responsible for their country's shortcomings and the disasters that have beleaguered it. They are accorded little or no credit for its achievements.

In much the same vein, Lebanon's legacy as an asylum, much of the economic allures it enjoyed during the 1960s and 1970s, as a haven for foreign capital and displaced minorities, are attributed to the chaos of surrounding Arab regimes. In short, rather than considering how Lebanon might have been made more vulnerable by such forces, we turn around instead and assail it for reaping the benefits of the disorders of others. The victim becomes, as it were, the avenger. In Sandra Mackey's words (1989), perhaps the latest example of those popularized obituaries of Lebanon, one finds typical expressions of such uncharitable views: "If Lebanon was pulsating in the 1960s, it was vibrating by early 1975. With the oil boom in the Arabian peninsula, every source of Lebanon's income had ballooned. Once more Lebanon's economy reaped the benefits of events beyond its borders. But this time the infusion of capital was Arab money." (Mackey 1989: 8). Awad is even more explicit in attributing the economic prosperity Lebanon enjoyed between 1950–1975 to either coincidental or external factors. This "remarkable growth was not the result of any coherent development strategy carried out by the public sector." Instead Awad argues, it was "coincidental, the product of external factors, such as the Arab-Israeli conflict, the closure of the Suez Canal or the nationalization of Arab economies" (Awad 1991: 83–86).

Can one not advance a more balanced and realistic assessment of the legacy of this inside-outside polemics? Much after all can be extracted from at least the country's blissful peacetime history to reinforce the more auspicious view; namely that when external disruptive sources are neutralized or contained, various Lebanese communities were able to evolve fairly adaptive and accommodating strategies for peaceful coexistence. This is a view persuasively argued and documented by, among others, Theodor Hanf, 1993; George Corm, 1988; Samir Khalaf, 1995; Charles Winslow, 1996; Farid El-Khazen, 2000.

For almost a century, from 1860 to 1958, an epoch marked by internal, regional, and global turmoil in the lives of new nations, Lebanon was comparatively peaceful and free of any manifestations of collective violence. Emerging from decades of bloody communal strife, it weathered the dislocations it was beset with as a plural society embroiled in the tumultuous transformations of a troubled region. Given its deficient civility, Lebanon might have never become a nation-state but was doomed instead to remain, as Albert Hourani would say, a "republic of tribes and villages." (Hourani

1988: 6). It was a republic nonetheless. With all its grievous faults, it survived the collapse and dismemberment of the Ottoman Empire, successive foreign penetrations and political rearrangements, ravages of a devastating famine, the ferments of two world wars and the sociocultural dislocations associated with swift, discordant societal transformations.

These are not trivial or ordinary accomplishments. A century is also a long time in the history of a young republic. Detractors of Lebanon, and they are many, particularly those who dismiss it as a genetically flawed, artificial entity or a victim of its own belligerent culture and innate proclivity for violence, are remiss when they continue to overlook this felicitous stretch of its eventful history.

Lebanon's less felicitous and darkest moments also need to be reexamined. At the least, its repeated encounters with political unrest must be explored in an effort to elucidate the belligerent nature and consequences of this persisting inside-outside dialectics. Each of the three major interludes or episodes of collective strife — the successive peasant uprisings and communal conflicts in the nineteenth century, the 1958 civil war, and the latest prolonged hostilities — have been subjected to an endless barrage of studies. There is clearly no dearth of information or speculation on each.

Some, particularly the circumstances and events associated with the sectarian massacres of 1860, have been perhaps over-studied from every conceivable perspective. Depending on archival sources and records consulted (i.e. Ottoman, French, British, missionaries or local chronicles) one is prone to emerge with markedly different readings or analyses (see, for example, three of the most recent studies: Akarli 1995; Fawaz 1994; Makdisi 2000). Hence, matters such as the identity of protagonists and/or perpetrators of the conflict, the issues or precursors which sparked it off, the unfolding character and pattern of violence, how it was sustained and compounded, and the eventual cessation of the conflict all remain open to question.

Similar ambiguities underlie interpretation of the 1958 civil war. The episode was clearly more limited in scope and magnitude when compared to the massacres of 1860 or the recent prolonged hostilities. It marked, though, a significant threshold in Lebanon's political history. For nearly a century Lebanon had managed to live with visible socioeconomic, cultural, and ideological differences and cleavages without breaking up into open armed conflict. What happened in 1958 to radicalize the tone of political discourse?

Since it was the first major breakdown in political order after such a long peaceful interlude, it provoked a massive volume of writing.[6] Access to declassified documents has recently revived interest in re-examining U.S. perceptions and its role in the crisis.[7] In all this, one discerns considerable controversy regarding the nature and consequences of the inside-outside dynamics. This is visible first in the plurality of nomenclatures and labels it acquired; ranging from "insurgency," "rebellion," "sedition," "insurrection," to "revolt," "counter-revolt," or "armed resistance." More substantively, there are differences in what was the crisis attributed to. Was it, as some argued, provoked largely by internal dislocations, socioeconomic discontent and other sources of instability associated with the struggle for power and political succession? Or was it the outcome of broader regional tensions exacerbated by the Palestinian-Israeli struggle and ideological rivalries in adjacent Arab regimes? If both, how did the interplay reflect itself in the unfolding pattern of violence? What, more concretely, motivated and mobilized embattled groups into armed conflict? Answers to these and other related issues are contested.

Treatment of the prolonged hostilities of 1975–90, at least if judged by the relentless literature about it, is much more perplexing. This is understandable, given the dizzying and changing number of protagonists and combatants (internal and external, identified and unidentified, controlled and undisciplined, zealots and mercenaries); who was fighting whom and why; the alternating pattern and intensity of violence; the swift and successive changes in issues involved; what sparked the episodes off; and how they were sustained, escalated, and resolved.

Here, as well, the unending polemics is not quelled. Indeed, it assumes at times a vigorous and contentious debate. There are those who see Lebanon as an inevitable victim of its own precariousness and internal contradictions; largely a reflection of the fragility of its plural and open democracy, its failed consociationalism or neglect and fears of a growing segment of its population. To Moshe Shmesh, for example, the very "structure of the regime set up in 1943 was flimsy from the outset. What was surprising about the civil war" he goes on to assert "was not its timing but how long it took to break out." (Shmesh 1986: 77). Meir Zamir goes further to assert that insecurity, suspicions, fear, hostility, which stem from a long history of sociopolitical conflict and sectarian violence, are deeply ingrained in the Lebanese national character. They are, as it were, a natural appendage of its national ethos. "Politics and violence," he tells us "have always been closely interwoven in Lebanon. The country's political leaders and their supporters are weaned on the idea of violence and regard it as a natural part of their existence" (Zamir 1982:4). Others are more inclined to view it as a victim of unresolved regional rivalries. Even to those who recognize the mutually reinforcing character of the inside-outside dynamics, it is the changes occurring in the regional order that are held accountable for initiating and sustaining the conflict. This is also apparent, it is argued, since hostility only ended when agreement was reached among the major external parties involved in the turmoil (See el-Khazen 2000).

2 The Radicalization of Communal Loyalties

"Most societies seem allergic to internal anonymity, homogeneity and amnesia."
— Ernest Gellner *Culture, Identity and Politics* (1988)

"A prolonged civil war is the most overt societal schism. In the preliminary civil discord — no matter how divisive and mutually contradictory are the elements involved, no matter how long-standing the opposing values or how deep-seated the distrust — a society, however strained or artificial, continues to exist. Once civil strife has passed the point of no return into civil war, however, the prewar society has, for better or worse, committed suicide."
— J. Bowyer Bell, *The Gun in Politics* (1987)

"It is more difficult to quell an impulse toward violence than to arouse it."
— Anthony Storr, *Human Aggression* (1965)

A defining element in Lebanon's checkered sociopolitical history, one that has had substantive implications for the character and magnitude of collective strife, is the survival and reassertion of communal solidarities. In fact, the three overarching and persisting features — (1) foreign intervention, (2) the reawakening of primordial identities, and (3) the escalation of protracted violence — are all intimately related. This is, after all, what informs the major thrust of this study. We will, in subsequent chapters, identify and account for the various forms foreign intervention has assumed. More explicitly, an effort will be made to explore how the unresolved regional and global rivalries have contributed to the protraction and escalation of conflict and the reassertion of communal solidarities. The aim here is to document a few of the persisting features underlying the survival of communal loyalties, particularly those aspects of Lebanon's "retribalization" exacerbated by the inside-outside dialectics. How and under what circumstances, to be more concrete, are communal loyalties radicalized?

By focusing on different episodes — ranging from peasant uprisings, factional feuds, and "class" and ideological struggles to other intermittent incidents of civil strife — it is possible to elucidate how, regardless of their origins and overt manifestations, they are all transformed (or deformed) into sectarian hostility. It is also then, as will be seen, that the conflict becomes bloodier, uncivil, and more mired into the tangled world of foreign intervention.

In effect what is being suggested here is that it is possible, for purposes of analysis, to identify three different layers or magnitudes of violence. There is first social strife, the product largely of socioeconomic disparities, asymmetrical development, ideological rivalries, relative deprivation, and feelings of neglect and dispossession. These, normally, are nonmilitant in character and express themselves in contentious but nonbelligerent forms of social protest and political mobilization. Second, if the socioeconomic disparities persist and the resulting hostilities are unappeased, particularly if accompanied by feelings of threatened communal legacy and confessional loyalties, conflict and discord are inclined to become more militant and bellicose. It is here that social discord is transformed into communal violence; or in the words of Bowyer Bell (1987) that *civil strife* passes the point of no return into *civil war*. Finally, civil violence is not, or does not always remain, "civil." When inflamed by the atavism of reawakened tribalism, enmity, and deep-seated suspicion of the "other," internecine feuds, and unresolved regional and global conflicts, collective violence could readily degenerate further into the incivility of proxy wars and surrogate victimization. It is here that violence acquires its own inherent self-destructive logic and spirals into that atrocious cycle of unrelenting cruelties.

Within this context, it is meaningful to identify and account for some of the circumstances associated with the tenacity of communalism and its various manifestations. An effort is also made to consider how social strife is deflected into communal violence and ultimately descends into further barbarism and incivility. Queries of this sort are not only of historic significance. There has been recently renewed theoretical interest in the nature, manifestations, and consequences of renewed "tribalism" and reassertion of local and communal identities, particularly as they relate to the forces of globalization and post-modernity.[1]

The Resilience of Communalism

For some time mainstream theoretical paradigms — i.e., those associated with modernization, Marxism, and their offshoots — were quite tenacious in upholding their views regarding the erosion of primordial ties and loyalties. Despite the striking ideological differences underlying the two meta theories, they shared the conviction that ties of fealty, religion, and community — which cemented societies together and accounted for social and political distinctions — were beginning to lose their grip and would, ultimately, become irrelevant. Indeed, to proponents of modernization theory, notions like familism, tribalism, confessionalism were not only pejoratively dismissed and trivialized, they were seen as obstacles to modernity. So-called "traditional" societies, in other words, were expected to break away and disengage themselves from such relics of pre-modern times if they are to enjoy the presumed fruits of modernity or to become full-fledged nation states. Given the resilience of traditional loyalties, some proponents made allowances for interim periods where "transitional" societies might linger for a while. Eventually, however, all such precarious hybrids will have to pass. They cannot, and will not, it was argued by a generation of social scientists in the sixties and seventies, be able to resist the overpowering forces of industrialization, urbanization, and secularization.

Likewise to Marxists, communist and socialist regimes were perceived as "giant brooms" expected to sweep away preexisting loyalties. If non-class attachments and interests survive or resurface, they are treated as forms of "false consciousness" to mask or veil fundamental economic and social contradictions. In short, ethnic and primordial loyalties were treated, as Theodor Hanf (1995) put it, as transitory phenomena by modernization theorists and as epiphenomena by Marxists. Both agreed, however, that primordialism was destined to disappear. Both, of course, have been wrong. It is a blatant misreading, if not a distortion, of history in both advanced and developing societies. It is a marvel in fact that such misrepresentations could have persisted given persuasive evidence to the contrary.[2]

Ernest Gellner (1988: 6–28) provides such evidence while exploring the nature of nationalism and cohesion in complex societies. He finds it conceptually fitting to reexamine the role of shared amnesia, collective forgetfulness, and anonymity in the emergence of nation-states. Among other things, he argues that the presumed erosion of primordial allegiances is not a prerequisite to the formation of cohesive nation-states. Likewise, the formation of strong, ruthless centralizing regimes is not the monopoly of any particular state or culture. Seemingly cohesive and integrated old states are not as culturally unified and homogeneous.

Of course here Ottoman Turkey became the prototype of the "mosaic" where ethnic and religious groups did not simply retain much of the so-called primordial and archaic identities, but were positively instructed — through edicts, centralization, fiat, etc. — never to forget. As such, the Ottomans were tolerant of other religions but they were strictly segregated from the Muslims. The various "millets," in other words, mixed but were never truly combined in a homogeneous and unified society. Today such a dread of collective amnesia is amply visible in the dramatic events surrounding the collapse of the USSR and the unfolding disintegration of Eastern Europe.

Nor are the nascent new nations today bereft of the loyalties and institutions often attributed exclusively to civil and secular nation-states. Perhaps conditions of anonymity are true in time of swift or revolutionary social changes and turmoil. But after the upheavals, when the deluge subsides, when social order is restored, internal cleavages and continuities resurface. New memories are invented when the old ones are destroyed. Indeed, "most societies," Gellner reiterates, "seem allergic to internal anonymity, homogeneity and amnesia." (Gellner 1988: 9).

Lebanon's political history, both in good and bad times, reinforces this self-evident but often overlooked or misconstrued reality. Throughout its epochal transformations — the emergence of the "principality" in the seventeenth and eighteenth centuries, the upheavals of the mid-nineteenth century and the consequent creation of the Mutesarrifate of Mount Lebanon (1860–1920), down to the creation of Greater Lebanon in 1920, the National Pact of 1943, the restoration of unity and stability after the civil war of 1958, and the aftermath of almost two decades of protracted violence — some salient realities about the ubiquity of recurring "retribalization" are reconfirmed. One might argue that Lebanon has not been detribalized sufficiently to be experiencing retribalization. The term, nonetheless, is being employed here rather loosely as a catchall phrase to refer to the resurgence of communal loyalties, particularly the convergence of confessional and territorial identities. As has been demonstrated by a score of socioeconomic and political historians, the sweeping changes Lebanon has been subjected to, from internal insurrections to centralized and direct rule by foreign powers or the more gradual and spontaneous changes associated with rapid urbanization, spread of market economy, and the exposure of a growing portion of the population to secular, liberal and radical ideologies, etc., did little to weaken or erode the intensity of confessional or sectarian loyalties. Indeed, in times of social unrest and political turmoil such loyalties became sharper and often superseded other ties and allegiances.[3]

Confessional loyalties have not only survived and retained their primacy, but also continue to serve as viable sources of communal solidarity. They inspire local and personal initiative, and account for much of the resourcefulness and cultural diversity and vitality of the Lebanese. But they also undermine civic consciousness and commitment to Lebanon as a nation-state. Expressed more poignantly, the forces that motivate and sustain harmony, balance, and prosperity are also the very forces that on occasion pull the society apart and contribute to conflict, tension, and civil disorder. The ties that bind, in other words, also unbind. (Khalaf and Denoeux 1988; Khalaf 1991).

As the cruelties of protracted violence became more menacing, it is understandable why traumatized and threatened groups should seek shelter in their communal solidarities and cloistered spaces. Confessional sentiments and their supportive loyalties, even in times of relative peace and stability, have always been effective sources of social support and political mobilization. But these are not, as Lebanon's fractious history amply demonstrates, unmixed blessings. While they cushion individuals and groups against the anomie and alienation of public life, they also heighten the density of communal hostility and enmity. Such processes have been particularly acute largely because class, ideological, and other secular forms of group affiliation have been comparatively more distant and abstract and, consequently, of less relevance to the psychic and social needs of the uprooted and traumatized. Hence, more and more Lebanese are today brandishing their confessionalism, if we may invoke a dual metaphor, as both emblem and armor: Emblem, because confessional identity has become the most viable medium for asserting presence and securing vital needs and benefits. It is only when an individual is placed within a confessional context that his ideas and assertions are rendered meaningful or worthwhile. Armor, because it has become a shield against real or imagined threats. The more vulnerable the emblem, the thicker the armor. Conversely, the thicker the armor, the more vulnerable and paranoid other communities become. It is precisely this dialectic between threatened communities and the urge to seek shelter in cloistered worlds that has plagued Lebanon for so long.

Massive population shifts, particularly since they are accompanied by the reintegration of displaced groups into more homogeneous, self-contained and exclusive communities, have also reinforced communal solidarity. Consequently, territorial and confessional identities, more so perhaps than at any other time in Lebanon's history, are beginning to converge. It is in this sense that "retribalization" is becoming sharper and more assertive. Some of its subtle, implicit, and nuanced earlier manifestations have become much more explicit. Political leaders, spokesmen of various communities, opinion-makers and ordinary citizens are not as reticent in recognizing and incorporating such features in their daily behavior or in bargaining for rights and privileges and validating their identities. Even normally less self-conscious and more open communities such as Greek Orthodox, Catholics and Sunni Muslims, are beginning to experiment with measures for enhancing and reinventing their special heritage and particular identity.

Recently such symptoms of "retribalization" have become, as will be elaborated in subsequent chapters, more pronounced. Ironically, during the prewar and pre-Taif periods when confessionalism was recognized, its manifestations and outward expression were often subtle and attenuated. Groups seemed shy, as it were, to be identified by such labels. More so during the decades of the 1950s and 60s when nationalism and often secular and so-called progressive and ideological venues for group affiliation had special appeal (See Melikian and Diab 1974).

Today, as the sectarian or confessional logic is consecrated by Taif and, to the same extent, by public opinion, the overt expression of communal and sectarian identities has become much more assertive. Political leaders and spokesmen of various communities, of all persuasions, are not at all reticent or shy in invoking such parochial claims. Indeed, dormant and quiescent communal identities are being reawakened, often reinvented, to validate claims for special privileges.

Universities, colleges, research foundations, voluntary associations, special advocacy groups, radio and TV stations are all being established with explicit and well-defined communal identities. So are cultural and popular recreational events and awards to recognize excellence and encourage creative and intellectual output. Even competitive sports, normally a transcending and neutral human encounter, have been factionalized by sectarian rivalries.

These and other such efforts can no longer be wished away or mystified. They must be recognized for what they are: strategies for the empowerment of threatened groups and their incorporation into the torrent of public life. The coalition of confessional and territorial entities, since it draws upon a potentially much larger base of support, is doubtless a more viable vector for political mobilization than kinship, fealty, or sectarian loyalties. Hence, as we will observe, it was not uncommon that protest movements and other forms of collective mobilization of social unrest, sparked by genuine grievances and unresolved public issues, were often deflected into confessional or communal rivalries.

Theodor Hanf (1995) coins the term "ethnurgy" to highlight such conscious invention and politicization of ethnic identity. Circumstances associated with the emergence and mobilization of such identities are instrumental in accounting for the pattern and intensity of intra- and interstate conflict. Since all societies are, to varying degrees, horizontally stratified with vertical cultural cleavages, conflict is bound to reflect both the horizontal socioeconomic disparities and the deep cultural divisions. By themselves, however, the strata and cleavages will not become sources of political mobilization unless groups are also made conscious of their distinctive identities. Differences in themselves, horizontal or vertical, become politicized only when those who share common distinctive attributes also share awareness of their distinctiveness. Analogically Hanf translates Marx's "class-by-itself" and "class-for-itself" into ethnic group loyalties. Hence, only an ethnic group "for itself" can become a source of political mobilization.

Within this context it becomes meaningful to identify circumstances in Lebanon's sociopolitical and cultural history that heighten and mobilize the political and radical consciousness of communal and confessional identities. Of course technically speaking, communal and confessional attachments are not strictly "ethnic" in character, if by that is meant that the assignment of special or distinct status, within a culture or social system, is arrived at on the basis of purely racial or physical characteristics. But if "ethnicity" is broadened to incorporate variable traits associated with religion, communal, ancestral affiliations, dialect, and other behavioral and subcultural distinctions, then confessional and sectarian identities may well assume some ethnic attributes (Horowitz 1985: xi). It is also then that these identities become sharper and more militant. They acquire a density of their own and coalesce around sentiments of solidarity and collective self-consciousness.

Popular accounts then were keen on depicting, often with noted amazement, the eagerness with which impressionable teenagers flocked to the barricades, just as their older brothers only a few years back had taken to frivolous pastimes, such as nightclubbing, fast cars, pinball machines, and sleazy entertainments. (Randal 1984: 112–13). This is all the more remarkable since we are dealing with a fairly quiescent political culture, one without much background or tradition in military service, conscription, or prior experience in paramilitary organizations.

In short, what these and other manifestations imply is that religion is not resorted to as a spiritual or ecclesiastical force. It is not a matter of communing with the divine as a redemptive longing to restore one's sense of well-being. Rather, it is sought largely as a form of ideological and communal mobilization. Indeed, it is often people's only means of asserting their threatened identities. Without it, groups are literally rootless, nameless, and voiceless.

Such realities, incidentally, are certainly not unique to Lebanon. In an insightful and thoroughly documented study of Hindu-Muslim rioting and violence in India, Sudhir Kakar (1996) reaches essentially the same conclusion. The author also draws on other historical encounters — such as the anti-Semitic pogroms in Spain in the fourteenth century, or sixteenth-century Catholic–Protestant violence in France, and anti-Catholic riots in eighteenth-century London — to validate the inference that all such instances of collective mobilization were more a byproduct of cultural identities and communalism than a reflection of religiosity or revitalization of religious zeal as such:

> If we look closely at individual cases around the world, we will find that the much-touted revival is less of religiosity than of cultural identities based on religious affiliation. In other words, there may not be any great ferment taking place in the world of religious ideas, beliefs, rituals, or any marked increase in the sum of human spirituality. Where the resurgence is most visible is in the organization of collective identities around religion, in the formation and strengthening of communities of believers. What we are witnessing today is less the resurgence of religion than (in the felicitous Indian usage) of communalism where a community of believers not only has religious affiliation but also social, economic, and political interests in common which may conflict with the corresponding interests of another community of believers sharing the same geographical space (Kakar 1996: 166–67).

To Kakar, communalism then is a state of mind elicited by the individual's assertion of being part of a religious community, preceded by the awareness of belonging to such a community. He goes further to maintain that only when, what he terms, the "We-ness of the community" is transformed into the "We are of communalism" can we better understand the circumstances which translate or deflect the potential or predispositions for intolerance, enmity and hostility and how these are ultimately released into outward violence (Kakar 1996: 192). Enmity after all can remain at a latent level. As will be demonstrated, hostility between the various communities in Lebanon did not always erupt in bloody confrontations. Rather, it managed, and for comparatively long stretches, to express itself in a wide gamut of nonviolent outlets and arrangements ranging from mild contempt, indifference, guarded contacts, and distancing, to consociational political strategies and territorial bonding in exclusive spaces.

This is why it is instructive to identify those interludes in Lebanon's checkered history — the critical watersheds so-to-speak — during which feelings of communal identity were undermined and when the vague, undefined threats and fears became sharper and more focused. As will be seen, it is also during such moments that communities sought efforts to reconnect and revive communal solidarity and mobilization. Identifying with and glorifying the threatened virtues of one's own group is heightened and rendered more righteous — as the psychology of in-group/out-group conflict reveals — if it is reinforced by enmity toward the outgroup. (For further elaboration, see Kelman 1987; Group for the Advancement of Psychiatry 1987). If uncontained, especially when amplified by rumors and stoked by religious demagogues, the hostility could easily erupt into open violence. By then only the slightest of sparks is needed for a violent explosion.

A drop of blood here and there, in moments of aroused communal passions, always begets a carnage. If I were to express this prosaically or more crudely, there is a relationship after all between hot-headedness and cold-blooded violence. The more impassioned and impetuous groups are, the more likely they are to be merciless and guilt-free in their brutality. Hot-headedness should not here be mistaken for mindlessness. Hard-core fighters, both by virtue of their youthfulness and effective resocialization, are normally impelled by an ardent, often sacrificial, commitment to the cause and strategies of combat. Hostility is thus made more legitimate by dehumanizing, depersonalizing and reducing the enemy into a mere category; a target to be acted upon or eliminated. The "other" becomes no more than an object whose body is worthy of being dispensed with (see Volkan 1979 and 1985; Keen 1986; Zur 1987). Assailants can now commit their cruelties with abandon and without shame or guilt. It is also then that collective violence degenerates into barbarism and incivility.

Social Strife and Communal Violence

By drawing on the rather prosaic distinctions we employed earlier between "horizontal" and "vertical" divisions, we can begin to isolate the circumstances which radicalize communal loyalties. At least we can better gauge and ascertain the magnitude and direction conflict is likely to assume as ordinary social strife is deflected into communal and fratricidal violence and how this escalates or degenerates into barbarism and incivility.

Horizontal socioeconomic disputes, at least as the experience of Lebanon is concerned, are more likely to remain comparatively mild and less belligerent. Affected strata are prone to experience various degrees of deprivation and neglect. Their social standing is undermined. They become less privileged. Like other impoverished, aggrieved, and dispossessed groups, they resort to collective protest to dramatize and, hopefully, correct the injustice and inequities. Such mobilization, however, unless it is deflected into confessional and communal hostility, rarely escalates into violent confrontations.

Communal and sectarian rivalries are of a different magnitude. While social strata are embittered by loss of status, material advantage, and privilege, "ethnic" groups (in this sense confessional and communal formations) are threatened by the loss of freedom, identity, heritage, and even their very national existence. As Hanf aptly puts it, "politicizing ethnic distinctions shift the struggle from divisible goods to indivisible principles" (Hanf 1995: 45).

It is at precisely such junctures, as socioeconomic and political rivalries in Lebanon are transformed into confessional or sectarian conflict, that the issues underlying the hostilities become "indivisible." The intensity of violence is bound to become more savaging and merciless. It is also then that prospects for resolving the conflict without belligerence become all the more unlikely.

In his probing analysis of civil strife in Ireland, Bowyer Bell (1987) expresses this poignant dilemma in terms which are quite applicable to Lebanon, particularly with regard to that fateful threshold when civil strife crosses over to the "point of no return into civil war."

A prolonged civil war is the most overt indication of an attenuated societal schism. In the preliminary civil discord — no matter how divisive and mutually contradictory are the elements involved, no matter how long-standing the opposing values or how deep-seated the distrust — a society, however strained or artificial, continues to exist. Once civil strife has passed the point of no return into civil war, however, the prewar society has, for better or worse, committed suicide. There can be no restoration of the uncomfortable but familiar past, for civil war can lead only to the ultimate triumph and imposition of a new society, cherished by the victors, inconceivable to the vanquished (Bowyer Bell 1987: 169).

Alas, this is a lesson the Lebanese have yet to learn despite their repeated encounters with both civil strife and civil wars. It is in this explicit sense that prolonged or recurrent wars are the most overt indication that something is not changing. The *belligerent equality* so-to-speak has never transformed itself into the *peaceful inequality* that entails the designation of one as victor and the other as vanquished. Despite the intensity, massiveness, and depth of damage and injury, the wars went on. They imperiled and demoralized everyday life. There was perpetual hurt and grief with no hope for deliverance or a temporary reprieve. Like a malignant cancer, it grows but refuses to deliver its victim from the anguish of his pain. The enfeebled patient lives on, doomed as it were to be rejuvenated by the very sources of his affliction.

This is why Lebanon's experience in this regard, both past and more recent, is not very encouraging. In fact, it is quite dismal. Throughout the hostilities of 1975–90, cycles of violence were interspersed with efforts of foreign emissaries interceding on behalf of their shifting client groups to broker a short-lived cease-fire or an abortive political settlement. Lebanon's political landscape is strewn with the wreckage of such failed efforts. Cease-fires, in fact, became the butt of political humor and popular derision. As soon as one was declared, it was summarily violated. These were more ploys to win respites from the cruelties of war and recoup losses than genuine efforts to arrest the fighting and consider less belligerent strategies for resolving conflict.

Incidentally, comparative evidence on the relationship between civil violence and conflict resolution is very instructive. Unfortunately, much of this evidence tends to reinforce Lebanon's bleak prospects. At least a recent analysis of how six other instances of civil unrest have ended — Colombia, Zimbabwe, Greece, Yemen, Sudan, Nigeria, and the American Civil War — suggest that in cases where conflict is primarily of an ethnic, communal character in contrast to those provoked by economic and/or political issues, the likelihood of a negotiated nonbelligerent resolution becomes very slim (Rutgers 1990). Indeed, all communal wars end in blood so-to-speak. There must be a victor and a vanquished before combatants begin to consider negotiation (Kaplan 1980).

Fred Ikle arrives at the same conclusion, particularly when he distinguishes civil conflict from international wars. "Outcomes intermediate between victory and defeat are difficult to construct. If partition is not a feasible outcome because belligerents are not geographically separable, one side has to get all, or nearly so, since there cannot be two governments . . . and since the passions aroused and the political cleavages opened render a sharing of power unworkable" (Ikle 1971: 95). More interestingly, even if any of the major adversaries is defeated, other participants may not admit or recognize such realities. This, too, has plagued Lebanon for so long. Defeat is a state of mind; everyone decides for themselves when they are defeated (Carroll 1980: 56).

Being entrapped in such a setting of unresolved and protracted hostility is inflammable. The most trivial slight or petty personal feud can become, as was to happen time and time again, an occasion for the shedding of blood. Also as Peter Gay reminds us, groups caught up in the frenzy of vengeful bloodletting do not normally resort to violence to avenge a slight. Rather, they are more prone to seek, or invent, a slight in order to release their impulse for aggression (Gay 1993:31). Hypersensitivity to being insulted or violated, nurtured by muted enmity, almost always provokes a tendency to retaliate out of proportion to the initial offense. This was clearly the case in the massacres of 1860, not as much in 1958, but much more pronounced in 1975–90.

Quickly during the early rounds of the war of 1971–76, the conflict started to display many of the features of confessional struggle. The two major combatants — the Christian Phalange and their allies and the Palestinians and the Muslim-Left Coalition — behaved as if their very existence was at stake. Little wonder that the fighting quickly descended into the abyss of a zero-sum deadly rivalry, where the perceived victory of one group can be realized only by annihilating the other. Spurred by the fear of being marginalized or swept by and subjugated in an Arab-Muslim mass, the Kata'ib reacted with phobic fanaticism to what seemed to them at the time as an ominous threat. They felt that they were resisting not only the violated authority of state sovereignty but also their way of life, unique heritage, and national existence. Often the threat was willfully dramatized to incite and awaken communal solidarity and, thereby, mobilize reticent Christians to the cause of militancy.

Moderation is hard to sustain in the midst of distrust and fear. Progressively the Kata'ib, more so perhaps than other Christian communities, departed from their earlier support of pluralist social arrangements and their preference for a democratic dialogue over progressive reform. They reverted, instead, to a more fanatic anti-Islamic rhetoric. Such awakened parochialism, associated with sectarian hostility, provided added stimulus from the cultivation of reflexive hatred.

Palestinians were likewise threatened by the fear of being liquidated. Lebanon, by the mid-seventies, was their last abode so-to-speak. It had become at the least their most strategic stronghold. After the loss of its Jordan base, the PLO was more entrenched in Lebanon. It also jealously guarded the political and strategic gains it had managed to carve there. The 1969 Cairo Accord, by placing Palestinian refugee camps under PLO control, rendered them virtually inaccessible to Lebanese authorities. The accord was therefore tantamount to an act of national liberation. The logistical and ideological support they were receiving from Arab radical and rejectionist regimes, particularly after the Egyptian-Israeli peace accord, made their presence in Lebanon all the more vital for their survival. Hence, they were protecting not merely the privileges and freedoms they had acquired in recent years, but also the political setting that had nurtured and safeguarded their very existence.

So both major combatants were locked into that deadly zero-sum duel. As the magnitude of sectarian fighting became bloodier, so did with each renewed cycle of violence, the intensity of vengeance, and enmity. Some time ago Anthony Storr warned that "it is more difficult to quell an impulse toward violence than to arouse it" (Storr 1968). Once aroused it acquires a logic of its own. It feeds on itself and becomes self-propagating. Again and again, the omnipresent binary categories of diabolic "them" and virtuous "us" resurfaced with sharper and more deadly intensity. The enemy is demonized further and the conflict is seen as a war between light and darkness, between the virtuous and the damned. As ordinary, quiescent citizens are drawn into the vortex of such bellicose hostility, they too become more amenable to being engulfed in this pervasive and ferocious enmity. Almost overnight they are transformed into passive, helpless pawns caught up in an inexorable process. Aroused communities are abuzz with pejorative anecdotes. Adversaries compete in assigning blame and trading invectives. Attribution and name-calling escalates to new heights. Indeed, especially in the early rounds of fighting, it was elevated to a high art of rancorous political discourse. All the repressed residues of the past resurfaced. Adversaries, once perceived as rigid, became hopelessly intransigent. "Isolationists" degenerated into bigots and traitors. Disenfranchised and unanchored masses became aliens with "green faces." "Borrowed ideologies" became repressive, chaotic and obfuscating. In short, the bad became worse; the unsavory and undesirable degenerated into the repulsive and the demonic.

One has only to read a sampling of war diaries and accounts of combatants, or even those of dispassionate observers or neutral bystanders, to highlight the war-like implications of such predispositions. This seething enmity and fanaticism was naturally more visible in the polemical platforms of warring factions, militias, and their affiliated political pressure groups and parties. It also permeated the rest of the society. Pamphleteering, local historiographies, position papers and public pronouncements became legion and more rancid and divisive in tone and substance. So were church sermons and Friday mosque *khoutbas*. Colorful wall graffiti, expressive street displays, propaganda campaigns, elaborate obituaries of fallen fighters also evolved their own popular images and art forms.

Though largely symbolic, in that such manifestations may not inflict direct and immediate damage, they are nonetheless responsible for preparing the psychological and moral justifications for outward aggression. Violence is thus rendered socially acceptable and tolerable. Even wanton and gratuitous violence becomes, in the words of Robin Williams, "virtuous action in the name of applauded values" (Williams 1981: 26–27).

Like other such "ideologies of enmity," as John Mack (1979, 1988) calls them, they all converge on three overriding but related objectives: First, the glorification of one's community and the ominous threats to it. Communalism in this regard becomes a rapacious scavenger. It feeds upon the awakened sense of a privileged but threatened territorial identity. Second, the propagation of mutual vilification campaigns whereby each group depicts the "other" as the repository of all the ills and pathologies of society. Ironically, the "other," as John Keane aptly puts it, is treated "simultaneously as everything and nothing" (Keane 1996: 125). The enemy is dreaded and feared, but it is also arrogantly dismissed as inferior and worthless. Finally, these inevitably lead to the legitimization of violence against the defiled other (For further details, see Mack 1988; Penderhughes 1979; Keane 1996).

The moral and psychological implications of such strategies, though self-evident, should not be overlooked. By evoking such imagery the "other" is transformed into a public menace, a threat to security and national sovereignty. Hence it becomes easier to inflict violence against him. At least the moral inhibitions, associated with such acts of aggression, are suspended or removed. Indeed, aggression against the "other" assumes a purgative value. It becomes an act of liberation, the only way to preserve or restore national dignity and integrity. More palliating, it obviates much of the guilt of having blood on one's hands. And this is not, as will be elaborated later, necessarily the blood of strangers and distant enemies. Remorse in these instances is not as poignant. But as the ferocity of combat descends into the callused atrocities of internecine, intracommunal, and turf warfare (as it did when Christian militias were eliminating their Christian rivals, the in-fighting between Palestinian factions or between Amal and Hizbullah), the blood is quite often the blood of brothers and kinsmen.

Alas, as the recent history of "ethnic cleansing" tells us, the alleviation of guilt in the frenzy of battle is only momentary. When wars are nurtured by religious passions and the visceral hatreds that go with them, they acquire a self-destructive momentum of their own and they spiral, inexorably, out of control. Altogether they become harder to forget and even much more difficult to resolve. Entrapped in such an unyielding and atrocious cycle of vengeance and reprisal, fighting in Lebanon started to display many of the pathologies of barbarism inherent in uncivil violence.

3 The Drift into Incivility

"Religion shelters us from violence just as violence seeks shelter
in religion."
— René Gerard, *Violence and the Sacred* (1997)

"It is the group boundaries that determine the extent of human
sympathy; within these boundaries, humanity prevails; outside
them torture is inflicted without qualm."
— Randall Collins, *The Three Faces of Cruelty* (1974)

When, why, and under what circumstances does collective
violence become uncivil or drift into incivility? More concretely, how is
latent enmity released into open but limited conflict and what exacerbates
this hostility to assume the pathological manifestations of random and guilt-
free violence? Other than implying, as is conventionally done in defining
civil violence (i.e., that civilians rather than regular armed forces are engaged
in such civil disturbances), what is so civil about civil violence? Can civil
violence, in the first place, ever be civil? Is it not a rhetorical conjunction
of incongruous terms, bordering on the oxymoron?

This interest in the link between violence and civility is not, of course,
of recent origin. The vision of the world as a battle ground, a blood-splattered
arena fit for atavistic gladiators, enjoyed currency long before social Darwinism became salient. Thomas Hobbes's savage portrayal of life in the state of
nature as solitary, poor, nasty, brutish, and short, no matter how blunt and
extreme, was not just a ringing metaphor. What it asserted, as every school-
boy came to believe, is that humans are one another's natural enemies. More
pertinent perhaps to the concerns of this study, Hobbes went further to
marvel how ordinary people would behave so atrociously during the English
civil war of the 1640s. His answer has lost little of its poignancy. In the
absence of government, he told us, the stage is set for a war of all against
all, in which no holds are barred. Denied the protection of an able and just
government, deprived and threatened groups would do anything to preserve
themselves.

More than a century later, Adam Smith espoused competition and ruthless struggle to maintain one's self interest as an enabling and constructive force in society. Freud, of course, went further in accounting for the disquieting implications of man's psychological insecurities. Even when the sense of physical security is not threatened, people are predisposed to protect themselves psychologically by pushing their personal insecurities onto others. It is always easier to get neighbors and kinsmen to vent their wrath and pent up hostilities on each other. Outlets for such displaced aggression are naturally more ravenous in an intimate and closely knit sociocultural setting.

Most nineteenth-century observers, early and late, had few doubts that the human is fundamentally an aggressive animal. Peter Gay (1993), in his insightful and probing analysis of the "cultivation of hatred" as a constructive and destructive force in Victorian society provides persuasive evidence through the views of some of the towering thinkers of the day to reinforce the notion that this "sentiment" or "instinct" for destruction is innate in man. To most nineteenth-century Christian believers, the conviction that mankind is "inherently wicked — greedy, sensual, mendacious, aggressive — came naturally" (Gay 1993: 4). To secular thinkers and unbelievers, particularly those influenced by the views of Herbert Spencer and social Darwinism, man's intrinsic combativeness was, of course, an irrefutable premise on both philosophical and scientific grounds. Herbert Spencer, though not strictly Darwinian, became the prophet for preaching the survival of the fittest even if it entailed nasty combativeness and pugnacious rivalry.

Around the turn of the century, William James summed up the post-Darwinism view when he asserted that "ancestral evolution has made us all potential warriors" (James 1902: 366). A few years later, Georg Simmel, the brilliant and enigmatic German sociologist, reiterated the same verdict: that the human mind is endowed with a "fighting instinct. . . . an inborn need to hate and fight" (As quoted by Gay 1993: 4).

By the time Ortega y Gasset (1932) warned of the "revolt of the masses," the polemics over the nature and consequence of violence took a sharper turn. For Ortega, the revolt of the masses signaled a most pathological form of barbarism. It marked a regression to a Hobbesian order and was sustained by the sheer pleasure of destructiveness. It found expression in random violence, protracted disorder, the impoverishment and demoralization of public life, and the erosion of civility and accepted standards of morality and decency.

Others, particularly writers like André Gide (1950), J.P. Sartre (1964), Albert Camus (1956), Paul Goodman (1964), R.D. Laing (1967), Frantz

Fanon (1966), and other spokesmen of Third World insurgency advanced, of course, a more "theraputic" and salutary view of violence. On some occasions, they argued, violence (even barbarism) arises as a necessary stage in the dialectic of self-discovery. In other words, there are times when barbarism can be understood and condoned as a return to sanity, an experience through which society seeks to recover its lost integrity and virtue. This can be witnessed in virtually all post-revolutionary epochs, which are marked by rapid and threatening socioeconomic and political change. In such instances acts of savagery and violence — even coarse, indecorous and boorish behavior — become legitimate moral responses to the rampant immorality and hypocrisy that pervade the social fabric and the body politic.

Such conceptions often border on the "romanticization" of violence and treat it as a rejuvenating and purging force — a sort of rebirth or regeneration through commitment to militancy. Sorel's (1961) assertion that a class can be resurrected through violence or other familiar refrains of insurgency (such as those articulated by Fanon, Debray and Mao), that individuals can become whole again by participating in violent politics, are frequently invoked as a rationalization for violence. In his attack on colonialism, Fanon (1961) goes further to assert that the powerless are entitled to kill their oppressors. By doing so, they are in effect killing two birds in one stone: the oppressor within and the oppressor without.

There has been renewed interest, in recent explorations of the changing incidence and character of armed conflict, in mapping out the interplay among globalization, reawakened communalism, and the "uncivil" character of so-called civil wars. The demise of the Cold War and the disintegration of the Soviet Empire and their tumultuous reverberations throughout the world have, among other things, brought about a perceptible decline in major wars between nation-states. These and associated global events — particularly reform and liberalizing movements in the USSR and Eastern Europe and the presumed homogenizing impact of Western consumerism and popular culture — have reawakened the polemics over the nature and consequences of such transformations.

Some, often in apocalyptic terms, see in these momentous events not just the end of the Cold War or a watershed of a fundamental historical movement, but "the end of history as such: that is, the end point of mankind's ideological evolution and the universalization of Western liberal democracy as the final form of human government" (Fukuyama 1989: 4). In a similar vein, others herald these epochal transformations as blissful signs of the "retreat from doomsday" or at least as manifestation of the longest stretch of peace in recent history when the cruelties, "repulsiveness and futility of war" have now come to an end (see Mueller 1989; Melko 1990, among others).

To Singer and Wildavsky (1993), the world now may be divided into two distinct zones; one of peace and another of violent anarchy. The so-called "democratic zone of peace," comprising roughly one-seventh of the world's population, contains the comparatively prosperous and open democracies. This felicitous zone forms a "security community" where the rhetoric of war and militancy has ceased to be the main instrument of politics. Instead, civil peace, mediated and reinforced through nonbelligerent dialogue, voluntarism, competitive elections, and other venues of political participation in public spaces, prevail as the norm. The rest of the world constitutes the "zone of violent anarchy and turmoil." Here societies are entrapped in protracted war, poverty, and lawlessness. Civility, security, stability are longed for but never realized. Instead, people are embroiled in chronic "coups and revolution, civil and international wars and internal massacres and bloody repression."

These celebrated views have not, of course, gone unchallenged. Rebuttals abound. The world clearly cannot fall into such clearly demarcated zones. Even those who live within the so-called democratic zone of peace are "as much if not more troubled by violence than the majority of the world's population" (Keane 1996: 4–5). Some are berated for positing such a unilinear vision of the uninterrupted progression of capitalism into an idyllic facsimile of a conflict-free liberal democracy. They contend that while the world is moving away from bipolarity, it is being beleaguered by new fractious tensions and the reawakening of dormant primordial and primitive hostilities. For example, competition for world markets is likely to generate trade wars, marginalization of growing segments of itinerant labor, and other grievous dislocations. New forms of East/West, North/South, interstate conflict and those provoked by environmental degradations and human rights abuses are also bound to be exacerbated. Nor are the alleged allures of cultural modernity likely to be accepted without resistance. Sharp increases in reactionary movements, fundamentalist militancy, and so-called identity conflicts concerned with the preservation of cultural authenticity, ethnic, and tribal purity attest to this.

In a celebrated and polemical book, Benjamin Barber (1996), avoids such sharp dichotomies and polarization. Instead, he anticipates a world in which the forces of parochial ethnicity and tribalism, as epitomized in *Jihad*, and those of cosmopolitan globalism, as expressed in *McWorld*, are intertwined. Although the two sets of forces underlying each appear antithetical, the dialectics between them are seen as the central paradox in human history in that both are tearing the world apart and bringing it together. "Jihad" is forged around "communities of blood, rooted in exclusion and hatred, communities that slight democracy in favor of tyrannical paternalism or consensual tribalism." "McWorld" forges global markets rooted in consumption and profit"(Barber 1996: 6–7). While the former are driven by parochial hatreds and thus re-create ancient ethnic borders from within; the latter, propelled by universalizing markets, are inclined to render national borders more porous from without. Both, however, Barber warns, are bound to undermine state sovereignty and democracy. Both harbor a strong "indifference to civil liberties."

Globalism and Uncivil Wars

Controversy over these and related issues notwithstanding, one can discern a convergence of views on a few issues.

First, while these changes are associated with the decline of major wars between nation states, they have left in their wake a trail of bewildering and destabilizing transformations. In some instances this has led to the consolidation of larger entities and the longing for "European Homeland" and the burgeoning interest in such global issues as the environment, human rights, labor migration, world terrorism, epidemics, drug, and trade wars. In others, we see unmistakable evidence of a sharp increase in the incidence of so-called low-intensity conflict (LIC), mostly internal and communal forms of strife fueled by ideological, ethnic, racial, sectarian, and tribal tensions and solidarities. In either case, as Hüppauf has urged recently, "the line dividing war and peace has been blurred beyond recognition and civil society does not lead to the eradication of but continues to co-exist with violence" (Hüppauf 1996:2).

More important, most of these internal wars are sustained with outside assistance and patronage, thereby reconfirming the complexities of the interplay among local, national, regional, and international rivalries. It is also then that they degenerate into "Dirty Wars"; i.e., the proxy battlegrounds for other peoples' wars and the surrogate victims of unresolved regional and global tensions. One prime characteristic of all such wars, of which Lebanon and Yugoslavia are often cited as poignant examples, is the deliberate targeting of innocent civilian groups and the pervasive mood of unrelenting terror and fear that blankets the entire population.

Second, these world-wide "uncivil wars" have the tendency to degenerate into conflagrations that depart from the old moral precepts of "just wars." In other words, the costs of these wars, in proportion to their ends, are both unjust and uncivil. They are unjust because they are much too costly. The magnitude of destruction — both to life and property — are too high in terms of the accomplishments of the wars. They violate what Michael Walzer calls "the maxim of proportionality" (Walzer 1992: xvi). They are uncivil because the violence and destruction are usually indiscriminate, random, reckless. Innocent civilians are disproportionately victimized.

It is not being suggested here that previous civil wars were bloodless. Rather that the bloodshed, as John Keane argues, had a structure and organized form. Many of today's wars by comparison seem to lack this coherent logic other than murder on an unlimited scale (Keane 1996: 137). Furthermore the wars are "uncivil" not only because they violate rational calculation strategies, but also because violence begins to take on a life of its own. Rather than being politics by some other means, violence becomes an end in itself. Its "perversely self-destructive dynamics" becomes, in the words of Keane, "self-propagating."

This "revolving-door" of relentless cycles of violence, quite often provoked by "unidentified assailants" became, as will be seen, the most striking feature of protracted strife in Lebanon. Each bloody episode was begetting its own avenging reactions. Curiously, the episodes appear to take place at moments preceded by inexplicable lulls in the intensity of fighting or, equally puzzling, when prospects for reconciliation seemed auspicious.

For example, on that infamous day Kata'ib Party leader Pierre Gemayyel made a reconciliatory visit to Damascus (December 6, 1976), the bodies of four slain Kata'ib activists were found on a hillside east of Beirut. Without waiting even for Gemayyel's return from Damascus, Kata'ib militiamen went on a rampage and rounded up and summarily killed more than seventy Muslims picked at random on the basis of their ID notification of their religious affiliation. This "Black Saturday," as the label that dark day acquired, became a grim threshold for ushering in other such mindless vendettas.

When in the fall of 1976 the Kata'ib and other Christian militias launched their "cleaning" up operations culminating in the siege and "liberation" of Tel al-Zaatar and other suburbs (such as Dbayyeh, Maslakh, Qarantina, Jisr al-Basha, Nabaa and other mixed neighborhood in areas under their control) the LNM and their Palestinian allies retaliated by besieging the Maronite town of Damour on the coast south of Beirut. More than 500 people, it is assumed, lost their lives in Damour, as was also the case in Quarantina.

When Kamal Jumblat was assassinated, along with two of his close associates, on March 16, 1977, on his way home in Mukhtara, his outraged Druze kinsmen sought revenge among their most likely surrogate enemies. Though the assassination was attributed to Syrian agents, his frenzied followers went on a rampage and slaughtered more than 170 Christians in adjacent villages. In a vengeful act of impassioned *quid-pro-quo*, the proverbial Christian–Druze coexistence in the Shuf was dealt a grievous and irretrievable blow.

Avenging the death of Bashir Gemayel was much more gruesome in substance and implications. When the youthful President-elect was killed in the massive explosions that ripped through the phalangist headquarters in East Beirut (September 14, 1982), it did not take long for his bereaved followers to retaliate for their stricken leader. The incident released a flush of contemptuous outrage. As in other such episodes, the fury was not, of course, directed against those who might have had a hand in the tragedy. Instead, it was discharged on the most vulnerable and accessible proxy targets: Palestinian refugees in Sabra and Shatila camps. Given the outrage and the protection the perpetrators of the massacre had received, the victimization was bound to be gruesome. It turned out to be more barbarous than all expectations. Though the area was monitored at the time by the Israeli Defense Forces (IDF), Gemayel's own militia, reinforced by members of Major Haddad's South Lebanese Army (SLA), managed to get through and indulged in two days of utter bestiality. Indeed, they were deliberately let in by the Israelis. Close to 2,000 people, mostly children, women and elderly, were butchered. The IDF, clearly did nothing to stop or contain the pogrom.

Even state-sponsored invasions were not averse to such tit-for-tat strategies. When no legitimate grounds for retaliatory measures were available, alibis or "provocations" were willfully fabricated. The Israeli invasion of 1982 was one fully documented instance of such strategies. Menachem Begin, as Israeli Prime Minister, had promised President Reagan that Israel would not launch an attack on south Lebanon without a clear provocation from Palestinian or Syrian forces. For more than a year the Lebanese Southern borders were fairly quiet. The "Sinai Observers Agreement" between Egypt and Israel was signed. Saudi Arabia issued their bold declaration, the first to be made by an Arab regime, regarding Israel's right to exist. The U.S., Egypt and Israel were engaged in negotiations toward some kind of self-rule for the Palestinians in the West Bank and Gaza. Yet, despite all these reassuring signals, Israel sought to officially annex the Golan Heights, which had been captured from Syria in 1967. Shortly before the invasion (May 9, 1982), Israel shot down two Syrian MIGs during a routine reconnaissance over Lebanon. But the real pretext, the immediate "provocation" for the invasion, came when the Israeli Ambassador to Britain was shot down and seriously wounded in London.[1]

The incivility and futility of strife became more visible precisely because such atavistic forms of self-administered retributive justice were bereft of any redemptive or restorative value. The more merciless the scope and intensity of vengeful violence, the more remote the likelihood of reconciliation. It is also then that the vertical divisions started to assume a more fractious character. Communities became more cloistered and, hence, less inclined to entertain schemes for coexistence and cooperation.

Cruelty not only begets cruelty. It also becomes the breeding ground for bigots and hard-liners. In the wake of those early confrontations, the Damour Brigade of the Lebanese Forces vowed to avenge their fallen townsmen and relatives. They swore not to stop fighting until all Palestinians were driven out of Lebanon. Other Maronite leaders declared that if they fail to curb or restrain Palestinian presence in Lebanon, they would advocate a secessionist-separatist all-Maronite enclave. The LNM and their leftist allies retaliated by declaring that they would take measures to foreclose the political isolation of the Kata'ib.

Third, observers are not concerned simply about the increasing incidence of such local uncivil wars. In many places in the world, their form and content are undergoing such sharp transformations that they can no longer be understood, it is claimed, by the conventional analysis of ordinary civil wars, such as class struggle, national liberation, youth protest or ideological rifts and party rivalries. To a considerable extent they are akin to, or at least have much in common with, what Keane labels as a "late modern regression into 'primitive' or 'tribal' warfare" (Keane 1996: 136). Likewise Robert Kaplan speaks about the emergence of "re-primitivized man: a jagged-glass pattern of city-states, shanty-states, nebulous and anarchic regionalism in the grip of low intensity conflict" (Kaplan: 1994: 56).

Much of the internecine and intracommunal rivalries between the major combatants took the form of such "turf battles." These conflagrations had, naturally, more in common with tribal and factional feuds than with conventional warfare, revolutionary struggles, or class and ideological conflicts. They are also much bloodier than the benign label "low intensity conflict" suggests. Indeed, they are all the more baffling and painful because the

bloodletting is endogenous; as incredulous and abhorrent as the muted cruelties of "intimate violence" or the futile victims of "friendly fire." All the
malevolent and self-destructive inner logic of violence is manifest here: i.e.,
the corrosive proclivity of groups embroiled in conflict to eliminate potential
competitors from within their own groups to enhance and consolidate their
belligerency against their enemies without.

Here again the original sources which might have provoked the initial
hostilities become irrelevant. Caught up in the frenzy of blood-letting, combatants began to kill those they can; not those they want. Little wonder that
such internecine violence turns out to be the most atrocious. Its ultimate
pathos is not only inherent in the heavy toll of innocent victims it generates,
but, more perfidious, it is often inflicted upon, and by, groups with known
identities and histories. People were literally killing their neighbors and
friends of yesterday. This is why in the early rounds of fighting, militias and
fighters in close combat often resorted to wearing masks to conceal their
identities.

Virtually all the militias have had their hands stained by the blood of
their own brothers. Initially, this was most apparent in the infighting between
and among Palestinian factions. Early in 1977, mainline Palestinians of the
PLO were already engaged in pitched battles with those of the PFLP-
General Command and the Arab Rejection and Liberation Fronts. At other
times, the Syrian-sponsored Sa'iqa were fighting others, particularly those
with leanings toward Iraq or Libya. Often rival factions within single camps
(such as those between Arafat and Abu Musa loyalists within Fateh), were
riven with fierce clashes.

Among Shi'ites, the infighting between Syrian-supported Amal and
Iranian-supported Hizbullah was equally ferocious. These conflicts were exacerbated by their shifting global and regional sponsors. For example, when
Iran became suspicious of Syria's rapprochement with Washington, after
1988, it gave Hizbullah a freer hand in undermining Syria's proxy powers
within the Shi'ite community. More perplexing, sometimes Hizbullah
would be at war with a Syrian-supported militia in the Beqa while fighting
on the side of another Syrian-supported militia in south Lebanon.[2]

The most ruthless, however, were the turf wars among the Maronite militias and their contentious warlords. Coalitions and alliances readily broke
up into fragmented factions, each vying to extend and consolidate its powers.
Bashir Gemayyel's swift political ascendancy was largely a byproduct of the
ruthlessness he displayed in eliminating potential rivals (e.g. Tony Franjieh
and Dany Chamoun, both presidential hopefuls) in his quest to claim the

leadership of the Maronite community and, ultimately, Lebanon. In May of 1978 he encountered little resistance when his Phalangist militias attacked the coveted and strategic region of Safra and destroyed the military infrastructure of Chamoun's Tigers, the militia of the National Liberal Party (NLP). The elimination of Tony Franjieh was far more gruesome. Masterminded and led by Elie Hobeika, Phalangist forces raided Ihden (June 13 1978) and massacred Franjieh, his wife and child, and twenty-five of his followers.

The rivalry and intermittent clashes between Samir Ja'ja and Elie Hobeika for the leadership of the Lebanese Forces and the final showdown in September of 1986, was costlier and much more divisive. Hobeika's militia, reinforced by Syrian-backed Muslims from West Beirut, crossed over to confront the Ja'ja-Gemayyel coalition. Though Hobeika's incursion into the Christian enclave was repelled, it was the first such fateful crossover. It left grievous repercussions other than the heavy toll of casualties and destruction.

By far the most destructive of the intra-Maronite turf wars was the final confrontation between Ja'ja and General Awn. This was more than just a turf war since it pitted two Maronite diehards who entertained two distinct visions for safeguarding and bolstering Christian sovereignty. Ja'ja was calling for a "Federal Lebanon" to be partitioned among its various sectarian communities. Awn, on the other hand, favored a broader more Lebanonist vision, reflecting a "Greater Lebanon" of the past, than the constricted Maronite nationalist view envisioned by Ja'ja and the Lebanese Forces. Much like the cryptic biblical story of Cain and Abel, the sibling rivalry between Ja'ja and Awn was equally enigmatic in the hidden meanings it evoked.[3] This morbid legacy was clearly alive in Lebanon and equally brutal. Given the urban density of the Christian enclave and the technologies of destruction available to both (thanks to Iraq's Saddam Hussein), the campaign was bound to be devastating in its terror and ferocity. Patriarch Nusrallah Sfeir, like other outraged Maronite leaders, bemoaned this round of bloodletting as "collective suicide." After six weeks of reckless fighting and abortive cease fires, more than 1,000 lives were lost. This was more, incidentally, than the toll of devastations spawned by six months of artillery bombardment by the Syrians in 1989 (Winslow 1996: 276–77).

Finally, Lebanon's encounters with collective violence reconfirm another compelling feature of the so-called "new uncivil wars," particularly in the manner with which such wars violate another fundamental attribute of just-war theory. As articulated by Walzer, civil wars are considered "just" if they are seen as efforts to restore the *status quo ante*. In this fundamental sense, the wars of 1975–90, more so perhaps than their predecessors, were "unjust" because they rendered any prospects for secular reform all the more remote. They also eliminated the return or restoration of the modicum of civility, along with the liberal and plural coexistence of the pre-war period.

The Pathologies of Protracted Violence

All wars are atrocious. The horrors spawned by the Lebanese wars are particularly galling, I have been suggesting, because they were not anchored in any recognizable and coherent set of causes nor have they resolved the issues that might have sparked the initial hostilities. It is in this poignant sense that they have been wasteful, ugly, and unfinished. All they did is foment and regenerate a deepening legacy of enmity, suspicion, and implacable chasms and widening rifts within and among its communities. I wish to go further and suggest that they have bequeathed a maelstrom of unforeseen cruelties of their own, which have compounded this drift or descent into incivility.

Though each of the episodes has been subjected to extensive and repeated study, no synthetic or composite effort has been made thus far to reexamine the interludes together to extract and highlight their defining elements. Despite their varied historical contexts, they do evince recurrent features, which elucidate the intimate interplay between the magnitude of collective violence, reawakened communal solidarities, and foreign intrusion. Some of these features have become distinctive characteristics of Lebanon's political culture. Others share much with instances of collective violence in comparable historical settings. A few merit brief mention here as a preamble to the elaborate and more substantive documentation in subsequent chapters.

First and, perhaps, most striking is the distinction that needs to be borne in mind between the factors which *initiate* the conflict and those which *sustain* and compound its magnitude and consequences. Hopefully, it will be made apparent that the circumstances which impelled marginalized and oppressed groups to political violence were not necessarily those which sustained their mobilization and informed the direction, character, and outcome of conflict. This outstanding feature, which incidentally is overlooked by both theoretical and empirical studies of conflict, was to resurface time and again in all the interludes under study. For example, all the peasant uprisings in nineteenth-century Lebanon were initially sparked off by a sense of collective conscience and a concern for public welfare. Yet, all were deflected, at one point or another, into confessional hostility. Likewise, episodes of communal conflict, originally provoked by socioeconomic disparities and legitimate grievances, were transformed (or deformed) into factional rivalry. The enthusiasm for "class" struggle and collective mobilization espoused by Christian peasants in the North during the peasant uprisings of 1820 found little appeal among their counterparts in the Druze districts. By arousing latent confessional enmity, traditional Druze leaders could easily manipulate such sentiments to ward off or caution against such involvement. The lapse of nearly forty years (from 1820 to 1860) had done little in other words, to transform the loyalties and attachments of peasants.

The brush with civil unrest in 1958, comparatively brief as it was, also displayed this dramatic turnaround from a socioeconomic and political rivalry over "divisible goods" into a belligerent and fierce struggle over "indivisible principles." As this happened the character and magnitude of strife became visibly more boisterous and bloody. Grievances, strikes, demonstrations, and other forms of collective protest were transformed into armed clashes and bitter sectarian warfare. The protracted hostilities of 1975–90 were replete with such instances where the fighting acquired a life of its own and was propelled into directions unrelated to the initial sources of the conflict.

Another defining element stands out, one that also will inform much of our composite portrait of protracted strife. Initially, the uprisings tended to employ nonbelligerent forms of collective protest such as rallies, mass gatherings, petitions, refusing payments of rent and other feudal impositions. On the whole, however, even when the confrontations became more contentious, the resort to violence involved little more than the ordinary rifles and hatchets common at the time in factional combat and local rivalries.

By the time regional and European powers were drawn into the conflict, violence, in most instances, had escalated into actual warfare with regular armies, reinforced by the technologies of mass destruction; e.g., massive troop movements, naval blockades, bombardment, heavy artillery and the like. It is also then the damage to life and property became inevitably more devastating (Smilianskaya 1972:81; al-Shidyaq 1954, II: 226).

Another related feature, one which prefigured most encounters with collective strife, became more manifest: Insurgents, peasants, rebels rarely acted alone. In all episodes of peasant uprisings, for example, organizational and ideological leadership was assumed by Maronite clerics. It was they who first articulated the peasants' revolutionary attitude toward the feudal system. They organized them into village communes and appointed *wakils* as spokesmen

for the *'ammiyyah*. In addition to ecclesiastical intervention, the peasants almost always received either the direct or moral support of Ottoman officials
and foreign consuls. As usual these were inclined to manipulate the uprisings
for purposes unrelated to the grievances of the peasants as a protest movement.
The Ottomans were always eager to undermine the privileged status of Mount
Lebanon and the local authority of feudal chiefs. Indeed, playing one group
against another became an apt euphemism for Ottoman repression.

Foreign powers, always eager to gain inroads into the Middle East and
win protégés, also reverted to the same divisive strategies. This was particularly apparent in 1840. While European powers (France, Britain, Russia,
Austria, and Prussia) were all acting in unison to release Syria from its Egyptian occupiers, each had their own diplomatic agendas. Sometimes discord
within any of the countries, globally or regionally, would leave its reverberations on the course and outcome of the rebellion. Hence, as will be seen,
many of the local uprisings would be deflected into a regional or global
crisis. Indignant peasants, already violated by the adverse effects of European
economic penetrations, were victimized further. Kisrwan, in the process, was
assailed into a proxy battleground for other people's wars.

The internationalization of the conflict in 1958 also contributed to the
protraction and escalation of hostility. Events outside Lebanon (i.e. the Suez
Crisis of 1956, the formation of the UAR in February of 1958, and the Iraqi
coup in July of 1958) raised the specter of growing Soviet influence in the
region and undermined Western interests. Heated debates in the Arab league
and the Security Council, riveting world attention and the ultimate landing
of U.S. troops, did little to address or assuage the internal sources of discord.
The intervention, as was the case on repeated occasions in 1975–90, served
only to polarize the factions and deepen sources of confessional hostility and
fear.

A third element was the way violence, both in the nineteenth century
and 1958, acquired its own momentum and began to generate its own belligerent episodes. Embattled groups were entrapped in an escalating spiral
of vengeance and retribution; a feature which became much more pronounced and devastating in 1975–90. In such highly charged settings, the
most trivial slight or petty personal encounter can become, as was to happen
time and time again, an occasion for the shedding of blood. Hypersensitivity
to being insulted or violated, nurtured by unresolved hostility, almost always
provokes a tendency to retaliate out of proportion to the initial offense.

This too became another indelible feature of Lebanon's entrapment in
recurrent and escalating cycles of vindictive violence. One has only to read

war diaries and accounts of combatants, dispassionate observers, or neutral bystanders to highlight the belligerent implications inherent in such predispositions. In times of combat and periods of heightened hostility, communities are abuzz with pejorative inflections, insulting innuendoes, and the arrogant rhetoric of boastful muscle-flexing. Each maligns the other. They trade invectives, fabricate incriminating episodes only to reconfirm all the abusive epithets they had harbored about each other for so long. Even communities with no such visible history of violence or enmity between them were drawn into the vortex of combat. No sooner, for example, did the fighting break out in the early rounds of 1975–76, than permeable neighborhoods of "West" and "East" Beirut become transformed into barricaded and partitioned enclosures with their own warlords, militias, media, war system, and subcultural manifestations.

Residents of "East" Beirut, with its predominantly Christian and Right-wing leaning groups, would depict the "Western" suburbs as an insecure, chaotic, disorderly mass of "alien," "unattached," and "unanchored" groups aroused by "borrowed ideologies" and an insatiable appetite for lawlessness and boorish decadence. In turn, residents of "West" Beirut portrayed the Eastern quarters of the city and its sprawling suburbs to the north as a self-enclosed "isolationist" ghetto dominated by the overpowering control and hegemony of fascist-like organizations where strangers are suspect and treated with contempt.

Finally, the relentless suffering of the Lebanese epitomizes another curious anomaly, which departs from the experience of conventional civil wars. As John Keane (1995) reminds us, not only is the defining and crucial attribute of any civil war inherent in the use of direct violence by the protagonists against their enemies, but also that at some point, after the conflict or insurrection explodes into the open, the outcome of the conflict must be decided. To Keane, a civil war normally may be considered to have ceased when one of the following three conditions has transpired: (1) When one faction forcibly subjugates its opponent as in the American Civil War; (2) when the warring parties manage to establish their independence from each other, as in the case of the separation of Holland and Belgium; (3) or when the combatants are mutually exhausted and they opt, as in the War of Roses, to arrange a temporary truce.

None of these circumstances have ever transpired in Lebanon. It is in this fundamental sense that the country's "civil" wars have been "uncivil." Perhaps because of the overriding ethos of "no victor, no vanquished," which has long characterized its checkered political history, even bloody and often decisive confrontations (as happened repeatedly in the nineteenth century), never ended, or were never permitted to end, by the unequivocal defeat or victory of one group over the other.

The role of foreign brokers, in earlier and more recent episodes of civil strife, in either mystifying or obstructing the decisive resolutions of such encounters, cannot and should not be overlooked. As we shall see, patrons (self-appointed or otherwise) often for considerations unrelated to the indigenous conflict, intercede on behalf of their respective client groups. Instances of such meddling are legion. So are the alibis. In the name of amity, equity, balance, stability, peace, geopolitical considerations; if not mercy or the empowerment of threatened communities, power-brokers have never shied away from such alibis to rationalize or disguise their intervention. In fact, at times, like the proverbial fearless fools rushing in, they too have been embroiled in the country's quagmire; thereby exacerbating the tension they were alleged to contain. Their embattled client groups are once again transformed, as in earlier such episodes, into passive, helpless pawns caught up in an inexorable process. Lebanon is perhaps unique among nation-states in that it has never fully or freely willed its entry or exit from war.

Virtually all the episodes of communal strife in the nineteenth century reconfirmed this anomalous ethos of "no victor and no vanquished." The events of 1958, as will be seen, were yet another costly repetition of this unheeded lesson of history.

The outbreak of fighting had hardly started in 1975 when the disruptive and escalating character of the inside-outside dialectic was already strikingly visible. Fuad Faris, a leading strategist of the left alliance, was plain and unambiguous in affirming this relationship. He was also revealing the belligerent underside of the egregious interplay and a basic premise of this study; namely that the forces which initiate strife are not necessary the same which sustain and heighten its brutality.

> It must be concluded that, while Lebanon contained the necessary ingredients for an armed confrontation between the internal opposing parties, the brutality and bloodiness of the Lebanese war, its prolongation and delayed outcome, are primarily due to the increased interference of external forces and the meddling of foreign governments (Faris 1976: 175).

Had any of the earlier episodes of political strife been more explicitly resolved, by designating a winner and a loser, and resolving, thereby, the decisive issues associated with each, then perhaps Lebanon might have been spared many of the costly trials and tribulations of subsequent turmoil. If there is, after all, any logic inherent in the structure of war; any war, just or unjust, it is normally a derivative of some of the assumed benefits the victors come to enjoy. For only at the end of the war do the rewards of injuring occur, particularly the enactment of the winner's issues.

Once again, Bowyer Bell delivers another instructive message. "Every civil war," he tells us, "ends with the effect of a revolution: the construction of a society with institutions and values that create an intolerable life for a substantial portion of the defeated, whose very identities had been first transformed by the polarization and then shattered. The vicious, almost permanent psychic wounds of civil war are less a result of the cruelty of the contest, the extensive violence, battles of vengeance, and wanton destruction, than of the 'intolerable' terms of defeat, which must be 'tolerated' by one side and imposed, year after year, by the other" (Bowyer Bell 1987).

All the adversaries in Lebanon must, doubtless, realize that they are likewise caught in this double-binding predicament. They, too, have opted to suffer the more "tolerable" cruelties of protracted strife rather than the "intolerable" psychic wounds of defeat. Since, to many, sustaining the war meant at times no more than a discourse of belligerency, with its warring postures and rhetorical gestures, it is clearly more dignifying than the humiliation of defeat. And defeat in Lebanon will most certainly involve, at least to the major adversaries, exclusion from the reality of the old dreams and/or unwillful participation in a new and abhorrent world.

More perhaps than any other foreign broker, Syria has been quite adept at maneuvering its brinkmanship in Lebanon to reinforce the circumstances in favor of this attenuated myth of "no victor, no vanquished." Indeed, when it dispatched Syrian-based units of the Palestine Liberation Army (PLA) into Lebanon early in 1976, Syria made very explicit what its avowed objectives were; namely to ensure that neither side in the war emerged as victorious or upset the delicate equilibrium of forces. In January of 1976, they restrained the Maronite forces when they were gaining the upper hand. Six months later they turned to contain the Palestinian and Muslim left coalition when the logistics of fighting swung in their favor. This same oscillating and adept reflexivity has characterized Syria's strategies in maintaining its patronizing relationship with all its client groups in Lebanon. No groups were allowed to gain sufficient supremacy or hegemony over the others. Even prominent leaders who evinced such predilections were either cowed into political subservience or eliminated.

Syria's role in the Ta'if Accord of 1989, which was supposed to have heralded Lebanon's Second Republic, was also predicated on the premise that the "no victor, no vanquished" formula is still a desirable and workable arrangement. The Accord though, judging by its contentious birth, is still riddled with uncertainties. It clearly has not, as we shall see, reassured or appeased all communities that there are no real victors or vanquished. Nor has it safeguarded the country's sovereignty or achieved the desired political consensus and national integration.

Foremost, Ta'if embraced the principle of abolishing religious affiliation for filling all government positions, yet few practical steps have been taken thus far to accomplish it. More critical, the corrective constitutional changes stipulated by the Accord (i.e. more equitable system of power sharing by way of redressing the pro-Christian and pro-Maronite bias of the earlier system) were supposed to be implemented without undermining the political standing of Christians or inviting their fears. Stipulations of Ta'if notwithstanding, large portions of the Christian community continue to harbor strong antipathies for what they term *al-ihbat al-Masihi* (Christian hopelessness and discontent). The de-facto balance of political power has visibly shifted toward Muslims. A whole generation of Maronite leaders — particularly those involved in the last phases of 1975–90 war — have either been jailed (Samir Ja'ja'), banished (Michael Awn) or were forced into exile (Raymond Edde and Amin Gemayyel). No alternate core of forceful leadership looms in the horizon. While all other communities appear to enjoy uncontested leaders or spokesmen, the Maronites seem leaderless, splintered and bereft of compelling voices apart perhaps from the Patriarch.

More disheartening Lebanon remains today virtually under Syria's hegemony; almost akin to a subservient satellite state. Such transgression of Lebanon's sovereignty could not have been sustained without international acknowledgement and tacit approval or support. Ta'if, for example (in which Damascus incidentally was one of its major architects), calls for the redeployment of the 30,000 Syrian troops stationed in Lebanon two years after the implementation of constitutional changes. This stipulation has been arbitrarily overlooked. At least it has been reinterpreted by Syrian authorities to mean that no substantial redeployment or withdrawal of their troops from Lebanon can be expected before a final Israeli pullout from Southern Lebanon. Incidentally, this is why the issue came to a head directly after the Israeli withdrawal.

Damascus is also allowed to meddle with the political life of the country; both the broader macro issues of destiny hinging on foreign policy and external security along with the intricacies of petty local politics. Recent measures reflecting growing state authoritarianism, curtailment of media pluralism and permissive audiovisual networks (e.g. 100 radio and 50 TV stations), and postponement of municipal elections are all done largely with Syria's tutelage and prodding. Lebanon's economy, however, is not tinkered with. The country's proverbial laissez faire and free enterprise, with its aggressive freewheeling entrepreneurs and open-market credit facilities are perceived as Syria's Hong Kong. Beirut is today, doubtlessly, the largest construction site in the Middle East. The massive reconstruction efforts, let alone drug trafficking in the Beqá and the rampant kickbacks from public projects, provides lucrative outlets for Syria's economy and its superfluous manpower.

Within such a setting, Lebanon remains hostage to circumstances that render the inveterate inside-outside dialectics all the more vulnerable. It does not take much for Syria to maneuver any of its key proxies to destabilize the internal security and thereby justify its continued presence in Lebanon.

The Sanctification of Cruelty

One poignant inference may be inevitably deduced from our discussion thus far: that Lebanon's encounters with civil unrest have been largely unjust and uncivil. Despite the immensity of suffering and victimization, the country today is in a less enviable condition, while the prospects of restoring prewar civility (always precarious at best) are much more remote and improbable.

In light of the above, the nagging question resurfaces and needs to be restated: How could this fairly peaceful and resourceful society, with a comparatively impressive history of viable pluralism, co-existence and republicanism, become brainwashed into so much barbarism and incivility?

We have thus far sought the answer, like most scholars seem to be doing recently, in the so-called inside-outside dialectics and, more concretely in the case of Lebanon, in some of the macro geopolitical forces of unresolved regional and global rivalries and the belligerency inherent in reawakened communalism. Part of the answer may still be sought, I have been suggesting, in the unfolding and escalating character of communal violence itself. Once unleashed, violence is hard to quell, while its perversely self-destructive dynamics acquire a life of their own. In more conceptual terms, violence in this case is no longer a dependent variable but becomes an independent variable propelling and reproducing its own consequences.

By shifting the focus of inquiry in this manner we can better understand not only the forces associated with the origin and antecedents of violence but also those circumstances which sustain, reproduce, and escalate its intensity. By doing so we can also make judicious use of some insightful theoretical contributions often overlooked in such explorations.

Foremost, the existential experience of Lebanon, particularly since it is entrapped in such an atrocious and unyielding cycle of vengeance and reprisal epitomize the three sociocultural elements Paul Ricoeur attributes to any form of human evil, namely: "defilement," "sin," and "guilt" (Ricoeur 1967). By defiling (debasing and demonizing) the "other," it is much easier to sanction his killing and, hence create conditions for guilt-free violence. Natalie Davis (1975) in her analysis of popular religious rioting in sixteenth-century France, also talks about the "rites of violence" to elucidate the strategies Protestants and Catholics engaged in to "defile," "pollute," "desecrate" the other. Here, as well, we are given vivid evidence of how victims were dehumanized, which generated conditions for "guilt-free massacres" (Davis 1975: 181).

One is struck, the lapse of four centuries notwithstanding, by how comparable the manifestations of communal violence are. The mutual vilification; how Protestants were viewed as "vessels of pollution," while Catholic priests were "lewd" and accused of converting churches into brothels and arsenal depots. Masses, on both sides, were considered "filthy," "vile," and "diabolic." Hence, combatants are made to feel more comfortable about the merciless suffering they inflict on their reinvented enemies. All other atrocities normally elicited by the cruelties of confessional bloodletting — the desecration of religious edifices and symbols, mutilation of corpses, dehumanization of victims, etc. — had their analogues in Lebanon (Davis 1975: 156–81).

The exploitation of religious symbolism by inciting sectarian bigotry and reawakening the predatory forces of confessional zealotry became, doubtless, the most atrocious feature of the prolonged hostilities of 1975–90. In a culture pregnant with religious consciousness and latent sectarian enmity, defamatory attributions become more volatile. Negative stereotypes, lodged in the collective memory of each community, are reawakened. Little wonder that conflict came to assume all the manifestations of a baleful and deadly contest. The ugly events of the war are strewn with such vengeful episodes. One sectarian massacre begetting another of more appalling proportions. Some "unidentified elements" or "undisciplined" assailants are always held accountable.

With or without such scapegoats to alleviate collective guilt and mask the true identity of assailants, the fighting descends into the abyss of a zero-sum fierce rivalry, where the perceived victory of one group is achieved by the deprivation of the other. Again and again, the omnipresent binary categories of diabolic "them" and virtuous "us" resurface with sharper intensity. Hence it is either a victory for "us" or a victory for "them." The enemy is demonized further and the conflict is seen as a war between light and darkness, between the virtuous and the damned.

Much can be extracted from the massive propaganda literature and pamphleteering at various stages of the 1975–90 Lebanese war to substantiate the strategies employed by adversaries for manufacturing enmity and sanctioning violence. A cursory content analysis of two such prominent documents — the Kaslik, on behalf of the Christian Lebanese Front and the so-called "Aramoun Summit," on behalf of the predominantly Muslim National Movement (LNM) — reveals the depth of the polemics, mutual vilification, and consequent sanctification of violence against the "other." Considering the vile attributions they assign to each other, fighters involved in such purifying bloodbaths are not only purged of their guilt. They are also glorified into patriots and national heroes.

Bowyer Bell accounts for the legitimization of violence in Ireland in almost identical terms:

> In sum, all the actors feel legitimate, and all act within a tradition that authorizes their strategies and limits their tactics. Each is a patriot, none a murderer. All are rational, some even reasonable, their course, if single-minded, set from a partially understood past toward a specific if improbable goal. As with most other lethal political questions, the ground has been strewn with myths, special pleading, fine slogans, and elegant rationalizations. The distant observer may select from the lot, but the burden here is relatively simple. Even if the perceptions of those involved differ from those of the alien eye, the gunmen are not mindless, and their strategies and tactics are shaped by tradition and policy (Bowyer Bell: 1987: 169).

The implication here is that we should not dismiss or account for violence as though it is merely a byproduct of crazed or deprived groups or those driven by the frenzy of aroused religious passions. Gunmen, in other words, Bowyer Bell tells us, are not "mindless." Rather, they are shaped and socially constructed within a cultural tradition that authorizes and legitimates their violence.

Natalie Davis also reiterates this view. The Protestant-Catholic rioting she explored in sixteenth-century France is explained not in terms of how crazy, frustrated, deprived, uprooted groups were (though they may sometimes have such characteristics), but in terms of the goals of their actions and in terms of the roles and patterns of behavior allowed by their culture. It is in this fundamental sense that religious violence is related here less to the pathological than to the normal (Davis 1975: 185–86).

By focusing on the "normalization" of communal and civil strife, one is able to avoid some of the pitfalls often underlying the conventional analysis of episodes of religious and ethnic conflict. Two approaches, in particular, stand out and continue to survive in accounting for the persistence of sectarian hostility. Occasionally they resurface and are extended to account for the pathologies of terrorism and radicalization of Islam.

One approach perceives religious violence as an extraordinary event, the product of frenzy or the frustrated and/or atavistic impulses of irrational and "primitive" minds. Such impulses are symptomatic of the reawakening of the deeply rooted hostility lodged in the "collective unconscious" of each of the communities. Another perspective is more likely to treat such violence as a more usual dimension of social behavior, but is prone to explain it as a somewhat pathological byproduct of certain kinds of economic deprivation, status loss, marginalization, or even child rearing practices.

Instead, by following the insights and suggestive hints one can extract from the seminal works of Girard, Davis, Collins, among others, one is able to emerge with a more sobering and realistic view of communal strife. At least the enabling and disabling attributes inherent in ardent religious and communal commitments become more plausible. Religion is not assigned only a pathological role in inciting violence but rather in providing moral venues for its sanctification. In other words, as long as those engaged in violence maintain a given religious commitment, they are less likely to display guilt or shame for their cruelties. This is, after all, what Girard has in mind when he argues that just as religion protects us from violence, it can also allow us to seek "higher" and "nobler" justifications for sanctioning it. Religion, he tells us, "shelters us from violence just as violence seeks shelter in religion." As this happens, communities are entrapped in that vicious circle of vengeance and reprisal. "The mimetic character of violence is so intense it cannot burn itself out. . . . Only violence can put an end to violence and that is why violence is self-propagating" (Girard 1986: 24–26).

Religion in such instances elicits strong emotions because it connects intimately with some of our noblest sentiments and aspirations, particularly those of self-definition, love, peace, compassion, benevolence, justice, and the like. But then precisely because religion connects intimately with such fundamental values, violence is bound to be more brutal and ferocious. No quantum leap of imagination is required to account for the persistence of such seemingly inconsistent manifestations.

Robin Williams must have had this in mind when he spoke of the "sanctified cruelty" and "virtuous bigotry" inherent in all holy wars. "The annals of the past as well as the daily news of the present are filled," he tells us, "with the records of virtuous bigotry, justifiable homicide, sanctified cruelty, censorious and primitive piety, obligatory revenge and retributive justice" (Williams 1981: 35). The more recent work of Sudhir Kakar (1996) has vividly demonstrated that every religion, under certain circumstances, holds a vision of "divinely legitimized violence":

> In the Semitic religions, we have the Holy War of the Christians, the Just War of the Jews, and the Jehad of the Muslims where the believers are enjoined in battle and destroy evildoers. In other religions such as Hinduism and Buddhism, with their greater reputation for tolerance and nonviolence, violence is elevated to the realm of the sacred as part of the created order. In Hinduism, for instance, there is a cycle of violence and peacefulness as the Kali Age is followed by the Golden Age. Buddhist myths talk of Seven Days of the Sword where men will look on and kill each other as beasts, after which peace returns and no life is taken. Although Islam (especially in its current phase) and medieval Christianity have had most violent reputations, the question as to which religions have unleashed the greatest amount of violence is ultimately an empirical one (Kakar 1996: 193–94).

Randall Collins (1974) carries this a step further by providing a comparative sociological framework for the analysis of cruelty. The essentially Durkheimian perspective he adopts takes us, I think, in a more appropriate direction for a fuller understanding of the form and magnitude violence has assumed in Lebanon. He seeks an understanding of cruelty not in purely religious passions or commitments, but in the interplay between morality and the boundaries of group inclusion and exclusion. "It is the group boundaries," he asserts, "that determine the extent of human sympathy; within these boundaries, humanity prevails; outside them, torture is inflicted without qualm" (Collins 1974: 417).

Since confessional and territorial identities are converging in Lebanon, the resulting sense of communalism, as a vector for group solidarity, has been reinforced and heightened. Hence, any threat to the group is bound, as Durkheim would argue, to reunify it in its "righteous indignation." It is this set of moral boundaries which may place groups beyond the pale of moral obligations. Violence in such instances becomes "not just morally indifferent but morally motivated" (Collins 1975: 419). Here again the double-edged significance of such reinforced communalism becomes much more pronounced. As we shall see, in times of widespread fear, panic, and insecurity, displaced groups seek shelter in such spatially bounded communities. By doing so they become all the more distant and detached and, hence, more likely to be ferocious and callous in their combat strategies and tactics. At successive stages of the war, as adversaries became more anchored spatially, they lost contact with and empathy for their enemies. Such detachment, reinforced by reawakened enmity and political resocialization, eroded what little residue of human sympathy was left. Cruelty was guilt-free; it was celebrated often with the exuberance and hoopla of boisterous and joyful events. The annals of the war are etched with such gruesome episodes and icons of inhumanity, almost akin to a "danse macabre." The most sinister and grim were the post-kill celebrations amidst charred and devastated settings, with the mangled disfigured remains of slaughtered fighters and casualties displayed boastfully as trophies of the ephemeral victories of battle.

The reterritorialization of displaced groups in cloistered communities had another ominous byproduct. The sheltered communities themselves became more vulnerable and accessible targets. This is more so, incidentally, among the warring and traditionally more belligerent communities, namely; Maronite, Druze, and Shi'ites. Their enclaves, by virtue of their stronger and more integrative communal solidarities, became much easier to identify spatially. In other words, the indiscriminate and so-called random shelling which pounded civilian groups in enemy territory was not that indiscriminate anymore. Likewise, the casualties of car bombs detonated at congested marketplaces or intersections were destined, given the confessional rehomogenization of neighborhoods, to be from one exclusive community.

Here again, in other words, the enabling and disabling features of communalism became more pronounced. By seeking shelter in cloistered communities, displaced and terrorized groups found security, benevolence, relief, and psychic reinforcement. They also, however, ran the risk of becoming more accessible targets for collective violence and pogroms.

The form and magnitude of violence also became deadlier. The hand-to-hand fighting, street and neighborhood battles, gave way to random shelling, car bombs, full-scale manhunts, methodical "combing," and "clean-up" operations, besieging and blockading sanitary and food relief, kidnapping, detention, and collective massacres.

Reinforced by the more sophisticated technologies of warfare, the magnitude of violence was bound to escalate. Automatic pistols and rifles, the emblematic AK47 (the Kalashnikov Russian assault rifle used by Palestinian militias and their allied groups), or the American M16 used by Christian forces, gave way to heavier artillery, mortars, mobile rocket launches, tanks, and ultimately to the even deadlier technologies of full-fledged conventional weaponry of state-sponsored armies. By the time of the Israeli invasion of 1982, fighter-bombers, heavy artillery, and naval gunfire were routinely employed against residential districts. Cluster bombs, incapacitating gas, and white phosphorous "smart" bombs were also used. In fact, epitomizing the ultimate in cruelty and incivility, there is evidence that Lebanon was used then to test the battlefield effectiveness of new weaponry.

In this poignant sense, not only had Lebanon become a proxy battlefield for relentless regional and global rivalries, but also it was further reduced pitilessly to a testing ground for the lethal technologies of future wars.

4 Peasants, Commoners and Clerics
Resistance and Rebellion: 1820–1860

"Warfare was a quicker as well as a more honorable route to
riches than trade."
— Ernest Gellner, *Nationalism* (1997).

The mimetic character of violence is so intense it cannot burn
itself out. . . . Only violence can put an end to violence and that
is why violence is self-propagating."
— René Girard, *Violence and the Sacred* (1977).

There has been reawakened interest in the forms that peasant resistance are likely to assume, particularly in historical situations where open defiance is either impossible or entails considerable hazards (Scott 1985; Colburn 1989). Under such circumstances, it is argued, peasant resistance is prone to remain in the "hidden realm of political conflict." Hence, it is less likely to take the form of open collective acts of violence such as riots, rebellion, sedition, or revolutionary movements. Since peasant uprisings, anyway, are "few and far in between," it is more meaningful, Scott and Colburn tell us, to shift analysis to the more prosaic means of everyday resistance. In such instances, petitions, rallies, boycotts, sabotage, footdragging, false compliance, pilfering, and other such acts of resistance become part of the arsenal of relatively powerless and subordinate groups. Or, more likely, such hidden or muted hostility is seen as an expression of groups deficient in class consciousness or denied access to collective forms of mobilization. Such ordinary forms of everyday resistance become, to employ James Scott's apt expression, the "weapons of the weak."

Lebanon's experience with peasant uprisings is, in this regard, instructive in more than one respect. First, peasant resistance did not remain in the hidden or quietist realm of political conflict. Nor were such acts confined to the conventional forms of everyday resistance that seemingly mute and helpless social groups resort to in mobilizing protest or redressing their grievances. Second, peasants in Lebanon, perhaps more than other such insurrections in the Middle East (Baer 1982: 275), evinced attributes of collective solidarity and class consciousness rare among movements in small and highly factionalized sociocultural settings. In some instances, Christian peasants were revolting against rulers and overlords who were also Christian. Collective class-consciousness in such cases, clearly assumed primacy over confessional and fealty ties. Yet, these uprisings rarely remained in their pure form. They either merged with intercommunal tensions, rampant at the time, or were deflected into confessional hostility. It is then, as will be demonstrated, that fairly contained forms of collective protest degenerate into random and reckless belligerency. Finally, the Lebanese experience departs in a striking sense from another basic feature commonly associated with peasant revolts; namely, that they "have been repressed far more often than they have succeeded . . . and that for them to succeed requires a somewhat unusual combination of circumstances that has occurred only in modern times" (Moore 1966: 479–80).

In an exhaustive comparative exploration of peasant rebellion in Egypt and the fertile crescent during the last 200 years, Gabriel Baer concludes that the only such successful instances in the nineteenth century took place in Lebanon. This is particularly true of the Kisrwan revolt of 1858–61, which to him stands out as a "unique phenomenon . . . different in most of its features from any peasant rebellion in the Middle East" (Baer 1982: 312). It was clearly the longest, having established a "peasant republic" which lasted for about three years. It adopted principles of equality and democratic government. It was inspired and initiated by the peasantry itself, incited by the Maronite clergy, and drew support from among the prosperous independent elements of the new bourgeoisie of small towns. It enjoyed a populist leadership, reinforced by an elected council of representatives *(Wakils)*. It also articulated a set of explicit demands and managed to bring about a profound redistribution of property between the lords and peasants. Finally, and most telling perhaps, it accomplished all this without much bloodshed or violence. Baer concludes his seminal study by asserting that "such a unique revolt could occur only in a country whose social features differed from those of all other areas in the Middle East" (Baer 1982: 312).

The legitimacy of this claim can be ascertained only if efforts are made to probe into that set of "unusual combination of circumstances," to invoke Moore's query, which might account for the comparative success of peasant uprisings in Lebanon.

My intention here is not to provide yet another chronicle of such events. There is one too many already. Indeed, no episodes in the social and political history of Lebanon have been, perhaps, chronicled as much. One has to wade through a medley of discrepant accounts, situate their authors, check with alternate sources to verify the authenticity and credibility of their version of the story. Fortunately, quite a few have already been edited and subjected to such meticulous scrutiny and reexamination, let alone the impartial accounts and interpretations of contemporary observers.

My task here, instead, is less ambitious: to extract from such accounts recurrent features to substantiate the changing pattern of collective protest. What inspired and motivated the insurgents to collective action? When and why did such action begin to assume more belligerent manifestations? Were the peasants acting on their own, or were they instruments and/or surrogate victims of other sources of conflict? What, if anything, did these episodes accomplish?

Since the uprisings were, to a large extent, a reaction to some of the institutions and loyalties of "feudal" society, it is pertinent to begin our discussion by identifying those features of feudal society of Mount Lebanon which could have initiated and sustained collective protest.

Feudal Society of Mount Lebanon

In its broad features, the socioeconomic and political organization of Mount Lebanon during the early part of the nineteenth century may be characterized as feudal. In both its origin and evolution, the *iqta'* system had much in common with other feudal societies: The system of vassalage and the institution of the fief, the idea of the personal bond, the hereditary and hierarchical nature of social relations, patron-client ties and obligations, decentralization of the power of the state and the consequent autonomy of feudal chiefs in the appropriation of justice, collection of taxes, and maintenance of law and order. These and other attributes were similar to the predominant form of European feudalism. Yet, the system of *iqta'* in Mount Lebanon had some peculiar features that differentiated it from both European and Ottoman prototypes.

As the term itself suggests, *iqta'* denotes a system of socioeconomic and political organization composed of districts *(muqata'as)* in which political authority was distributed among autonomous feudal families *(muqata'jis)*. The *muqata'ji* was subservient to the amir or hakim who, as supreme ruler, occupied an office vested in a family — in this case the Shihabi Imarah or principality. Within the context of the Ottoman system of government, the sultan was formally the highest authority over the rulers of Mount Lebanon and their subjects. The amir received his yearly investiture through one of the sultan's representatives, the *walis* of Saida, Tripoli, or Damascus, under whose administration Lebanon and its dependencies were divided. Through the pashas, the amir also forwarded his annual tribute *(miri)*, which he owed the Ottoman Treasury. In effect, however, neither the sultan nor the *walis* — with the noted exception of Jazzar's governorship of Saida (1776–1804) — meddled very much in the internal affairs of Mount Lebanon. The amirs enjoyed considerable autonomy in exercising their independent authority. They had the double task of dealing with the demands of the Ottoman pashas and acting as arbitrator among the muqata'jis in case of internal conflict. The specific duties of collecting taxes, maintaining peace and order, requiring a limited annual amount of unpaid labor from peasantry *(corvée)*, and exercising judicial authority of first instance over all local, civil, and criminal cases involving penalties short of death were all part of the traditional authority of the *muqata'ji*.

Four rather unusual political features of the iqta' system of Mount Lebanon, all of which have implications for understanding the special character of peasant uprisings, can be emphasized:

First, and perhaps most striking, the *muqata'as* in Lebanon were not organized as military fiefs. Nor were the fief holders expected to perform any military duties in return for the *muqata'as* allotted to them, as was the case in Syria, Egypt, Palestine, and Iraq. The feudal sheikhs of Mount Lebanon lived in rural estates and not in garrison towns. The Shihabi amirs did keep a small number of retainers mostly for administrative purposes, but they had no significant armies or police force.

Second, the nonmilitary character of Lebanese feudalism was an expression of the personal nature of political authority and allegiance. Legitimacy was more a function of personal loyalty between protector and protégé than an attribute of coercion or impersonal authority. The amir, in other words, did not have to resort to coercion to generate and sustain conformity to his authority. Instead he relied on the good will of his *muqata'jis* and the personal allegiance of their followers *(atba'* or *uhdah)*. This generated a measure of mutual moral obligations and feelings of interdependence. Typically, such relationships assumed the form of a patron-client network. They involved the exchange of support for protection. The client strengthens the patron by giving him support, and receives aid and protection in return. Primordial as it was, this form of allegiance was not sectarian. The *muqata'ji* usually presided over districts that were religiously mixed. In contrast to this nonconfessional system stood the government of *iltizam* where only Sunni Muslims had the right to hold authority (Harik 1965: 420).

Third, the *muqata'ji* was a hereditary feudal chief whose authority over a particular district was vested within a patrilineal kinship group. He lived in his own village and maintained ties of patronage with his *atba'*. In contrast, the *multazim* was not idigenous to the tax farm he controlled. He was more akin to government official than a feudal sheikh.

Finally, the *muqata'jis* enjoyed more independence in exercising their control at the local level. Unlike the *multazims* in other provinces of the Ottoman Empire, they were autonomous feudal chiefs and not officials in a decentralized Ottoman hierarchy.

The system of taxation was flexibly, obscure, and generally irregular in its exactions. A system, however, did exist. Whether the fiscal organization was technically an *iltizam*, or something peculiar to the *iqta'* of Mount Lebanon is a moot point still debated by some historians, (Polk 1963: 32; Chevallier 1971: 82:89). What is undisputed, however, is that the Shihabi amirs were charged with the duty of forwarding taxes to the Ottoman Treasury by way of the governor of Saida, and that neither the amount of this yearly tribute *(miri)* nor their tenure in office were fixed.

Officially, the *miri* was supposed to be levied upon all sown land, and the amount of the tax depended upon the crop sown (Volney 1788: 66). Yet neither in its assessment nor collection was the system consistent or regular. Indeed, the tribute was arbitrarily set and varied considerably with changing circumstances. Rather than being proportional to wealth (Burckhardt 1822: 188; de Lamartine 1835: 294), the *miri* was often a reflection of the amir's power or special standing vis-à-vis the Ottoman pasha. In instances, when the Ottoman policy played rival amirs against one another, the governorship of Mount Lebanon normally went to the highest bidder.

The *miri* was not the only form of taxation demanded by the Imperial Treasury. In addition, a poll tax *(kharaj or jizya)* was imposed on non-Muslims who, for religious reasons, were not subject to military service. Another head tax *(fardah)* was also levied on occasion.

During the early nineteenth century, the system of *metayage* was beginning to transform the peasant-proprietor into a mere farm hand or *metayer*. As metayers or sharecroppers, the farmers were expected to pay their feudal landlord a specific share of the harvest, the size of which depended on conditions such as the type of crop cultivated, whether the *metayer* owned seeds and implements, and the existing irrigation conditions. Typical of the *metayage* system common in Western Europe during the eighteenth century, the Lebanese sharecropper paid rent in kind and was bound by personal obligations of subservience to his feudal lord: he did not have the right to marry without the lord's permission, and he was also forbidden to leave this feudal lord at will, whereas the latter could forcibly transfer him to another estate. Furthermore, the abusive practice of corvée often entitled the ruling amirs and feudal chiefs to demand free labor from peasants for construction of palaces, forts, and other public works.

In addition, the peasants owed their landlords other traditional payments and presents *(idiyya)*, which symbolized their fealty loyalty and obligations. These often took the form of prescribed presents on holidays, weddings, and other ceremonial occasions (Chevallier 1959: 48–50; Porath 1965: 78–80). These and other such taxing obligations indicate that the peasants' dependence on their lords was not entirely economic in character. For example, a newly born Christian boy was anointed in oil and baptized in order to symbolize his fealty to the lord (Porath 1965: 80; Aowad 1933: 130). The landlords often told their tenants what to grow, even on their private plots. Most intrusive, perhaps, a peasant had to secure a license from his landlord, for a fee, in order to get married (Churchill 1853, vol. 1: 45; Porath 1965: 80).

It is curious that despite the seemingly deplorable conditions of the peasants and the general impoverishment of the country, the economy of Mount Lebanon at the end of the eighteenth century was still considered by several observers as being relatively prosperous and viable. (See, for example, Polk 1963: 75). Although the land is constantly referred to as *miri*, it was actually the private property of the person or group holding the *miri* rights. At the end of the eighteenth century, Volney estimated that about one-tenth of the Lebanese land was held directly by the *muqata'jis* as their estate *(arzaq or aqarat)*, often committed to managers. The remainder was held by their vassals *(atba')* — who became in effect the hereditary farmers of the village — and by Christian monasteries and churches (Volney 1788: 64; Poliak 1939: 58).

The economy of Mount Lebanon was also remarkably self-sufficient. The Biqa valley was a major source of grain and animal products. Caravans from Hawran and other parts of inland Syria imported grain and rice from Egypt, which made up for the shortages not covered by what was grown locally. Cottage industry supplied much of the daily wants of the peasants.

The backbone of the Lebanese economy was, of course, its silk production. For centuries, Lebanon's highly prized silk had been the most prominent item of its industrial and agricultural exports. The production of silk was compatible with the basic features of Lebanese agriculture and its labor-intensive household economy. For example, mulberry trees, suited to the climate and moisture pattern of the mountain, were relatively easy to grow and could be exploited for a variety of uses. Likewise, much of the process of cultivating and reeling silk did not require the peasant to interrupt his daily tasks; and virtually all age groups could be productively engaged in the activity (Guys, 1850: 170). European demand for Lebanese silk increased sharply during the eighteenth century and with the introduction of modern processing methods by local and European entrepreneurs, entire village communities experienced considerable prosperity.

Some of the sociocultural features of Lebanon at the time were also striking and account, in part, for the successful integration of its pluralistic and differentiated social structure. Vertically, the society was highly stratified with marked social distinctions on the basis of status and kinship affiliation. A recognized hierarchy of ranks among the feudal elites had evolved as a rather formalized system of social prestige sustained by elaborate forms of social protocol and rules of conduct. The distribution of prestige among the different families was not arbitrary. It reflected a continuity of traditional considerations. A few of these salient features deserve brief mention. The most striking was the real power each of the families wielded. This was visible in the hierarchy of noble titles differentiating that of an amir, *muqaddam* and sheikh. Such rigid social stratification was naturally an expression of the vintage of their kinship genealogy, and the esteem the families enjoyed in the eyes of the ruling Shihabs. For example, only three houses held the title of amir (Shihab, Abil-lama, and Arslan), one *muqaddam* (Muzhir), and several (Jumblat, Imad, Abu Nakad, Talhuq, Abd al-Malik among the Druze; and Khazin, Hubaysh and Dahdah among the Maronites) were entitled to the rank of sheikh. Together these eight sheikhly families formed a special stratum of "great Sheikhs" (*al-mashyikh al-kibar*), differentiated from other feudal families (such as Azar, Dahir, and Hamadeh) in terms of titular prestige and the extent of their feudal tenure and control over their respective *muqata'as* (Shihab 1933; Aouad 1933; Salibi 1965; Harik 1968; al-Shidyaq 1970).

Property in itself was not the principal factor in determining one's social position. More precisely, the social honor the notables enjoyed in their respective communities did not vanish with diminished wealth. Given this intimate association between kinship and social status, it is little wonder that the family survived as the fundamental socioeconomic and political unit in society. So strong was this consciousness of lineage that families were closely identified with the particular *jib* or *bait* ("branch" or "house") they descended from. The whole spatial configuration of a village or town and the physical arrangement of housing patterns into well-defined quarters and neighborhoods reflected kinship considerations. Such cloistered territorial entities played, as will be seen, a crucial role in reinforcing communal identities and intensifying the magnitude of factional violence.

Kinship solidarity was further reinforced by the prevalence of strong en-
dogamous ties. Marriage outside one's family or village was rare. Doubtlessly,
economic and moral considerations, such as the desire to concentrate wealth
within the family, to avoid payments of dowries, and the concern for family
honor and virtue all played some part in sustaining endogamy.

Typical of highly stratified society, there was also little intermarriage between the various strata and even fewer instances of social mobility. The
possible exceptions were the movements of Abillama *muqaddams* into the
rank of amir and a few others — Talhuqs, Abd al-Maliks, Ids, Junblats — who
were bestowed with their sheikhly titles by the Shihabi amirs after the battle
of Ayn Dara in 1711. While the feudal aristocracy could be readily differentiated into well-defined strata of amirs, *muqaddams*, and sheikhs, no such
hierarchies characterized the commoners. They were all lumped into one
undifferentiated strata of *ammiyyah*.

Apart from the distinctions of status and kinship, the social structure of
Mount Lebanon was differentiated horizontally into isolated and closely knit
village communities. The mountainous terrain and the natural divisions of
the country into distinct geographic regions, each with its own particular
customs, dialect, folklore, and social mannerisms, rendered the village community a fundamental unit in the society of Mount Lebanon. Strong en-
dogamous ties, continuities in the patterns of residence and landownership,
attachments to feudal families who also resided in the village, along with
the geographic isolation from other communities, all tended to reinforce
village loyalties and make the village more conscious of communal interests.
So strong were these loyalties that village identity often superseded kinship,
religious, or class attachments.

The convergence of this unusual combination of strong village solidarity,
rugged mountainous terrain, and consequent isolation from centers of government authority and control must have incited the predisposition for collective protest. Several social historians have, incidentally, singled out such
ecological considerations as basic preconditions for peasant rebellions all
over the world (Baer 1982; Mousnier 1970: 337; Wolf 1971: 264–65). Eric
Wolf, in particular, is very explicit on this point. He asserts that the "tactical
effectiveness of rebellions in peripheral areas is tripled if they contain also
defensible mountainous redoubts" (Wolf 1971: 264).

Despite these divisions, the integrative institutions of feudal society managed to maintain a state of harmony and balance among the various sects
and strata in society. If there were any tensions, they at least did not break
up into open hostility until early in the nineteenth century. Indeed, the

Druze and Christians, in the words of an impartial observer, had "lived together in the most perfect harmony and good-will" (Churchill 1862: 25).

New Forms of Collective Protest

The state of harmony and security did not, however, survive for long. During the first half of the nineteenth century, Lebanon witnessed various forms of societal change that began to dislocate feudal relations and disrupt the balance of forces between the various groups.

Although the three uprisings were sparked off by different circumstances and expressed varying grievances, they had, nonetheless, much in common. They were all manifestations of the same socioeconomic and political changes that began to weaken the feudal system and challenge the legitimacy of hereditary feudal authority. The more specific issues provoked by the uprisings — such as taxation, land tenancy, conscription, disarmament — were all reactions to essentially the same phenomena: attempts by successive Ottoman pashas to impose tight controls on Mount Lebanon, and an enfeebled feudal aristocracy trying to preserve its eroding power and privilege. The uprisings were also an expression of an emancipated peasantry and clergy who were articulating a new spirit of collective consciousness. All those features were making their presence felt at the turn of the century.

From a broader historical perspective, the uprisings in Lebanon substantiate the three major patterns of political conditions which, according to Baer (1982: 255–263), have contributed to the outbreak of peasant rebellions. First, they are more likely to occur in situations where the central government has been weakened. The two earliest rebellions, that of 1784 and 1790, took place at a time when the rule of the Shihabi Amir Yusuf was undermined by the civil war initiated by Jazzar Pasha. Second, they are also likely to occur under the opposite conditions; namely, when the central government, through the imposition of central rule, becomes stronger. Under such circumstances, the feudal lords are weakened to such an extent that the peasants, as was the case in the Kisrwan uprising of 1857, were able to exploit the situation and revolt against the Khazins. Finally, when local feudal lords are strong and influential enough among their subordinate peasants, they become more empowered to react against the impositions of central government. This is, in fact, what happened during the 1840 uprising. Some of the Khazin sheikhs incited their peasants to revolt against Bashir II and his Egyptian allies who were coercing him to impose the exactions associated with direct rule, such as taxation, conscription and *corvée*.

The Uprising of 1820

At the turn of the nineteenth century, Lebanon had just emerged from three prolonged and turbulent decades of the oppressive tyranny of Ahmad Pasha al-Jazzar. Appointed by the Ottomans to the pashalik of Sidon in 1775, Jazzar managed to become the dominant figure in Syrian history until his death in 1804. Partly by intrigue and partly by inciting confessional rivalry and quarrels between Druze factions, he asserted his authority over bickering feudal chieftains, controlled lawlessness in the countryside, and was fairly successful in exacting and remitting the necessary dues to the Imperial Treasury. He detached Beirut from Mount Lebanon and proceeded, as he had intended, to bring the Shihabi Emirate under his complete control.

Jazzar's rapacious and tight control of the vilayet of Sidon offers the classic instance of monopolization of a province. He was in complete possession of the agricultural lands and had them cultivated for his own profit. He was virtually a partner of merchants and artisans, imposed himself as their money-lender and banker, fixed arbitrary prices for their goods, and demanded excessive custom duties. He increased the revenues from direct taxation by farming out the towns and districts of his province at exorbitant sums. Growing insecurity in the countryside, usurious rates of interest, poor means of transportation, shortages of credit, and the primitive state of agriculture were beginning to deplete the modest economic prosperity the Mountain had enjoyed thus far.

The effects of all this were momentous. Jazzar had in effect converted the Druze amirs into "instruments of oppression on behalf of the Turkish authorities" (Gibb and Bowen 1957: 68). In doing so he contributed, in no small part, to the decline of feudal authority. With Jazzar's exit, Amir Bashir proceeded to restore the diminished prestige of the Shihabi Emirate. To this end he sought to consolidate his position by curbing the power of the feudal families, particularly the Druze *muqata'jis*.

Between 1804 and 1819, Bashir was the unrivaled master of Lebanon. He had eliminated all possible sources of local rivalry. He opened up the country to persecuted Christians, Druze, and other dissident Muslims and fugitives from the interior of Syria. He launched upon an impressive array of public works and substituted his own stern but benevolent justice for the caprice and tyranny of feudal amirs and sheikhs. Consequently he could pose as the champion of the Ottomans in Syria (Salibi 1965: 23–24). Circumstances, however, took a sharp turn for the worse in 1819 and generated the set of events that were to plunge Lebanon into a series of protracted crises.

In 1819 Abdallah Pasha succeeded Suleiman as governor of Akka. Like his notorious predecessor, Jazzar, he did not relish the prospect of a strong and autonomous amir in Mount Lebanon. Accordingly, shortly after his appointment, he started his incessant demands for an exorbitant tribute from Bashir. When the Amir showed reluctance, the Pasha applied pressure by arresting Bashir's subjects who happened to be in Sidon and Beirut at the time. Eventually, Bashir was compelled to concede to the Pasha's demands and had no recourse but to send his agents to collect the additional tribute. The tax agents had hardly started their work when the peasants of Kisrwan and Matn, incited by the clergy and two of Bashir's cousins coveting the emirate, (Amir Hassan and Amir Salman) rose in rebellion against Bashir. Unable to contain the uprising or to collect the needed revenue, Bashir went into voluntary exile to Hawran.

The central feature of the *ammiyyah* uprising remains no doubt the changing perspective of the Maronite clergy and their emergence as a powerful group in challenging feudal authority and in generating new forms of Maronite consciousness and communal loyalties. A brief consideration of how these transformations came into being becomes vital for understanding the role of the clergy in mobilizing peasants and commoners and inciting them for collective and organized resistance.

Typical of ties of patronage, the relationship between the *muqata'jis* and the clergy in the North until the end of the eighteenth century was one of mutual benefit and support. The *muqata'jis* provided the church with their protection and in return the clergy pledged their spiritual and material support. The Khazin sheikhs, throughout the period of their feudal authority in Kisrwan, which dates back to the early seventeenth century, had almost total control over the wealth of the district. Together with the Hubayshes and Dahdahs, they virtually owned all the land. They also exercised considerable control over the administration of the affairs of the church. Since it was part of their family prerogative to select prelates, they influenced the election of patriarchs and had almost complete control over the appointment of archbishops and bishops.

This convergence of interests between the *muqata'jis* and the church survived until the end of the eighteenth century. Under the impetus of new ideas, reform-minded clerics began early in the nineteenth century to advocate measures to rationalize church bureaucracy and to reorganize its economic resources in a more enterprising manner. Achievement criteria and merit were introduced to replace nepotism in recruiting and promoting clerics. Efforts were also made to render the Church free from interference by notables and more economically independent.

To this end monastic orders with considerable autonomy were established early in the eighteenth century. Typical of other monastic organizations, the orders led a disciplined, austere, but productive life. Since individually the monks were not entitled to possess any private property or wealth, they worked hard as collective bodies to secure their economic independence. Through their own labor, donations, gifts, and religious services (such as education for which they were compensated in land), they were able to extend cultivable land under their control and augment their wealth. One estimate claims that by the middle of the nineteenth century they occupied "nearly a fourth of the entire surface of the Mountain" (Churchill 1853: 88–89). The orders were also very active in industrial crafts such as wine, spirits, bookbinding, and printing. To free themselves from the domination of *a'yan*, they secured in 1812 a decree that deprived the latter of the right to levy taxes on the order's monasteries. Instead, the monks themselves were now authorized to collect and remit the *miri* directly. Nowhere was this more apparent than in the recruitment process. For example, while in the eighteenth century the upper echelons of the Church's hierarchy were almost an exclusive preserve of the notable families, in the nineteenth century the proportion of commoners in the same offices was significantly larger than that of the notables (Harik 1968: 122–26).

More important for understanding the active involvement of the clergy in the *ammiyyah* uprising was their role as articulators and carriers of a new Maronite ideology, one which reinforced the identity and solidarity of the Maronite community within Ottomany Syria, and in doing so undermined further the supremacy of the feudal system (Salibi 1959 1988; Hourani 1962: 226–45). In one sense or another they were articulating a new form of communal consciousness, which challenged the sense of personal allegiance, and kinship ties which were the hallmarks of feudal society. In fact, it was the clerical rather than the secular writers who first defined the community's revolutionary attitude toward the *iqta'* system (Harik 1968: 165–66). As we have seen, up until the last few decades of the eighteenth century, feudal society was held together by primordial ties of kinship and patron-client loyalties. Recognition of Mount Lebanon as a sort of national home for the Maronite community, ethnicity, and confessional allegiance, was emerging as a new source of political legitimacy.

The Church, early in the nineteenth century and particularly in North Lebanon, was in a favorable position to assume the intellectual and political leadership necessary for changing the world view or political outlook of the peasants. The priest was doubtless the most ubiquitous and central figure in the village. He was not only entrusted with the task of attending to the spiritual needs of his community and administering sacraments at various stages of the life cycle such as baptism, communion, marriage and death, but was also authorized to resolve family disputes and marital problems, and was often sought as mediator in factional conflict and village rivalry.

The enterprising monks were also a source of employment to the surplus manpower of the village. They were active in establishing voluntary associations and religious societies. But most important, perhaps, they virtually monopolized the school system and the printing press — the only media available at the time. Education was almost entirely under their control. Graduates of the Maronite College in Rome had, since 1584, been returning to Mount Lebanon and the clerical profession was the only vocation compatible with their advanced training and knowledge.

Prominent schools like 'Ayn Turah (1734) and 'Ayn Waraqah (1789) were established by graduates of the Rome College and served as models for other schools in Mount Lebanon. So fundamental was the instruction in these schools that almost all the individuals, both lay and cleric, who played a central part in the political and cultural awakening of Lebanon in the nineteenth century had received their training there (Hitti 1957: 401–11; Salibi 1965: 122–27; Antonius 1938: 37–38). So did many of the secretaries and assistants to the Shihabi amirs and Ottoman Pashas. Several of the graduates, particularly those who occupied the key office of *mudabbir* (administrative assistants or managers who, among other things, served as scribes, financial controllers, political advisors, and in some instances military commanders), rose to positions of great influence during the Shihabi *Imarah*.

In short, there was hardly an aspect of the secular life of the community that remained untouched or unaffected by the omnipresence of clerics or clerical education. Second to the family, no other group or institution figured as prominently in the daily lives of individuals. With a ratio of roughly one priest for every two hundred lay Maronites, (Harik 1968: 154), their presence was bound to be pervasive, let alone their growing prestige and influence.

The point being emphasized here is that even if the Church had chosen not to, it is doubtful whether it could have restrained itself from becoming involved in the political life of Mount Lebanon. Furthermore, no other group could have offered the organizational and intellectual leadership necessary for challenging the political legitimacy of the *iqta'* system. Clerics were far from selfless in this regard. They had a stake in undermining the supremacy of feudal families. So when the occasion availed itself, as it did in 1820, they had their share in inciting and organizing the *Ammiyyah* uprising.

The immediate issue at the time was taxation. A newly appointed pasha at Sidon had demanded an extra tribute from Bashir II. To be exact, the new impositions amounted to doubling the levies on peasants intended to satisfy the rapacious demands of the Ottoman Pasha along with Bashir's lavish expenditure on his palace and private mercenaries (Smilianskaya 1972: 68–69; al Shidyaq 1970, 2: 144–45). The Druze community in the South was solidly united under the leadership of Sheikh Bashir Jumblat, and would have certainly resisted such demands. Accordingly, the Amir turned to what he thought were the leaderless *muqata'as* of the North. He did not anticipate that organized sedition was already in the making.

Bishop Yusuf Istfan (1759–1823), as recognized by several historians, emerged as the prime mover and architect of the rebellion. As founder of the College of 'Ayn Waraqah and Christian judge for North Lebanon he had already assumed a prominent role in the affairs of the Mountain. His background and eventful life is instructive for understanding the role of the clerics in mobilizing the *'ammiyyah*. Like many clerical recruits, Istfan was an orphaned child of humble origins and a descendent of a family with extensive contacts within the church. He also had the benefit of a good education and opportunities, through contacts with foreign travelers and scholars (e.g. Burckhardt and Jirmanous Adam) to acquire knowledge of law, foreign languages, and exposure to western intellectual and political trends. Early in his career as an amateur historian and a young priest, he displayed an active interest in the wellbeing of the Maronite community. Later on, as titular archbishop, patriarchal secretary, and judge, he pursued such interests with devotion, often bordering on zealotry.

Istfan's relationship with Bashir was strained precisely because he had seen in some of Bashir's actions a threat to the hegemony and welfare of the Maronite community. His special affinity to the poor and common folk aroused his outrage against Bashir's taxation policy. He was equally incensed by the Shihabs' ambivalent treatment of their true religious identity, and the proclivity of the Amir in particular to disguise his Maronite faith in public. One particular episode in 1818, disclosing the strained relationship between church and state during the period, compounded Istfan's indignation. Amir Bashir had issued an order to his kinsmen to fast during Ramadan and to present themselves as Muslims in public (Harik 1968: 212). These and other such episodes offended religious susceptibilities and heightened the level of discontent, particularly among the lower clergy. By the time Bashir sent his tax agents to collect the added impositions, Bishop Istfan was already in a contentious and rebellious frame of mind.

Discontent was widespread. Many of Istfan's colleagues (particularly Bishop 'Aynturini) were similarly inclined to mobilize insubordination and protest. They also received the tacit support of Patriarch Hilou. The movement, however, was clearly Istfan's brainchild. His innovative leadership proved instrumental in one significant respect: he organized the peasants into village communes and asked each village to chose a *wakil* (representative) as a spokesman who could act on their behalf with other *wakils* and government authorities (al-Shidyaq 1970, 2: 145; Shihab 1933: 685; Churchill 1862: 38). Simple as it may seem, this innovative institution had revolutionary implications for transforming the political perspectives of peasants and challenging feudal authority and the nature of political allegiance to it. Insurgents from the Maronite districts of the North (Christians of the Druze-dominated districts of South Lebanon did not participate) drew up a covenant (composed by Bishop Istfan) in which they pledged their solidarity as *ammiyyah*, their unrelenting loyalty to their *wakils*, determination to oppose additional taxes, and to struggle collectively in safeguarding their communal public interest. A similar covenant was drawn between the village of Bash'alah and their wakils on August 15, 1821. Iliya Harik provides the following text of this interesting document:

> We the undersigned, all the natives of Bash'alah in general, old and young, have freely accepted and entrusted ourselves and our expenses to our cousin, Tannus al Shidyaq Nasr, and whatever is required of us in general and in detail with respect to the ammiyyah. His word will be final with us in all matters of expenses and losses. Regarding the call to arms, we shall obey him in the recruitment of men in our interest and that of the common people. We shall not disobey or relent, and whoever disobeys or relents in what we have written here shall incur upon himself our hostility and severe punishment.
>
> This is what has been agreed upon between us and him [i.e., the wakil], and he shall act according to his conscience, not favoring anyone over the other nor relenting in the questions of our interest. Whatever he arranges as the tax, we shall accept; and if he relents in pursuing our interest, we shall hold him accountable. . . .
>
> If we suffer a loss, it will be shared by all of us equally. We should all be united as one person, having one word and paying one tax. . . . (Harik 1968: 213–14).

Both the substance and tone of the covenant makes it clear that the uprising should not be dismissed as a mere localized grievance against the heavy exactions imposed on the peasants. Underlying such concrete demands lurked other more subtle issues and perspectives. First, and perhaps most important, the uprising reveals that *iqta'* society was far from a closed system incapable of internal transformation. The very fact that the sedition was sparked off by the joint efforts of clerics and peasants is sociologically significant. It is one indication that the personal allegiance to the *muqata'jis* did not restrain the *ammiyyah* from entertaining other forms of allegiance. Second, by choosing a *wakil* from among the *ammiyyah* and entrusting him with the task of being their spokesman on all matters of common interest, the covenants were, in effect, articulating a new concept of authority that necessitated a shift from the ascriptive ties of status and kinship to those based on communal and public interest. Third, this also involved a change in the peasant's political perspective: he no longer perceived himself as being bound by personal allegiances to his feudal lord. Instead, and perhaps for the first time, he was made conscious of his communal loyalties and the notion of public welfare *(al salih al umumi)*. Finally, inspired by the Maronite ideology of the clerical and secular writers of the day, the uprising embodied a spirit of Maronite communal consciousness against Druze aspirations for domination and privilege. It also articulated a nationalist fervor and a desire to seek greater autonomy and independence from Ottoman control (Abraham 1981: 41–46; Harik 1968: 221).

By standards of the day it managed to mobilize a fairly large number of participants. More than 6,000, it is estimated, were present at the Intilias mass rally when the *ammiyyah* covenant was drawn up (al-Shidyaq 1970, 2: 145; al-Hattuni 1884: 242; Daww 1911: 155). Faced with such massive resistance, Bashir opted to retire from the government of Mount Lebanon. Abdallah Pasha, the wali of Saida, had no option but to call for the investiture of two of Bashir's cousins (Salman and Hassan) to fill the abandoned post. The peasants and their supporters were, of course, jubilant and marched in triumph to Dayr al-Qamar to celebrate the ceremonial investiture. Their jubilation was, however, short-lived. Promptly, the two amirs dispatched their tax collectors to levy the added impositions demanded by the wali of Saida. Once again, the *ammiyyah* were outraged. They rose in protest and expelled the tax collectors. The Ottoman wali had no choice but to recall Amir Bashir from his voluntary exile.

Upon his return Bashir sent his sons to collect the *miri* from the Maronite North. The peasants again resisted and mobilized another mass rally at Lihfid. Their demands this time were not confined to the issue of taxation. They insisted on being treated at least on equal terms with the Druze and, more far-reaching perhaps, they were demanding that their governor should not be invested by an Ottoman wali and that he should be one of them (al-Shidyaq 1970, 2: 155; Harik 1968: 218).

The defiant, revolutionary, and independent spirit of the Maronite *ammiyyah* was too much for Bashir. He rejected categorically all their demands and called upon his mercenaries and Druze supporters in the Chuf for military assistance. It is at this point that the uprising, thus far bloodless, became more belligerent. Fighting broke out in various towns and villages; particularly Lihfid, Kisrwan, and Jibbat Bsharri. In one of the most violent encounters, a largely spontaneous and unprovoked scuffle near Ihmij, sources speak of almost 80 casualties (Daww 1911: 173; al-Shidyaq 1970, 2: 156). Even the leaders of the revolt were not spared. Bishop Istfan fled to Akkar, vowing to lead a life of worship and solitude. He was denied such felicitous longings. Being pardoned by Bashir, he went to pay his respects in 1823 only to be poisoned and die shortly after leaving the Amir's palace. Al-Aynturini met the same cruel fate. He too was caught, tortured and died soon afterward in a Maronite convent in Jubayl (Yazbak 1955: 159).

Despite the enthusiasm touched off by the initial stages of the rebellion the *ammyiyyah* sedition had some peculiar, often anomalous, features that detracted from its credibility as a genuine peasant uprising.

First, the initiative for political change remained essentially a Maronite phenomenon and was predominantly confined to the Christian *muqata'as* of the North. Only one Druze feudal family (the Imads of the Yazbaki faction) expressed willingness to support the *ammiyyah* cause. Efforts to seek the assistance of others in the South proved futile. The uprising clearly failed to spark the same spirit of revolt among the *ammiyyah* of the Druze. The Druze sheikhs, in fact, looked with aversion at the prospects of participating on equal terms with commoners, let alone the Christians of the North. When, for example, the two Shihabi amirs (Hassan and Salman) espoused the cause of the uprising and called upon the Talhouq Druze Sheiks to do likewise, their response to Tannus al Shidyaq who was acting as messenger at the time displayed deep repugnance. He was told: "We do not get led by the Christian commoners of that country . . . it is held a shame by us" (al-Shidyaq 1970, 2: 154). Given this enmity, one may infer that the ideological nationalism generated and encouraged by the Maronite clergy was parochial not civic. Even when perceived as a "class" rivalry, the commoners of the South remained loyal to their feudal sheikhs. They refused to heed the call of "class" or "public" consciousness articulated in the North.

Second, the *ammiyyah* was, to a considerable extent, *ammiyyah* in name only. At least in terms of sources of inspiration and leadership much of the support came from outside the ranks of peasants and commoners. The clergy provided the intellectual and ideological justifications and much of impetus for organization. A Khazin sheikh, initially, was chosen as leader. Other *ayan*, sheikhs, and amirs, were drawn into the movement because of factional rivalry and competition for office. They did not, clearly, harbor much genuine interest in the ultimate welfare of commoners.

Third, the uprising was not an entirely local affair. The great powers, particularly England and France, were already embroiled in the internal affairs of Lebanon in the aftermath of Napoleon's retreat from Palestine. Bashir, concerned about Lebanon's autonomy and neutrality, refused to come to the aid of the French general. This naturally endeared him to the British whose patronage he willfully used in his struggles with the Ottoman walis. During Bashir's brief exile in Egypt he negotiated with Muhammad Ali and his son, Ibrahim Pasha, the prospects for Egypt's expedition into Syria in an effort to secure Lebanon's independence from the Ottoman Empire (Abraham 1981: 52–53).

Altogether, the *ammiyyah* uprising was the first instance in which some of the established beliefs and institutions of iqta' society were seriously challenged. Significant as it was, however, the challenge did not signal the obsolescence of the *a'yan*, nor did it radically rearrange the forces that held the society together. Initially, the uprising brought about the exile of Bashir and the deposition of his successors. This is no mean accomplishment. Bashir's exile, however, was very brief. With the help of the Druze *ayan* he was, after all, able to crush the rebellion and reestablish order in the country. He also succeeded in collecting the taxes he had originally intended, and in imposing additional penalties for insubordination.

In this respect all that the rebellion did was to initiate the transition from the traditional ties of kinship, status and personal allegiance to a more communal form of social cohesion where the sources of political legitimacy were defined in terms of ethnicity and confessional allegiance. In short, it substituted one form of primordial loyalty for another.

The Uprising of 1840

The uprising of 1840 came in the wake of a decade of Egyptian occupation when Mount Lebanon was subjected to a thorough and intensive form of centralized control. Some of the reforms and changes introduced by Ibrahim Pasha, particularly in the economic sphere, were far reaching. The growth of public security, reforms in the fiscal system, rationalization of land tenure, growth in foreign trade, movement of capital, and the opening of village society, etc., produced a pronounced shift in the relative socioeconomic and political positions of the various groups and communities. The delicate balances that had held the society together were deeply shaken.

Evidence of disenchantment with the Egyptian presence (particularly the despised measures of conscription, *corvée* and taxation) began to appear earlier in the decade. The magnitude and intensity of all these dreaded impositions witnessed a sharp increase. Taxation became more oppressive. The 1820 uprising, as we have seen, was largely a revolt against the doubled tax Amir Bashir had imposed; hence, the rally-cry of the Intilias covenant "*mal wahid wa jizya wahida*"; i.e. that taxes should be levied only once a year. By 1840, taxes were being collected several times a year. Ibrahim Pasha went even further and sought to levy the polltax for seven years in advance. Taxes also increased enormously, at least if measured by revenues acruing to the Ottoman treasury. Citing Russian and French diplomatic sources, Smilianskaya (1972: 40–41) reports that the Lebanese *Jizya* amounted to not more than 150,000 piasters in the 1770s and 600,000 at the end of the century. By 1820, a sum of 2.5 million piasters was collected. This figure leaped to 8.75 million for the time of the Egyptian occupation, i.e. a five-fold increase accounting for currency depreciation. What compounded the outrage of the peasants was that revenues from these rapacious exactions were used for the maintenance of the Egyptian army and the wars waged by Ibrahim Pasha.

The system of *corvée* also became more ruinous. As we have seen, a measure of forced labor for public and welfare needs was common and considered legitimate, particularly if perceived as part of the fealty obligation peasants owed their feudal sheikhs. Under the Egyptians, however, *corvée* became much more abusive. It was extracted for contemptuous and disagreeable services such as the transportation of munitions and provisions to army camps and labor in the deplorable conditions of the coalmines of Salima and Qurnayil. These, and other such offensive measures, such as the billeting of soldiers with peasants to secure the payment of taxes (Baer 1982: 264), provoked the added outrage of villagers.

Of all the abuses associated with the Egyptians, conscription was by far the most widely feared. Like other exactions, it too witnessed a sharp increase. Prior to the Egyptian occupation, one out of three males was recruited in each family. By 1840, the proportion increased to one out of two (Baer 1982: 263). The dread conscription provoked was understandable. Since it involved a prolonged absence from a village or town, it imposed a drain on the economic resources of Mount Lebanon. It meant isolation from kinship and other primordial ties which are sources of personal reinforcement and support in village society. Indeed, it was so despised that potential conscripts would do their utmost to avoid its terrors. Beiruti Muslims — and their coreligionists in Saida and Tripoli — were known to seek refuge in European consulates and foreign residences, hide in caverns and excavations, or take to the sea in vain efforts to flee from the pursuit of Egyptian officers. Druze sought immunity in baptism or conversion, and there were cases of mutilation and emigration.

As early as 1834, there were uprisings in Palestine, Tripoli, and Lattakia against the imposition of such measures, and in each case Ibrahim Pasha was successful in subduing the insurrections with the assistance of Amir Bashir. He then turned to Mount Lebanon and requested from Bashir the conscription of 1,600 Druzes to serve for the regular fifteen-year term in the Egyptian army.

The initial success of the major Druze insurrection of Hawran in 1838 encouraged their coreligionists in Mount Lebanon to take up their arms in support of the same cause. Through French and European consular intervention, Christians had gained a temporary respite from conscription. They were, however, dragged into the confrontation in a more damaging manner. Ibrahim Pasha requested Bashir to recruit some 4,000 Christian mountaineers to assist in subduing the Druze rebels. In appreciation of such assistance, the Maronites were allowed to keep possession of their arms and promised no additional tax increases (Hitti 1957: 124).

This request was uprecedented in the history of Mount Lebanon. So far the "tradition of asylum" and the sort of peaceful confederacy that evolved between the various communities prevented any direct clash between them. For generations Lebanon was torn by internal strife, but it was the strife of factions and feuding families. Little of it took the form of religious rivalry. The Hawran episode, by pitting Christian against Druze, was bound to arouse bitter confessional hostility.

In 1840, however, Muhammad Ali reversed his decision and insisted on disarming all Christians of Mount Lebanon, which was correctly perceived by the population as a step toward general conscription. Even in normal times, mountaineers are generally reluctant to abandon their rifles. Indeed, village folkways have it that "the Lebanese would rather part with his wife than with his rifle" (al-Halabi 1927, 2: 6).

By then Bashir II had been reduced to a mere instrument of his Egyptian masters. Despite his initial reluctance, he had no recourse but to succumb to Mohammad Ali's commands. Accordingly, in May 1840 he summoned the

Druze and Christians of Dayr al-Qamar to surrender their arms. Throughout the months of April and May, in fact, Mount Lebanon was in a state of ferment and widespread anxiety. It was rumored that Muhammad Ali was conscripting Lebanese medical students in Egypt and that Egyptian officers were already rounding up recruits in Tripoli and Baalback. Indeed, shortly thereafter an Egyptian vessel called on Beirut, reportedly to carry off able-bodied males for military service (al-Shidyaq 1970, 2: 225; Farah 1967: 110).

The outcry, this time, was total. First in Dayr al-Qamar and then in other towns and villages the call for armed struggle became more audible. Christians, Druze, Sunni Muslims, and Shi'ites temporarily suspended their differences and acted collectively to resist Bashir's orders. The first phase of the insurgence began on May 27, when a handful of Maronite and Druze leaders met at Dayr al-Qamar and pledged to resist the conscription campaign. A covert committee, composed of ten Maronites and two Druze, was organized to solicit funds and arms. Secret dispatches went out urging villagers not to surrender their arms and to shelter their sons from the reach of conscription officers.

From its inception, it was apparent that the insurgents were not acting alone. Indeed, growing sources of internal unrest notwithstanding, much of the impetus for the uprising was largely a byproduct of superpower rivalry. The British, at the time, were still convinced that an Ottoman-controlled Syria would be a better safeguard for their trade routes to India; hence the successful diplomatic efforts of Palmerston in forging a delicate alliance among Britain, Russia, Austria, and Prussia to rescue Syria from its Egyptian occupiers. Russia, eager to widen the rift between France and Great Britain, endorsed Palmerston's plans. So did Metternich. With the exception of France, all the concert powers had perceived their national interests to be better served by evicting the Egyptians from Syria. None of the allies, however, were willing to commit the necessary forces to engage Ibrahim Pasha in ground battles. Inciting the armed struggle of local insurgents, already outraged by the abusive policies of the Egyptians, seemed a less hazardous course. It was certainly less costly to the concert of European powers.

France, because of its friendly relations with both the Maronites and the Pasha of Egypt, was in an awkward diplomatic predicament. Official opinion in France was divided and inconsistent. One faction, led by Prime Minister Thiers, was supporting Muhammad Ali; another, close to King Louis Philippe, was advocating a policy of reconciliation and appeasement (see Farah 1967: 110–113). The King, in fact, dispatched his nephew, Comte d'Onfroi, to assist the insurgents. The Comte came reinforced with a letter from the Pope to the Maronite Patriarch urging and blessing the call for armed struggle (Guys 1850: II, 266).

The Pope's blessings were needed because the higher echelons of the Maronite clergy in Mount Lebanon were also divided. Beirut's Maronite Bishop, Butrus Karam, had ordered the inhabitants of Dayr al Qamar to desist from any acts of hostility against Amir Bashir and his Egyptian masters. The appeal was not heeded; particularly in Kisrwan, Jubayl, Sahil, and the southern districts of Shahhar and Manasif. In all these Muqata'as, the sheikhly feudal families — Khazin, Abi Lama', Nakad — were embittered by the way Bashir had undermined their traditional authority. Other regions, however, especially the predominantly Greek Orthodox, Sunni, and Druze towns of Hasbayya and Rashayya, were reluctant to take up arms against Bashir.

Much like the 'ammiyyah of 1820, leadership did not devolve entirely around the commoners. For example, initially, the Beirut branch of the rebellion was led by two commoners. Soon, however, Francis al Khazin took over. Other descendents of notable families, "Wujuh al-'amiyyah" as they were popularly labelled, assumed leadership.

Comte d'Onfroi managed to solicit enough support to raise a force of about 10,000 Maronite fighters. Early in June, rebel leaders, mostly dispossessed feudal sheikhs and relatives of Amir Bashir, gathered at Intilias, elected Comte d'Onfroi as their "French Commander of Troops," expressed firm determination to resist the oppressive injustices of Egyptian rule, and pledged "to fight to restore their independence or die." They also drew up a covenant outlining a set of explicit grievances to abrogate the abuses of conscription, disarmament, corvée, and taxation. Reminiscent of the 'ammiyyah of 1820, the covenant evinced the same confessional and class-consciousness. "We have come together in a real Christian unity free from (personal) purposes and from spite, made rather for the welfare of the common folk (jumhur) of the community" (Harik 1968:248).

Similarly, the rebels of 1840 were calling for the end of foreign rule and the restoration of Mount Lebanon's autonomy and independence. They were also demanding the reorganization of the administration by forming a new administrative council representing the various communities to assist the amir in governing the public affairs of Mount Lebanon.

Military operations were masterminded by d'Onfroi who had established his headquarters at the little town of Zuq al-Kharab near Junieh. He kept the insurgents well supplied with ammunition, crosses, and French banners. For logistic purposes, they were split into two groups; one led by d'Onfroi and the other by Yusuf Shihab, a dispossessed cousin of Amir Bashir. A Jesuit missionary was assigned to counsel the inexperienced Yusuf along with other leaders. Bourée the French consul, also played an active part in helping French agents secure military supplies for the insurgents through Cyprus. So did the consuls of other Catholic powers; particularly Austria and Sardinia. (For these and other details see Farah 1967: 110–117.)

Such blatant intervention only served to arouse the hostility of Amir Bashir and the Egyptian Pasha. They called upon further troop reinforcements. On June 20, Muhammad Ali's son, Abbas, landed in Beirut with 12,000 troops. Ibrahim Pasha mobilized another 12,000. Suleiman Pasha, the Ottoman wali at Saidon, committed around 20,000. So did Amir Bashir. The combined forces, almost six times the size mustered by insurgents, converged on their strongholds and easily overwhelmed them.

The first phase of the revolt (roughly between mid-May and the end of July 1840) ended with failure. Towns and villages in Matn and Beqa' were sacked, insurgents surrendered their arms and fifty-seven of their leaders were exiled to Egypt. By then, however, the "Eastern Question" was attracting the attention of European powers. During this second phase, it was the turn of the British consuls and their agents to mobilize the insurgents. Richard Wood, who had served as British observer on two earlier occasions, was dispatched to Lebanon in 1840 with explicit instructions from the British Ambassador at Istanbul, to incite the Lebanese against the Egyptians (Farah 1967: 110–116).

Reinforced by the terms of the London Treaty of July 1840, in which the Quadruple Alliance had agreed to expel the Egyptians from Syria, the British spearheaded the massive naval and military campaign launched for that effort. By September, they had succeeded in amassing twenty-two warships, joined by a token number of Austrian and Turkish naval units. An allied ground force of more than 11,000 troops was also mobilized. In the words of one observer it was, indeed, "a strange spectacle, Metternich and Palmerston inviting rebels to revolt against Ibrahim, an Austrian archduke fighting for freedom and helping a British admiral to foil the designs of France." (Temperley 1964: 117).

On September 9 Beirut was bombarded from the sea, followed the next day by a landing of troops at the Bay of Junieh, seat of the Maronite patriarchate. So thrilled was the patriarch that he offered the British commander a church to serve as headquarters of the operations. While the allied forces established their dominance over the coastal regions, insurgents engaged Egyptian troops in the hillsides of Matn and Kisrwan.

Within two weeks the allies occupied the main towns and cities, and by early November the Egyptians withdrew their demoralized forces from Syria. The defeat of Ibrahim Pasha carried with it the humiliating downfall of Bashir's illustrious reign of more than half a century. He had steadfastly supported the Egyptians and had no recourse but to deliver himself up for exile.

More damaging, perhaps, was the sectarian enmity the Egyptian interlude left in its wake. By pitting Maronites against Druzes in 1838 and then Druzes against Maronites in 1840, Muhammad Ali violated the spirit of asylum and the culture of tolerance which had characterized communal relations. Mount Lebanon was also made more accessible and vulnerable to foreign intervention. From then on, communal hostility and internationalization of its polity were destined to become inveterate features of its political destiny.

The Uprising of 1857–60

The peasants' involvement in the political events of 1840 might have contributed to putting an end to both the Egyptian occupation and the eventful reign of Bashir II. They did little, however, to transform the underlying loyalties of peasants or those aspects of the feudal system that were the source of their grievances.

Indeed, by the mid-fifties Mount Lebanon continued to display all the ingredients of a feuding and fractured social order: factional conflict between rival feudal chiefs, family rivalry between factions of the same extended kinship group, a bit of "class" conflict between a feudal aristocracy eager to preserve its eroding power and privilege and an emerging Maronite clergy and the mass of exploited peasantry determined to challenge the social and political supremacy of feudal authority. This intricate network of competing and shifting loyalties was reinforced, often deliberately incited, by Ottoman pashas playing one faction against another or the intervention of Western powers each eager to protect or promote the interest of its own protégé.

By and large, however, civil strife was largely nonsectarian. At least until 1840, nineteenth-century travelers and local chroniclers continued to be impressed by the spirit of amity and harmony that characterized communal relations. From then on, cleavages began to assume a more confessional form. One outburst of factional strife provoked another until they culminated in the harrowing massacres of 1860.

What brought about this convergence of social protest and intercommunal strife? Why were the former — seemingly genuine peasant uprisings

sparked by collective outrage and a measure of revolutionary consciousness — muted or deflected into bitter and bloody sectarian hostilities? In the
language of our study, how and why did the largely "civil" forms of social
unrest and collective protest degenerate into "uncivil" violence, the type that
became a protracted cycle of often indiscriminate and self-destructive blood
letting? This is of particular relevance to our exploration because the change
in the pattern of conflict also brought with it a marked increase in the
magnitude of violence.

Doubtless, this is a reflection of the confluence of internal and external
sources of disruptive transformations Lebanon was witnessing at the time.
The great power rivalry and the consequent internationalization of Lebanese
politics had already left their toll. Foreign powers, eager to gain inroads into
the region, sought to pit one religious community against another. The centralized policies of the Ottomans, directed at undermining the privileged
status of Mount Lebanon and the local authority of feudal chiefs, exacerbated the tension further. So did the liberal policies of Ibrahim Pasha and
the egalitarian provisions of the Ottoman reforms.

A decade of Egyptian rule opened up the village society of Mount Lebanon to all sorts of societal changes and secular reforms while generating a
pronounced shift in the relative socioeconomic position of religious communities. The precarious balance that held society together and sustained
confessional harmony was disrupted. The Ottoman Tanzimat did little to
assuage these dislocations. On the contrary, the secular and innovative tones
of the reforms were a threat to the vested interest of traditional Muslims,
and the egalitarian provisions of the edicts provoked further hostility between
the sects. (For further details, see Khalaf 1979: 45–63; Porath 1965: 81–86).
The escalation of hostility is also a reflection, as has been propounded by
another premise of this study, of its own self-propagating character. Once
initiated, violence quickly acquires a life of its own and is sustained by forces
often unrelated to the initial sources that had provoked the hostility.

The communities were already seething with confessional enmity and
required little provocation. The downfall of Bashir II and the appointment
of his incompetent cousin, Bashir III, as his successor, gave the Ottomans a
welcome opportunity to undermine the local autonomy of Lebanon's feudal
chiefs. Upon the insistence of the Ottoman authorities, Bashir III organized
a council or diwan of twelve men (two from each of the dominant sects;
Maronites, Druze, Greek Orthodox, Greek Catholics, Sunni Muslims, and
Shi'ites) to assist him in the administration of justice. Both Druze and Christian feudal sheikhs saw in this an encroachment of their traditional authority

and refused to cooperate in this arrangement. Druze sheikhs in particular, especially the Junblats, Arslans, and Talhuqs, who were eager to restore the rights and privileges they had lost during Bashir II's reign, were not prepared to suffer further usurpations. More provocative was the circular issued by Patriarch Yusuf Hubaysh, and signed by leading Maronite families, calling on their coreligionists in the Druze districts to assume the judicial authority traditionally held by the feudal chiefs. "This was tantamount to an assertion by the Patriarch of the power to withdraw authority from the Druze sheikhs" (Kerr 1959: 4).

Following a dispute in October 1841 over the distribution of taxes, a party of Druze led by the Abu Naked sheikhs attacked Dayr al-Qamar, set the town on fire, pillaged Christian homes, and besieged Bashir III. The incident touched off other sectarian clashes throughout the Shuf, Biqa, and Zahle. This was the first sectarian outburst, and it left a staggering toll: a loss of about 300 people, the destruction of half a million dollars of property (Churchill 1862: 63–64), the dismissal of Bashir III under humiliating conditions, the end of the Shihabi Emirate, and a large residue of ill-feeling and mutual suspicion. (For further details, see Churchill 1862: 46–62; Hitti 1957: 434–35.) The animosity was further aggravated by the complicity of the Ottoman authorities. Not only were they suspected of having been involved in the initial Druze plot against the Christians (Salibi 1965: 50; Hitti 1957: 434–35), but also there were instances in which Ottoman troops participated in the acts of plundering. Such instances gave rise to the saying common then among Christians: "We would sooner by plundered by Druzes than protected by Turks" (Churchill 1862: 52).

By 1842 it was becoming apparent that an irreparable breach was drawing the religious communities further apart. The Maronite-Druze confederacy, which had sustained Lebanon's autonomy for so long, suffered its first serious setback. The Ottomans were eager to step in and impose direct rule over Mount Lebanon. They declared the end of the Shihabi Emirate and appointed Umar Pasha "al-Namsawi" ("the Austrian") as governor. The Druze, already jealous of Christian ascendancy in power and prosperity, greeted the downfall of the Shihabs with enthusiasm, without realizing that the introduction of Ottoman centralized rule would ultimately have adverse effects on their own community. The Christians, naturally, refused to recognize the new arrangement and insisted on a restoration of the Emirate, which could only be achieved with Druze cooperation (Salibi 1965: 53).

Umar Pasha's main concern was to gain support for his efforts to establish direct Ottoman rule. He turned first to the Druze and Maronite feudal sheikhs who had been dispossessed by the Shihabs. By restoring their estates and traditional prerogatives and appointing several of them as his advisors and agents, he won their support for the new regime. Second, he was eager to demonstrate to European powers that direct Ottoman rule enjoyed wide support in Lebanon. To this end, agents were hired to circulate petitions and secure signatures (a sort of plebiscite by coercion) in favor of direct Ottoman rule. He resorted to bribery, entreaties, false premises, threats, intimidation, blackmail, and "every species of personal indignity" (Churchill 1862: 66–75) to procure the necessary signatures. So flagrant were the extortionist pressures that European consuls in Beirut collectively protested against the use of such measures, and declared the petitions to be "completely unrepresentative of true Lebanese opinion" (Salibi 1956: 55).

In the meantime, internal alignments within Lebanon were being swiftly redefined. The petitions had hardly been circulated, when the Druze had serious afterthoughts about direct Ottoman administration and their place within it. They had considered themselves responsible for the collapse of the Shihabi Emirate and the establishment of Ottoman rule, and were therefore reluctant to assume a subservient position and accept the arbitrary dictates of Ottoman officials. Confronted with such Druze pretensions, and in desperation, Umar Pasha turned to the Maronites for support and started his policy of ingratiation to win their favors. This only aroused the suspicion of the Maronites and the bitter resentment of the Druze. So intense was Druze opposition that Umar Pasha was forced to arrest seven of their prominent sheikhs. The outrage was instantaneous. An open Druze rebellion was declared demanding the immediate dismissal of Umar Pasha, immunity from conscription and disarmament, and exception from taxes for a three-year period (Salibi 1965: 62). Despite strong resistance, a contingent of Turkish and Albanian troops forced the surrender of Druze leaders.

The rebellion, nonetheless, was a clear indication that direct Ottoman control was disagreeable to both Druze and Maronites. Efforts for a new Druze-Maronite coalition had failed, but the insurgents enjoyed the moral support of Maronite leaders (Kerr 1959: 5–6; Churchill 1862: 64–79). Druze feudal sheikhs were resentful of the loss of the traditional prerogatives and the arbitrary arrests and imprisonment they were subjected to under the autocratic control of Umar Pasha. The Maronites were equally appalled by the demise of the Shihabi dynasty and, with it, the frustration of their hopes for establishing an autonomous Christian Imarah (Harik 1968: 268). In the face of such opposition, the Ottomans were forced to dismiss Umar Pasha before he completed his first year in office. So ended this brief interlude of

direct Ottoman rule. More important, this interlude had intensified the enmity between the religious communities. The desperate efforts of the Ottomans to assert their direct authority over Lebanon prompted them to resort
to their time-worn ploys of inciting sectarian suspicions and hostility.

European intervention (particularly on behalf of France and Britain) prevented the Ottoman government from imposing direct control over Lebanon, but failed to reconcile the Druze and Maronites. Consequently, the
five powers and the Porte agreed in 1843 to a scheme of partitioning: a
northern district under a Christian *qa'immaqam* ("sub-governor"), and a
southern under a Druze *qa'immaqam*, each to rule over his coreligionists
and both responsible to the local Ottoman governor residing in Beirut. The
Beirut–Damascus road was used as an arbitrary line of demarcation. The
partition scheme was a compromise plan (advanced by Prince Metternich)
between the French and Ottoman proposals. The French (supported by the
Austrians) continued to hope for a restoration of the Shihabi Emirate; while
the Ottomans (backed by the Russians) insisted on the complete integration
of Lebanon into the Empire and opposed any reinstatement of Lebanese
autonomy.

The double *qa'immaqamiyyah* was an ill-fated plan from the day of its
inception. The partition was an artificial political division that aggravated
rather than assuaged religious cleavages. In the words of a contemporary
observer, "it was the formal organization of civil war in the country" (as
quoted by Salibi 1965: 64). According to the scheme, each *qa'immaqm* was
to exercise authority over his own coreligionists. The religious composition
of the two districts, however, was far from homogenous. This created the
problem of how to treat those who belonged to one religious community
but happened to be living under the political authority of another, especially
in areas like the Shuf, Gharb, and Matn.

To overcome the jurisdictional problems created by the mixed districts,
the Porte decided to limit the authority of each *qa'immaqam* to his own
territory, thus denying Christians in the Druze districts the right of appealing
to a Christian authority in judicial and tax matters (Kerr 1959: 607). As usual,
European powers intervened on behalf of their protégés. France, as the protector of Maronite and Catholic interest, opposed the Ottoman plan and
encouraged the church to remove Maronites from the jurisdiction of the
Druze *qa'immaqam* and to place them directly under the Christian one.
Britain, eager to safeguard the prerogatives of the Druze feudal sheikhs,
approved the revised scheme. In the meantime, Russia maintained that the
Greek Orthodox community of 20,500 was populous enough to justify the

creation of a special *qa'immaqamiyyah* (for further details, see Salibi 1965: 63–66). In the face of such conflicting expectations, an arrangement was arrived at whereby in each of the mixed districts, a Christian and Druze *wakil* would be chosen, each with judicial authority over his coreligionists and responsible to the *qa'immaqam* of his sect. Mixed cases, involving Christian and Druze, would be heard jointly by the two *wakils*. The wakils were also empowered to collect taxes, each from his own sect, on behalf of the feudal chief (Kerr 1959: 8–9; Salibi 1965: 66–67).

A fresh outbreak of hostilities in the spring of 1845 finally convinced the Ottomans of the inadequacies inherent in the double *qa'immaqamiyyah*. Nevertheless, the Ottomans opted not to resort to a thorough reorganization of Mount Lebanon. Instead, they modified the existing arrangement by settling the jurisdictional problems of Christians living in Druze districts. A review of the articles and provisions of the Règlement Shakib Efendi, as the plan is identified by historians, reveals that altogether it reinforced rather than undermined the prevailing social and political power of the feudal families (For further details, see Jouplain 1908: 297–353; Chevallier 1971: 174–79; Poujade, 1867: 34–35).

It is against this background that the confluence of peasant uprisings and communal hostility should be viewed: the demise of the Shihabs, growing disparities between religious communities, increasing foreign intervention, and the eagerness of the Ottomans to impose direct rule on Mount Lebanon and to undermine all vestiges of its local autonomy.

Peasant agitation in Kisrwan, which began gaining considerable momentum in 1858, can still be better understood when viewed within the context of the economic transformations (particularly the expansion of European trade and the consequent emergence of an urban bourgeoisie) which weakened the stability of the feudal economy. "From the middle of the nineteenth century onwards," Gabriel Baer asserts, "peasant revolts in Egypt and Lebanon were no longer caused by fiscal pressure alone or by political coercion of fellahs . . . but rather by economic processes which brought about the deterioration of their position" (Baer 1982: 264).

These transformations, at least in Mount Lebanon, were not exclusively the byproduct of the inevitable transition from a subsistence agricultural economy to one based on cash crops. The French Revolution, crisis in silk trade in the wake of the Crimean War, and a host of natural calamities all severely affected the status of the Khazins as suppliers of raw silk to the French spinners.(For further details, see Buheiry 1989, Dubar and Nasr 1976: 51–59, Saba 1976). By the mid nineteenth century silk trade with Europe was restored, but in a modified pattern: European traders now re-exported the silk to Lebanon in processed form, thereby competing ruinously with the local cottage manufacturers. The situation deteriorated further when the French set up modern spinning mills in regions closer to Beirut's harbor, such as the Shuf and Matn, but further away from Kisrwan (Baer 1982: 266; Porath 1965: 85).

The burgeoning urban middle class (mostly Christian merchants and agents for European traders) continued to prosper. The rest of the society, particularly craftsmen, artisans, peasants, and small traders, were adversely affected by the growing dependence of the Lebanese economy on European production and trade. The new trading patterns deprived a large portion of the rural society of its traditional sources of livelihood and rendered the economy sensitive to external circumstances. Any disturbance in the European economy had its reverberations within Lebanon. The French consul general in Beirut noted that the French financial crisis of 1857–58 had had "disastrous consequences for Syrian business. Numerous and important bankruptcies, and extraordinary financial uneasiness felt until the end of 1859, loss of credit everywhere, and all this added to by two years of poor harvest" (Chevallier 1968: 219). Furthermore, in violation of the Anglo-Turkish commercial Treaty of 1838, which established the principle of free trade and laissez-faire, the Ottomans imposed a tax on silk cocoons at the place where they were raised, an act which contributed to the consequent ruin of many of the local reeling factories (Issawi 1967: 115; Chevallier 1968: 218).

Feudal families tried to curtail their growing indebtedness and recoup their losses by intensifying the forced exactions and taxation on peasants. Others ceded or sold portions of their land to villagers and then tried to reclaim them forcibly through their armed retainers. These abusive strategies were more apparent in the Christian districts since, unlike the Druze *qa'immaqamiyyah*, there were no *wakils* there to protect the peasants or bargain on their behalf.

The impetus for mobilization was, once again, initiated in the predominantly Christian districts of the north. The clergy were openly active in inciting and organizing the protest. As in earlier episodes the conflict also created an unlikely coalition, this time pitting the Khazin sheikhs against the *qa'immaqam*, the peasants, and the clergy (Porath 1965: 84). Early in 1858 the protest continued to assume rather civil and contained forms of gatherings — public rallies to vindicate grievances, draft petitions, and organize delegations of protest.

Appropriately, the first such public gatherings took place in towns like Zuq Mikhayil, Ajaltun, and Mazra'at Kafr Dubyan, whose livelihood and relative prosperity was largely linked to silk processing and trading. The gatherings were fairly small. The largest, claimed not more than 200 people. They were spontaneously organized, often independent of each other and with no evidence of coordination or concerted planning. They also displayed little traces of radicalism; other than announcing the formation of *Shuyukh al Shabab* (youth organizations), electing *wakils,* and forging alliances with other oppressed villages and towns. "We band together," one of these petitions declared, "in a spirit of unmalicious love, refraining from any deed that might give offence." (Porath 1965: 91). At one of those gatherings, Salih Sfeir, the moderate *Sheikh Shabab* of Ajaltun, was elected *wakil'am* or supreme commander of the villages.

The demands of the peasants, at that early phase of the rebellion, were concerned only with the cessation of some of the oppressive measures they were being subjected to. They did not challenge the legitimacy of the Khazin's authority, nor were they making claims to expropriate any of their estates. They were merely demanding that government authority, exercised by the Khazins, be invested in three of its members as *ma'mur* (government official).

The "unmalicious" and "unoffensive" demands, well-intentioned as they might have been, clearly did not remain so. By early May of the same year, participants in a mass rally at Bhannis were already carrying arms and talking about rebelling against the Khazins. From then on the tone and structure of the movement became more confrontational. Peasant agitation began to assume violent forms. In one village after another, *sheikh shababs* organized village councils, usurped power, and demanded further concessions from their feudal lords. The reluctance of the notables to grant these concessions only provoked added bitterness among the peasants. Leadership also passed into more radical hands. The relatively moderate Salih Sfeir was replaced by the more intemperate, arrogant, and ambitious Tanyus Shahin of Rayfun.

The transfer of leadership to Shahin, the illiterate farrier who had "little to recommend him other than his tall and muscular frame and violent temper" (Salibi 1965: 85), was a turning point. The day he was proclaimed general commander of Kisrwan, Shahin launched an aggressive campaign to collect arms and funds and to extend the rebellion to the more moderate northwestern regions. Almost overnight he became a folk hero; the avowed and undisputed spokesman of peasants and their redeemer from feudal tutelage. His adulators sang paeans in his praise. His arrival in villages and towns was greeted by volleys of rifle fire. He clearly enjoyed the deference and respect normally accorded to a legitimate ruler. He was even addressed as "Bey," a title that bore Ottoman administrative connotations (For these and other details, see Porath 1965: 94–117; Kerr 1959: 49).

The heightened belligerency of the movement was first visible in the intransigent and escalated concessions the rebels were demanding: full equality of status between sheikhs and peasants; an end to the exactions of gifts, dues, and the imposition of forced labor; an abolition of contrived taxes on land already sold by the sheikhs to peasants; and the abolition of the right to authorize marriages and administer floggings and jail sentences (Porath 1965: 100–101).

The intransigence of rebels was not confined to the grievances and new claims they were making. Their belligerency acquired more hostile dimensions as they set out to drive the Khazins out of Kisrwan. Often without much resistance, the Khazins abandoned their estates in Rayfun, Ajaltoun, Ghadir, Dar'un and sought refuge in villages further north and Beirut. Accounts of these events do not reveal much by way of violence. It was not, in fact, until mid-July 1859 that the first fatal casualties were reported when the wife and daughter of one of the Khazin sheikhs were killed in Ajaltoun.

Another striking feature, particularly during episodes of evicting the Khazin and confiscating their property, was the absence of wanton acts of violence. It is estimated that 500 Khazins were driven from their homes and their estates were taken away (Porath 1965: 98). Of course, there were instances of looting food, household utensils, tools, and supplies. Orchards, particularly olive groves and mulberry trees, were willfully destroyed and vandalized. Herds of goats and sheep were grazed in devastated woodlots. Villagers in the northwest who demurred from accepting Shahin's authority were subjected to harassment and coercive ploys. Their houses were mauled and robbed. Others were victims of extortion and involuntary tributes of food supplies and money.

On the whole, however, on reading the diversity of accounts, one emerges with a relatively tame portrait: not of rootless brigands on the rampage, eager to wreak vengeance in acts of unrestrained terrorism but of socially-minded rebels bent on correcting injustices and rooting out oppressive features of feudal society. Tanyus Shahin comes out more in the image of a Robin Hood than an insolent bandit. For every act of unrestrained looting attributed to his partisans, one encounters others where confiscated property and crops were collected and redistributed for the common welfare.

Shahin clearly was not acting alone. It is rare for uprisings of this sort to be inspired and sustained by local initiative only. The peasant movement enjoyed, it seems, the moral encouragement of the Ottoman authorities and

Patriarch Mass'ad. At least they were not very eager to contain the rebellion. Some observers go even further to maintain that since the Ottoman's ultimate objective was the establishment of direct rule, the uprising was the outcome of their explicit incitement in an effort to eliminate or undermine Christian hegemony in Lebanon (Hattuni, 1884: 332–34). England and France continued to display their discrepant viewpoints and roles. While the British consul was a fervent supporter of the Khazins, the French were more sympathetic to the rebels though they had reservations about Shahin's style of government. As in earlier instances, the Maronite clergy, partly because of their humble social origins and their anti-aristocratic sentiments, offered more than just moral support, though it remained suspicious of Shahin's character and personal ambitions (See Porath 1965: 137–46 for further details concerning the type of assistance the clergy offered).

By the spring of 1859, the peasant insurrection became a full-fledged social revolution; at least in the Christian districts of the North. The Khazins and other feudal families were evicted from their homes and stripped of their possessions. Feudal property, household provisions, and ammunition were parceled out among the peasants, and Tanyus Shahin was issuing his commands with the "authority of the people" *(biquwat al-hukuma al-jumhuriyya)*. (Kerr 1959: 53; Churchill 1862: 111–12; Porath 1966: 115).

It is not clear what Shahin might have meant by these sublime catchwords. As a protégé of the French Lazarite monks who ran, it seems, a school in his own village of Rayfun, he was probably reiterating populist sentiments evoked by the French Revolution and its aftermath in Europe (Porath 1965: 115). What is clear, however, is that Shahin was recognized as governor of Kisrwan, that he governed with the assistance of a council empowered with the maintenance of public order, the regulation of judicial proceedings, and "taking cognizance of acts of disobedience" (Churchill 1862: 127). It is odd that a rebel and maverick of sorts, notorious for his intemperate character, dreaded as a "riot-monger," should be dispatching instructions to religious dignitaries imploring them to caution villagers against drunkenness during festivals and other acts of public disorder (Churchill 1862: 127). He did. He also managed the affairs of government as though the sources of legitimacy were inherent in the will of its people. By so doing, he won more than just the devoted allegiance of aggrieved peasants. Even the Patriarch recognized him as the lawful ruler of Kisrwan.

It is also apparent that the organizational structure of government, such as it was, rested on village *wakils*; a total of 116. Some were appointed by Shahin himself; others were chosen by the villagers (Churchill 1862: 127).

As in earlier '*ammiyyahs*, a fairly large number of those were drawn from wealthy and notable families. At least ten were priests and around 25 figured among the signatories of the agreement to restore the Khazins to Kisrwan (Porath 1965: 114).

Successful as the peasant revolt had been in raising the hopes of other peasants throughout Lebanon, the movement remained predominantly a local upheaval. There were efforts, whether spontaneous or deliberate, to "export" the rebellion to other regions of Lebanon. The Khazins, in fact, in their petition to the British consul, spoke in alarming terms of how the "evil spirit" of revolt had spread to al the *muqata'at*. It is understandable why the Khazins might have deliberately exaggerated the magnitude of disorder provoked by the revolt in order to invite the intervention of central authorities. There were incidents in Batrun, al-Matn, and al-Qati'. By the time agitation reached the Shuf and other southern regions, early in 1860, it began to change its character. Rather than inciting the peasants to social revolt against their óverlords, the rebellion started to assume an intercommunal strife. It is at this point that the social unrest in Kisrwan merged with the sectarian tensions in the central and southern districts. The convergence proved disastrous. It is also then that manifestations of barbarism, wanton violence, and incivility became visibly more cruel and treacherous.

Druze peasants were apprehensive about taking similar action against their own feudal sheikhs. Indeed, the peasant movement in the Druze districts assumed a sectarian rather than a "class" conflict. Druze sheikhs were successful in muting and deflecting the grievances and discontent of their own peasants by provoking sectarian rivalry, particularly in the religiously mixed communities of the Shuf and Matn. The communities, as we have seen, were already seething with confessional enmity and required little provocation. After the first clash of 1841, both Druze and Maronites continued to rearm themselves. The supply of arms and ammunitions that cleared Beirut customs in the years preceding the war was quite voluminous (Buheiry 1989: 499–511; Tibawi 1969: 123).

The two communities had also been preparing for the confrontation, although Christians went about it much more openly, and with greater deliberation and boasting, often taunting their adversaries. Several of the Christian villages, for example, were in a state close to actual mobilization. Units of armed men, with special uniforms, led by a *sheikh shabab*, were organized in each of the villages. In turn, these small units were placed under the command of higher officers. In Beirut the Maronite Bishop himself organized and headed such an armed group, while wealthy Maronites competed with one another in raising subscriptions for the purchase of arms and ammunition (Jessup 1910: 165–66).

Confrontations started in earnest when appeals for help and military assistance, from the religiously mixed regions, reached Kisrwan. Tanyus Shahin responded by mobilizing expeditions to rescue his besieged coreligionists. Christians in Shuf, Jazzin, and Dayr al-Qamar feared the hostility of Druze; those in Zahle and Biqa dreaded their Shi'ite neighbors. Somehow, the expedition faltered. Partly because of Shahin's illness, his rivalry with Yusuf Karam the popular leader vying to displace him or, as other sources claim, the involvement of Ottoman forces, the expedition failed to accomplish its mission (Scheltema 1920:92–96). Indeed, the arrival of Christians from the north sparked off the conflagration and fuelled the aroused hostility of the Druze. More disruptive, perhaps, it gave the Ottomans the pretext to step up their direct intervention. Rebel areas in the north were embargoed. Economic sanctions were imposed by interdicting the Kisrwan coast and prohibiting the importation of wheat and other amenities. The army, dispatched by Khurshid Pasha to separate and pacify the embattled communities in Matn, accomplished just the opposite. It blocked efforts of other Christians to reach and assist their coreligionists and was, some sources claim, directly involved in butchering Christians (Scheltema 1920: 68–69; Porath 1965: 124).

Once ignited, the religious character of strife became more pronounced. Confessional agitation and violence were readily sparked. The ferocity of fighting intensified. Priests enticed recruits and accompanied fighters to battle. Shahin made reconciliatory contacts with the Khazins to renunify Christian forces.

Although the Maronites, with an estimated 50,000 men, were expecting to overwhelm the 12,000 Druze forces (indeed they often boasted of exterminating their adversaries) early in the struggle, the Druze manifested superiority in fighting effectiveness. In one battle after another, they defeated and humbled the Maronites.

So sweeping was the Druze victory that historians talk with amazement about the "flagrant temerity of the Druzes . . . and the seemingly inexplicable Christian cowardice" (Salibi 1965: 93). The Druze forces were better organized, disciplined, and fought more fiercely and menacingly; while Christians suffered from inept and bickering leadership (Churchill, 1862: 142–43). The magnitude and intensity of violence was most astonishing.

Sometimes within hours entire villages and towns would fall, often with little resistance. Townsmen, seized with panic, would abandon their villages and homes to be burned down, plundered, and pillaged and seek refuge in Christian strongholds. Other fugitives on their way to Beirut or Sidon were often overtaken, robbed, and killed indiscriminately by their assailants. Even the Christian strongholds were not spared. In fact, it was in these towns that the worst atrocities were perpetrated. First in 'Ayn Dara, then in Babda, Jazzine, Hasbayya, Rashayya, Zahle and Dayr al-Qamar the same savage pattern of violence repeated itself with added intensity. The Ottoman garrison commander would offer the Christians asylum in the local seraglio, request the surrender of their arms, and then stand idly by watching the carnage.

In the short span of four weeks (from mid-May until June 20), an estimated 12,000 Christians lost their lives, 4,000 had perished in destitution, 100,000 became homeless, and about £4 million worth of damage to property had been done (Churchill 1862: 132; Hitti 1957: 438; Salibi 1965: 106). Added to this devastation of life and property was the legacy of confessional bitterness the war had generated. Lebanon was in urgent need of swift and sweeping measures to pacify, rehabilitate, and reconstruct the fabric of a dismembered society. It was also clear that more than a mere restoration of order and tranquility was needed. The political reorganization of Mount Lebanon became imminent. Once again, Lebanon was both a victim, and at the mercy, of foreign intervention.

Through French initiative, major powers (Great Britain, Austria, Russia, Prussia, and Turkey) convened and decided to set up an international commission to fix responsibility, determine guilt, estimate indemnity, and suggest reforms for the reorganization of Lebanon. After eight months of extended discussion, agreement was reached on June 9, 1861 on a new organic statute (*Règlement Organique*) which reconstituted Lebanon as an Ottoman province or Mutasarrifiyyah (plenipotentiarate) under the guarantee of the six signatory powers.

Inferences

During the relatively short span of forty years, Mount Lebanon experienced successive outbreaks of collective strife. Typical of small, highly factionalized societies, many of these episodes often assumed a befuddling medley of factional feuds, peasant insurrections, and sectarian rivalries. As we have seen, on at least three occasions — 1820, 1840, and 1857 — peasants and commoners were incited to rebel against some of the repressive abuses of feudal society.

Despite the varied historical circumstances associated with these episodes, they evinced recurrent features which elucidate the changing character and magnitude of communal strife. Some of these features, as will
become apparent in subsequent chapters, have become distinctive characteristics of Lebanon's political legacy. Others share much with instances of
collective violence in comparable historical settings. It is possible, nonetheless, to extract a few inferences regarding the nature of participation, as well
as the timing, location, and form protracted conflict is likely to assume.

1. *The circumstances which impelled groups to resort to political violence
were not necessarily those which sustained their mobilization and informed the
direction and outcome of conflict.* All three uprisings, as we have seen, were
initially sparked off by a sense of collective consciousness and a concern for
public welfare. Yet, all were deflected, at one point or another, into confessional hostility. Likewise, episodes of communal conflict, originally provoked
by socioeconomic disparities and legitimate grievances, were transformed (or
deformed) into factional or confessional rivalry. Again and again, in other
words, struggles over "divisible goods," i.e., contests of distributive justice as
to who gets what and how much, are deflected into struggles over "indivisible
principles," those embedded in primordial loyalties and the inviolable attachments of faith, creed, community, and family. The enthusiasm for "class"
struggle and collective mobilization among Christian peasants in the North
found little appeal among their counterparts in the Druze districts. By arousing latent confessional enmity, traditional Druze leaders could easily manipulate such sentiments to ward off or caution against such involvement. The
lapse of nearly forty years, (i.e., between 1820 and 1857) in other words, had
done little to transform the loyalties and attachments of peasants. Expressed
more concretely, confessional, local, and feudal allegiances continued to su-
persede other public and collective interests. A Druze remained a Druze first,
a Jumblatti second, a Shufi third and then, a fellah or part of the *'ammah.*

2. *The form and magnitude the conflict assumed was also distinctive.* Unlike
other comparable protest movements, all three insurrections were not confined to prosaic acts of everyday resistance so common among powerless and
furtive social categories. The insurrections managed to mobilize a fairly large
number of participants. The Intilias *'Ammiyyah* of 1824 recruited around
6,000 insurgents. By 1840, the figure leaped to about 20,000. During the latter
stages of the 1858 uprising, close to thirty villages and towns in Kisrwan were
directly involved. The rebellion was also sustained for three years.

Initially, the uprisings employed nonconfrontational strategies of collective protest. Rallies, gatherings, petitions, mass agitation were very common. In some instances, particularly in 1858 when peasants felt strong enough to resist impositions of their feudal lords, they often ceased payments of rent they owed their Khazin sheikhs. When these strategies failed, rebels had no aversion to experiment with other, more contentious ones.

Indeed, in all three uprisings, conflict spiraled into violent scuffles, armed hostilities, and frontal clashes between masses of armed peasants and state-sponsored armies. In some instances, particularly in 1840, peasants employed the conventional logistics of guerrilla warfare, such as ambushing and attacking Egyptian convoys transporting ammunition and supplies (Smilianskaya 1972: 81; al-Shidyaq 1970, 2: 226). On the whole, however, the instruments of violence involved little more than ordinary rifles and hatchets common at the time in factional combat and local rivalries. By the time regional and European powers were drawn into the conflict, violence had escalated into actual warfare with regular armies, reinforced by the technologies of mass destruction; e.g., massive troop movements, naval blockades, bombardment, heavy artillery and the like. It is also then that the damage to life and property and other manifestations of incivility became more devastating.

3. *Inevitably, strife generated by the insurrections assumed a vast array of forms.* There was much, however, in its underlying pattern and character to support René Girard's (1977) insight regarding the nature of "surrogate victims." Given the multilayered hierarchical structure of feudal society, compounded by regional and global rivalries, all the protagonists (powerful and weak, rooted and marginal, internal and external) were equally embroiled in juxtapositions of competing interests and shifting loyalties. Hence, many of the episodes of strife were replete with situational ironies, often creating unlikely coalitions of awkward political bedfellows. European powers and their protégés and agents, Ottoman sultans with their *walis* and *pashas*, feudal sheikhs, *'ayan*, clerics, *Wakils*, *Shuyukh Shabab*, and an undifferentiated mass of commoners were all caught up in an intricate hierarchy of contentious relationships.

In such a milieu, to paraphrase Girard, when hostility is unappeased, it seeks and always finds surrogate victims. Groups and individuals responsible for its original fury are promptly replaced by others. Such proxy targets of renewed hostility are victimized only because they happen to be vulnerable and accessible (Girard 1977). Examples of such displaced victimization are legion. A Sultan, eager to ingratiate himself with a given Western power, spares its local protégé or protected communities but oppresses others. An amir, unable or unwilling to defy the rapacious exactions of a pasha turns to leaderless muqata'as. Rebellious peasants, not powerful enough to confront their main adversaries (central government), vent their vengeance on weaker groups (Khazin Sheikhs).

4. *The character, manifestations and consequences of violence displayed by the three uprisings provide vivid evidence in support of the two broad perspectives on civil strife.* As elucidated by James Rule (1988), one encounters much to substantiate the "consumatory" or expressive character of collective strife — the kind which is incited and sustained by group solidarity, the sharing of revolutionary excitement engendered by the insurrections. Here, the flux of events themselves, the unfolding episodes associated with the outbreak of hostilities served to draw insurgents together. Conflict and the threat of violence became, in the words of Alain Touraine (1981) the "glue" which cemented groups together. Mass rallies, animated gatherings, collective agitation, Shahine's charisma, the resourcefulness of *wakils*, the camaraderie of *shuyukh al-shabab*, and the exhilaration of combat all contributed to this. It is also here that one sees manifestations of emotional contagion, the frenzy of aroused peasants incited by anger, rage, vengeance and, hence, their predisposition to vent their wrath through unrestrained looting and plunder. In short, the appeals of expressing solidarity with one's group, assailing one's enemy, and the destruction of hated symbols provided the catalyst for collective violence.

However, one also sees perhaps more evidence of the "instrumental" character of collective strife, the type that bears closer affinity to the rational calculation of costs and benefits inherent in protest movements. Here rebels were driven not only by an impulse to correct injustices and seek some reprieve from feudal abuse but also by a desire to secure material benefits and basic necessities. As we have seen, acts of looting and confiscating the Khazin's property and crops were merely parts of organized operations designed to place expropriated property at the disposal of the rebellion. Hence, they were not symptoms of unrestrained acts of marauding and pillaging or a compulsion to wreak vengeance for its own sake. Indeed, particularly in 1858, the expulsion of the Khazins lasted long enough to be accompanied by their de-facto expropriation and, hence, a substantial redistribution of property in favor of commoners (Baer 1982: 300–301).

This instrumental character of warfare — i.e. the employment of war as a shortcut to wealth and material well-being — is neither unusual nor unique to Lebanon. Gellner, in fact, attributes it as a generalized feature for most agrarian societies. In medieval Spain, he tells us, "warfare was a quicker as well as a more honorable route to riches than trade" (Gellner 1997: 18).

Mount Lebanon's geography, the density of village settlements, and the personal allegiance and loyalty inherent in the system of *iqta'* must have inhibited the emergence of peasant brigandage typical of "primitive rebels" and wanton banditry (Hobsbawm 1985).

5. *Unlike other instances of peasant uprisings which are, generally, deficient of resources and organized leadership to mobilize and institutionalize political participation, peasants in Kisrwan were comparatively successful in translating their disaffection into political action.* Indeed, Gabriel Baer argues that Lebanon was a "conspicuous exception" in this regard (Baer 1982: 305).

Because of the educational activities of the Maronite church, Lazarists and other missionary orders, Kisrwan peasants enjoyed a comparatively high degree of literacy. Western contacts, enterprising monks, and local initiative generated a relatively prosperous and viable economy with an appreciable degree of security of life and property. Despite some of its abusive features, feudal society remained open to sociocultural innovation. The institution of *wakil*, as elected representatives, reinforced by bands of *shuyukh shabab* provided a pool of integrated resources amenable to mobilization.

In his analysis of the French Revolution of 1848, Marx argued that the revolt was the work of a temporary coalition among the Parisian proletariat, the petty bourgeoisie, and an enlightened fragment of the bourgeoisie. They joined in toppling the regime, "as a miserable but incoherent peasantry sat by" (Tilly 1978: 12). The Kisrwan peasants were miserable but they were neither incoherent nor did they sit idly by. They had a consciousness of common interest, collective vision, and a readiness to be mobilized.

Villagers in the predominantly Druze districts of the South suffered the same indignation and were victims of similar abuses. Yet they never displayed the same enthusiasm for collective mobilization. Their stronger fealty and communal ties muted and deflected the public grievances they shared with other peasants. They also possessed little of the resources available to their Maronite counterparts in the North.

6. *Peasants rarely acted alone.* In all three instances, to varying degrees, organizational and ideological leadership was assumed by Maronite clerics. It was they who first articulated the peasants' revolutionary attitude toward

the *iqta'* system. They organized them into village communes and appointed *wakils* as spokesmen for the *ammiyyah*.

In addition to ecclesiastical intervention, the peasants almost always received either the direct or moral support of Ottoman authorities and foreign consuls who manipulated the uprisings for purposes unrelated to the grievances or interests of the 'ammiyyah as a genuine protest movement. The Ottomans, as we have seen, were eager to undermine the privileged status of Mount Lebanon and the local authority of feudal chiefs. Indeed, pitting one group against another, through alternating strategies of ingratiation and manipulation, became a popular shorthand for Ottoman barbarity and repression.

Foreign powers, eager to gain inroads into the Middle East and win protégés, also reverted to the same divisive strategies. This was poignantly apparent in 1840. While European powers — France, Britain, Russia, Austria, and Prussia — were all acting in concert to rescue Syria from its Egyptian occupiers, each had their own diplomatic agendas. Sometimes, discord within a country (e.g., the conflict in France between Prime Minister Thiers and King Louis-Philippe) left its reverberations on the course and outcome of the rebellion. Consequently, a genuine local uprising was, literally, appropriated and deflected into a global crisis. Indignant peasants, already violated by the adverse effects of European economic transformations, were victimized further.

7. *Finally, a disconcerting but explicable inference stands out.* It is one with prophetic implications for the course and magnitude violence was to assume in the future. As long as the conflict remained a "class" rivalry, exacerbated by fiscal pressures, socioeconomic disparities, political coercion and the like, it was comparatively bloodless. If and when, however, it was transformed or deflected into a confessional or communal hostility, the magnitude and intensity of violence became much more menacing.

This, as René Girard reminds us, bears even more ominous implications. "Religion shelters us from violence just as violence seeks shelter in religion." As this happens, communities are entrapped in a vicious circle of vengeance and reprisal. "The mimetic character of violence is so intense it cannot burn itself out. . . . Only violence can put an end to violence and that is why violence is self-propagating" (Girard 1986: 24–26).

5 Civil Strife of 1958: Revolt and Counter Revolt

"Lebanon is a country which must be kept completely still politically in order to prevent communal self-centeredness and mutual distrust from turning into active and angry contention."
— Edward Shils (1966): 4.

For almost a century, from 1860 to 1958, an epoch normally marked by internal, regional, and global turmoil in the lives of new nations, Lebanon was comparatively peaceful and free of any manifestations of civil strife or collective violence. Emerging from decades of bloody communal strife, it weathered the dislocations it was beset with as a plural society embroiled in the tumultuous transformations of a troubled region. Handicapped by a fragmented political culture, uneven development, dissonant growth, inept archaic polity, and deficient resources, Lebanon managed to evolve into a fairly liberal, democratic, prosperous, and vibrant little republic.

Given its deficient civility, Lebanon might have never become a nation-state. Instead, it might have been doomed to remain, as Albert Hourani would say, a "republic of tribes and villages" (Hourani 1988:6). It was a republic nonetheless. With all its grievous faults, it survived the collapse and dismemberment of the Ottoman Empire, successive foreign penetrations and political rearrangements, ravages of a devastating famine, the ferments of two world wars, and the sociocultural dislocations associated with swift, discordant societal transformations.

These are not trivial or ordinary accomplishments. A century is also a long time in the history of a young republic. Detractors of Lebanon, and they are many — particularly those who dismiss it as a genetically flawed, artificial entity or a victim of its own belligerent culture and innate proclivity for violence — are remiss when they continue to overlook this felicitous stretch in its eventful history.

Certainly, Lebanon was not and could not have remained conflict-free. Very few societies are. It has had its fair share of unresolved tensions, recurrent cycles of public protest, and militant mobilization of collective grievances. On the whole, these were nonviolent. Its struggle for independence, for example, was bloodless; "child's play compared to the struggles through which other nations have won their independence" (Hourani 1966: 28). Political conflict in the post-independence years assume, generally, the form of personal feuds between rival political factions seeking to extend their clientage support or bickering over the spoils of office. Even crises of political succession were nonbelligerent. Bishara Khoury's tenure in office as first president of the republic (1943–52) ended with a so-called "Rosewater Revolution." When his otherwise stable and successful administration showed growing signs of corruption and nepotism, a powerful coalition of sectarian leaders and a national strike mobilized by a "Committee of National Liberation" compelled him to retire.

The military in most adjacent regimes was already, often through a succession of violent putsches and coups d'état, the main vector of revolutionary change. In Lebanon, in this as in earlier political crises, the army opted for a neutral, timid or reconciliatory role. Indeed, the whole tone of political mobilization in the post-independence decades was quiescent.

Lebanon also has no substantial urban mob of unemployed, beggars, cast-offs, and rejects from the routines of society or idlers extruded from an overcultivated and underproductive agriculture. Lebanon has its boot-blacks, taxi drivers, loitering errand boys, indolent household servants absenting themselves from their tasks. It has a little of the tinder of street conflagrations, or the frontline fighters who involve themselves in altercations with the security forces, the first crystals around which mass demonstrations are formed. But on the whole it has too few idle or unemployed loungers, and thus far no great demagogues whose eloquence can arouse slumbering ideological propensities and dormant demands (Shils 1966: 7).

Even when the various communities did not genuinely love each other they coexisted at tolerable degrees of enmity. The "National Covenant" of 1943 (*Mithaq al-Watani*), an unwritten pact to secure Lebanon's independence from France, evolved into a pragmatic political strategy to alleviate the tension engendered by the two inveterate and nagging issues in the country's political history: national identity and confessional harmony.

As will be shown later, despite some of its noted shortcomings, this largely gentleman's agreement, a sort of solemn pact between the two leading spokesmen of their respective communities, managed for nearly three decades to contain communal enmity and ensure more that just a modicum of prosperity and political stability.

There is considerable legitimacy to the claims made by a growing number of observers that the destabilization of Lebanon, at least at the critical juncture, was more the outcome of broader regional tensions, particularly the creation of the State of Israel and the consequent Palestinian-Israeli struggle and ideological rivalries in adjacent Arab regimes than internal disparities and/or deeply-rooted communal hostilities (See Harik 1987; Scruton 1987; Corm 1988, 1989; Messarra 1988, among others). Druze and Maronites, despite their ingrained enmity, managed to coexist for three centuries as participants in one commonwealth. The political stability and economic prosperity Lebanon enjoyed in its post-independence years helped in converting Muslim adherents to the Lebanese state. Ideological and socioeconomic differences were visible but did not erupt into belligerent confrontations.

It is in this sense that the crisis of 1958 marked a significant watershed in Lebanon's political history. It was the first major breakdown in political order, a foreboding signal that the *Mithaq* might not be able to contain or mitigate the sources of simmering tensions for too long. Until then impartial observers could still marvel over Lebanon's propensity to preserve itself as a virtual island of calm in a region raging with fury and political turmoil. Even after the civil unrest of 1958, Edward Shils prefaced his celebrated essay on the prospects for Lebanese civility by saying:

Contemporary Lebanon appears to be a happy phenomenon, uniqe in the third world, a prosperous liberal country. It has a parliamentary body, freely elected in the competition of a plurality of independent political parties. Its politicians are, as politicians go, relatively reasonable men. The tone of public debate is not strident. The Chamber of Deputies is an orderly assembly. Elections are conducted with a minimum of violence, and reports of coercion of the electorate are rare. Lebanon enjoys freedom of association and freedom of expression. Its press is literate and not too sensational or abusive. Its citizens, freely organized, feel free to approach their parliamentary representatives either as individuals or through their organizations. It is a law-abiding country in many important respects and passions are held in check; public order is maintained without a large display of force. People do not disappear in the night. . . .

Strikes, violent demonstrations, angry class antagonisms are relatively infrequent for a country of growing economic differentiation. Finally, the country is prosperous (Shils 1966: 1).

Shils, of course was not oblivious to the underlying tensions exacerbating Lebanon's deficient civility. Given its deeply rooted communalism, lack of national attachments, or a sense of identity and consensus which transcends subnational loyalties and interest, it is not unusual that Lebanon should display symptoms of fragmentation. What, however, compounds this situation further is that this "incivility" is not confined to the mass of the population whose access to, and interest in, the center is normally feeble and sporadic. More unsettling is how far this phenomenon had pervaded the elite and Zu'ama, those who dominate and speak of behalf of the primordial and religious communities.

Shils's guarded optimism is also a reflection of the country's vulnerability to regional and international sources of instability. "Lebanon," he maintained, "is a country which must be kept completely still politically in order to prevent communal self-centeredness and mutual distrust from turning into active and angry contention" (Shils 1966: 4). In 1958 the country began, perceptibly, to experience the disquieting symptoms of progressive erosion of such political stillness.

When compared to the massacres and mayhem of 1860 and the protracted cruelties of the 1970s and 1980s, the 1958 crisis seems benign and pacific as a civil war.[1] Oddly enough, it was also happening at a time when this so-called "Merchant Republic" was at the peak of its golden age, a period when peace and prosperity were miraculously combined (Owen 1988: 36). It was a civil war nonetheless. Whether instigated by a massive infiltration of subversive elements or saboteurs (as pro-government forces claimed), or inspired and sustained by a genuine and spontaneous uprising (as the opposition maintained), it had all the ingredients of civil strife. Various groups within the population resorted to armed struggle. Political order broke down; authority at the center disintegrated; leaders normally reticent about violent politics became progressively more involved in it. As in earlier episodes of communal conflict, a bewildering plurality of factions, driven by shifting allegiances and motives, were entrapped in an escalating spiral of hostility. Predominantly nonsectarian, involving issues of presidential succession, constitutional amendments, foreign policy, political grievances, and the like, the crisis degenerated willy-nilly into a confessional hostility; thereby reawakening religious enmity and heightening the intensity of violence.

Here again this dialectical and escalating interplay between reawakened confessional enmity, the heightened intensity of violence, and the drift into all the cruelties of incivility became more compelling. As in other such episodes, the original issues provoking the conflict receded. Lebanon was increasingly embroiled in the regional and international conflicts of the period and became, once again, an object and victim of cold war rivalries.

What changed the non-strident tone of public debate and how did it become more belligerent? How and why did the contentious groups in the conflict resort to, or drift into, insurgency? How did they rationalize their participation in political violence and what form did such violence assume?[2]

Drift Into Insurgency

To assert that the drift into political violence was largely a byproduct of the interplay between internal dislocations and external pressures is, in many respects, an affirmation of the obvious. Yet, it is an affirmation worth belaboring given some of its persisting features and consequences. Early in the 1950s the destabilizing consequences of this interplay were already much in evidence.

Lebanon's economic prosperity, impressive as it was, was not evenly spread. The dislocations were exacerbated by rapid urbanization, growing disparities in socioeconomic standards and symptoms of relative deprivation. These were visible in the mounting, predominantly Muslim, grievances against the political order denying them equal access to benefits and privileges. They were also critical of the government's neglect of outlying regions, rampant corruption, and favoritism.

The upsurge of Pan-Arab nationalist sentiments, inspired by Nasser's charismatic and messianic leadership, had gained considerable inroads in Lebanon; particularly among disenfranchised and marginal groups who were openly resentful of the avowedly pro-Western foreign policy of the government. Nasserism, with its anti-imperialist, nationalist fervor, and ideological support for the mobilization of underprivileged masses, awakened muted spirits of rebellion and defiance. It also undermined the authority of traditional Muslim leaders and aroused the anxiety of the Maronite political establishment.

Early during Chamoun's tenure in office (1952–58) his foreign policy was already suspect because of his predisposition to place Lebanon's external sovereignty in the hands of Western and, more particularly, British interests.

By the time of the Suez crisis in 1956, the pro-Western policies of the regime were becoming more pronounced. Chamoun, for example, refused to sever relations with Britain and France or to condemn the aggression; thereby provoking an outcry among Muslim leaders and the resignation of the Prime Minister, Abdallah Yafi, and Minister of State Saeb Salam. He supported the Baghdad Pact of 1955 and cultivated closer ties with anti-Nasserist Arab regimes like Iraq, Jordan, Saudi Arabia, Iran, and Turkey. In open defiance of the ascendant public mood, prodded perhaps by Dr. Charles Malik, his Foreign Minister and arch proponent of a pro-Western and activist foreign policy role for Lebanon, Chamoun was too hasty in endorsing the Eisenhower Doctrine, launched in 1957 in an effort to curtail the spread of radical and leftist ideologies in the Middle East. The outcry, this time, was more outrageous. Prominent figures (e.g. Rashid Karami, Sabri Hamadeh, Ahmad As'ad, Hamid Frangieh) resigned from the government in protest. The internal cleavages were aggravated further by electoral reforms of 1957, which undermined the parliamentary constituencies and popular bases of support of some of the leading traditional zua'ma. Indeed, despite Chamoun's open political style and demeanor and his fondness for reaching out and responding to the needs of ordinary citizens, he managed to alienate a sizeable cross-section of the country's political leaders and their respective constituencies. Hence, regions like Tripoli, Beqaa, Southern Lebanon, the Chouf, Zgharta threw their weight with the opposition, thereby undermining the territorial base on which Lebanon's internal sovereignty was predicated.

The pattern and heightened intensity of conflict became predictable. In the early phases of mobilization, the opposition had no intentions of resorting to political violence. Nor did it demand the resignation of Chamoun. Instead, it perceived the forthcoming parliamentary elections of May 1957 as a popular referendum on its policies as opposed to those of the government. Because of its mistrust of the Sami al-Solh cabinet, particularly its open-Western and anti-Nasserist strategies, the opposition was demanding its resignation in favor of a more neutral caretaker cabinet to oversee the elections. Hence, on May 30, 1957, they called for a general strike and peaceful demonstration to mobilize popular support on behalf of their demands.

As in many such instances, the peaceful demonstration degenerated into a violent scuffle between the opposition and security forces, with each side accusing the other of firing the fateful first shot. When the fighting was over, the opposition claimed that 15 persons were killed and more than 200 wounded; while the government official communiqué declared that only four men and one women were killed, accused foreign agents and agitators for inciting violence, even staging a coup d'état.

What was certain, however, was that firearms and tear gas were used and two politicians (Saeb Salam and Nassim Majdalani) were wounded and taken to hospitals under custody. Overnight, Salam, already prominent, became a national hero. In a dramatic gesture, from his hospital bed he went on a hunger strike until the government resigned. It was at this point that General Chehab, commander of the Army, stepped in as a mediator. A compromise was arrived at where Chehab assumed full control of security forces and two so-called "neutral" ministers were added to safeguard the honesty and freedom of elections.

Results of the elections (held for security reasons on four successive Sundays beginning on June 9) were a stunning and resounding victory for the government. The opposition barely sneaked in with only 8 of the 66 seats of the new Chamber. Virtually all the veteran politicians and prominent leaders of the opposition — Saeb Salam (Sunni), Kamal Jumblat (Druze), Ahmad As'ad (Shi'te) — were displaced in favor of pro-government candidates. Outcries of foul play, intimidation, bribery, and vote tampering were very audible. In fairness though, observers were more inclined to assign blame not so much on outright fraudulence as on Chamoun's disingenuous electoral reforms and gerrymandering, which stripped the zua'ma of their traditional bases of support.

From then on tension mounted. After a short and deceptive lull, the incidence of violent episodes increased. Clan feuds, sabotage, bombings, arms smuggling, as well as clashes between armed bands and security forces became virtually daily occurrences. Slowly, but perceptibly, Lebanon was descending into anarchy and anomie.

A cursory review of the chronology of events, for at least two years prior to the outbreak of hostilities, reveals that ferment was already building up. Here again, the "inside-outside" character of episodes of political violence was starkly visible. Taken together, changes in the pattern and magnitude of violence reflect some of the troublesome, often intractable, issues underlying the crisis; namely, socioeconomic disparities, the grievances of neglected groups and regions, factional rivalries, sectarian hostility, and the heated polemics over Lebanon's national identity and foreign policy orientation. The pattern of violence, as a consequence, falls ostensibly within four generic categories; ranging in intensity from strikes, demonstrations, and rioting, to subversive acts of sabotage, terrorism, and political assassinations:

1. *Waves of strikes*, particularly those of October 1957, in which workers and employers, in both the private and public sectors were demanding higher wages and better working conditions.

2. *National elections in Lebanon*, rent with schisms and factional rivalry, are an occasion for mass mobilization and display of emotionalism. The parliamentary elections of 1957 were particularly turbulent and ideologically charged, with claims and counter-claims of government intervention, bribery, and fraudulence. For security reasons, balloting was phased out over a period of four successive Sundays, with restrictions on public gatherings and rallies. This, invariably, led to scuffles, mob rioting, and politically motivated murders.

3. *Anti-Western demonstrations* in the wake of the Israeli attack on Egypt and mounting terrorist activities against British and French targets and interests.

4. *Episodes of infiltration and subversive activities attributed to political dissident groups*, particularly Palestinians, Syrians, Egyptians, and other political refugees. The Syrian and Egyptian regimes, in particular, were openly hostile to the Chamoun administration. They had launched a sustained invidious media campaign against its pro-Western policies and were directly involved in providing funds, as well as tactical and arms assistance to the opposition. The Egyptian Ambassador in Beirut, Brigadier Abdul Hamid Ghaleb, kept close and personal contacts with leaders of the United National Front (UNF) and the Embassy's residence in West Beirut became virtually the oppositions headquarters (see Qubain 1961: 55 for further details). During periods of heavy fighting, gun-running and arms smuggling across the Syrian borders became very common. Armed bands of volunteers were crossing and recrossing the frontiers at will. The intervention was so flagrant that the government was compelled periodically to ban Egyptian and Syrian papers, jam their radio programs and take coercive measures to deport infiltrators from there (Qubain 1961: 51–60).

An inventory of a selective sample of such recurrent episodes should suffice by way of identifying their character, diversity and magnitude.[3]

- Beirut was placed (November 21, 1956) under army control following violent anti-Western demonstrations.
- An Egyptian military attaché (November 22, 1956) was linked to a terrorist campaign of bombing British and French buildings in Beirut. Two hundred "Arabs" were arrested in connection with these and other subversive activities.
- Several new caches of arms were discovered (November 26, 1956), in a round-up of subversive elements.

- Col. Ghassan Jadid, a leader of the Syrian Nationalist Party (PPS) in exile in Beirut, was assassinated (February 19, 1957) by a gunman.
- Pre-election rioting broke out in Beirut (May 30, 1957) when security forces attempted to halt a demonstration and a strike led by former premiers Saeb Salam and Abdallah al-Yafi. Eight persons were killed and more than 20 wounded.
- Security forces (May 31, 1957) broke up two small demonstrations by opposition groups in Beirut.
- Twenty persons were killed and thirty wounded (June 16, 1957) in pre-election clashes in the Northern village of Miziara.
- It was revealed in Beirut (September 3, 1957), that during the past 48 hours security officers had seized 15 Czechoslovak sub-machine guns coming from Syria.
- Three gendarme and six arms smugglers were killed (September 12, 1957) in a gun fight near Deir al Ashayir on the Syrian frontier.
- The government (September 25, 1957) indicted 400 persons, including former Premiers Abdallah al Yafi, Saeb Salam and Hussein Oweini, on charges of attempting an armed coup and inciting to riot during the election campaign the previous May.
- The Lebanese Security Department announced (October 5, 1957) the arrest of seven persons charged with bombing newspaper plants under orders of Syrian Army Intelligence Bureau.
- A Lebanese gendarmerie post was raided (December 5, 1957) by bandits operating from Syria.
- The Lebanese army has reported to have taken over (December 8, 1957) the border zone of the northeast where raiders from Syria attacked.
- A band of 150 mountaineers (December 21, 1957) attacked a police post in North Lebanon resulting in the death of at least 18 persons and 50 wounded. This attack increased pressure on the Government to put the area under martial law.
- Twenty-three persons, most of whom were Palestinians, were sentenced (February 24, 1958) to terms of imprisonment ranging from three to 15 years for acts of terrorism.
- Four persons reported killed and at least 10 wounded in Tyre (April 2, 1958) in riots protesting the sentencing of three youths accused of defaming the Lebanese flag during pro-Nasser demonstrations.

In response to such growing manifestations of disorder the government introduced successive repressive measures to curb infiltration and to control

sabotage and terrorism. Early in 1957 the Lebanese Internal Security Council was already recommending strict control of the Lebanese-Syrian border,
a ban on movements of political refugees as well as any form of political
activity on their part. For that purpose the government announced, on January 16, the formation of a new national guard for sentry duty at important
installations. Likewise, rigid controls were imposed over all Palestinian refugees. Abdel Aziz Chehab, director general of the Interior Ministry, went
further to declare that in an effort to end terrorism, Lebanon was considering
establishing "concentration camps for foreigners who are suspect, where we
can keep them under surveillance." He confirmed that the measure is aimed
at Palestinian refugees (*Middle Eastern Affairs* 1958: 81).

Such impositions were visibly more stringent during elections. Frontiers
with Syria were closed on such occasions. There was a ban on the importation of Syrian and Egyptian papers. Palestinians were confined to their
camps. All arms permits were suspended. So were the sales of alcohol and
the licensing of political meetings.

The government was also displaying greater indignation and sensitivity
to criticism. This is seen in the flurry of decrees and the enactment of
successive legislations intended to curb the freedom of the press and the
mobilization of dissent. A selective inventory of such measures is, again,
instructive by way of identifying their magnitude and intensity.[4]

- The Government issued (May 12, 1957) a military warning to newspapers, with penalties up to five years imprisonment for publishing anything considered as inciting the population or criticizing the army.
- Jon Kimche, editor of the *Jewish Observer* was expelled (May 14, 1957).
  On the same day, all copies of the no. 5 issue of the *Manchester Guardian*, which carried a critical dispatch of Beirut City Administration, were
  confiscated.
- Prior censorship concerning the army, the rebels and anything regarded
  as likely to endanger security, cause sedition, or criticize the government
  was imposed (May 28, 1957) on all press reports.
- Decree (June 9, 1957) allowing the government to cancel the official
  status or job security of any government employee who joins a strike,
  does anything that damages the interest of the state, or belongs to a
  political party.
- Editor of an opposition paper was arrested (June 19, 1957) for violating
  censorship regulations. Warrants were issued for six others.
- Arrest warrants were issued (June 20, 1957) for 15 opposition leaders on
  a charge of inciting disturbances.

- The Cabinet approved a bill (June 26, 1957) authorizing the detention before judicial inquiry of any journalist whose writing was considered to offend the government.
- The Beirut daily newspaper *Le Jour* announced (July 18, 1957) that it would suspend publication indefinitely since there was no freedom of the press.
- The Ministry of Information banned the entry of the *New York Times* for publishing reports considered defamatory to Lebanese officials.

By early May of 1958 Lebanon was entrapped in a spiral of escalating violence; almost a textbook expression of the threefold manifestations of injustice, revolt, and repression inherent in virtually all forms of political violence. (Brown 1987: 8–13; Camara 1971). First, a growing segment of the population was already perceiving itself as violated by a deepening sense of injustice, social dislocation, inequity, and disaffection with the government's policies and its rampant favoritism and corruption. Second, these largely subtle and symbolic forms of deprivation were becoming more acute and oppressive, particularly after the elections of 1957. Outraged leaders, stripped of their traditional constituencies, called for open revolt against those held accountable for the abuses and usurpation of their power. Third, confronted with mounting symptoms of disorder and threats to its hegemony, both by the mobilization of internal dissent and infiltration of dissident groups, the government resorted to repressive measures, which only compounded the hostility and militancy of the adversaries.

Two events, predictably external and internal, provided direct impetus for the outbreak of fighting. The creation of the United Arab Republic (UAR) by the union of Syria and Egypt in February of 1958 generated added enthusiasm among the Lebanese already outraged by Chamoun's anti-Nasserism. Jubilant students, particularly those affiliated to the Maqassed Sunni Benevolent Society, took to the street.[5] There were widespread celebrations, rallies, and popular manifestations of adulation in support of Nasser's heroic political feats during the Suez crisis. Early in 1955 the Mufti of Lebanon was already sending telegrams to Nasser as "the Arab Muslim President . . . in the name of the Muslims of Lebanon we greet you and endorse your magnificent stand . . . and your defense of the Arab cause and Islam." On the occasion of the nationalization of the Canal, 30,000 signatures of support were collected from Tripoli alone (Atiyah 1973: 240). Nasser's imposing portraits, insignia, and graffiti overwhelmed the urban scene. So did the vitriolic press and radio programs, particularly the acrimonious campaigns the "Voice of the Arabs" launched against the "Villainous trio": Chamoun, his maligned

Sunni Prime Minister (Sami al-Solh), and Foreign Minister (Charles Malik), who were depicted as infatuous stooges of the West. At the Maqassed school, observed Desmond Stewart who headed its English program, "Every class-room had its portrait of Nasser, never of Chamoun; every wall-newspaper told of Nasser's exploits, whether in getting the British to evacuate the Canal Zone, or in distributing the land of the Pashas to the landless, and in uniting the Arabs" (Stewart 1959: 14). An unending steam of visitors and delegations from Lebanon went to Damascus to pay homage to Nasser. Some leaders of the UNF, in riveting speeches, implored him to involve himself directly in the internal affairs of Lebanon. These and other such popular manifes-tations aroused suspicion and hostility and widened cleavages between the already polarized political coalitions.

What, however, triggered the insurgency was the assassination of Nassib al-Matni on May 8, 1958, an independent Maronite journalist and an ardent critic of the regime. If an episode may be singled out as the "Sarajevo" of 1958, doubtless this event merits the label. The motive for the assassination, rumored to have been entirely nonpolitical, was never discovered; neither were the suspects. Leaders of the UNF nevertheless charged that Chamoun's henchmen were responsible for this and other "crimes" and were clamoring not only for their punishment but also for the resignation of the president himself. The fact that al-Matni happened to be a Maronite Christian served as an expedient alibi for a Muslim insurrection, muting thereby the sectarian sentiments fueling the hostility. Leading spokesmen of the opposition were also claiming that their call for a general strike was a purely internal conflict, directed against the pervasive corruption of the regime, and that they had no intention of undermining Lebanon's integrity and independence.

Both these claims, incidentally, i.e., the nonsectarian and internal char-acter of conflict, were challenged and discredited by the unfolding events. No sooner had the peaceful strike been called for that it escalated into violent confrontations in different regions of the country with clear evidence of massive infiltration of arms, fighters, and other modes of interventions from across the Syrian borders and the UAR.

The spark that touched off and fostered organized manifestations of col-lective violence elsewhere in the country ignited in Tripoli on May 10. Internal security forces (gendarmerie) clashed with demonstrators killing ten and wounding more than sixty persons. The outrage was instantaneous and widespread. In West Beirut, Sidon, and Tripoli, streets and quarters were barricaded. Sporadic clashes and kidnappings terrorized the population and threatened order and daily routines. Leaders of the opposition, particularly

Saeb Salam in West Beirut and Kamal Jumblat in the Chouf, openly called
for armed struggle. So swift were the incursions, doubtless evidence of earlier
preparation and coordination, that in less than two weeks the opposition was
in control of more than two-thirds of Lebanon's territory — much of the
coastal regions, along with Beqaa, Akkar, the South, and the Chouf.

President Chamoun tried in vain to draw the army into the struggle.
General Fuad Chehab, however, demurred. Sensing the dangers of involving the military in what was perceived at the time as a factional struggle, he
feared that such intervention would split the Army. Chamoun had no recourse but to fall back on the Gendarmerie which was poorly equipped and
factionally splintered. In desperation, he solicited the help of the Kata'ib and
the Syrian Socialist National Party (PPS), exacerbating thereby the sectarian
character of the conflict.

Given the profusion of Pan-Arabist sentiments, particularly in the wake
of the UAR union under Nasser, and the cultist appeal he was generating
among Lebanese Muslims, no wonder that many Christians perceived the
insurgency of their compatriots in threatening terms; i.e., as efforts to engulf
Lebanon in a messianic wave of Arab nationalism and to undermine its
autonomy and independence. Indeed, Chamoun incited such fears to solicit
the support of the Kata'ib and the PPS, who despite their ideological differences showed a common enmity against the onslaught of Pan-Arabism.

It was also understandable, given the interplay of internal and external
sources of unrest, why the Lebanese crisis was internationalized. Lebanon
was getting more deeply embroiled in the post-Suez ferment and the Cold
War rivalry raging at the time. Each group was also accusing the other of
soliciting outside support. In their daily communiqués and press releases
each side went to great lengths (by supplying photos, confessions, personal
documents) to reveal the identity of such infiltrators and "hired agents." The
opposition continued to insist that the crisis was an internal uprising, inspired
and supported by internal forces. It was the government, they charged, that
was arming its supporters among the Maronites and PPS, deploying the
armed and security forces, and receiving secret and illegal military and financial aid from the U.S., Turkey, Iraq; even British officers in Arab clothes
(Karami 1959:187) in crushing the rebellion. The government, on the other
hand, was more likely to incriminate Syrians, Egyptians, Palestinians, communists and other such subversive elements and "outlaws." Indeed, the government filed an official complaint accusing the UAR of massive intervention in Lebanon's internal affairs and in undermining the country's
independence. When recourse to the League of Arab States failed to reduce

tension, the U.N. Security Council was convened. In his address to the Security Council (June 6, 1958), Dr. Malik provided detailed substantiation of six sets of facts (supplying arms, training in subversion, the participation of UAR civilians and government agents, press and radio campaigns, etc.) as evidence of "massive, illegal and unprovoked intervention." A United Nations Observer Group (UNOGIL) was dispatched to observe and report on such allegations.[6]

The internationalization of the crisis took a sharper and more dramatic turn on July 14, in the wake of the Iraqi revolution which destroyed the Hashemite monarchy, the seat of the Baghdad Pact. Alarmed by the renewed frenzy of anti-Western sentiments, growing Russian influence in the region, and the prospects of further turmoil in Lebanon and Jordan, the U.S. promptly dispatched, in less than 24 hours, Marines to Lebanon. Within hours of the coup in Baghdad, Chamoun was already asking the U.S. ambassador for immediate intervention, insisting that "unless this took place within 48 hours, he would be a dead man, and Lebanon would become an Egyptian satellite" (Thayer 1959: 28). On that hot summer day in mid-July about 2,000 Marines, in full battle gear and supported by its amphibious forces, landed on the sandy beaches south of Beirut. They were reinforced shortly after by 15,000 men along with the mobilization of the entire Sixth Fleet, consisting of about 70 ships and 40,000 troops, in the eastern Mediterranean.

Robert Murphy, Eisenhower's emissary, was clear and unequivocal regarding the circumstances associated with that momentous event:

Settlement of the Tunisian conflict in 1958 did not bring peace to other Mediterranean countries, and machinations by Arabs throughout the Middle East created a perilous situation. This highly sensitive area was of political importance to the United States, and even more important to our European allies who depended on it as their major source of petroleum. Among other danger spots, the state Department was particularly concerned about the Republic of Lebanon. That small country had about a million and a half inhabitants, normally balanced delicately between Christians and Moslems, but now distorted by the presence of three hundred thousand Moslem refugees who had fled from Palestine. Many of these refugees were desperate men, bitter against the United States because it supported the State of Israel which had caused their exile. We learned that Arab nationalists, under the direction of President Nasser of Egypt, were spending money to influence the swollen Moslem population of Lebanon and were sending clandestine arms to rebellious elements there. The prospect of the spread of Nasserism into Lebanon, one of the most pro-Western countries in the entire area, awoke lively reactions in Washington. Congress expressed considerable interest in helping our friends, especially when some Lebanese factions openly revolted against the duly constituted Government. By early June the situation had deteriorated badly, the country was in a state of civil war, and a vociferous radio and press campaign in Egypt was calling for the overthrow of the Republic of Lebanon (Murphy 1964: 396–97).

The Marines' landing was eventless, at least if compared with the calamitous consequences of subsequent interventions. Here again Murphy's recollection of that stirring, albeit bizarre, event is worth quoting in full:

By the time I arrived in Beirut, almost seven thousand Marines had landed and were patrolling the vicinity with tanks, armored amphibians, and self-propelled atomic howitzers, although no nuclear weapons were unloaded. The landings had been made with eclat, with no unfortunate incidents and no casualties. By July 18 about seventy or seventy-five warships of the Sixth Fleet were near Beirut Harbor, providing quite a spectacle for the fashionable diners on the terrace of the Pigeon Rock restaurant. Marine columns were marching past the luxurious St. George Hotel, where girls were sunning themselves on yachts in the hotel's private basin while Navy jets from the carriers Saratoga and Essex were shrieking over the city. By July 25 the American shore forces numbered at least 10,600 men — 4,000 Army, 6,600 Marines — more than the entire Lebanese Army.

As our forces had come to Lebanon at the invitation of Chamoun, the first thing I did in Beirut was to pay my respects to the President at his official residence. There I found a tired and worried man, who for sixty-seven days had been a self-made prisoner. Apparently he had not so much as looked out of a window during that time, and this undoubtedly was wise as his chances of assassination were excellent. Under the Lebanese constitution the President of the Republic was limited to one term in office, but Chamoun was proposing to amend the constitution and seek a second term, and this political issue was one of the main reasons for the civil war.

Since Berlin in 1945, I had not been in a more trigger-happy place than Beirut was at that time. Wild fusillades, bombings and arson were the order of the day and more especially the night. Almost across the street from the presidential palace was the Basta, a complex of ancient streets and buildings forming the type of district sometimes called the Casbah. The British Ambassador had asked for the protection of a Marine guard and this was assigned to him. But the first night the Americans were on duty, the British Embassy was peppered by shootings from the Basta which narrowly missed some of our Marines. President Chamoun told me that he had ordered and begged General Fuad Chehab, who was in command of the Lebanese Army, to clean out the Basta, but without success. My immediate reaction was that Chehab ought to be fired, a competent new commander appointed, and action taken to restore order and authority of the Government. I found it was not quite that simple (Murphy 1964: 399–400).

While Western allies applauded the intervention, Russia decried it as a "direct act of war and open piracy" and warned that the Soviet Union could not remain "indifferent to events creating a grave menace in an area abutting on its frontiers." Nasser, of course, was equally indignant and condemned the landing "as a grave violation of the U.N. charter and a flagrant threat to the Arab countries" (Agwani 1963: 340).

Within Lebanon the Marine landing polarized the adversaries. Chamoun expressed "profound gratitude" and felt "happy and honored." The opposition, on the other hand, was stunned. Saeb Salam, its leading spokesman, declared bitterly that "imperialism had returned with its armies" and issued a call to "repel the enemy" (Agwani 1963: 341). Eventually, however, Murphy was able to lend support to the mediation efforts of the so-called "Third Force," a nucleus of moderate politicians working for a nonbelligerent resolution of the conflict. A compromise was arranged and General Chehab was prevailed upon to become the new President.

Embattled Groups and Regions

No sooner had the fighting started than the country was divided into five regions: virtually independent territorial enclaves, war zones, or "fiefdoms" under the control of one of its local Zu'ama. Perceptions of the crisis — its underlying causes; rationalization for armed struggle; the pattern, intensity and timing of violence; the degree of organization and motivation of partic-

ipants, mobilization of resources, and the forms collective strife assumed —
differed from one region to another. Invariably, however, they also displayed
some common attributes.

Beirut

In Beirut, the city and its suburbs were split into its two traditional communities on largely sectarian grounds. Western Beirut, particularly the predominantly Muslim quarters of al-Basta, Museitbeh and Mazra'a, was under
control of the opposition, while the Christian quarters of Eastern Beirut
remained under the control of loyalist forces. Leaders on both sides of the
divide made repeated appeals and pronouncements to ensure that civil strife
did not slip into confessional conflagrations. Yet, despite these efforts the
fighting in Beirut almost inevitably degenerated into a bloody communal
war between the Christian quarters to the east and the Muslim quarters in
and around al-Basta. Strongholds and quarters of adversaries were already
akin to embattled war-zones. They needed little by way of provocation. In
the words of Robert Murphy, they were "trigger-happy, seething with wild
fusillades, bombings and arson."

Initially, the opposition-held quarters in West Beirut were independent,
loosely coordinated groups of insurgents falling, generally, under three separate commands: Saeb Salam, Mu'in Hammoud, and Adnan al-Hakim as
head of al-Najjadah party, something of a Muslim counterpart to the Maronite Kata'ib. Efforts to unify the groups failed, in part because of intense
rivalry between Salam and al-Najjadah. The latter, established in 1939 as a
youth movement, never succeeded in broadening its constituency beyond
the limited appeal it inspired among the urban Sunni Muslim underclass.
With the upsurge of Nasserism and Arab Nationalist sentiments, the party
became more of a paramilitary mass movement espousing extremist views
such as uniting Lebanon with the UAR, even at a time when Muslim
Zu'ama and Nasser himself were only calling for cooperation and a certain
degree of foreign policy coordination. Doubtless, al-Najjadah were drawing
on the appeal of such populist sentiments and the glamour of paramilitarism
in its bid to undermine the clientelism of the traditional zu'ama.

As leader and spokesmen of the opposition, Saeb Salam was very reluctant
to abandon his nonbelligerent strategies in challenging the loyalists and
their allies. Like other leaders, he spoke of being coerced into insurgency
in self-defense against the repressive and criminal deeds of the regime.

Indeed, in accounting for the causes of unrest, Salam identified the "regrettable" stages which transformed "the popular, peaceful uprising into a bloody revolution." Initially, Salam asserts that the uprising took the form of a "popular opposition to foil the conspiracy hatched by the President against the constitution with the aim of renewing his term for another six years. . . . The suppression, oppression, terrorism and criminal acts committed by the President and his clique, however, transformed the battle into a peaceful popular uprising to preserve the sanctity of the Constitution and national unity" (Agwani 1965: 72).

On May 12 the armed insurrection in Beirut broke out with an almost identical replay of the bloody rioting in Tripoli two days earlier; namely the sacking and burning of the USIS library and blowing up of the IPC pipelines. Given the savagery of the events, the government promptly decreed a state of alert and imposed a curfew. Foreign Minister Charles Malik hastened to protest to the government of the UAR the "massive interference in the events now unrolling in Lebanon . . . and the streams of armed men still pouring in from Syria" (*Middle Eastern Affairs* 1958: 240).

Of course, leaders of the opposition were outraged by such charges. Five days after the outbreak of hostilities in Beirut, Salam went further to declare that:

> The President did not respect the will of the people, but resorted to steel and fire, thus transforming this peaceful political struggle into a bloody revolution in which the people have been forced to defend themselves and their principles in the face of instigation, aggression and murder. Hundreds have been killed and wounded in Beirut and elsewhere.
>
> The President, Foreign Minister Charles Malik and their clique were not satisfied with their methods aimed at dominating the majority of the people, who opposed their stupid policy. They turned to more serious and shrewder methods. They are now attempting to deal the heart of national unity a mortal blow by inciting communal disputes and civil war.
>
> We are convinced that the vigilant Lebanese people, who have defeated previous conspiracies by Chamoun, Malik, and their former supporters, will now defeat these evil conspiracies. The revolution of the people will remain purely nationalist. There is no room for communal exploitation. We are all true Lebanese working in the interests of the Lebanon alone. Today we do our utmost to resist this evil conspiracy and prevent civil war (Agwani 1965: 72–73).

So alarmed by the escalation of rioting and violence, particularly after a bomb explosion in a Beirut streetcar killed, on May 26, eleven persons and injured dozens more, the Cabinet passed a decree authorizing the recruitment of a civilian militia to help quash the rebellion. The move was bitterly denounced by religious leaders including the Maronite Patriarch Paul Ma'ushi who went further and demanded the replacement of Chamoun by General Chehab since he considered the situation too grave for a compromise (*The Middle East Journal*).

By the time U.S. troops were landing in Lebanon (July 15, 1958), Salam invoked national duty and honor and called upon "valiant youth" to defend their country.

Valiant youth of the people's resistance, today we turn to you while the country is passing through the most sordid period in its current history. There is grave danger, and imperialism has returned with its armies to the beloved homeland in a hideous plot hatched with the traitor agent Camille Chamoun and his criminal gang. National duty calls upon you to comport yourselves on the field of honour as daring heroes in defence of your country, territory and freedom. You have fought and struggled to liberate your country from the atrocities and afflictions of imperialism. But here is traitor Chamoun, who has pledged loyalty to the homeland, betraying his trust and pledge and calling on the enemy to occupy the country. In this way Chamoun unmasks himself and discloses his intention. He is a traitor to his country and a plotter against those who believe in sovereignty and independence (Agwani 1965: 293).

Signing his declarations as "Commander-in-Chief of the People's Forces," he condemned the invasion and warned the aggressors to withdraw their forces from Lebanese soil. Even after Chehab's election (July 31, 1958), welcome as it was to the opposition, Salam continued to insist on the downfall of Chamoun and the withdrawal of the forces of aggression; otherwise the popular resistance would not abandon their resistance (Agwani 1965: 377).

From the Kata'ib's perspective the crisis was not simply a conflict over political succession, the quality of leadership, or a consequence of the dislocations and grievances generated by a corrupt and unjust political system. Rather, it was seen as an expression of a fundamental tension involving the very nature of Lebanon's national identity and growing anxiety over the country's autonomy and sovereignty as an independent state. Indeed, to leaders of the party, the issue of presidential succession was dismissed as an expedient alibi employed by the pan-Arab and Nasserite elements among the insurgents in their effort to discredit, fragment, destroy, and then reconstitute Lebanon's polity into something approximating the other "revolutionary" and "progressive" regimes in the region.

The old atavistic fears of the Christians, particularly the Maronites, that they are an endangered minority about to be engulfed in a sea of Islamic states and the impassioned frenzy of Arab masses were once again reawakened. President Chamoun was savvy enough to work on such fears in soliciting the support of the quietist and politically inactive elements of the Christian community. Manifestations of such confessional consciousness were already apparent in Maronite communities and did not require much by way of incitement. Desmond Stewart, living in Junieh at the time, had this to say:

> Living among Maronites, one might have thought that the Christian religion had started on the Seine, not the Jordan. There were French priests in soutanes; bells rang more frequently than I remembered them in Oxford. . . . The spirit of Junieh — despite its beauty, a lugubrious town — came alive on religious feasts such as Assumption or Pentecost: then the pavements were jammed with Maronites, then floats covered with allegorical groups moved from the central square, with its French municipal building, towards a church: sweating enthusiasts posed in the sunshine, Crusaders in tinfoil with scarlet crosses, a moslem dragon, turbaned enemies of the Faith, transfixed. After the floats would come a lorry with priests saying Mass at an altar. Odd occasions, and very fervent.

> Most of the handsome stone-built houses were owned by people who had fawned on the French, then on the British, and who now cast interested glances towards America. They boasted of being quite unlike the Arabs. Sometimes they claimed to be Phoenicians, sometimes the by-blows of Frankish crusaders. They were proud of speaking French; in Arabic they had referred to France as umm al hannoun, the nourishing mother. They rang the Angelus, a challenge to the minarets, not so far away, in Beirut and Tripoli. If you asked, "Are there any Moslems here?" They would look astounded and reply, "Here, in Junieh? Not one: we are all Maronites" (Stewart 1961: 10–12).

Chamoun's predicament was very critical, particularly since some prominent and visible Maronites (e.g. the Patriarch, former President of the Republic al-Khuri, the Franjiyehs, Ammouns) and members of the "Third Force" (i.e., Emile Bustani, Henry Far'awn, Charles Helou, Alfred Naqqash, Philip Taqla, Ghassan Tueni) were already supporting the opposition, at least on the issue of succession. In impassioned editorials, Tueni, perhaps the most outspoken of this group, repeatedly cautioned against the use of violence, foreign patronage, the incitement of confessional enmity, and implored both — loyalists and insurgents — to transcend their petty squabbles and spare Lebanon the foibles of a specious "revolution."

As a member of the "Third Force," Tueni attempted to mediate a compromise solution between the two sides. He did not, though, hesitate to rebuke both sides sharply or to address candidly some of the most sensitive issues underlying the conflict. In an editorial on March 15, two months before the outbreak of violence, he remarked that the Muslims of Lebanon look to Nasser for leadership almost to the point of deification; thereby provoking Christians to transform Chamoun into such a symbol. "Provocation was met by provocation. . . . The jubilant gunfire in the air in celebration of either of the deified leaders was only a small step away from gunfire in the street. This step, which could easily exacerbate Lebanon's eclipse, is accessible to the folly of any foolhardy or trigger-happy mercenary" (Tueni 1958: 5).

Tueni's and the "Third Force's," criticisms of Chamoun rested on two issues: reelection and the internationalization of the crisis. While insisting that Chamoun should complete his legal term rather than resign at once as the opposition demanded, Tueni nonetheless insisted that Chamoun's duty was to renounce publicly all thoughts of a second term, and that his failure to do so only lent moral support to the opposition. Tueni was also critical of the government's action in taking their complaint against interference from the UAR to the Arab League at the UN, not on the grounds that there was no such interference, but because appealing for outside aid would only enhance Lebanon's proclivity for such dependence. The real crisis Tueni cautioned was apt to resurface once the fighting ceased: "the problem of deciding the destiny of a country which we have made a state, but which we have not known how to make into a nation" (Tueni 1958: 38).

The day after the Marines landed on July 15, Tueni was sharper and more poignant in his criticisms of combatants.

To certain Christians who still tell themselves that the age of protectorates and Crusades is not over, we say quite frankly that the Sixth Fleet did not land its troops to protect them, but to protect its own vital interests; and that its vital interests have no religion, but that if we must give a religious label to those with whom its interests lie, we should say that it is the Muslims with whom the West will try to make friends (Tueni 1958: 54).

Likewise, he repeatedly taunted the opposition leaders for allowing themselves to become prisoners of their own followers' extremism, for sustaining the insurrection long after the reelection of Chamoun was out of the question, and for being more interested in their own personal political status than in the country's welfare. He declared, in another impassioned editorial, that much as he longed to see radical reform in Lebanon, he could not support the revolution because it promised little worth the shedding of a drop of blood. "Shall we liberate the people with the tribes of Sabri Hamadeh or the gangs of Suleiman Franjiyeh?" (Tueni 1958: 41).

It did not take much, incidentally, for Chamoun to whip up sectarian sentiments. In Lebanon, religious phobias have long been easy to ignite. This why little is required, by way of provocation, to transform civil strife into the treacherous cruelties of uncivil wars. Chamoun was partly successful in winning the loyalty of a sizeable portion of the Christian Community. For example, most of the lower clergy and several of the bishops deserted Patriarch Ma'ushi. In some instances, priests exhorted their flock during mass and religious ceremonies to support Chamoun (Qubain 1961:83). It was also evident that the government went as far as to arm some of them (e.g. supporters of Mughabghab in the Chuf) in lieu of its repeated failure to draw the more active involvement of security forces into the conflict.

The Kata'ib, contrary to prevalent assumptions, were not uncritical admirers of Chamoun of his regime. Privately, as well as in public pronouncements and successive editorials in the opinion columns of *al-Amal*, the organ of the party, they were adamantly opposed to any attempt at amending the constitution to permit Chamoun, or any other incumbent for that matter, to renew his term. In other words, while Chamoun to them was dispensable, the system was not. The party was also leery of aligning itself too closely with a regime about to lose its credibility. Nor was the Kata'ib particularly happy about the confessional undertones and religious fervor the conflict was arousing — a feature they attributed to the opposition along with the explicit incitement of Egypt and Syria.

With the polarization of the conflict into pro-Arab and anti-Chamoun rivalry, the Kata'ib had no choice but to shift its allegiance and started to perceive any apposition to Chamoun, at least by implication, as a design or conspiracy to undermine Lebanon's sovereignty and nationalist loyalties. It is then that they became unequivocal and steadfast in their support of the government.

Initially, however, this support did not manifest itself in any militant activity or involvement in street fighting, despite its burgeoning image as a paramilitary movement sparked by the fanaticism of supervigilantes and the machismo of the devoted hard core striking force of its younger recruits (Staokes 1975). Indeed, the party did not relish its paramilitary role — especially since it perceived civil strife as an instigation of foreign elements and "borrowed ideologies" conspiring to enfeeble the internal social fabric of the state and, thereby, generating conditions germane for such foreign intervention.

For sure, the Kata'ib, along with the PPS and Armenian Tashnaq, offered assistance to government security forces in fighting insurgents. By all accounts, however, the role of the Kata'ib was limited; particularly when compared to the PPS, who assumed the brunt of the heavy fighting, often waging battles and provoking confrontations of their own in virtually all areas of conflict. On the whole, the Kata'ib's involvements were limited to Beirut and the Christian strongholds of Mount Lebanon. Even there their activities consisted of little more than assisting the gendarmerie in patrolling the streets (Qubain 1961: 84; Entelis 1974: 176). Doubtless, this explains why much of the opposition literature on the crisis spared the Kata'ib the pugnacious outcries it leveled at Chamoun, Malik, al-Solh and the PPS.

This seemingly bizarre collaboration between the Kata'ib and the PPS deserves, nonetheless, brief explication. Despite their deep-seated hostility and ideological differences, and by an odd confluence of circumstances, they found themselves part of the same tenuous but expedient alliance. Crises in Lebanon, as elsewhere, render the cohabitation of such strange bedfellows more plausible. This is simply one of recurrent instances rooted in the factionalism of a fragmented political culture sustained by shifting political alliances and personal rivalries.

Other than the transient hostility they harbored against the insurgents, they had little else in common. Indeed, clashes between the two parties, shortly before the outbreak of hostilities in May, were very common. The very ideology of the PPS was, after all, antithetical to the existence of Lebanon as an independent entity. As such the party has no genuine interest in Lebanon's long-term stability. Nor did it relish, given its avowed secularism, the preservation of a plural society sustained by confessional and primordial loyalties.

Like other political parties and movements rooted in the 1930s struggle for independence, the PPS espoused nationalist and emancipatory sentiments. Ideologically, it professed a secularist, progressive, anti-feudal program and advocated a doctrine of Syrian nationalism committed to the reunification of so-called "Natural Syria," encompassing the fertile crescent, along with Iraq and Cyprus. Sparked by the charisma, powerful intellect, and adroit manipulation of its leader and founder, Antoun Saadeh, and reinforced by a tinge of European fascism and totalitarian discipline, the party grew from a small, ostracized secret society to a sizeable party of about 25,000, drawn largely from a cross-section of intersectarian groups (Yamak 1966, Suleiman 1967; Showeiri 1973).

Its failure to achieve power or even gain legitimacy intensified its feelings of frustration and, with time, increased its leanings toward violence. In fact, since 1949, violence had become the only method by which it hoped to create favorable conditions for the realization of its objectives. In 1951, it plotted and successfully carried out the assassination of Riad al-Solh, several times Prime Minister of Lebanon. In 1955, under the direct orders of the president of the party, a party member assassinated Col. Adnan Malki.[7] In 1956 and 1957, the party was implicated in a plot against the Syrian government. It was suppressed in Syria and many of its leaders were either jailed or sentenced to death (Yamak 1966: 146).

Its anticlerical, secular ideology and its claims for advancing a rational philosophy to address and reform the pathologies of Near Eastern Sociocultural, political, and economic life was very appealing to a generation of intellectual idealists, political activists, and extremists. The party's mystique of active combat also attracted a large reservoir of militant zealots from the disenfranchised and uprooted elements of society.

The PPS had little to lose. It was driven by pure enmity and bitterness. The party's distrust of Communism, the Ba'th, and Nasser's brand of Arabism was compounded by its seething fury over the treacherous execution of Sa'adeh. Ostracized and despised everywhere, Lebanon was its last battlefield. Yet, it evinced no loyalty to Lebanon's independence or its preservation as a political entity. It was clearly not motivated by any such idealistic fervor but by a desire for self-preservation. A victory for the opposition would have spelled its liquidation. Hence, they fought recklessly and everywhere.

Although the PPS was banned in Iraq, Syria and Jordan, the Iraqi regime found it expedient, nonetheless, to support its subversive activities in Lebanon largely because of their mutual hatred of the Syrian regime and the recently established UAR. Much of the party's support, both in funds and arms, came from Iraq. Its armed militias of about 3,000 waged some of the most vicious battles with little regard to the havoc and destruction the fighting generated in vital and infrastructural facilities.

Tripoli

Civil unrest in Tripoli, by far the fiercest and most damaging, displayed patterns of mobilization and violence quite distinct from those observed elsewhere. The overall character of the "Popular Resistance," much as in Beirut, Mount Lebanon, and Sidon, was largely insurrectionist. As in other predominantly Muslim regions at a time of ascendant Arab nationalist sentiments, Tripoli was bitterly opposed to the pro-Western foreign policy of Chamoun's regime. Rashid Karami, the scion of a long line of urban zua'ma was spared the humiliation of defeat other traditional leaders suffered in the infamous elections of 1957. He was, nonetheless, openly critical of the N-government's neglect of Tripoli, his political constituency, and the second-largest city in the country. He also decried the corruption and favoritism of the Chamounists and their allies.

All other similarities, however, end here. The sparks that touched off waves of civil unrest throughout the country were, it must be recalled, initiated in Tripoli. The ensuing tension and fighting was sustained, at escalating intensity, throughout the five-month interlude of civil strife. In Beirut, by comparison, much of the heavy fighting took place over one weekend — that of June 14 and 15. The ferocity of violence in Tripoli was largely a reflection of the bitter rivalries between the PPS, Ba'th, and Communist parties, compounded by the cross-cutting loyalty the great mass of Tripolitanians felt for the Karami family.

Incidentally, the fragmented political culture of Tripoli had been a source of political strife for quite some time. Early in December, six months before the outbreak of hostilities, the government had already declared the northern district as a "military area" because of the escalating incidence of bombings, attempted assassinations, and other acts of sabotage. It is clear that the insurrectional movement was initiated by these parties and was touched off, characteristically, by the plundering of the American Information Office (USIS) and the Iraq Petroleum Company (IPC) — favorite targets of nationalist demonstrators. The local PPS headquarters, the mortal enemy of the Ba'th, was also sacked and burned (Hottinger 1961: 132–33). In one day of rioting, May 9, fifteen persons were reported killed and 128 wounded (*Middle East Affairs* 1958: 239).

The army was also more heavily and directly involved. Elsewhere, because of Chehab's intent to maintain its neutrality, the role of the army was comparatively incidental. Only during rare, critical confrontations was Chehab persuaded to commit armed forces into the battle. In Tripoli, the army assumed major responsibility, employing armored cars, tanks and heavy artillery. Casualties, as a result, were much heavier. It is estimated that close to 170 persons were killed in the city and its harbor, al-Mina (Karami 1959: 256). Since the figures are derived from sources close to the insurgents, they most probably exclude the equally heavy casualties loyalists and government security forces suffered. Physical destruction was also comparatively heavier in Tripoli. Dense urban quarters, in both the old city and the harbor, were demolished through shelling and counter-shelling.

The army's direct involvement might well be a reflection of local political developments in the region. Zgharta, traditionally the Christian counter-weight against Muslim Tripoli, was embroiled at the time in a bloody lead-ership struggle of its own; a replay of the endemic factional rivalry between its feuding clans. The Chamoun government had tried, in compliance with its "antifeudal" strategies, to bolster the Dwaihis, the anti-Fanjiyah faction of Zgharta. The heated preelectoral campaign had degenerated into an in-famous shootout (June 15, 1957) in an open church courtyard ("la tuerie de Miziara") where thirty-eight innocent victims were slain and more than thirty were wounded. The involvement of the Dawihis in their strife-torn town in the north, prevented their participation in the broader national crisis being waged in Tripoli. The armed forces most probably stepped in to act as surrogate.

Much like Beirut, Tripoli was also split into two main war zones. The Old City — with its labyrinthian quarters, covered souks and pedestrian alley-ways, with al-Mansuri Mosque at its epicenter — came under the control of the rebel forces. Together, the Old City and al-Mina, had a predominantly Sunni Muslim population of about 40,000. Fervor for Nasser and Arab Na-tionalism was intense and highly voluble. Impassioned masses, public slo-gans, graffiti, and Friday mosque sermons were openly idolizing Nasser and calling for unity with the UAR. The other outlying new suburbs, with reli-giously-mixed groups of relatively more recent out-migrants from the Old City and adjoining towns and villages, were largely pro-government. (See Gulick 1967 for demographic and sectarian composition of various neigh-borhoods in Tripoli.)

The insurgent movement in Tripoli also appears to have been better organized. It may not approximate the features of a "Paris Commune," as one enthusiastic observer claimed (Stewart 1958: 110). It did, though, display a clear organizational structure with an eight-man central command and a seven-man executive office with explicit chains of command and division of responsibility. A revolutionary court and other auxiliary appendages of government were also established. Rashid Karami was more than just a titular head. By virtue of his kinship descent and professed enthusiasm for Nasserist and Arab nationalist ideologies, he wielded considerable authority and popularity among a broad cross-section of his constituency. His subordinates in commanding positions (e.g. al-Rafi'i, 'Adra, Ma'sarani, Hamzah, al-Baghdadi) were of like-mind and background; drawn largely from prominent urban Sunni Muslim families with Ba'thist and Nationalist leanings.

There is also evidence, suggestive if not conclusive, that Tripoli's "Popular Resistance" benefited from a much larger volume of infiltration of arms and men from the Syria and other sources. The bulk of the northern frontier area was held by the opposition, which, along with the inaccessible nature of the terrain, doubtlessly accounts for such massive infiltration. Published chronologies, extracted from local sources, confirm such tendencies. Early in 1957, one encounters entries involving smuggling of guns, ammunition, and the participation of UAR civilian nationals and government officials in subversive activities or in the direction and mobilization of the insurrection (*Middle Eastern Affairs* 1957, 1958; *Middle East Journal* 1957, 1958).

The Chuf Region

Some of the heaviest and sustained fighting took place in the Chuf where Kamal Jumblat, reaching beyond other opposition leaders, declared his own autonomous local government in defiance of state authority. The rudiments of administrative units were established to regulate provisions and supplies, security, police, justice, and armed forces. Jumblat's imposing family estate and palace at al-Mukhtarah served as capital and headquarters of his insurgent movement. He clearly relished the rebellious role he was playing and often went about it with aplomb and studied fanfare. The international and local media played up to him and sensationalized their coverage of the battles in the Chuf, in part because of the dramatic turn of events there and the images they evoked of yet another Druze–Maronite bloody conflict — a replay of the massacres of 1860.

It was not difficult for Jumblat to justify his resort to armed rebellion. As a passionate reformist, often a doctrinaire revolutionary pamphleteer, and something of a wide-ranging intellectual dilettante, he could easily conceal his parochial and personal interests behind the guise of radical political rhetoric and the call for liberation. He prefaced his impassioned book, largely a seething political tract written shortly after the civil war of 1958, by lambasting the "anarchy, crass materialism, hypocrisy . . . and the corrupt and corrupting influence of mercantilism rooted in the Phoenician heritage . . . and the opportunism, clientelism of Lebanese politicians and the foreign hands which squandered its resources and fragmented its political culture" (Jumblat 1959: 10–15). He spares no one. Of course, Chamoun and his "stooges," particularly al-Solh and Malik, emerge as prime culprits. They are held responsible for betraying Arab nationalist sentiments, being lackies of Western imperialism, deepening sectarian hostility, and violating morality of public life. "Prostitution, white-slave traffic, drugs, gambling . . . reached their zenith" Jumblat charged, in Chamoun's "accursed regime" (Jumblat 1959: 33). To Jumblat, it is these and the complicity of other self-serving politicians which account for the failure of the insurrection in bringing about a radical transformation of society and its despicable political institutions.

In advancing his socialist program he maintains that:

The theory of liberalism, or absolute freedom in politics, is a mistake as far as Lebanon is concerned. It has bequeathed to us this individualist anarchy in our public and private life, so that people in this country have become selfish and wrapped up in their own interests, heedless of everything except what directly concerns themselves, exerting themselves only for what falls within their narrow horizons, interested in nothing that does not bear them a definite advantage (Jumblat 1959: 161).

To him, much of the economic prosperity Lebanon was enjoying was due in large part to the fact that Beirut had become "a nightclub for the royalty and capitalists of the Arab world and a cosmopolitan center for licit and illicit commerce" (Jumblat 1959: 33).

The turning point, however — and Jumblat is quite explicit on this — was his failure to regain his parliamentary seat. It was a devastating blow to his credibility and stature, particularly since an electoral position in the National Assembly was seen as an inevitable appendage to his feudal ancestry. The failure was a decisive watershed which prompted him to entertain, not without agonizing hindsight, more militant forms of opposition. Thus far, often

invoking Gandhi's strategies of passive resistance, he had refrained from
considering such radical options. From then on, however, all such restraints
melted away. Curiously, being cast out of parliament and his exclusion from
the assembly, and its open forum for public debate, meant to Jumblat that
he was thrust back into feudal society with its contentious and warring
predispositions.

> Our failure in the Chuf . . . after Chamoun used his armed gangs,
> (gendarmes and civilians) to terrorize the Christian villages to force
> them to vote against us, was the third incitement in the crisis. . . .
> When I became certain of my personal failure. . . . I left the house
> secretly through a back door, to Beirut, for fear that my brethren would
> revolt if I remained among them . . . and in fact, a few hours later,
> news of the Chufites reached us. They immediately cut telephone
> lines, congregated on public roads, and carried out provocative acts
> against authorities, who accepted them and avoided facing them for
> fear that they would develop into something more serious. We tried
> the impossible to stop such acts. . . . For tens of armed men stationed
> themselves in our house in the Chuf refusing to leave it. . . . Our
> remaining in Beirut near the security forces, who could detain me
> anytime they wished, was the only guarantee that the revolt in the
> Chuf would not break out before we have prepared for it. . . . From
> that hour (i.e. after the election defeat), we began to think that the
> revolt had become inevitable . . . and after a short interlude of rest,
> mixed with feeling of despair, disgust and resentment of politics and
> its vile practitioners, we started to think that revolt was necessary and
> inevitable. Otherwise, we would have been guilty of failure in har-
> nessing and directing the legitimate rage of the new generations of
> radical change (Jumblat 1959: 83–89).

It is revealing that Jumblat's espousal of violent politics, despite the depth
of his outrage, was ambiguous and tentative. This was visible in the way he
justified and accounted for the initial and increasing involvement of his
followers in acts of terrorism and sabotage. He was equally evasive as to the
sources of arms and military assistance he received. "our men and supporters
had only a small number of rifles, not more than thirty. We made contacts
with those that had to be contacted. Despite our efforts we lost control and
could not restrain the enthusiasm of nine determined men who climbed

Mount Kanisah and launched terrorist acts in retaliation. Bridges, railroads, hydraulic installations, electric and telephone networks, municipal head-quarters were ambushed and destroyed. This small but heroic adventure served as a safety valve to release pent-up aggression and a training ground in live ammunition and actual combat" (Jumblat 1959, 86). In glowing terms Jumblat went further to depict of impact of such "redemptive acts" in gen-erating self-sacrifice, valor and manly virtues. Those imbued with such spirits "rushed to their death as if it were a spring betrothal, a joyous and regen-erative celebration" (Jumblat 1959: 87).

Benign as these "little excursions" were, they awakened Jumblat and his followers to the impact of violence in exposing the vulnerability of Chamoun and his exploitative regime. "It is the irony of fate," he exclaimed, "that we too should become versed in the new art of instilling terror and fear among those in power without violating their lives as was to happen, unfortunately, in subsequent episodes of urban strife" (Jumblat 1959: 88).

In this, as in other justifications of his initial guarded entry and growing involvement in political violence, Jumblat was in effect exonerating his own participation as a defensive strategy to curb the arrogance and cruelty of those in power. Since the state, he argued, in Chamoun's era had degen-erated into a collection of armed bands, the only legitimate response was to organize one's own armed bands. "A police state," he declared, "can only be resisted by similar rebellious and coercive measures" (Jumblat 1959: 90).

Once the fighting started it acquired an escalating momentum of its own; more so, perhaps, than in other regions of conflict. The bitter personal en-mity between Chamoun and Jumblat, the mixed interconfessional compo-sition of villages and towns with strongholds of government loyalists coexist-ing in close proximity to rebel forces, along with Jumblat's threatening intentions to march on Beirut and occupy the presidential palace to force Chamoun's resignation heightened the ferocity of fighting.

The Chuf battles started in earnest on May 13, just three days after the bloody clashes in Tripoli. On the 9th the UNF had taken the decision to launch the armed revolt to be spearheaded by Jumblat's offensives in the Chuf. Just a day after Jumblat reached al-Mukhtarah, rebel forces under his command attacked the presidential palace at Bayt al-Dine, thereby initiating armed hostility. So swift was the progression of events that they clearly be-speak of a high level of anticipatory mobilization and preparedness.

The battle of Bayt al-Dine raged for three days. Accounts of the fighting, men, casualties, movements, extent of destruction, etc. varied markedly with claims and counter-claims made by government and rebel sources (see

Qubain 1961: 76–78). It is clear, however, that Jumblat's forces were successful in occupying the greater part of the town and were about to reach
the Palace before being repelled by the army garrison stationed there and the
reinforcements of loyalist supporters; mostly PPS and followers of Na'im
Mughabghab, Majid Arslan and Qahtan Hamadeh. Another attack, the next
day, also failed to break government defensive positions.

On May 15, government forces launched a major counterattack with the
objective of occupying al-Mukhtarah and capturing Jumblat. Accounts of
the fighting by rebel sources are very dramatic, colorful, and suffused with
exaggerated tales of townsmen, armed with little other than ordinary rifles,
resisting the massive incursions of troops with automatic weapons, armed
vehicles, heavy artillery, and air cover.

At this point, a shift in the sectarian alignment of forces occurred; reminiscent of similar episodes of communal strife in the nineteenth century.
Druze spiritual leaders (*uqqal*) made efforts to reconcile the warring factions
within their own community by invoking communal solidarity and the perils
of internecine strife. Thereby, Majid Arslan (Minister of Agriculture at the
time) and subsequently Qahtan Hamadeh withdrew from battle and disbanded their followers. Once again, in other words, sectarian loyalty prevailed over ephemeral ideological and political interest.

With the withdrawal of Druze forces, the Chamounists had to rely more
heavily on the PPS, the gendarmes, and other loyalists, particularly Na'im
Mughabghab's , who remained throughout one of Chamoun's staunch and
loyal supporters.[8] As in other embattled areas, the PPS were also heavily
drawn into the fighting. Their irregular recruits and disciplined party members fought ferociously. In the meantime, Jumblat was also reinforcing his
own forces with volunteers from among the Druze in Syria. Throughout the
month of June, pitched battles were fought for the control of villages in the
central Chuf (e.g. Batlun, Fraydis, and 'Ayn Zahalta). Some of the fiercest
fighting, sustained for a full week in early July, took place on the strategic
ridge overlooking Beirut's International Airport. Confessionally mixed villages of Shimlan, 'Ainab and Qabr Shmul and surrounding hilltops were
the scenes of successive attacks and counterattacks, with each side claiming
advances and accusing the other on relying on infiltrators, foreign agents
and mercenaries (see Karami 1959: 187–90; Qubain 1961: 77–79).

So deep were some of the offensives mounted by the rebels that at least
on two such occasions (at 'Ayn Zahalta on June 13 and Shimlan on July 2)
the army felt it necessary to respond to President Chamoun's appeals for
intervention, employing tanks, field guns, armored cars and jets for air cover.

By the end, faced with such forces along with the failure of the opposition in Beirut to deliver their anticipated support, Jumblat bitterly abandoned his plans of storming and occupying the capital. He wrote with visible anguish: "Our forces had reached ten kilometers from the capital, Beirut. . . . Suddenly by strange magic direction, the operations and skirmishes of the popular resistance forces in Beirut ceased, and left us alone in the field battle" (Jumblat 1960: 9–10).

Ba'lbak and Hermel

In this region, comprising approximately half the country, the situation was considerably more obscure and complex. By virtue of the plural and diverse political subcultures that coexisted, the area clearly lacked the single unified pattern of command and leadership witnessed in other dissident territories. For example, the area north of Tripoli, stretching from the coast to the northeast frontier with Syria, was under the control of Karami and Hamzah. Southward along the border other relics of the Ottoman feudal fiefdoms, with their inveterate zua'ma and tightly circumscribed constituencies, were still very much in evidence. The local leaders (Hamadeh, Haydar, al'Aryan, Skaf) were each in control of their own district. With the exception of Zahle, which was entirely pro-government, and a few other PPS strongholds, mostly small villages like Nabi Uthman, much of the region was in support of the insurgent movement. Indeed, the entire Beqa'a and northeast region became virtually a "no man's land." Several belligerent tribes, particularly the Ja'fars, sustained their private wars with the army and gendarmerie. The few Christian villages in the area made "pacts" with the Muslim armed bands, affirming their "neutrality" in the national struggle and securing, in compensation, the injunction of keeping the bands out of their fields. The peasants tried to patrol their own boundaries (Hottinger 1961: 134).

The pattern of violence, predictably, displayed a bewildering array of forms: ranging from tribal feuds, acts of sabotage and terrorism to confrontations between security forces and Lebanese army, UN observers, and bands of infiltrators and smugglers. Because of its proximity to the Syrian border, however, much of the strife involved confrontations between security forces, often patrol and customs guards, and infiltrators and armed bandits from Syria. For example, as early as December 6, 1957, the UN Security Council was already meeting in an emergency session to discuss the raiding and looting of a gendarmerie post near Akroun, in the northeast, by bandits operating from Syria (*Middle Eastern Affairs*) 1958: 42). Recurrent acts of sabotage, terrorism, smuggling, infiltration of armed men, were becoming so massive that at least on two occasions (May 27 and June7) air force planes, stationed in Riyaq, were deployed to strafe columns of mules carrying ammunition through the Beqa' and to deploy rockets and napalm bombs to smash a column of 500 men smuggling arms and explosives down the main road from Homs to Ba'lbak (Middle East Journal 1958: 309).

Of all the rebel forces in the Beqa'-Hermel region, those under the leadership of Sabri Hamadeh were the most cohesive and numerous. They were also relatively better equipped, given their access to sources of smuggled arms and ammunition from Syria. The only opposition they received, short of direct government intervention, was from the PPS who managed to retain a camp for military training in one of the fortified villages and a radio transmitter under the name of the "Voice of Reform." Despite its fairly large number of fighters, the PPS stronghold could not resist attacks of the opposition forces. Following a fierce battle in mid-May PPS partisans were hunted down and rooted out of the area. Many were killed; others sought refuge in government-controlled regions.

By late May, all that remained of the devastated pro-government forces in the area was an army unit stationed at a fortified hilltop on the outskirts of Ba'lbak. The army, assisted by the air force, was able to repulse repeated attacks of the opposition, and managed to retain control of that strategic fort throughout the crisis. The government's successive attempts to penetrate areas under rebel control were likewise met with failure (Qubain 1961: 88).

Sidon

In Sidon the insurgency also assumed, more so than in other regions, the manifestations of a local insurrection. While other parts of south were dominated solidly by Shi'i feudalists, particularly the As'ad family, Sidon's militancy was inspired and controlled by Ma'ruf Saad, a burly ex-police officer, a "man of the people" who had risen to political prominence swiftly by defeating the government's candidate in the elections of 1957.

Saad's charisma and populist appeal evinced features of Hobsbawn's "primitive rebels," or social banditry so characteristic of incipient and inchoate mass uprisings. This is apparent in the political memoir he wrote shortly after the

civil war; a rather idealistic tract rationalizing the sources and motivation underlying his recourse to armed struggle. There is a bit of the Robin Hood syn-
drome; the avenger and fighter for social justice infused by a nationalist fervor
for emancipation and liberation (Saad 1959). His background and political
tutelage were also strikingly different from other leaders of the UNF with
whom he collaborated. All the other compatriots in the struggle (Salam, Jumblat, Karami, As'ad, Hamadeh, etc) were, as we have seen, scions of traditional
zua'ma threatened or embittered by the usurpation of their power; hence the
label the civil war had acquired as a "Revolt of the Pashas" (Petran 1987: 50).
Other than his humble social origins, Ma'ruf Saad was directly involved in
militant activities. He interrupted his high school education in 1936 to vol-
unteer as a fighter in the Arab resistance in Palestine, where he was imprisoned. Upon his release in 1945 he became a protégé of Riad al Solh, the
nationalist Sunni Muslim leader, taught athletics at the Maqased Benevolent
Society school in Sidon, and then became an avid follower of Nasser. He also
maintained close ties with the Palestinians. Their presence in large numbers,
as displaced refugees in camps in Sidon and adjoining areas, gave him opportunities to be involved in supportive activities on their behalf. They reciprocated by providing military assistance.

Much like Jumblat and other opposition leaders, he, too, speaks of a
"popular armed uprising," an intifadah and not a revolt. The uprising, he
maintained, was spontaneous. "We were driven into it. We never entertained
carrying arms. . . . We had no access to weapons at the time. We only wanted
to declare a strike until the government resigned" (Saad 1959: 13). Events,
he went on to say, particularly the assassination of Matni, Chamoun's opposition to the UAR, the government's repressive measures, the Sixth Fleet,
etc., developed in directions they had not intended or welcomed. Ma'ruf
Saad had no problems consolidating his control over the town. A central
command was formed and various revolutionary committees (security,
courts, training, publicity, etc.) were organized.

The "popular uprising" was able to recruit at least a thousand fighters
and other volunteers. In successive skirmishes with loyalist and security
forces they were able to repel all efforts to break up their resistance. Throughout the five-months of civil hostility, they kept Sidon free from government
interference and often assisted the UNF by dispatching volunteers to neighboring areas. On the whole, however, insurgents in Sidon were predominantly interested in maintaining their hegemony over the city. Hence, they
refrained from attacking regions where they had no traditional influence
over the inhabitants.

Kata'ib's Counterrevolution

The election of Chehab on July 31, 1958 marked the resolution of at least one major contentious issue underlying the crisis; namely presidential succession. This was, after all, one professed justification for America's intervention although Chamoun had never publicly stated that he would either amend the constitution or attempt to succeed himself. Sami al-Solh, speaking on behalf of the government on May 27, before the landing of American troops, reconfirmed that the government had not and would not seek such an amendment, nor would the parliament entertain the likelihood. At any rate Chehab's election brought about a perceptible relaxation in the level of hostility.

The transition to normalcy, in the wake of civil strife, is rarely free of tension. As in "Thermidor" the dread of eruption and return to the terror of war, is always there. Once aroused, violent impulses are not readily quelled. More so when necessary agencies of law and order, let alone the collective desire for reconciliation, have not as yet been embedded in the new order. Chehab was elected on July 31, but was not to be sworn in and assume power until September 23. This seven-week interlude proved fateful.

Early encouraging manifestations of the return to normalcy were visible in virtually all regions of conflict. Clashes between rebels and security forces were becoming less frequent, ceasefires were in effect, roads were opened to traffic, security forces were ordered to confiscate all arms, shops in the central business district were permitted to remain open until 11:00 P.M., clandestine radio stations were closed down. Even in remote regions of Beqa' and Hermel, leading factions declared their allegiance to the new government.

Beneath such signs of a return to order, however, new forms of violence, more personal and vengeful, surfaced. Acts of banditry, hooliganism, theft, pillage, looting, disdain for public order became more recurrent. So did kidnappings, torture, reprisals, and other religiously motivated offenses. For a few days, out-of-control masses rampaged, venting their rage and unprovoked hostility against innocent targets. These self-destructive manifestations, as I have been repeatedly arguing, epitomize some of the most decadent forms of uncivil and guilt-free violence. Two features disclosed the seriousness of such seemingly atavistic and free-floating violence. First, they were carried out mostly by followers without the consent or knowledge of leaders and often without their control. Second, many of these episodes assumed a pronounced Christian-Muslim character, revealing thereby the confessional amity aroused by the conflict. While these largely nonpolitical forms of violence surged, the country was also undergoing a contentious political battle over the composition of the first cabinet under the new regime. Cabinet crises in Lebanon, even in normal times, are fractious and cumbersome; more of a hazardous high-wire act than a benign game of musical chairs. This one, in particular, had much at stake. Coming in the wake of a bloody but unresolved civil war, the embattled communities were each upping the ante, so-to-speak, to reap the lion's share of seats in the new government and thereby tilting the outcome of the war in their favor.

Late in August a delegation of opposition leaders presented president-elect Chehab a statement which called for the formation of a government composed of opposition leaders and "other faithful persons" to fulfill the goals of the revolution and return the country to normal. The statement also accused "subversive and foreign elements . . . for inciting communal agitation, delaying the withdrawal of U.S. troops, and Chehab's assumption of his duties . . . with the aim of resisting the national movement and preventing it from achieving its aspirations" (*Mideast Mirror*, August 31 1958: 5).

The next day government loyalists came forth with their own set of demands. In the name of a United Parliamentary Bloc, a group of twenty-three deputies insisted that an ultimatum be issued to all armed elements to surrender their arms; that those responsible for riots, terrorism and arming of insurgents — i.e., opposition leaders — intended "to carry out a plan aimed at destroying political and economic conditions and Lebanon's existence" be brought to trial. They also declared that they would refuse to cooperate with any future government which included any leader of opposition, and thanked Chamoun for having realized the aspirations of the Lebanese people (*Mideast Mirror*, August 31 1958: 6).

In this heady political atmosphere — one teetering between the dread of rekindled anarchy and violence and the hopeful prospects of a new peaceful order — any episode, spontaneous or provoked, could tilt the metamorphosis of society in their direction: reconciliation and coexistence or further bloodletting. The ominous event occurred early afternoon of September 19 when Fuad Haddad, assistant editor of al-'Amal the organ of the Kata'ib, was kidnapped and presumed to be assassinated. If the assassination of Nasib al-Matni on May 8 was the spark that touched off the revolt and ensuing civil strife of the past five months, Haddad's abduction can be similarly singled out as the event that triggered the revival of political tensions and much of the tumultuous circumstances associated with what has come to be known as the "counterrevolution." As in earlier such episodes, particularly when the political setting becomes volatile and highly charged, any event or alibi can serve as the spark to unleash all the pent-up hostilities and set in motion that deadly cycle of vengeful violence.

The Kata'ib's response was instantaneous and equally deplorable. They issued an ultimatum to the opposition forces demanding the release of Haddad within two hours and, in reprisal, kidnapped a number of their men, thereby generating the treacherous cycle of random kidnapping. The "Voice of Lebanon," the Party's clandestine radio station, resumed its transmissions, which had been suspended a few weeks earlier with Chehab's election. Their messages this time were more vociferous and threatening; calling for merciless reprisals if the journalist were not released. On the 20th of September, they declared a general strike to start on September 22 in protest against Haddad's kidnapping. The reprieve was intended to give mediators the time to find and release him (for further details see al-'Amal, September 20 1958; Entelis 1974: 178–79).

The three alleged kidnappers were soon arrested and Saeb Salam, as leader of Beirut's insurgents, denounced all kidnappings and denied any involvement in this particular incident. The Kata'ib, nonetheless, did not suspend their call for a general strike. What aggravated matters was the assassination of yet another prominent party member (Cesar Bustani) the evening of the 20th of September. From then on the Kata'ib escalated their militancy and were heedless to all appeals made by Maronite leaders (including President Chamoun and Chehab) to call off their strike. Suspecting that these events were the work of infiltrators and saboteurs, they erected barricades in their own quarters just as the UNF did earlier under the Chamoun administration in the Basta quarter of West Beirut.

The Kata'ib, though, went much further. They discovered that day that they could, given the strategic location of their suburbs and villages around the capital, actually sever Beirut and the government from the rest of the country. By blocking a few of the main thoroughfares, they could besiege and embargo the city. For several days all kinds of merchandise, even two of the newly appointed ministers, were denied passage into the capital. Much of the ensuing fighting was, in fact, over the control of roads and transport in and around Beirut. Politically, the formation of the new cabinet, announced by President Chehab on the 24th of September, just a day after being sworn in by the Chamber of Deputies, only added insult to injury. The eight-man cabinet, under the premiership of Rashid Karami, was heavily tilted in favor of the opposition. The Kata'ib could hardly contain their outrage and perceived the new government as an unjustified victory for the rebels, and threatened to escalate their protest.

Once again the central issue of Lebanon's national identity awakened the Kata'ib's anxieties. From their perspective, if they did not act forcibly to challenge the skewed composition of the new government, Lebanon's precarious equilibrium could be fatally upset in favor of Muslim-Arabist elements. Hence to them the cabinet was not merely an ordinary squabble for seats or greater access to the privileges of office. The hegemony of the Christian community was in jeopardy of being compromised. They were adamant in strenuously resisting all such threats.

Throughout the earlier summer months of turmoil, the Kata'ib had perceived the crisis as essentially one of presidential succession. Hence their support did provide military assistance but it generally took the form of patrolling. The strategy of the party at the time, given the overwhelming petite bourgeois character of its constituency and its predilection for the preservation of Lebanon's laissez faire and economic liberalism, was largely defensive. All it desired was to protect the sources of its own economic vital interests; namely the Matn and free access to downtown Beirut, the port, and adjoining suburbs.

The Kata'ib saw the formation of the Karami cabinet, with its avowed intention of "harvesting the fruits of revolution" (see Agwani for the full text 1965: 388–89) as a new threat — heralding the advent of greater measure of state control and undue restraint on free enterprise. More ominous, perhaps, Pierre Gemayyel was distrustful of the personal admiration both Chehab and Karami bore to Nasser and, hence, dreaded the prospects of seeing Lebanon engulfed further in the ascendant wave of Arabism. In short, to the Kata'ib the composition of the cabinet with which Chehab inaugurated his regime was more than just an unjustified victory for the opposition. It imperiled the foundations of Lebanon's economic order and undermined its political autonomy as a Christian-Maronite homeland.

For roughly three weeks (September 20–October 14), the country slid further into anarchy and violence, with all the sordidness that such events generate. The general strike was rigidly observed in Beirut, Mount Lebanon, and Zahle. As districts were being barricaded the army was compelled to impose a curfew on the capital that led to the suspension of all activities except, of course, the upsurge in violence. And violence began to assume more pernicious forms. Initially, much of it involved anti-government demonstrations and clashes between Muslim merchants and shopkeepers in the central business district of Beirut and the "storm-troops" and partisans of the

Kata'ib entrusted to enforce the general strike. Soon these activities degenerated into vicious, spiteful acts of sectarian violence: kidnapping, torture, and gangster-like operations became more recurrent and were committed with unprecedented savagery and display of religious bigotry. For the first time, and on both sides, religious symbols and edifices were desecrated. Tortured victims were often branded with religious insignia. And, of course, leaders on both sides hastened to disclaim any responsibility for such acts and assigned blame on "irresponsible elements," "hired agents," "saboteurs." In so doing they were, doubtless, disclosing their own inability to restrain the frenzy of aroused masses.

Alarmed by the symptoms of such fanatic outbursts of confessional enmity, Christian and Muslim religious leaders made repeated appeals for calm and established a "Committee of Union," on October 11, to alleviate the sectarian hostility exacerbated by the conflict. Political leaders also made frantic efforts to arrive at an acceptable compromise. Finally, intense political negotiations among all factions, through President Chehab's persistent personal interventions, began to result in some easing of tensions. Embattled communities seemed, for the first time, on the verge of considering more reconciliatory options for resolving the crisis. The first such auspicious sign, one which was to become a political landmark of sorts, occurred on October 10 as a result of a meeting between Gemayyel and Prime Minister Karami. This was, incidentally, the first such meeting between these two archrivals in more than three years. Both emerged from it with pronouncements of reconciliation, appealing for harmony and an end to bloody discord. More explicitly, they professed their support for the "no victor, no vanquished" formula — an ironical but expedient diplomatic ploy for suspending hostility without addressing or resolving the issues provoking it.

A compromise government was formed which received the overwhelming support of all adversaries and factions except the PPS. In his policy statement Karami reiterated the major tenets of President Chehab's acceptance speech; namely the withdrawal of foreign troops, the strengthening of relations between Lebanon and the Arab states, the revival of the economy, abiding by the National Covenant of 1943, and cooperation with all countries on the basis of friendship and equality (for the complete text of these and other supportive declarations of other leading spokemen see Agwani 1965: 373–94).

Reactions were swift and reassuring. The Kataeb responded by calling off their strike, dismantling the barricades, and suspending their clandestine radio station. Warring factions and partisans of the UNF followed with similar measures. Barricades cordoning off other quarters in Beirut, Tripoli, Sidon, and Zahle disappeared. The curfew, in operation since May, was lifted. Roads and thoroughfares linking Beirut to the provinces were opened. Economic and commercial activities gradually started to recapture their pre-war vitality. Even Jumblat, the most recalcitrant of the insurgents disbanded his private army and reintegrated his partisans into the normal routine of village life.

Inferences

The events of 1958 mark a significant watershed in the political history of Lebanon. They stand out as the first major breakdown in political order after nearly a century of relative stability. Some go further to herald the insurrection as the "first fully sustained popular revolt in the Arab world . . . one that did not wither away, and that was not suppressed" (Stewart 1959: 109). This might well be an exaggerated claim. What is true, however, is that until then internal and external sources of tension were, as we have seen, present but never erupted into belligerent confrontations. In 1958, Lebanon began to lose its political tranquility. Limited and sporadic as the events were, they served as an ominous warning that the precarious balance, delicately held together, could be easily disrupted.

Indeed, from then on, the tone of political discourse started to undergo some visible changes. Consent, manipulation, compromise, bargaining, guarded contact, avoidance, "mutual lies" — thus far the hallmarks of the political process — were giving way to more contentious and malevolent forms of political confrontations.

Politics in Lebanon has long had elements of playfulness, often bordering on the tragicomic theatrics so common in other forms of public entertainment and sporting contests. One has only to read the memoirs of some of the veteran politicians, themselves scions of established political families, to realize how deeply-rooted this feature of competition for public office is in the ethos of Lebanon's political culture (see, for example, al-Khuri 1960; al-Solh 1960; Riyashi 1953). Discontent and grievances, much like competition for public office, found outlets in street demonstrations, rallies, and heated and acrimonious debates. Of all forms of political mobilization, however, elections were doubtless the most appealing and colorful. They became much-anticipated popular events charged with emotional intensity, something akin to a spirited and absorbing national pastime.

At times the whole country would be engulfed in a succession of relentless electoral campaigns: presidential, parliamentary, by-elections to fill vacated seats in the National Assembly, and municipal and other public contests for elected officers of professional and voluntary associations. They were launched with much ado and popular enthusiasm. Parliamentary elections in particular became overindulgent affairs involving lavish expenditures of money and passions. Spaced, for security reasons, over a four-week period, the whole country would be transmuted and would peak in a national mood of frenzy and high expectations. Voters were transported en masse in their electoral districts in boisterous motorcades and convoys. Performing one's civic duties was more a festive occasion to revisit one's ancestral village or town — a nostalgic excursion rather than a display of ideological commitment or a demonstration of one's concern over public issues.

The aggrieved in rigged elections — and elections were rarely free of pressure, vote tampering, or other nefarious strategies to manipulate the outcome of balloting — normally cried foul. Attempts to assuage one's injured political stature and public image would often lead to scattered incidents of violence. These, however, rarely became the basis for the mass mobilization of armed men.

The crisis of 1958 began to change all this. Emile Bustani, a prominent public figure and a presidential hopeful until his resourceful life was cut short when his private plane crashed in 1963, had this to say about Lebanon's transformation into a "nation of disputants."

> With its population made up almost equally of Arab Christians and Arab Muslims, Lebanon was bound to be a house divided against itself politically, as well as on sectarian grounds, no matter how cordial a front it might display to the outside world. The schism that existed was in many ways a legacy of past years, when the Turks taught the Muslims to hate the Christians and the French taught the Christians both to fear and hate the Muslims. . . . Following the allied victory in the second World War, the Lebanese became a nation of disputants. What had been a long-term bone of popular contention, a subject of leisurely mental and oral strife, turned dramatically into an issue of political life and death. . . . The two groups became at once more closely knit among themselves and more hostile to each other (Bustani 1961: 80–81).

In retrospect, the brush with civil unrest in 1958 has been instructive precisely because it marks the threshold at which the character of political contests dramatically changed from a subject of "leisurely mental and oral strife into an issue of life and death." Or, in the language of Theodor Hanf invoked earlier, it is then that the conflict degenerates from a struggle over "divisible goods" to a struggle over "indivisible principles." The moment, in other words, socioeconomic rivalry is transmuted into confessional or communal enmity, with all its attendant fears of marginalization, erasure, threats to identity and collective consciousness, that hostility descends into the incivility of atavistic violence.

Episodic feuds, personal slurs, grievances, and minor provocations normally dismissed as tolerable manifestations of a fractious political culture were transformed into sources of bitter hostility and polarization. Any move by either side became suspect and was always interpreted as motivated by the worse possible intentions. Parliamentary debates, electoral campaigns, political pronouncements became forums for exchanging insults and invectives. Being barred from entering parliament was, suddenly, a legitimate justification for armed insurrection. Attribution and demonization of the "other" evolved into common strategies for rationalizing belligerency. Insurgents became "outlaws," "infiltrators," "terrorists," "unanchored masses" wreaking havoc in society and undermining its sovereignty and autonomy. Loyalists became a malicious "clique," a den of "criminals," "traitors," "western stooges" and "infidels." Every atrocious misdeed from political corruption and bigotry to prostitution, drugs, and thievery was attributed to Chamoun and his maligned "gang" (Jumblat 1959: 32).

Enmity, in such a charged political milieu, can become highly combustible. It is then that politics becomes, to borrow Henry Adams's axiom, "the systematic organization of hatred" (Wills 1990: 3). When provoked, it could easily spark off hostility and heighten the predisposition to belligerency. This is, in fact, what was transpiring at the time. Grievances, demonstrations, and other forms of collective protest were being transformed into riots, clashes, and violent confrontations. Charting the networks of such enmity, i.e., who hates whom, where, and why provides at times a better understanding of the shifting character of political alliances than ideological disputes and public issues.

As an "uprising," "sedition," "insurrection," "revolt," or "civil war" — to mention a few of its many labels — it must not be judged by the structural transformations it unleashed. By standards of the day, the ensuing violence and destruction was massive. It took a toll of some 3,000 lives, had dire economic consequences, deepened communal enmity, and rendered Lebanon more vulnerable to regional and international rivalries. Yet, the insurrection did not result in any fundamental restructuring of society or its political system. Indeed, since the call for armed struggle was largely made by a disgruntled political elite, demanding little more than the resignation of President Chamoun, the "revolt" ended by the restoration of the status quo.

If measured against the protracted cruelties of the 1970s and1980s, it pales by comparison. It seems more of a benign and sporadic excursion into violent politics. Yet, it jolted the country. It drew together, albeit on a limited scale, diverse elements that had not before been commonly engaged in collective protest. In that sense it offered political tutelage and initiated a wide spectrum of individuals and political parties into the fray of political mobilization and violent politics. Leaders of the insurrection had little in common, other than their hostility to the regime and its pro-Western policies and, to a lesser extent, a transient ideological infatuation they shared with Nasserism. They were drawn from different regions, articulated varying justifications for their participation in an armed struggle and displayed distinct political styles. It is rather odd that a coalition of tribal feudal chiefs, landlords, urban gentry, clerics, revolutionary pamphleteers, intellectual dilettantes, militant commoners, etc. should all find common cause in rebellion. They did. They also drew around them a coterie of young political upstarts and activists, mostly intellectuals, journalists, artists, and professors, sparked by the novelty and idealism of collective struggle and the prospects of launching a career in public life. In addition to the organized commands, councils, and other revolutionary committees, leaders in the various war zones established, they also relied on an informal network — an array of close relatives, friends and hangers on — of personal assistants and advisors. These often served as self-appointed think tanks; they gave interviews, issued press releases, drafted speeches, suggested strategies. Saeb Salam, for example, relied on Walid Khalidi (his brother-in-law, an Oxford don and recently appointed professor at the American University of Beirut), Clovis Maksoud, Rashid Chehab al-Din, Abd al-Karim Zein. Rashid Karami, drew upon the help of Tal'at Karim, Abd al Majd al-Rafi'i and Amin Hafez. Kamal Jumblat sought the advice of partisans like Gibran Majdalani, Nauwaf Karami and Shafik Rayyes. To Ma'rouf Saad, Muhannad Majthoub served as his political confidante and intellectual counsel.

Mass support was also a broad and loose coalition of peasants, blue-collar workers, lower-middle-class elements, progressive students, and other marginal recruits and volunteers. Armed men received nominal wages, family allowances, and a daily ration of cigarettes, beverages, and snacks in return for their services. Palestinian refugees, already in Lebanon for nearly a decade, many of whom had strong pro-Nasserist sympathies, took an active part in the fighting. At the time, Palestinians in the diaspora were not as yet politically organized. Their involvement, nonetheless, sent a warning signal and provoked the fear of the Christian community.

To many of the participants at all three levels (that of leadership, hard-core assistants, and the mass of rank-and-file activists and fighters) the events of 1958 served as a venue for their initiation into militancy; the clamor of street fighting and communal strife. Since many of the actors were still around in 1975, their experience came in handy. Indeed, to activists like Ibrahim Qulailat, an impressionable adolescent of 18 at the time, he had hardly completed his high school education in 1958. Like other lower-middle-class Sunni Muslims from West Beirut, he was a Nasser enthusiast, maintained close ties with Fatah and radical and populist elements of the "street," and was involved in successive acts of violence. Shortly after 1958, he established *al-Murabitun* as an independent Nasserist movement, which was to play a prominent role in the civil war of 1975.

Altogether, the nature and consequences of the events of 1958 reinforce certain attributes that have become embedded in Lebanon's rather unusual legacy with civil strife. One sees relics of the earlier forms of communal and factional hostility, those aroused and sustained by deep-seated animosities, atavistic fears of local groups coexisting in close and dense sociopolitical settings. But one also sees features that prefigure much of what was to come; namely, the violence of deprived and dislocated groups, Lebanese or otherwise, inspired by nationalist and secular ideologies, transcending endemic sources of conflict and with nebulous allegiances to Lebanon or concern for its sovereignty. Obviously the involvement of groups like the PPS, Ba'th, Palestinians, Communists; the coalitions they formed and the character of their militancy was bound to be different from those of the more endogenous factions. Much of the violence in this latter instance became more proxy in character and more devastating in its cruelties. It was also then that Lebanon became, because of its political vulnerabilities, a battlefield, so-to-speak, for the wars of others.

Within a more conceptual context, the events of 1958 provide persuasive evidence to support a basic premise of this study; namely, that the sources often associated with the initiation of political violence are not necessarily those which sustain or exacerbate its intensity. Several inferences can be made in this regard, especially by way of highlighting those features which were to become more pronounced in the protracted strife of the seventies and eighties.

1. *Clearly, the resort to collective violence was initially rooted in grievances, legitimate or otherwise, which various groups perceived as sources of injustice.*

Socioeconomic disparities and imbalances in regional development, the role of the state in privileging Maronite communities, government corruption and favoritism, electoral reforms, and opposition to the state's pro-Western policy, all played a role in initiating or predisposing groups to entertain armed struggle. So did the repressive measures launched by the government to control the insurgency and its incursive elements.

Drawing again on the mundane distinction made earlier between "horizontal" and "vertical" divisions, one may better understand or at least elucidate the difference between "civil" and "uncivil" violence. As long as disputes remained predominantly horizontal in character (i.e., grievances over distributive justice, feelings of relative status and material well-being, deprivation, even political succession), the conflict is likely to remain fairly mild and contained. Deprived, neglected, underprivileged groups feel that their socioeconomic standing is being undermined. They resort, as we have seen, to various forms of collective mobilization (street protest, demonstrations, boycott, public outcries of dissent) to dramatize their dispossession or political marginalization. These, however, remain "civil" in at least three senses: civilians are the ones generally involved in initiating and mobilizing discontent; the conflict is likely to be less belligerent and, finally, as long as it remains a genuine socioeconomic rivalry it is less predisposed to turn into a proxy and surrogate venue for other sources of conflict.

2. Primordial rivalries, like other "vertical" alignments, are usually incited and sustained by factional, personal, communal and sectarian loyalties. Adversaries here are not as much embittered by feelings of socioeconomic deprivation, loss of status, or privilege. They are, instead, threatened by the more ominous fears of loss of identity, heritage, autonomy, and freedom. One's very existence is at stake. Reawakened communalism allays such fears, which are more likely to exacerbate the intensity of tension and sustain the communal character of violence. The initial issues underlying the conflict were nonsectarian. So were the composition and motives of the main adversaries. Both insurgents and loyalists were broad and loose coalitions of religiously mixed groups. Yet, fighting in urban and rural areas assumed at times a religious character. Indeed, leaders on both sides incited such sentiments to reawaken communal solidarities and extend the basis of their support.

3. The internationalization of the conflict also contributed to the protraction of hostility. As Lebanon became increasingly embroiled in the regional and international conflicts of the period, it could not be sheltered from the destabilizing inter-Arab rivalries and Soviet-American power struggles. As this occurred, the original issues provoking the conflict receded. In short, Lebanon once again became an object and victim of cold war rivalries. Events outside Lebanon (the Suez crisis of 1956, the formation of the UAR in February of 1958 and the Iraqi Revolution in July of 1958) threatened Western interest in the region, raised the specter of growing Soviet influence, and legitimized the internationalization of Lebanese politics. Heated debates in the Arab League and the Security Council, riveting world attention and the ultimate landing of U.S. troops, did little by way of addressing or assuaging the internal sources of discord. The intervention, as was the case in similar earlier and subsequent instances, only polarized the factions and deepened sources of paranoia and hostility.

4. *As violence unfolded it acquired its own momentum and began to generate its own belligerent episodes.* Embattled groups were entrapped, as it were, in an escalating spiral of violent confrontations; a feature that became much more pronounced in 1975. Leaders themselves often helplessly admitted that once incited, violent episodes were escalating out of control and there was little they could do to quell the fury of aroused passions. This, too, supports another basic premise of this study — that the origin of violence is not necessarily located in enduring structural and attitudinal conditions but in the flux of events associated with the outbreak of hostility. Here as well one is able to account for another seeming paradox inherent in collective violence; i.e., the initial reluctance of leaders to entertain belligerency but that once it erupts, they are inclined, as Saeb Salam, Kamal Jumblat, Ma'ruf Saad, among others did, to romanticize its redemptive and regenerative attributes.

5. *The forms of violence also displayed some anomalous features.* These made it seem more of a "structural" and "negotiated" phenomenon than one primarily driven by an irresistible urge to inflict reckless injury and damage on others. There was, clearly, a discrepancy between the outward, often dramatic and stirring, rhetoric of war and the rather cautious and non-deadly form combat actually assumed on the ground. The war, in short, was much too voluble on words but short on casualties.

Indeed, the unfolding pattern of violence seemed surrealistic at times; more of an incredulous spectacle, and "opera bouffe" than a real insurrection: an army that would not fight; opposition leaders officially declared as "rebels" with warrants for their arrest, yet free enough to circulate, hold press conferences, and appear on public television; pitched battles that would suddenly stop to permit army trucks to supply rebel forces with amenities and rescue casualties (Qubain 1961: 71; Hottinger 1961: 132). Emile Bustani, who kept contacts with both factions and bore close witness to the actual course of fighting, observed that the "uprising was both launched and contained with a certain old-fashioned courtesy more in keeping with a private duel between members of the nobility than a political revolt" (Bustani 1961: 86).

Accounts of fighting are replete with episodes displaying similar symptoms of disarming courtesy and concern for the niceties of conduct. Fighters, for example, were known to apply for curfew passes before they staged their raids. Others took out licenses for carrying arms. Fighting in Beirut usually took place in the afternoon and at night; often over weekends, as if not to disrupt too drastically the orderly regularities of daily routines. Truces were mutually arranged to relieve the pressure of combat. After a particularly fierce bout of fighting in the Chouf, a cease-fire permitted Christian villagers to be provisioned from Beirut. In return, wounded Druze were brought to Beirut for medical treatment (Hottinger 1961: 32). Deliberate efforts were made, by both sides, to avoid random and unnecessary victims. Explosives were placed at time when it was reasonably certain that premises would be vacant. Desmond Stewart, who claimed acquaintance with a bomb-thrower named Adnan, noted that he "has undoubtedly taken scrupulous care only to make noises, symbols. When he bombed Dory Chamoun's shop, he made sure there was no one in the house upstairs at the time" (Stewart 1959: 61).

The role of the army is perhaps most intriguing in this regard. It maintained its neutrality, refusing, despite its superiority, to crush the insurrection. It acted as an arbiter between the embattled factions. Often it went further to shelter one group from onslaught of the other. For example, it repelled advances of the rebels upon regions inhabited by partisans of the government. It also gave protection to the rebels by prohibiting the PPS from starting fighting in Beirut. During the Marines' landing, it acted as a buffer between American troops and the insurgents (Hottinger 1961: 134).

These and other symptoms of the domestication and routinization of violence became much more pervasive in the seventies and eighties. It is, nonetheless, instructive to encounter such manifestations in 1958, whereby some of the grotesque features of the war were already becoming a form of discourse or political language stripped of any belligerent undertones. This was also happening in a political culture where light arms are accessible and widely used on festive occasions.

6. *The conflict was also sustained and rendered more problematic by a bewildering maze of factions, shifting allegiances, and sources of external pa-*

tronage. These, as we have seen, made for some unlikely and awkward coalitions and accounted for the diverse manifestations violence assumed.
These turf wars were largely factional feuds and confessional rivalries fueled
by personal and local animosities. These were also aggravated by the squabbles of partisanship, ideologies, and nascent "haves" and "have nots." Hence
the patriotic vigilantes of the Kata'ib were collaborating with, often pitted
against, mercenaries with little, or at best, idiosyncratic attachments to Lebanon. The Ba'th, Communists, Najjadah, started the war on the side of the
insurrection. By the end, the Ba'th and the Communists became mortal
enemies; mostly a consequence of Syria's persecution of Communists. When
Karami ran into some difficulties with the Ba'th in Tripoli, the Communists
were more than eager to give him largely unwelcome support (Hottinger
1961: 137). Just as cleavages within the ranks of the loyalists created tenuous
and shifting alliances, so did the personal squabbles between and among
leaders of the opposition. Tension between Salam and Karami, Salam and
Jumblat, Salam and the Najjadah, Tashnak and Khantshak, were always
resurfacing and affecting thereby the course and direction of hostilities.

7. *Fnally, the events of 1958 reconfirmed another curious attribute of collective strife in Lebanon; namely the ethos of "no victor, no vanquished."* This,
as we have seen, also characterized much of the earlier episodes of communal conflict in the nineteenth century. Somehow, violent confrontations
never ended, or were never permitted to end, by the unequivocal defeat or
victory of one group over the other. From one perspective, this might be
taken to mean that disruptive as the events were, they did not dispel the
hope for reconciliation and compromise between the warring communities.
More explicitly, it could well mean that the differences and grievances which
led to armed struggle had not quite reached the point where they could not
be reconciled. Leaders of the major factions in the conflict were, as we saw,
still able to take part in the same coalition government.

But the "no victor, no vanquished" formula also carries less auspicious
implications: that the Lebanese have not as yet heeded the lessons of their
troubled history with recrudescent civil strife. Had any of the earlier episodes
of political violence been more explicitly resolved, by designating a winner
or a loser, and resolving thereby the issues associated with each, then perhaps
the country might have been spared many of the cruelties of subsequent
strife.

6   Lebanon's Golden/Gilded Age: 1943 — 1975

> Fabulous, yet perfectly authentic, stories are told of the transfer of gold from Mexico to India and China, of the shipment of copper from Franco's Spain to Stalin's Russia and of the sale of a huge consignment of toothbrushes from an Italian firm to a neighboring one — and all directed from and financed by some mangy-looking business house in Beirut. In 1951, when Lebanon's gold trade was at its peak, it was estimated that 30 percent of world gold traffic passed through the country.
> — Charles Issawi, "Economic Development and Political Liberalism in Lebanon" (1966)

> Lebanon's singular brand of democracy is doubly wondrous. It works and, for its continued growth and functioning, has depended heavily from birth on the international community.
> — J.C. Hurewitz, "Lebanese Democracy in its International Setting" (1963)

The brief interlude between the relatively benign civil war of 1958 and the protracted cruelties of 1975 stands out as a perplexing often anomalous epoch in Lebanon's eventful political history. It is a period marked by sustained political stability, economic prosperity, and swift societal transformations, the closest the country ever got to a "golden age" with all the outward manifestations of stupendous vitality, exuberance, and rising expectations. But these were also times of growing disparities, cleavages, neglect, portends perhaps of a more "gilded age" of misdirected and uneven growth, boisterous political culture, conspicuous consumption, and the trappings of frivolous life-styles masking creeping social tensions and other ominous symptoms of political unrest.

Perhaps because of such marked asymmetry, observers differ in their assessment of this interlude. Those who see it as a prelude to war tend, with the benefit of hindsight, to exaggerate the country's internal contradictions and hold them accountable for much of the subsequent havoc and collective violence. A growing number of writers, in fact, speak of "self-destruction," "self-dismantling" as if Lebanon and the Lebanese are collective victims of some form of national suicide. Others, along the same vein, dismiss Lebanon as a myth, an archaic, artificial entity, created from the outset on shaky and flimsy foundations and therefore doomed to self-destruction.[1]

Others, with a more optimistic frame of mind, are more inclined to see this period as a rather fortunate interlude, a testimony to the resourcefulness and ingenuity of its people. We are often reminded by a score of such authors that when the state of greater Lebanon as a political entity was ushered into the world in 1920 it was already enfeebled by two calamitous disasters: the famine and ruinous consequences of World War I and the great depression of the 1930s. The famine alone decimated thousands in cities and much more in rural areas.

Most devastating were doubtless the physical and immediate effects of war. No sooner had Turkey entered the war (October 1914) than Jamal Pasha — the commander-in-chief of the Fourth Army and military governor of the area — promptly occupied Lebanon, abolished its autonomy, suspended the Administrative Council, and ushered in the worst reign of terror the country had ever known. Until the end of the war, Lebanon was placed under Ottoman rule. Jamal Pasha imposed military conscription, requisitioned beasts of burden, and summoned people to relinquish much of their provisions to support his troops. Even trees, often entire groves, were cut down and used as fuel for army trains. The mulberry groves in the Biqa', and a considerable portion of the country's forests, were decimated for that purpose (Al-Aswad 1925:247).

Anyone suspected of anti-Ottoman, Pro-Arab, or Pro-French sentiments lived under the constant fear of being imprisoned, banished or condemned to death on charges of high treason. An infamous military court was established and dealt arbitrarily with all such cases. Evasion of Military service, guilt by association or hearsay, membership in any of the burgeoning secret societies and clubs, or even a passing critical remark in a letter from a relative abroad were all punishable charges (Hitti 1957: 483–84).

Of all the Ottoman provinces, Lebanon suffered the worst and most damaging hardships. Foreign remittances, tourism, and revenue from summer resorts, by then major sources of national income, came to a sudden halt. A tight blockade was imposed on food, medical supplies, and clothing. Staple items and basic commodities were scarce. Prices rose and shortages became more widespread. By the fall of 1916, famine, successive swarms of locusts, epidemics (particularly typhoid, typhus, malaria, dysentery, bubonic plague) hit an already enfeebled and demoralized population. Entire villages were deserted. Others were left in partial or total ruin, depleted of their manpower and other resources. Altogether, some 100,000 out of a population of 450,000 are estimated to have lost their lives. Many of the remaining were in a pitiful state of destitution (For further details see Hitti 1997: 483–86; Khatir 1967: 197–201; el-Maqdisi 1921: 53–59).

The backbone of Lebanon's economy, its silk industry, was to suffer its fateful woes by the entry of "synthetic silk" (rayon) into the world market. Whatever prosperity Lebanon had enjoyed by then quickly vanished, leaving more people destitute. Forced migration, which had begun in the wake of the 1860 sectarian strife, reached its peak in the early 1930s. Heart-rending accounts of the day bespeak of the immensity of collective suffering. The anguish of migration seemed welcome in comparison to the visitations of pauperism, hunger, conscription, and Ottoman repression and persecution (For further details, see Safa 1960; Khalaf 1987; Saliba 1981; Abou 1980).

In no time, however, Lebanon managed to resuscitate itself. With no resources to speak of, other than a temperate climate and scenic beauty, the country emerged as one of the most dominant commercial and cultural centers in the Arab world.

The gradual transformation of the economy from a subsistence to a market system was accompanied by marked shifts in the position of various groups within the social hierarchy. Peasants in Mount Lebanon, both Christian and Druze, acquired real estate and became land owners. In the large towns, prosperous communities of merchants and money lenders gained social prominence and political influence. In the coastal cities of Beirut and Tripoli, swift commercialization and the opening up of urban society to Western contacts and new economic opportunities provided favorable conditions for the emergence of a new urban "aristocracy."

Concomitant with these changes — possibly because of them — Lebanon witnessed an educational and intellectual awakening that began to transform the social and cultural life of the country. The extension of foreign and missionary education activity, initiated in the middle of the nineteenth century, encouraged further indigenous initiatives in the field of popular education. Benevolent, literary, scientific, and other voluntary associations participated more effectively in the intellectual and reform movements of the day. Literacy became more widespread. Presses published a variety of books, periodicals, and newspapers covering a broad range of topics and reaching an audience beyond the confines of Lebanon. It was then that Lebanon

acquired — deservedly or not — the slightly arrogant and overbearing reputation of being a "center of illumination" (*balad al-isha*).[2] It was also then
that the popular and catchy saying "Happy was he who had a goat's enclosure
in Lebanon" became more widespread.

To many of Lebanon's admirers such realities are further proof that if and
when external sources of instability are contained (e.g. 1860–1914, 1943–
58, 1958–75), the country was able to survive — as it did during these interludes — as a viable and stable parliamentary democracy. Charles Issawi,
in two concurrent articles (1956 and 1964), provided persuasive documentation to support these claims. He explored the economic and social foundations of democracy in the Middle East and came to the conclusion that
Lebanon was the only country in which most of the prerequisites for parliamentary democracy are met.[3] Issawi also maintained that the survival of
parliamentary democracy in Lebanon, after it had been broken down in so
many others, was not just an accident of history. On the contrary, it is a
"triumph of ingenuity over nature."

It is generally agreed that this remarkable development has been
achieved by the enterprise of private Lebanese citizens, and has owed
little to the help of either nature, or foreigners, or the government.
Except for a pleasant climate and a beautiful scenery, nature has been
niggardly towards Lebanon. Lebanon has not received even a small
fraction of the huge oil deposits, vast alluvial plains and broad rivers
with which some of its neighbors have been endowed. This trading
community does not even have a good natural harbor with easy communications with the interior, such as Haifa and Alexandretta. The
development of Beirut into the leading port in the Eastern Mediterranean is a triumph of ingenuity over nature (Issawi 1964: 280–81).

Kamal Salibi's (1966) assessment of the "merchant republic" during the
inaugural terms of Khoury and Chamoun (1943–58), concurs with this
felicitous profile. While both regimes left a rather unsavory residue of government neglect and corruption, they were also responsible for engendering
the kinds of developments associated with the country's phenomenal prosperity and stability.

It would be unfair, and also misleading, not to give the merchant
republic of Khoury and Chamoun its due of credit. In 1943 Lebanon,
tiny and lacking in any important natural resources, was barely devel-

oped and its economic viability was subject to doubt. By 1958 it had been transformed into a highly prosperous country with considerable social development, well-ordered foreign relations, and a remarkable degree of stability. The unbridled capitalism which the Christian oligarchs secured was chiefly responsible for the country's phenomenal prosperity, as it was also responsible for the maintenance of Lebanese democracy. At a time when dictatorships were emerging everywhere in the Arab world and abolishing democratic practice, the Lebanese merchant republic bravely championed the ideal of constitutional life and guaranteed the freedom of enterprise which is essential to capitalism. In a part of the world where people were rapidly losing their liberties, Lebanese freedom became proverbial and provided the basis for genuine stability (Salibi 1966: 214–15).

A recent assessment of Lebanon's political economy as a "Merchant Republic" — particularly the implications of its service-oriented, open and deregulated economy on nation-building and political stability — is a bit more guarded. Carolyn Gates (1998) in a thorough and well-documented study, provides persuasive evidence to account for the success of the so-called "Lebanese Miracle" — at least in the two decades after the Second World War. Lebanon's outward-looking economy managed to institutionalize an economic order which sustained a strong currency, mobilized domestic private capital, attracted foreign investment, and promoted a growing variety of service exports. Altogether these accomplishments, doubtless a testimony to the ingenuity of its economic and political elite which had embraced the liberal economic vision of the "New Phoenicians," managed also to instill a modicum of international confidence in Lebanon.[4]

These propitious circumstances, it should be emphasized, are not, as often assumed, the outcome of serendipity or historic coincidence. It has become fashionable lately to dismiss Lebanon's success story as largely the byproduct of fortuitous and unintended windfalls rather than deliberate and willful planning or rational debate.

One economist, for example, argues unequivocally that whatever prosperity Lebanon enjoyed was the result of what he termed the "Economics of coincidence and Disaster." The Lebanese economy, Fuad Awad (1991) tells us, was largely shaped by external fortuitous events such the Arab-Israeli conflict, the closure of the Suez Canal, the nationalization of Arab economics, and the severance of Arab–U.S. diplomatic relations in 1967. While such exogenous factors account for Lebanon's momentary and lopsided prosperity, they made it vulnerable to external shocks. He goes further to assert that the socioeconomic disparities generated by such coincidental and ex-ogenous circumstances — "camouflage by artificial prosperity" — account for Lebanon's downfall (Awad 1991: 83). The overall assessment of a recent conference which hosted a collection of credible Lebanese experts at Ox-ford's Center for Lebanese Studies also reiterated the view that Lebanon's past miracle was mainly based on a spurious or misbegotten combination of luck and external factors (Fattouh 1998: 1). Another, (Waines 1976) derides the shrewd and hard-driven Lebanese entrepreneur, and the mercantile and middleman economy they created, as more the result of Adam Smith's "in-visible hand" than any rational planning. To Moshe Shmesh, the very struc-ture on which the "Lebanese Miracle" was founded was "flimsy from the outset. . . . what was surprising was how long it took to break down. . . ." (Shemesh 1986: 77).

Such partial and lopsided views are clearly inconsistent with the eco-nomic realities of the period. They can be faulted or questioned on at least two counts: first, the emergence of the "Merchant Republic" and how it came to embrace an outward-looking, noninterventionist, open and service-biased laissez-faire economy was not the result of coincidence. It came about after heated political debate and protracted controversy over the likely eco-nomic strategies Lebanon was to adopt in its post-independence and post–World War II interlude. The polemics at the time took the form of an open public debate among three overriding groups and their contentious constit-uencies and coteries and personal advisors and ideological spokesmen. Sec-ond, the outcome of such open debate was far from disastrous. To a consid-erable extent, the model they had forged, reinforced by the National Pact of 1943, which envisioned Lebanon being ruled by a partnership of Maro-nite and Sunni Merchants, bankers and landowners, managed to ward off a succession of debilitating challenges and survive, rather robustly, until the outbreak of civil hostilities in 1975. Economic historians have, on repeated occasions, reconfirmed such realities. To Roger Owen, the wartime regime had stimulated the economy in such a way that Lebanon had "the highest per capita income in the Arab East, the lowest rate of illiteracy, the best developed infrastructure and, for all its emphasis on banking and services, the largest share of manufacturing within national income. This too gave the country an important vested interest in maintaining and expanding its regional economic role" (Owen 1986: 28–29).

The so-called "Lebanese Miracle," even in its golden age was, of course, far from faultless. Although the economy enjoyed high growth rates, it was not, as will be seen, evenly spread. Its vibrant private sector, which siphoned off much of the wealth generated by Beirut's entrepôt and transit trade, walked away with its lion's share. The basic economic needs of the majority of the population were not adequately met. The system was also less successful in contributing to civil liberties, nation-building or in bridging the sociocultural disparities. Indeed, symptoms of relative deprivation, because of the ostentations of the privileged few, seemed starker and more injurious. Equally unsettling and, much like the pitfalls of nineteenth century economic and diplomatic dependency, by aligning Lebanon even further to external markets and sources of political unrest, made it more vulnerable to the vagaries of global and regional transformations (for further details, see Gates 1998; Khalaf 2001).

Stark as the internal disparities were at the time, they could not alone have triggered much unrest. As in earlier such encounters, the sparks were fanned or ignited from without. Indeed, the first threatening clouds on Lebanon's horizon gathered early in Charles Helou's term in 1964. He was so eager to preserve Lebanon's "Arab face" that his first official act was to attend the Arab summit, convened in Cairo, to protest Israel's plans to divert Jordanian and Lebanese water. More ominously, he also granted permission to Ahmad Shuqayri, Nasser's appointee to head to newly established PLO, to train guerrillas in his own village retreat.

The first cracks in Lebanon's protective armor widened. The interplay between the frayed communal solidarities and unresolved regional and global rivalries became volatile. Two recent observers in fact (Winslow 1996 and El-Khazen 2000) trace back the origins of Lebanon's destruction to those fateful events and not, as often attributed, to the outbreak of fighting in the spring of 1975. From then on, the country was inexorably drawn into the region's most bitter and belligerent hostilities.

The polemics over Lebanon's "golden/gilded" age have not been confined to the weighty, ponderous discourse of scholars or the sensational accounts of journalists and other popular writers. Literary figures, poets, essayists, intellectuals have been equally perplexed by Lebanon's (particularly Beirut's) paradoxical character. The cruelties of the war simply gave them added graphic evidence to evoke and epitomize this alternating character of Lebanon. Instances of such contrasts or seeming paradoxes are legion:

- An accommodating and hospitable society, sustained by sentiments of charity, love, compassion, and feelings of neighborliness and extended obligations; but one also fractured by factional, almost tribal, and deep-seated hostility and distance between communities.
- A place of refuge, an asylum, a sanctuary, or a corridor for persecuted and displaced dissidents; yet also an open and free place.

- An arresting natural environment and scenic beauty, a source for romanticized often idyllic inspiration; but also a boisterous political
  culture.
- Pervasive religiosity and divisive sectarian and confessional loyalties coexisting with manifestations of a secular liberal and cosmopolitan life
  style.
- A convivial society sparked by ethos of play, gregarious, festive and fun-
  loving outlets; yet one also riddled with symptoms of paranoia, fear, and
  grief.
- A sense of opulence, extravagance, even profligacy, being vied contemptuously by a mounting underclass of less privileged and dispossessed
  groups.
- A fashionable resort, a "playground" with all the glitter, sleaze, and gaudy
  commercialization of a tourist-oriented culture, interlaced with pockets
  of creativity and genuine concern to preserve and enrich its threatened
  heritage and the high quality of its scholarly and artistic legacy.

These and related questions will be addressed in the next chapter. It is
necessary that we probe first into the character and consequences of the
salient socioeconomic and political transformations associated with this
rather luminous and peaceful interlude. The chapter, accordingly, explores
two related dimensions. First, an attempt is made to reassess some of the
outstanding economic, sociocultural and political features engendered in
this epoch by way of arriving at a more balanced and realistic appraisal of
its overall legacy. Second, by employing the rather slack but expressive label
of a "playground" we can better, in my view, elucidate those attributes which
may account for Lebanon's almost Janus-like, dichotomous character;
namely, features which underlie its "success story" and those which render
it more vulnerable to internal and external contradictions.

Lebanon as a "Success Story"

There was nothing mythical about the stability and prosperity the country
enjoyed during this blissful interlude. Nor were their manifestations as mysterious. They were visible in virtually all dimensions of society: political,
socioeconomic, and cultural. There was also more to Lebanon's "success
story" than the outwardly shoddy, often corrupt, and garish symptoms of a
"merchant" or "tribal" republic geared and sustained by primordial and

clientelistic loyalties or the enticements of foreign capital and tourism. To Lebanon's detractors, who became legion after its downfall, the state was little more than an "estate" to be plowed, harrowed, and then reaped for the aggrandizing few entrusted to be its benevolent guardians. None of its political regimes were spared such epitaphs. In varying degrees they all suffered some of these clientelistic abuses. Yet it is too rash; if not unjust, to deny Lebanon's accomplishments or to claim that a predatory and rapacious few had successively reduced the country's potential to the edges of chaos and despair. One may easily advance, as I intend to do, a more salutary image which in my view is more consistent with the realities extracted from its history. Accordingly I will argue that since its independence in 1943, partly by its own ingenuity and partly because of the misfortunes of adjoining regimes, Lebanon was already displaying some of the enviable symptoms of political stability, economic prosperity and sociocultural mobilization. The best I can do is briefly highlight some of these features by was of substantiating their manifestations and consequences.

Economic Performance

It may be overstating the case a bit to call Lebanon's economy a "miracle." Any assessment, however, of its overall accomplishments, by all conventional indicators, reveals a few remarkable, if not "miraculous" features. At least three such attributes stand out. First, for nearly twenty-five years (from 1950 until the outbreak of hostilities in 1975), the economy experienced a sustained and often accelerating expansion. Second, there was also considerable change and viable diversification in the performance of its major economic sectors. Finally, the country witnessed a decrease in both overall income and regional disparities in living standards (for further details see, Labaki 1981; Hanf 1993; Owen 1988).

These propitious changes, it must be emphasized, predated the inflow of Arab oil capital by more than a decade. They were largely an indigenous reaction to some of the favorable economic circumstances generated by World War II. Unlike the massive privations and suffering inflicted on Lebanon during World War I, the Second World War brought nothing but gain. Wartime conditions, which had reduced international trade, transport, and communications and created new markets for domestic production, had at least temporarily "reshaped the Lebanese economy. Unemployment was virtually eliminated. Physical infrastructure was improved; and wide-ranging regulatory policies were imposed . . . with extraordinary Allied expenditures in the region, Lebanon's foreign reserves and domestic savings grew substantially" (Gates 1998: 109).

The expenditure of Allied Forces, along with expanded employment opportunities generated appreciable revenues, particularly among the entrepreneurial and working classes.

> The tales of spectacular profiteering and the Horatio Alger stories of the time are part of the folklore of modern Lebanon. From the peasant who found a job as chauffer with the British 7th Army to the *homme d'affaires* who made a fortune selling tank barricades, nearly everybody benefited. The boom has never really ended. Twenty years after the expulsion of the Vichy regime, the inhabitant of Beirut, rich or poor, can hardly avoid the ultramodern world around him (Hudson 1968: 71).

Reserves accumulated during the war exceeded $100 million (Issawi 1966: 284) and were judiciously invested in building and extending the country's infrastructure, particularly its airport, road network and electricity. By the early 1960s, thirty-seven international airlines were already making daily flights into the airport. In no time Beirut evolved into the main financial center of the Middle East and one of the leading centers in the world.

> Fabulous, yet perfectly authentic, stories are told of the transfer of gold from Mexico to India and China, of the shipment of copper from Franco's Spain to Stalin's Russia and of the sale of a huge consignment of toothbrushes from an Italian firm to a neighboring one — and all directed from and financed by some mangy-looking business house in Beirut. In 1951, when Lebanon's gold trade was at its peak, it was estimated that 30 percent of world gold traffic passed through the country (Issawi 1966: 284).

It was also then that Lebanon began to upgrade its stature as a transit center. In early 1950s, and clearly much earlier than the impetus it was to receive from the Persian Gulf shaykhdoms, Lebanon was already acting as the main trade intermediary for the neighboring countries. Some 50,000 passengers and 400,000 tons of goods, other than petroleum, were transmitted through Lebanon in that year. Likewise, Beirut was already the headquarters of a growing number of multinational firms (Issawi 1964: 285). This is at least another indication that Lebanon's economic growth had preceded the oil boom. Nor was it, as often assumed, merely the outgrowth of free enterprise and reckless private initiative. Even the presidency of Bishara Al-Khoury (1943–52), notorious for championing tenets of economic liberalism, did not release the state from its prerogatives and policies of investment on public utilities and services. Camille Chamoun (1952–58) likewise, despite his ardent laissez-faire leanings, did not undermine the role of the state in either enacting legislation to favor such intervention or in establishing special institutions to encourage economic development. Close to a dozen such government agencies were founded during his six-year term. Among them were the Institute of Industrial Research, Economic Planning and Development Council, the Silk Bureau, the Agricultural Industrial and Real Estate Credit Bank, the Independent Fund For Energy.

During the presidency of Fuad Chehab (1958–64), the link between economic planning and balanced regional development, social justice, and national unity assumed, of course, more pronounced dimensions. It was then, as Boutros Labaki (1993: 100) argues, that Keynesian precepts were grafted on to classical liberalism. It was also then, as will be amplified later, that Chehabism became coterminous with central planning and the growing dependence of the governing elite on a network of experts and advisors unconnected to the traditional political system.[5] Chehabism, in this regard, naturally meant a much greater portion of public spending and increase in government subsidies for industry, tourism, agriculture, applied and scientific research and education. It also involved the introduction of economic reforms in an effort to tame and control the excessive pecuniary desires and caprices of private enterprise (see Salibi 1965: 222 for examples of reforms). The establishment of councils and special government bureaus with explicit development and welfare agendas increased exponentially. Of particular importance were the National Council for Scientific Research, Higher Council for Urban Planning, Council for the Implementation of Construction Projects, Bureau of Animal Protection, and the like. More than the two previous regimes, Chehab's Presidency was marked by a much more substantive investment on public projects and, hence, a visible expansion of utilities — particularly health, water, electricity, road networks, and the modernization of ports. More important, the country's phenomenal prosperity was no longer left to chance or entrusted to the whims of individual administrators, political zua'ma, or unbridled appetites of greedy capitalists.

Coming in the wake of the unsettling disruptions of 1958, the Chehab regime may be legitimately credited with two added accomplishments: The promotion of a much-needed sense of national unity and the establishment of public order. Both the internal and foreign policies of the regime were directed toward allaying the fractious divisions within society while making judicious concessions to ascendant Arab nationalist sentiments without compromising the country's sovereignty. Political strife in 1958 had also, as we have seen, unleashed residues of acrimonious and strident political passions, in the form of "street" and populist manifestations. Armed gangs, henchmen, and client groups of traditional zua'ma and communal leaders needed to be restrained. The regime's excessive reliance on its notorious and often repressive security forces (Deuxième Bureau), was largely an effort to restore public order.

Charles Helou's term (1964–70) was unfortunately marred by a succession of debilitating economic and political crises which deflected the energies and public concerns of the regime. The Intra Bank crisis of 1966, the Six Day war of 1967 and the disruptive confrontations with a recalcitrant and radicalized Palestinian resistance movement were all understandably unsettling in their consequences. Most critical, perhaps, they rendered the country more vulnerable to unresolved regional conflict. Helou's Presidency, because of his own personal and ideological leanings toward Chiha's brand of economic liberalism, also marked a gradual departure from planned development strategies. Nonetheless, at least the sociocultural and economic legacy Helou bequeathed to his successor was far from discreditable. Most prominent, particularly in terms of their long-term implications, were efforts to rationalize the banking sector, stimulate economic growth, industrial development, and the modernization of the Lebanese University. The state also continued the large-scale public schemes and projects begun in earlier regimes and launched a satellite station to upgrade and extend the country's international communication networks.

The presidency of Suleiman Franjieh (1970–76) was also marked by this same juxtaposition of rapid economic growth interrupted by growing symptoms of socioeconomic unrest and mounting political tension and violence. The state managed though to introduce some critical legislative reforms (such as the decree of 1943) for the regulation of industry, particularly pharmaceuticals and petroleum refineries. New ministries (e.g. Petroleum and Industry, Housing and Cooperatives) and other governmental agencies (Social Security and Health) were introduced. Among the noted public projects were efforts to modernize thermal electric power stations and secondary and higher education.

In general, observers might differ in their assessment of the magnitude of economic growth. They all concur, however, that the country managed to sustain a rather impressive economic record. Some go even further to maintain that this thirty-year interlude was also characterized by a decline in the socioeconomic differences among and between the various strata of society (Labaki 1993: 101). Roger Owen gives an overall growth rate of about seven percent a year, over this entire period. Accounting for population increase, this would have still meant a rise of about three to four percent per capita (Owen 1988: 33). That its proverbial tertiary sector (trade, banking, services) should continue to play so vital a part in this prodigious growth is a tribute to the historic intermediary role it has served in this regard. The share of this sector in the gross domestic product increased from 62 percent in 1950 to nearly 75 percent in 1970; perhaps one of the highest rates in the world (Nasr 1978: 3).

A compelling index of this growth is the increase in banking institutions and volume of deposits. The total volume of bank deposits multiplied by 38 percent since 1950. As a result, the proportion of total to national income leaped from 20 percent in 1950 to 122 percent in 1974. This, too, is one of the highest recorded rates in the world (Nasr 1978: 4). The number of banks also increased from 10 in 1950 to 93 in 1966, with more than 20 being branches of foreign banks (Issawi 1964: 285). The brief recession the country suffered, in the wake of the Intra Bank crisis of 1966 and the Arab-Israeli war of 1967, was offset by the inflow of "petro-dollars." Dubar and Nasr (1976: 71) maintain that about two-thirds of the gulf-oil surplus passed through Lebanese hands between 1956 and 1966. Much of the construction work and real estate development Beirut and other cities were undergoing at the time was financed by such capital inflow. This massive inflow also permitted the country to pay off its large import surplus.

Naturally, this growing dependence of the Lebanese economy on foreign capital, as exponents of dependency theories would have us believe, is bound to carry with it some pitfalls.[6] It exaggerated Lebanon's global image or national identity as a transit economy or entrepôt and, thereby, made it more vulnerable to external exigencies. More important it reinforced the monopolistic privileges of a handful of well-connected entrepreneurs. By virtue of the clientelistic political network they enjoyed (such as favorable import quotas), it was estimated that not more than five such families or houses (Abu-Adal, Chiha, Faroun, Fattal, Kettaneh) had virtual monopoly over two-thirds of all foreign imports (Labaki 1971: 12). Nasr provides further evidence to prove that for the most part the same groups who dominated local production were also those who extended their controls over the import sector. Hence, cartel agreements in such vital ventures as construction materials, food products, textiles, sugar, poultry, and cement also came under the control of a few monopolies (Nasr 1978: 6).

Contrary to popular misconceptions, much of this wealth, apparent in spectacular economic growth and outward manifestations of ostentatious materialism, was not voraciously consumed or reinvested into the financial sector of Christian capitalists and oligarchs. Nor was Lebanon merely an entrepôt or a transit center. Large sums were invested to develop other sectors of the economy, particularly agriculture and industry. It was during this period that agriculture witnessed a remarkable upsurge, triggered by a shift to high-value products drawing heavy investment in labor and capital. Since the mid-1940s the magnitude of expansion in cultivable and irrigated areas was sustained at a fairly high rate of 3 percent per annum (Issawi 1964: 286). Extensive terracing of Lebanese mountainous slopes, coupled by more efficient use of fertilizers, pesticides, seeds, and improvements in processing and marketing of produce, generated appreciable increase in yield and income, particularly apples, citrus, bananas and poultry.

While in 1959 about half the country's labor force was engaged in agriculture, within just another decade the proportion had dropped to only one-fifth. What is remarkable, it was in this period that the sector experienced its greatest growth. Albert Badre puts it at an astonishing 5 percent a year (Badre 1972: 164–65). Doubtless, this is a reflection of increasing specialization in farm technology and the introduction of agro-business and other forms of agrarian capitalism. This was particularly true of crops like apples, citrus, poultry, tobacco, and sugar beets. By 1975 output in these crops together made up about two-thirds of total value (Owen 1988: 35).

It was also these crops (particularly tobacco in the south, sugar beets and potato in the Beqa'a and Akkar, citrus in the coastal plains and apples in Mount Lebanon) which were receptive to profitable capitalist ventures. It was then that Lebanon's rural and mountainous landscape was being subjected to intensive cultivation. The proverbial resourcefulness of villagers was, once again, put to edifying use. Reclaimed land was increasing at the rate of three percent a year and agricultural production doubled several times (Toubi 1980: 93). The mulberry groves of old, which had sustained Lebanon's thriving cottage silk-reeling industry in the nineteenth century, were converted to terraced orchards to accommodate the lucrative demand for apple crops. In fact, farmers were so anxious to capture the allures of the market that apple growing became almost a compulsive national enterprise, a fad as hazardous as the "tulip mania" of seventeenth-century Holland. Fortunately, the almost inelastic demand for the coveted Lebanese apple, along with other perishable fruits, spared the country that fateful Dutch analogy. By 1974, Arab markets alone were absorbing more than 90 percent of all fruit production (Nasr 1978: 6).

Here again such profound transformations brought with them some inauspicious consequences. Two in particular have been severely unsettling. First, the growth of agro-Business brought about a significant decline in sharecropping, the traditional lifeline of Lebanese farming. Small farmers and sharecroppers, who had constituted in 1950 about 25 percent of the active agricultural population, declined to not more than 5 percent by 1970. Displaced farmers were either forced to migrate or suffer the status of being reduced to hired hands or wage laborers. Both were equally disparaging. Migrants became part of that swelling mass of disreputable and pauperized "misery belt" of Beirut's suburbs. Those compelled to become wage laborers had to suffer the indignities of competing with that cheap pool of itinerant labor, mostly Palestinian and Syrian refugees.

The magnitude and nature of the rural exodus, perhaps one of Lebanon's most grievous problems, was by far more disruptive in its consequences. Estimates and reasons underlying this persistent and accelerating outflow are varied. Initially, some of the conventional push and pull factor (exploitation, lack of employment opportunities, enticements of city life etc.) accounted for much of the exodus. After 1967, however, the growing insecurity of border villages because of incessant Israeli incursions generated waves of massive involuntary out-migration. Results of the only national manpower survey (undertaken in 1970) revealed that nearly one-fifth of Lebanon's rural population during the 1960s had migrated to towns or, more likely, to Beirut's suburban fringe. This exodus was particularly disruptive because it was largely a one-step jarring encounter rather than a two-step process observed in other instances of rural displacement. In other words villages were compelled to suffer the alienation of city without any intermediary and more accommodating interlude. Exodus from the south, as shown in table 6.1, was as high as one-third. During the early 1970s the magnitude increased sharply to envelop 65 percent of the rural population of the south and about 50 percent of the Biqa'a (see Nasr 1978: 9–10). Little wonder that by early 1970s such displaced and disgruntled groups became, as will be seen, easy fodder and accessible pools for any forms of political mobilization.

Altogether the performance of the agriculture sector, despite some of its grievous pitfalls, is not as adverse as often assumed. It is customary, for example, to site its declining share to the national product as evidence of its inherent flaws. Of course, the relative share of agriculture in the national

TABLE 6.1 Rural to Urban Migration

Province	Total Population of rural origin	% of Pop. migrated to towns in province	% of pop. migrated to Beirut or suburbs
Mount Lebanon	344,000	2.1%	17.4%
North Lebanon	204,435	8.6%	7.4%
South Lebanon	242,085	2.8%	29.3%
Beka'a	178,425	1.7%	16.9%
Total	758,670	3.5%	18.1%

Source: Salim Nasr, "The Crisis of Lebanese Capitalism" MERIP Reports No. 73 (December 1978): 10

economy dropped from about 20 percent in 1950 to 9 percent in 1973. So had the proportion of the agricultural labor within the national labor force. It declined from 50 to 20 percent during the same period. Yet such inevitable macro trends should not disguise some of the tangible accomplishments realized at the micro level. Indeed such accomplishments are all the more remarkable given the structural constraints farmers had to grapple with.

The ingenuity of small farmers and their predisposition to experiment with novel forms of crop rotation and judicious use of fertilizers, insecticides, and fungicides were effective in maximizing yield. The peasants' relentless attachments to their own ancestral land, tracts, and homesteads reinforced their commitments and resourcefulness. Their tenacity to hold on was matched by efforts to safeguard and upgrade the cherished values inherent in this primal heritage. Hence, contrary to mistaken, often exaggerated, views, small and independent farmers were not the hapless victims of absentee landlords, decadent feudalists, or the burgeoning class of rapacious capitalists and exploitative intermediaries. By the second half of the 1960s about 90 percent of the inhabitants of Mount Lebanon owned land of varying sizes. There were naturally some regional variation: 81 percent in the north, 75 in the Beqa'a, and 70 in the South. Altogether, though, some three-quarters of Lebanon's rural population owned land parcels to which they displayed varying degrees of attachments (see Nasr 1978 for these and related estimates).

In some notable instances private initiatives—both small and large— were inventive in responding to strategies of capital-intensive and technological innovations. The state, particularly during the Shihab regime (1958–64) had also launched impressive programs of rural development, schooling, and welfare programs.

The popular misconception that Lebanon's economic success story was nothing but a fortuitous accident of history engendered and enshrined by the mercantile ethics of a "Merchant Republic," is also challenged by the unusual performance of its industrial sector. As shown in table 6.2, industry witnessed the most substantive growth; twice in fact of the increase in trade. Throughout the 1950s and 1960s it expanded rapidly enough to maintain about 12 to 13 percent of its share of the national product. By the early 1970s, however, it "exploded" according to Owen (1988: 35) to raise its contribution to somewhere between 20 and 25 percent (see Kanovsky 1983/4 for a slightly more moderate estimate of this expansion).

Accounts of this vigorous growth normally converge on a set of distinctive attributes. Some single out diversification, where no one product had exercised a leading role for any extended period of time (J. P. Bertrand, et al 1979). Others note the predisposition of industrialists to innovate, as reflected in their willingness to experiment with complex and state of the art systems of production and technology. By directing their output to meet the demands of a rapidly expanding export industry, Lebanon also evolved, "far and away, as the most important Arab supplier of manufactured goods to the

TABLE 6.2 Structural Change of Economy
Selected year: 1950–73

	Percentage Shares					
	1950	*1955*	*1960*	*1965*	*1970*	*1973*
Agriculture	19.7	16.2	14.1	11.6	9.2	9.0
Industry	13.5	12.7	12.1	13.1	15.9	21.0
Construction	4.1	4.3	3.5	5.7	4.5	4.5
Transportation	4.1	5.4	3.9	8.2	8.2	8.5
Trade	28.8	28.8	32.0	30.6	31.4	33.0
Finance & Insurance	3.8	5.1	6.3	3.4	3.4	4.0
Real Estate	9.2	8.4	11.0	7.6	8.8	10.0
Government	6.9	6.0	7.8	8.0	8.7	10.0
Other Services	9.6	12.0	9.2	11.3	9.9	

Source: Roger Owen (1988: 34).

rest of the Arab World. . . . Altogether the rich oil states provided a market for exactly half of Lebanon's goods sold before the civil war" (Owen 1988: 35–36).

It was also during this period that daring individuals, with little by way of established capital or political connections other than their ingenuity and resourcefulness, launched successful contracting, engineering, consulting, aviation, and other venturesome projects which served as models and sources of inspiration for subsequent generations of equally spirited entrepreneurs. Family firms and establishments, likewise, outgrew their timidity and their nepotistic and paternalistic inclinations and evolved into some of the most enterprising and dynamic industrial organizations. In textiles, food processing, tanning, wooden and metal furniture, soap, metal works, pharmaceuticals, family enterprises like Ghandour, Jabre, Badaro, Esseily, Cortas, Kassarjian, Fattal, Doumit, Frem etc. demonstrated remarkable readiness to innovate and expand without betraying some of the traditional and rational norms and practices (Khalaf 1987: 159; Sayigh 1962: 87).

Mention must be made of the relationship between the fairly small and moderate size of industrial firms, the character of patrimonial management, and the incidence of industrial conflict. The industrial census of 1971 reveals that there were close to 11,000 small-scale firms or workshops employing less than twenty-five workers. This sector, which draws more than half of the active industrial labor force, accounts for nearly 33 percent of total production, 40 percent of the value added and 42 percent of the wage earners. On the other hand, there were only 300 establishments that employed more than 25 workers. These represent only 10 percent of the total industrial units and account for two-thirds of total production (for further details, Direction Central de la Statestique 1972).

Here again some scholars are prone to exaggerate some of the abusive or disabling features engendered by the survival of fairly small and craft-oriented industrial establishments. To Salim Nasr, for example, this "limited and crude industrialization" accounts for much of the crisis of the industrial sector; particularly its marginal standing within the Lebanese economy and its role in reproducing the hegemony of exploitative capitalism (Nasr 1978: 10–12). Yet it is these comparatively small establishments that displayed more human concern for the welfare and well-being of their workers. Such investment in benevolent human relations did much, as empirical surveys revealed, in reducing manifestations of industrial tensions and labor-management disputes. (Khalaf 1964). Except for an inevitable portion of itinerant casual labor recruited on daily or seasonal basis, the labor force on the whole enjoyed more than just a modicum of employment security and adequate working conditions.[7] The country, particularly when compared to neighboring totalitarian regimes and overregulated state economies was also buttressed by an accommodating system of labor legislation and a fairly open labor movement.

Such circumstances were bound, as they were, to be reflected in favorable measures of sustained growth. This was particularly evident in increases in number and size of enterprises (e.g. metal, mechanical, electrical, chemical, and pharmaceutical), capital investment, labor force participation, production, and energy utilizations. Value added also witnessed appreciable expansion, particularly during the decade following the crisis of 1958 (Hudson 1968: 60–70; Iskandar 1962: 33).

Social Mobilization

It is it is in the area of social mobilization where Lebanon displayed, perhaps, its most impressive accomplishments. On virtually all the conventional indices of exposure to modernity (i.e. magnitude of urbanization, literacy and school enrollments, mass communication, food consumption, and other public health and quality of life measures), Lebanon was not only substantially better but actually had had a head start of several decades over its Arab neighbor (See Hudson 1968: 80).

By almost any comparative yardstick, Lebanon's experience with urbanization has been phenomenal and accounts, perhaps, for much of the asymmetry associated with its golden/gilded age. The country's urban population more than tripled and attained an 80 percent degree of urbanization within the short span of 30 years. This, incidentally, is disproportionately higher than rates observed elsewhere in the world. The magnitude of the increasing scale of urbanization in most other developed countries is normally gradual and moderate. Indeed, it took most Western societies approximately two centuries to reach a 70 percent level of urbanization. Lebanon's experience is striking not only because of its magnitude but also because of the sharp and sudden leaps with which it occurred. In two decades, during the 1950s and 1960s, the proportion of urban residents increased from 27.7 percent to close to 60 percent.

The same intensity of growth was sustained during the mid-1970s. Of course much of this growth was absorbed by Beirut and its already teeming suburbs. In fact, rates of growth of Beirut's urban agglomeration (at a level of 6.5 percent a year) was among the highest in the world. With the exception of the unusual circumstances associated with cities like Baghdad (9.4 percent) and Kuwait (12.2 percent), other comparable rates ranged between 1.5 and 4.0 percent in developed countries and 2.5 and 6 percent in most Asia and Latin America (see Tabbarah 1977: 5, for these and other details).

The disruptive consequences of such swift and jarring transformations are grievous and will be amplified shortly. Urbanization, nonetheless, remains Lebanon's quintessential great multiplier and social mobilizer, the vector through which much of its encounters with modernity have been realized. Deservedly or not, it was then that Beirut's image as a cosmopolitan, sophisticated, polyglot meeting place of world cultures was being embellished.

All the indicators, crude and refined, attest to this overriding reality. From the sharp increases in the flow of domestic and foreign mail, number of telephones, passenger vehicles to the more stupendous growth in the volume and diversity of media exposure (particularly TV, radio, and movie attendance), all bespeak of appreciable increases in degrees of physical and psychic mobility and high levels of consumption throughout the strata of society. On these and other related indices, Lebanon enjoyed disproportionately higher rates than those observed in adjoining Arab states. Shortly after independence, for example, Lebanon could already boast of over 8,000 passenger vehicles, or about 7 per 1,000 people, which was considerably more than what Syria, Jordan, Iraq, and Egypt had in 1960. By then Lebanon had leaped to 73,000 or close to 40 cars per 1,000, compared to an average of 4 to 6 among those neighboring Arab states (UNESCO statistical yearbook 1985; Khalaf 1992).

On other vectors of mass communication Lebanon was even more notorious, almost an oddity. Early in the 1950s, if measured by the number of movie seats per capita, Beirut was already living up to its reputation as the movie capital of the world. By then, per capita movie attendance was five per year. In another decade, it increased by fivefold, a close second to Hong Kong (UNESCO 1965). During the same period, the number of movie theaters leaped from 48 to 170, an increment of 12 new houses per year. The accessibility of such theaters, rendered more appealing by the variety of films, plush surroundings, and low prices, only served to whet the voracity of the Lebanese of all classes for this form of public entertainment. Indeed by then, before the advent of TV and home videos, anticipating, attending, and talking about movies was already the undisputed, most popular, and most absorbing national pastime.

In addition to its claim to be the movie capital of the world, Lebanon was, more importantly, also a "nation of journalists." The nation's accomplishments in this field are both pace-setting and of long-standing. Since the appearance of its first newspaper in 1858, the Lebanese have long displayed a distinct predilection and talent for establishing papers and periodicals sustained by an irresistible compulsion for reading them. As in other dimensions of public life, this striking penchant the Lebanese evinced for journalism was nurtured and cultivated within a network of family tradition. This intimate association between families and careers in journalism is of long standing. Families, in fact, more than ideological parties, advocacy groups, or political platforms have been the settings within which some of the most gifted journalists received their tutelage and commitments for journalistic careers. Illustrious families such as Aql, Khazin, Taqla, Tueini, Zeidan, Sarruf, Jemayyel, Tibi, Mukarzal, Awad, Taha, Nsouli, Machnouq, among others, have all produced successive generations of journalists. Fathers served as mentors and role models and, often, had direct impact in initiating scions into the venerable family tradition and in honing their skills and cultivating contacts (For further graphic autobiographical details see Tueni 1995).

This journalistic urge was not, incidentally, confined to Lebanon itself. In diaspora, displaced Lebanese intellectuals were instrumental in establishing everywhere they went some of the leading papers and periodicals. In the fertile crescent, Egypt, North Africa, European capitals, Australia and the two-Americas, such ventures were crucial in maintaining links with the two worlds and as platforms for mobilizing dissent against Ottoman and foreign oppression.

Indeed, despite restrictions imposed by colonial or national governments, the Lebanese managed by the turn of the century to establish sanctioned press associations and syndicates and a fairly large number of licensed publications. By 1927, 256 newspapers and more than 140 periodicals were already registered, albeit many were short-lived. During the struggle for independence the press became much more vociferous and strident. By the early 1950s the number leaped to more than 400 political publications. Clearly, the repressive ideologies and stringent state controls prevalent in adjacent totalitarian regimes were an inducement. Publishers in the region came to Lebanon to print what they could not print in their own countries. The abuses of such a free-far-all setting became much too grievous. In 1993 the government imposed restrictions by issuing a decree forbidding the granting of any new licenses for political publications. To create a new publication, two licenses had to be purchased. Also, any periodical which went out of circulation for more than six months would have its license revoked. As a result, the number of periodicals since has been stabilized at 105 licenses, including 53 dailies, 48 weeklies and 4 monthlies. Readership and circulation, however, increased appreciably and continued to do so until the outbreak of hostilities in the mid seventies. For example, by the mid-sixties circulation was about 200,000 or 120 copies per 1,000 with 85 percent of the Beirutis and 77 percent of the Lebanese in general indicating that they were frequent readers (Hudson 1966: 73). These estimates, incidentally, are considerably higher that the sum total of newspaper circulation in the entire region (UNESCO Statistical Yearbook 1985).

    By 1975 Lebanon had more than 400 valid publication licenses. For a country of about 3.5 million, this is an incredible density of newsprint; perhaps the highest in the world. The majority were politically independent, though a small number might be associated with political groups. Indeed, the press had become so independent that it evolved into an autonomous institution, a "Fourth Estate," along with the executive, legislative and judicial authorities. Rare among the Arab press, Lebanese newspapers and periodicals extended their devoted readership outside its national boundaries. Indeed, the circulation of a handful of its leading newspapers was larger outside than inside the country. Much of its appeal and success derived no doubt from its credibility for trustworthy, enlightened, and critical journalism. More important was the genuine diversity and almost unfettered freedom it enjoyed. All significant currents of Arab thought and ideological leanings had a voice or corner in the press. Even when censorship was imposed, particularly in times of acute political crises, papers demonstrated their autonomy by printing blank spaces; a signal to readers that they were censored. Incidentally, this recalcitrant but benign gesture was not permitted elsewhere in the Arab world.

    The pluralism and relative freedom of the media, in themselves manifestations of a broader laissez faire political culture, had been at times readily abused. The more the press acted as a spirited gadfly in arousing public discontent and mobilizing collective grievances, the more it became a target of manipulation, often through outright sponsorship and patronage of dissident groups and regimes outside Lebanon.

    Altogether the "Fourth Estate," particularly in times of political succession and electoral contests, wielded immense powers. A few of the prominent papers, particularly *An-Nahar*, have often been sought directly by leading candidates or vociferous members of the opposition to launch campaigns or articulate platforms on their behalf. On more than one occasion such efforts were instrumental in tilting the results of tightly contested campaigns (see Tueni 1995 for further documentation).

Intellectual and Cultural Awakening

Concomitant with the sweeping socioeconomic transformations, or perhaps because of them, Lebanon was also undergoing a cultural and intellectual awakening of far-reaching proportions. In fact, something akin to a "silent Revolution" was slowly taking place. This was apparent on at least three broad cultural dimensions. First, and perhaps most explicit, it was manifest in the type of questions and issues, ideological and otherwise, the burgeoning intelligentsia was beginning to probe and address publicly at the time. Second, it was visible in cultural intellectual products — both high and lowbrow — particularly those which displayed symptoms of daring and experimentation in painting, sculpture, photography, performing arts, and other popular cultural expressions. Finally, it was also visible in some of the unobtrusive but fundamental changes in everyday life. A word about each, by way of elaboration, is in order.

At the ideological level, this cultural awakening was heightened, as suggested earlier, by the critical political transformations overwhelming the region at the time. This was, after all, the period of national struggle marked by growing hostility toward Ottoman, French, British, Zionist, and other colonial and occupying forces. It was a time of upheaval and bafflement, fraught with the fearsome specters of Ottoman oppression, ravages of famine, the cruelties of two world wars, and the hopes and frustrations of the struggle for independence and self-determination. It was during this period that Arab thinkers were grappling with the nagging question regarding the nature of nationalist sentiments, political identity, and cultural heritage and how to forge autonomous political states without alienating themselves for Pan-Arabist sentiments.

The traffic in ideas and personages Beirut witnessed during the interwar period was prodigious, both in number and diversity. Autobiographical accounts recall nostalgically the incessant stream of Arab and other dignitaries who visited Beirut at that time. (See, e.g., Al Khalidi 1978; Qurtas 1983, and Al Solh 1984). The diversity of books, periodicals, daily newspapers, opinions, and world views they were exposed to was as dazzling in its variety as it was far-reaching in its impact. They were equally impressed by the new cultural activities (e.g., public lectures and debates, organized sports, concerts, youth clubs), awakened national sentiments (participation in political parties, protest movements and street demonstrations, and mass rallies), and subtle changes in mannerisms and social behavior (opportunities for the sexes to mix freely, and the appearance of new styles of conduct, etiquette, and social conventions). Ras-Beirut, in particular, because it was able to accommodate waves of itinerant groups and immigrants, was comparatively more receptive to such diversity than other communities. To a large extent, all the intelligentsia at the time were asking essentially the same questions: Who are we? Who is to blame for our fragmentation? Who are our friends and enemies? Where do we go from here? The answers they gave, however, depending on their own particular sociopolitical milieu, were strikingly different.

At the risk of some oversimplification, one can discern three broad groups or responses. The first consisted of "isolationists," mostly romanticized zealots and chauvinists, who were eager to preserve what they regarded as Lebanon's privileged and unique cultural and historic attributes. Other than sustaining friendly contacts with France, they were opposed to any policies or involvements that would draw Lebanon into the quagmires of its neighbors or undermine their country's sovereignty and independence. Emile Edde's Nationalist Bloc is largely an outgrowth or expression of such sentiments. Second, were the "Arabists," who saw Lebanon's political destiny and well-being in a closer alignment with its Arab heritage and the nascent nationalist and ideological platforms and emancipatory movements. Finally, and between the two rather polemical extremes, once can place the Chiha-Khoury coalition and the "constitutionalists" who were advocating a reconciliatory perspective one that recognizes Lebanon's distinct plural character but is open to both its Mediterranean and Arab heritage.

For example, members of the French-educated Maronite intelligentsia living mostly in the Eastern suburbs of Beirut, who were frequent contributors to *La Revue Phénicienne*, had different perceptions of Lebanon's identity and its future than had the Sunni Muslim intelligentsia. The latter were more inclined to espouse Islamic, Pro-Ottomanl, and ultimately Pan-Arab and Arab Nationalist causes consistent with their political constituency and readership. Furthermore, what readers in the Christian suburbs found appealing in *Al-Bashir*, their counterparts in the Muslim quarters sought in *Thamarat al-Funum, al-Mufid, al-Nida', al-Haqiqa*. The journals and periodicals around Ras-Beirut — earlier ones such as *Kawkab al-Subh al-Munir, al-Nashra al-Usbuiyya, al-Junayna* and eventually *al-Abhath* and *Al-Kulliyah* — were considerably more open to a diversity of viewpoints and world views, more moderate in their opinions and more receptive to secular and liberal ideas.

It was also in this period that the first generation of Western-trained local scholars started to return to Lebanon. For example, in virtually every discipline or program within AUB — initially in Arabic, History, Education, and then gradually in the Social, Physical and Medical Sciences — a critical mass of resourceful and spirited scholars was emerging to assume a more prominent role in the intellectual life of the community (see Khalaf 1994). The small nucleus of local scholars (Yaqub Sarruf, Faris Nimr, Jabr Dumit, and Bulus Khawli) who had accompanied the University since its inception, was joined by another handful (Mansur Jurdak, Jurjus and Anis Maqdisi, and Philip Hitti) at the turn of the century. It was not, however, until the 1920s and 30s that the first sizeable group of local scholars returned to AUB after receiving their advanced training in the U.S. The intellectual and cultural life of the community, as well as the enhanced stature of the University, has not been the same since. Any methodical intellectual history will doubtlessly reveal the seminal and vital character of their contributions and how deeply they have influenced the subsequent course of teaching and research in the region.[8]

Much like their American mentors they too devoted the most productive years of their career to the University, and immersed themselves in the life of the community, many of them not leaving AUB until their retirement. Their presence served as a source of inspiration to successive generations of younger scholars. More distinctive perhaps, they had a broad and public conception of their role, a feature that served to deepen the sphere of their influence and enhance their public image. Partly because of their exceptional gifts and the unusual circumstances of the time, they did not confine their intellectual concerns within the narrow walls of the campus. They were sparked by a spirit of public service and a longing to participate in debating and resolving the critical problems and public issues the Arab world was then facing.

This is quite apparent in both the nature of their scholarly output and the extent of their public involvement. While the earlier generations excelled in establishing local periodicals and popularizing issues (e.g., *Al-Kulliyah, Al-Muqtataf*), addressing themselves primarily to Arab audiences, this "middle generation" extended and internationalized the scope of their intellectual and professional interests without ignoring the cultural needs of their local and regional constituency. They launched scientific research projects, published in professional foreign journals and produced what were to become standard reference works for years to come. A cursory review of their bibliography reveals the impressive range and diversity of their intellectual concerns.[9]

What was particularly rewarding, and surviving members of this generation continue to reflect on those years with considerable nostalgia, was the spirit of open dialogue that pervaded and animated their lives. Intellectuals rarely remained in solitude. There were intimate circles and personal networks to provide a sense of fellowship, camaraderie, and solidarity. These circles brought together individuals with diverse backgrounds, ideological leanings, and religious denominations. The search for knowledge and devotion to free inquiry helped them to transcend their parochial differences. So did the opportunities to participate in several of the publications, cultural and scientific organizations, and voluntary associations which they helped establish. Some of these communal and parochial voluntary associations broadened and diversified the scope of their activities to incorporate more civic and national attributes. Hence, they became more effective in meeting the welfare and benevolent needs of disenfranchised groups and in alleviating the void left by an inefficient and often mistrusted government bureaucracy.

Incidentally, it was out of such small cliques that some of the most resourceful endeavors, distinguished scholars, and public figures emerged. One such striking instance is the handful of scholars drawn from a variety of disciplines — Said Hamadeh, Charles Malik, Constantine Zurayk, George Hakim, Charles Issawi, Husni Sawwaf, Halim Najjar, Anis Frayha, and Zeine Zeine — who collaborated together in editing volumes and publishing *Silsilat Al -Abhath Al-Ijtima'iyya* (Series of Social Studies) in the early 1940s. Similar such collaborative efforts, often sparked by little more than the enthusiasm of like-minded colleagues, produced other impressive landmarks in the form of journals (*Al Abhath, Middle East Forum, Middle East Economic Papers, Berytus*), research centers (Economic Research Institute, Middle East Area Program, Arab Chronology and Documents), international conventions (The Middle East Medical Assembly) and associations (The Alumni Association, Al-'Urwa Al-Wuthqa, Civic Welfare League).

It was during the interwar period that participation in such activities, along with the burgeoning facilities for competitive sports, public performances, music, art, and theatre, began to attract wider appeal. As in other more serious endeavors of research, seemingly more frivolous and playful pursuits which often underlie competitive athletics and expressive artistic events also allowed individuals and groups to transcend their parochial identities and melt into a common cosmopolitan subculture.

It was precisely this open and cosmopolitan milieu that enhanced the appeal and stature of communities like Ras-Beirut. Liberals from other communities in Lebanon and elsewhere in the Arab world converged on it in successive waves and in increasingly large numbers. Munah al-Sulh, a prominent Sunni Muslim liberal and political analyst, singles out this same feature in accounting for his own political socialization. He pays tribute to his teachers at the Islamic Maqasid of Beirut (e.g., Zaki Naqqash, Umar Farrukh, Ibrahim Abd al-'Al) for sharpening his awareness of Arab heritage. He also notes with pride the influence of popular journalists and political activists (e.g., Abd al-Qadir al-Qabbani, Abd al-Ghani al-'Uraysi, Ahmad Tabbara, Ahmad Abbas) in intensifying his nationalist sentiments. But then he goes on to admit it was at AUB, at Faysal's restaurant, at the Arab Cultural Club, and in the private homes of his Protestant friends that he became cognizant of other "voices" and novel modes of conduct (al Solh 1984).

Though visibly more vibrant, Ras-Beirut did not have a monopoly over the cultural life of the city. Around the University of Saint Joseph (USJ), an equally spirited and productive circle of scholars was also asserting and consolidating its intellectual and scholastic influence. Initially, a handful of mostly Jesuit scholars (Most noted among them are fathers Louise Cheikho, Boulus Masa'ad, Istphan al-Bashaalani, Yusef al Jumayyel), the circle grew in number and stature and started to attract a secular but predominantly Francophone group of scholars and public intellectuals. Father Louise Cheikho, as founder and editor of *Al-Mashriq*, served as mentor and gadfly to successive generations of productive colleagues. The early volumes of *Al-Mashriq*, which was first a virtual monopoly of this group, attest to its prolific output and overriding interests in the socioeconomic and political history of Lebanon, manners and customs, law and jurisprudence, church and Maronite history, and related topics.

Because of the critical mass of productive scholars drawn into USJ's faculty of Law, Political, and Economic Sciences (founded in 1913), the output and research interests during its formative years were inevitably skewed in the direction of law and jurisprudence. The ground breaking research of distinguished scholars like Emile Tayan and Jean Baz on Muslim law stands out. So did the work of Bechara Tabbah on political and civil law, Choucri Cardahi on law, ethics and morality, Antoine Fattal on international law and diplomacy, Pierre Gannage, Jawad Osseyran, Negib Aboussouan, and Pierre Safa on comparative law.

Like AUB, the USJ also felt the need, early in its academic development, to establish its own professional journals. Soon after *Al-Mashriq* was published in 1898, the *Mélanges* followed suit in 1906. *Travaux et Jours*, which also enjoyed fairly wide circulation, came into being in 1961. Each of the independent faculties produced their own annual or bi-annual volumes or special series. Of note are the *Anuales* (1945), the *Proche Orient* (1967) — both juristic and economic — *Etudes de Droit Libanais* (1964).

Scanning through the USJ's *Livre D'or* (1995), commemorating the eight-
ieth anniversary of the faculty of law is almost akin to consulting a "Whose
Who" in Lebanon. Clearly, a disproportionate number of the country's political and public elite had received their tutelage under this select group of
mentors. No less than 30 percent, by the way, of all parliamentarians were
USJ graduates. Receiving a law degree, and until the early 1960s of the USJ
was the sole institution offering such education, was almost a prerequisite
for launching one's political career. Hence it is no surprise that 40 percent
of all parliamentarians since independence were graduates of law schools
and a significantly larger proportion, if one were to consider those who
received their education in Europe at French-Oriented secondary schools,
were French-educated (Khalaf 1980: 249).

The rivalry between the two sister institutions, a relic of the bitter hostility
between French Jesuits and New England Protestants, had given this competition a rather creative and vibrant edge. If AUB took the initiative to
establish a journal, host a conference, or sponsor a series of events, the USJ
reciprocated by doing likewise. The converse was also true. The beneficiary,
of course, was the effervescence of culture and other intellectual and artistic
byproducts. This was most visible in the effusive mood of cosmopolitanism
and savoir-faire in the burgeoning metropolitan life in Beirut and beyond.
When the USJ launched, in 1940, their annual conference (convened during the last week of April) as "Les Seminaires Semaines Sociales de Beyrouth," their counterparts in AUB responded by establishing their interdis-
ciplinary "Series of Social Studies." Of the two, the former was much more
of a public and coveted event; clearly a precursor of other such ventures
which became more fashionable in subsequent decades. Each year the conference addressed a particular issue such as public morality, schooling and
national education, agriculture and national resources, the Lebanese family,
the Lebanese economy, or social progress. These annual events always managed to engage some of the country's most notable scholars and gifted public
speakers: Michel Chiha, Fouad Boustany, Bichara Tabbah, Fouad Ammoun,
Hector Klat, Edmond Rabbath, Charles Ammoun, Joseph Donato, Antoine
Khalifé, Albert Badre, Fouad Saade, Soubhi Mahmassani, René Habachi,
Jean and Francois Bebbané, George Asmar, Jawad Boulos, George Hakim,
Paul Klat, Elie and Pierre Gannagé.

By the late 1950s and early 1960s, and much like AUB, the ranks of the
faculty at USJ began to be infused with fresh blood. It was also then that the
various divisions and faculties of the Lebanese National University were
being established. The marked upsurge in research output and publications

during the sixties is a reflection of such swelling numbers. It is also a testimony to the resourcefulness and elevated scholarly standards this new generation of scholars had set for itself.[10]

Another equally radiant landmark in the intellectual life of Lebanon during its vibrant post-independence epoch was the founding of the Lebanese Cenacle in 1946. It was a critical threshold that signaled the emergence of indigenous initiative for self-determination and national discourse. The times were auspicious. With the evacuation of all foreign troops, Lebanon's independence became a reality. The specters of World War II had disappeared. In quick succession, the country won international and regional recognition by being ushered into the Arab League and the United Nations.

The founders of the Cenacle intended it as an open forum for the articulation of the various ideological views and visions underlying Lebanon's national character as a pluralistic society. It was hoped that the open discourse would invite concerted efforts to forge the outlines of a coherent national identity with a modicum of consensus on its political, sociocultural, and aesthetic philosophy. As alluded to earlier, three different viewpoints were contesting for dominance. The first affirmed that the country was much too small to form a viable independent state. Hence it should be absorbed in the larger Arab World. The second, even more negative, asserted that in its present composite form the country was too fragmented and cumbersome to manage politically. Hence the most viable prospect was to reduce its size still further by ridding itself of some of its unwanted elements. Only by so doing could its survival be assured, albeit as a diminished and isolationist entity. The Cenacle opted for a third and more realistic perspective, one more consistent with Lebanon's pluralistic structure and prospects for harmonious coexistence among its differentiated parts. Cofounders of the Cenacle shared the optimistic view that through open dialogue it is possible to approach consensus on the common constituent elements defining Lebanon.

Those defining elements they held converge on the following set of beliefs: Lebanon, as a Mediterranean country, is heir to a long succession of Mediterranean cultures — Phoenician, Greek, Roman, Byzantine, Hittite, Ancient Egyptian, and Arab. In addition to language, it shares with its neighboring Arab states a common culture and common political destiny. Lebanon's Arabness is more than just an accident of history. Eminent Lebanese scholars literary figures of the caliber of Faris Shidyaq, Nassif and Ibrahim Yazigi, Butrus and Salim Bustani, and Adib Ishaq have contributed significantly to its nationalist ethos and Arab cultural and literary revival. But Lebanon has also an international character. By virtue of its strategic position and multiculturalism, it has been, since the 22nd century B.C. open and receptive to world cultures. It is both Arab and international, a gateway between East and West but, above all, it has its own personality and unique national identity.

The articulated credo of the Cenacle was not, naturally, uncritically endorsed. All its underlying premises and visions invited heated public debate. The periodic lectures of the Cenacle became eagerly awaited public events. They attracted some of the country's most eminent intellectuals and polemical figures. More telling, at a time when political discourse in adjacent Arab regimes had already degenerated into the belligerent and militant rhetoric of radical change and bloody confrontations, Lebanon opted for the pacifist give and take of open dialogue.

The Cenacle lectures always drew some of the eminent persons of the day. There were no holds barred on the topics to be discussed. Discretion of speakers was the only form of censorship. Politicians like Kamal Jumblat, Habib Abi Shahla, Saeb Salam, Hamid Franjieh, Micheal Khoury, Ghassan Tueni — representing a wide spectrum of views — spoke freely and critically. Likewise historians such as Fuad Bustani, Charles Corm, Jawad Boulos; even Arnold Toynbee aired their distinctive visions of Lebanon. The same was true of ideologists like Pierre Jumayyel, Alfred Naccash, Takieddine Solh, Edmond Naim, and Jamil Jabre.

Coming in the wake of a recently won independence, the concerns of the Cenacle converged understandably on three vital issues: Lebanon's foreign relations, its philosophical groundings, and some of the unsettling socioeconomic problems the country was grappling with at the time. Philip Taqla, Emile Bustani, Muhieddin Nsouli, Fuad Ammoun, Ibrahim Ahdab, and Manuel Yunis addressed foreign relations and diplomatic issues. Lebanon's philosophic and metaphysical perspectives were left to Charles Malik, Michel Chiha, René Habachi, Kamal Hajj, and Jean-Marie Domenach. Finally, specialists and policymakers in the fields of education, administrative reform, and economic and fiscal problems were invited to address their issues. So were problems of youth, women, the Lebanese family, and the creative and performing arts. The Cenacle was also venturesome enough to launch its own series of publications to stimulate the circulation of prominent Lebanese writers like Khalil Sarkis, Al-Akhtal as-Saghir, Said Takieddine, and Amin Rihani.

What the Cenacle had inaugurated in the mid 1940s was enhanced and enriched by other, often overwhelming, intellectual and cultural transformations Beirut was beginning to display at the time. These, inevitably, were associated with the intensive urbanization and commercialization the city was also undergoing. It must be recalled that the first evidence of an increasing scale of urbanization as measured by the intensity of construction activity did not really begin in Beirut until the early1950s. Until then, the city continued to assume its horizontal, even skyline with the traditional suburban villas overwhelming the urban scene. The intensity and pace of urbanization was not evenly spread throughout the city. Ras-Beirut, both spatially and culturally, was considerably more open than the other communities, enabling it to accommodate the growing demand for urban space. Since no confessional or ethnic group had complete dominance over the area, Ras-Beirut became particularly receptive to successive waves of marginal Anglo-Saxon groups, who could not have had an easy entry into other communities.

The sweeping sociocultural, political, and commercial transformations the area witnessed during the 1950s and 1960s reinforced and complemented, at least initially, the cosmopolitan and pluralistic character of Ras-Beirut. Beginning in 1948, waves of Palestinian migrants started taking up residence in the area. Political events in both Syria and Egypt, particularly after the Suez crisis of 1956, generated another influx. Armenian refugees, particularly professionals and semi-professional groups who had settled elsewhere in Lebanon (after the massacres of 1914), also started to converge on Ras-Beirut.

Despite their divergent backgrounds and the varying circumstances underlying their uprootedness, all these groups had much in common: they were drawn predominantly from highly literate, urban and middle-class families with Anglo-Saxon traditions and a predisposition for socioeconomic mobility. Though they were all displaced groups, they retained little of the attributes of refugee and marginal communities. They evinced, from the very beginning, a noticeable readiness to be assimilated into the nascent urban fabric of Beirut. They were also instrumental in accelerating the pace of change by adding to and enriching the cultural and economic vitality of the area. The upper- and middle-class Palestinians, many of whom managed eventually to acquire Lebanese citizenship, brought with them professional skills; a comparatively high proportion of them were professors and university graduates. A mere listing of a few of the names of those who joined the University during the 1950s indicates how vital this generation of Palestinians has been in upgrading the quality of professional and intellectual life of the area.[11]

Not only AUB, but other colleges, schools, and cultural centers were going through a period of growth and expansion. The inflow of capital from

the Gulf and the concomitant speculation in real estate provided other employment opportunities. In addition to providing a handy reservoir of professional talent, Palestinians (and this is also true of Egyptians and Syrians
who left the UAR after episodes of nationalization of private enterprise)
ventured into profitable and enterprising sectors of the economy. This was
particularly visible in banking, insurance, business services, and retail. The
Intra Bank, Arabia Insurance Co., and other consulting and contracting
firms (such as Dar Al-Handasa and ACE) come to mind. Armenians were
equally resourceful. They, too, contributed their own ethnic and occupa-
tional skills, particularly in professional and semi-professional vocations such
as pharmacy, dentistry, nursing, photography, and electronics.

By the late 1950s areas adjoining Ras-Beirut in particular were already
displaying all the characteristic features of increasing commercialization and
rapid growth. Urbanization was so swift, in fact, that in less than two decades
their spatial character was almost totally transformed. Mounting pressure for
urban space, the invasion of commercial establishments, and the sharp rise
in land values and speculation in real estate resulted in large-scale construction and corporate financing. The attractive red-tiled villas, which once
graced the suburban landscape, soon gave way to a more intensive form of
land utilization. Towering structures in reinforced concrete with glittering
glass facades and prefabricated aluminum frames began to overwhelm the
urban scene.

The sense of neighborhood and the homogeneous residential quarters
which housed regular and stable families were also threatened by a more
impersonal form of residence, such as single men's apartments, furnished
flats, and rooming houses to accommodate a growing itinerant population.
It was not uncommon, for example, to have the basement of a building
utilized as a stereo-club, bar or night-club, or possibly a garage or warehouse;
the ground floor as a movie house, side-walk café, restaurant, or display
parlor; the first few floors as bank and financial premises, executive and
administrative branch offices of foreign companies, marketing research out-
fits, insurance companies, transportation and airline agencies, single or collective doctor's clinics, or offices of other professionals — side by side with
shops, Swedish massage institutes, haute couture, and boutiques; and the
upper floor utilized for residential units, penthouse apartments, and roof
gardens (Khalaf and Kongstad 1973).

Gradually, Ras-Beirut started to lose its cohesive and wholesome character as a residential neighborhood and became, instead, a tempting ground
for sightseers, shoppers, tourists, and other transient groups, who sought ref-

uge in its anonymity and permissive outlets for casual and titillating forms of entertainment.

Despite these inevitable transformations, the area remained, until the early 1970s, the most dominant and arresting urban center in the Arab World. It retained its mixed composition and displayed, because of rampant consumerism, an even greater propensity to experiment with novel forms of cultural expression. The commercialization of popular culture as profitable ventures, reinforced by a permissive political climate and free and uncensored media, encouraged further eclecticism and sensationalism. The highbrow exclusive periodicals of the early 1960s (e.g. *Hiwar, Mawaqif, Sh'ir, al-Adab, al-Adib, al-Fikr*) were supplemented by a plethora of new tabloids and glossy magazines. Even daily newspapers broadened their coverage to reach the growing pseudo-intellectual interests of its readership. Many, for example, started publishing literary and cultural supplements. In ground breaking, often courageous and venturesome essays, writers were challenged to break loose of conventional and inherited modes of classical expression and to invent a new vernacular — a narrative prose better equipped to confront the broader human and universal issues.

Art, theatre, music, and dance displayed a variety of genres ranging from serious surrealistic expression to mediocre manifestations of poor taste and low aesthetic standards. Traditional folklore and arts and crafts were not spared. They too, were victimized by the ethos of cash and excessive commercialization. Publishing houses, with an eye to quick returns, were also eager to publish almost anything. Book exhibits became celebrated events and book stores continued to sell, despite the inevitable debasement of literary standards, perhaps the richest possible variety of books and periodicals found anywhere in the Arab World.

Universities like AUB and St. Joseph were no longer exclusive cultural sanctuaries. Other centers and outlets emerged to satisfy this aroused appetite for popular culture, ideas, and ideological discourse. Politically motivated cultural and information centers, sponsored by adjacent Arab regimes and ideological groups, established their own programs and publications or subsidized particular newspapers (e.g., *Dirasat 'Arabiyya, Journal of Palestine Studies, Dirasat Filastiniyya, Shu'un Filastiniyya, al-Hawadith* etc.). So did many of the foreign embassies and their affiliated cultural missions: The Kennedy Center, British council, Goethe Institute, University Christian Center, Italian, Spanish and Russian cultural centers, Arab Cultural Club, Islamic Cultural Center, The Orient-Institute, Centre d'Etudes et de Recherches sur le Moyen-Orient Contemprain (CERMOC) etc. — all contributed to the diversity of "voices" and "scripts." More important, one was at liberty to listen and incorporate what was heard.

As scholars pursued their research and teaching in an atmosphere of intellectual freedom, so did the growing ranks of freelance writers, editorialists, columnists, and opinion makers. Caustic political humor became a popular pastime. Ziyad Rahbani's gifted sketches and musical comedies, portraying the deepening pathologies of Lebanon's pluralism and the futility of sectarian violence, were reminiscent of Omar al-Zi'inni's biting poetic ditties of the 1930s and 1940s.

Such popular and other pseudo-intellectual voices became more audible and appealing. Some, in fact, were beginning to overwhelm those of the more serious and dispassionate scholars. The restless and baffled among the young read the musings of Unsi al-Hajj and Adonis with the same intensity that earlier generations had approached Constantine Zurayk's essays on Arab Nationalism or René Habachi's discourses on existential philosophy. It was intellectually fashionable to be engagé. There was an air of chic about it. The avant-garde, of all shades, flaunted their causes célèbres with considerable abandon and self-indulgence. They, too, had their own networks and social circles. Sidewalk cafés, snack bars and restaurants, much like the formal headquarters of other explicit groups, became identified with particular kinds of intellectual and ideological clients and subcultures.

The role of coffee houses and sidewalk cafés as venues for spirited public debate and lively discussions must not be overlooked or trivialized. In a culture predisposed for the jocular; for frivolous, festive, and ceremonial encounters, coffee houses in Beirut replaced or transformed such "idle" and "debased" spheres into productive and creative leisure. Traditionally, coffee houses, as elsewhere in the Arab World, were mostly sites for carefree, gregarious and light-hearted gatherings; at best they offered release from the petulant cares and drab routines of daily life. Gradually, they evolved into meeting grounds, rendezvous, and places of assignation for spirited and animated debate. Some, like "Faysal," "Diplomat," "Horseshoe," "Chez Paul," "Express," and "Ajami," became almost subterranean meeting places for left-wing and recalcitrant intellectuals and journalists. To dissidents out of favor in adjacent Arab regimes and other displaced groups, these places offered expedient outlets to mobilize their dissent. The fairly open media and permissive political culture were, naturally, very conducive in this regard.

The 1950s and 1960s also witnessed an upsurge in photography, art, music, folklore, and theatre. As in other cultural products in interludes of free expression and excessive experimentation, there was a great deal of mindless, often compulsive, borrowing. There was also, however, efforts to preserve and embellish local traditions and vernacular. Beirut, incidentally, was far from a wilderness or cultural tabula rasa awaiting the infusion of foreign incursions. If and when the cultural scene was ignited by foreign artists, it would be met by a pool of gifted local talent and an equally receptive audience and sponsors. The ebullience of photography and painting, much like the flowering of popular music, theatre, folklore and modern dance, owes much to such inventive symbiosis.

Clearly this cultural exuberance of the 1950s, 60s and 70s did not just suddenly mushroom out of thin air. Photography, for example, had made its appearance in Lebanon almost a century earlier. Credit is often attributed to the Bonfis family (Felix, his wife Lydie and son Adrien) who had set up their studio in the center of Beirut's business district in 1877. From then on, we are told, this gifted and indefatigable family transformed Beirut into the undisputed image-making capital of the Middle East. As John Carswell put it "there was no corner of Syria, Palestine, and Egypt, no topographical, religious, ethnic, social or incidental aspect of everyday life that was not grist to the Bonfils will" (Carswell 1989: 17). It was also then that commercial photography started to gain an edge over religious painting and iconography, which for a long time had been the most venerated genre of traditional painting and artistic expression. In quick succession local artists, particularly studios like Sarrafian, Sabunji, El-Ferkh, Nowfal, Dakouni, Aoun, Ferneini, Tabet, Srour, Mourani, Rabbat, Tarazi, became very prominent. They also managed, judging by the popularity of family and personal portraits among the notable and nascent urban bourgeoisie, to establish thriving business ventures (for further details see Fani 1995).

As in journalism, family and kinship networks were judiciously exploited in harnessing vocational skills and exporting such enterprises to other parts of the Middle East. For example, there were at least five Sabunjis: the Reverend Louis and his brother George and their offspring Daoud and Philip. Mention is also made of Chibli who had accompanied Cornelius Van Dyck in 1864 on his sightseeing expeditions. They all tended their trade and jealously guarded its vocational secrets in Beirut and Jerusalem. In Jerusalem they competed with rival establishments associated with the American colony who at the time were preoccupied with their own series of photographs of the Holly Land.

Displaced Armenian refugees were crucial in enhancing the professional and artistic stature of photography. They too, as an uprooted and marginalized ethnic community, displayed all the protective attributes of family and communal consciousness. Successive generations received their tute-lage and cultivated their professional skills in close association with other more accomplished family mentors. Some, like the Sarrafians in Beirut and the Orfilians in Tripoli, had a virtual monopoly over their profession. (Car-swell 1989; Yamin 1999). The Orfilians alone produced five reputable pho-tographers in three succeeding generations: Noubar, perhaps one of the earliest emigrants to Tripoli who took residence there in 1830, and his son Baghdasar and three of his grand children (Yabrum, Lyon, and Noubar).

Like other photographers they supplemented their trade by also painting; often they retouched portraits to comply with the idiosyncratic tastes of fas-tidious clients. The close link between the two art forms has been recognized by art historians. The history of both has been, likewise, intimately associated in Lebanon — at least in the formative years of development. Clearly, the commercial success of photography was not oblivious to the generation of early Lebanese painters. A photographic perspective began to impinge on their art. This is clearly seen in the output of some of the founding fathers of Lebanese classical painting, particularly Daoud Corm and Khalil Saleeby.

The relatively early preponderance of painting in Lebanon and its pop-ular appeal is doubtlessly a byproduct of the three primary prerequisites noted earlier, namely: a potential pool of talent, a receptive public, and private patronage. All three, to varying degrees, were evident in Lebanon long before formal instruction and schooling in art became available. It was after all not until 1937 that the Lebanese Académie de Beaux-Arts was es-tablished. For about two decades, this was the only venue for art instruction. Given its Francophile leanings, much of the output of the pioneering gen-erations of local artists remained within the fold of such French cultural traditions.

The other direct impetus that spurred a public enthusiasm for art would not appear until the mid 1950s, when the American University of Beirut established its Department of Fine Arts. Two innovative and spirited young American artists — Maryette Charlton and George Buehr — were recruited to spearhead the program. Schooled at the renowned Art Institute of Chi-cago, they brought with them many of its pedagogical precepts, some of which were rooted in the legacy of Bauhaus. Among other things, this meant that instructors had to be active, practicing, and exhibiting artists. More important, although art-making was perceived as a pervasive mundane ac-tivity, accessible virtually to everyone, it should be taught in a formalistic and not a stylistic manner. The art seminar introduced by spirited teachers, first hesitantly received, soon caught on. Largely because of their open, democratic character, they drew a large audience outside the university community. The public program of lectures, hands-on demonstrations and instructions engendered an enabling sentiment that almost anyone, if given an opportunity, could well discover untapped inner sources of creativity longing to be unleashed.

As in other dimensions of cultural and intellectual life, Lebanon was the beneficiary of this lively French-American rivalry to gain a measure of hegemony over the country's cosmopolitan cultural setting. As the French embassy stepped up its cultural exchange program by inviting renowned French avant-garde expressionists, the John Kennedy Center retaliated by launching a series of itinerant exhibits of high-profile American artists. One, in particular was John Ferren a leading abstract expressionist who took up residence in Beirut in 1964 and who had a captivating impact on a string of young Lebanese artists. His studio at Manara became a refuge for lively debate and free experimentation. Many trace their self-discovery and artistic sensibilities to such sessions.

This momentum for art was abetted by the establishment of art galleries and studios. During the 1950s and 60s such outlets, in fact, became successful business ventures which doubtless played a part in the commercialization of art and, hence, in debasing and bastardizing its standards. The quality of the exhibitions in the burgeoning art galleries did not always meet the desired critical standards of high art. In most, in fact, the line between decorative interior design and serious art was blurred, if not inexorably betrayed or overlooked. There were a few notable exceptions, however, which made efforts to safeguard the threatened standards of high art. *Gallery One*, founded by the poet Yusif al-Khal and his gifted Lebanese-American wife, Helen, was very influential in this regard. So was *Contact*, established by Waddah Fares, an Iraqi dissident artist who was instrumental in opening up exhibitions to artists elsewhere in the Arab World.

Another encouraging feature was the emergence of art criticism. Special literary supplements of leading newspapers started to devote portions of their weekly editions to art and art criticism. *L'Orient* itself hosted a series of avant-garde exhibitions in its premises in downtown Beirut. The annual Lebanese "Salon," most likely modeled after its European counterparts, sponsored public exhibitions. Its rather inclusive character meant, naturally, that the quality of large portions of the output was of dubious artistic credibility. The Sursock Museum, a privately endowed foundation, was more selective and discriminating in its exhibitions. In the late 60s and early 70s it hosted a series of thematic exhibitions (e.g. on iconography and Islamic art) accompanied by scholarly essays by reputable art historians of the caliber of Endré Grabar, Basil Grey, and Jules Leroy (Carswell 1989: 19).

Another compelling indigenous initiative was the founding of Dar Al Fan by a group of largely decentered public intellectuals under the leadership of Janine Rubeiz. Judiciously run by Rubeiz, it evolved as a vibrant site for intellectual camaraderie and free-spirited discussion. It drew together intellectuals, artists eager to reinvent the liberalizing encounters some of them enjoyed in comparable settings in Europe and the U.S.

One serendipitous but auspicious byproduct of this upsurge in art was the unprecedented participation of women, both as artists and enterprising patrons. They did so, judging by empirical evidence, in comparatively large numbers. Until the mid 70s Lebanon had the largest number of women artists in the Arab world (around 40 compared to 10 or less in each of the adjacent countries). More significant, the proportion of professionally active women (1/4) and those accorded a prominent status (1/3) among the leading artists of the country is perhaps unmatched elsewhere in the world (see Khal 1989: 15 for these and other features).

It is not too difficult to trace answers to such striking realities in both the sociocultural milieu of Lebanon at the time and the biographies of the artists themselves coming into their own during that spirited period. If Lebanon ever enjoyed a "Belle Epoque" it was then. These, as we have seen, were times of opportunity, exuberance, experimentation in life styles, and exposure to the novelties of art galleries, exhibits, and the commercialization of cultural products. But these were also times of conflict and uncertainty, marked by discordant societal transformations and asymmetry in gender expectations and, hence, ambivalence and tensions in personal options.

The vivid profiles of prominent resident artists — their background, the circumstances associated with their careers, the role that art came to play in their lives, and their perception of its impact on their status as women — attest to the underlying tensions engendered by the "polarized forces of freedom and restriction" they experienced (Khal 1987: 21). This poignant interplay between their biographies and the repressive sociocultural realities they were entrapped in should be instructive to researchers interested in documenting the marginalization and empowerment of women in the Arab World. In short, how do "excluded" or "secluded" groups seek strategies for enhancing their individuality, self-esteem and zones of autonomy without threatening their protected status in society?

Willfully, or otherwise, art came to play this enabling role in their lives. Some had no illusions about it. While it offered an effective medium for self-expression, it did little by way of transforming the lives of other women. One can easily extract common threads and themes—both manifest and latent—which inform this process. The following stand out: First, they were all drawn from a diverse background of ethnic, national, religious, or cultural pluralism. They also experienced and sustained such diversity through their own education, marriage, and other cross-cultural contacts. None of them, in fact, grew up or remained as "pure" or indigenous Lebanese. Second, their initiation into the arts was largely a byproduct of their adolescent socialization as a "safe" and decorative pastime. Much like music, dancing, drawing, or embroidery, it was an acceptable outlet at the time for girls of privileged and Francophile families. Either abroad or in the burgeoning art academies in Lebanon, they were exposed to the stimulation of an inspiring tutor or milieu that encouraged and channeled their creative energies. Third, and with rare exceptions, they all experienced successive emotionally unsettling encounters—diaspora, exile, divorce and tensions endemic to their gender roles—which transformed their dabbling with the arts into a consummate form of self-expression. To many (e.g. Caland, Saikali, Khal, Kazemi, Seraphim) their art acquired an explicit sensual quality, and they spoke about it, often unabashedly, as a means to "explore the sensual possibilities of the human body," "erotic and feminine sexuality" or color as a form of "quiet seduction" (Khal 1989: 30–31). Finally, it is at that point that their art became an enabling force in their life; a source of potency, identity, self-worth and inner strength to cope with the vicissitudes of public life and a palliative, fickle as it is, for the emotional void and existential angst they were beset with. "It is one of the new permissible windows in her 'herem'. Through it, she can discreetly express all that she feels and thinks. She paints now as in the past she embroidered poems to her beloved on a soft, silk handkerchief, with care and fine taste for "Zakhrafah" (decoration) as well as for depth of emotion. Most of them now still paint poems, but for a few it is their path for liberation" (Khal 1989: 31).

The music scene was also becoming more vibrant. If measured by the professional quality of local performers or the presence of autonomous and endowed national orchestras, Lebanon was clearly below par early in the 1960s. On other less visible indicators, however, public awareness, interest in music instruction, and public performance were growing perceptibly. Here again, as in other cultural and artistic expressions, conventional forms of music appreciation were being supplemented by more professional and discriminating opportunities. Traditional coffee houses, once sites for idle, gregarious, and convivial leisure were, as we have seen, transformed into places for spirited public debate. Likewise, art seminars converted and enriched the folk art of *Zakhrafah*, decorative design and embroidery, into a professional outlet and creative venue for self-validation, autonomy and personal worth.

The upsurge in music was also undergoing this enabling dialectical change. Writing in the mid 1960s Diana Taky Deen (1969: 217), an accomplished concert pianist herself, noted:

The Lebanese music-lover has once and for all adopted the concert hall as both replacement of and a complement to his gramophone. Fifteen years ago, a musical connoisseur was considered as well-informed as his pile of records at home was high and heavy. Today a season ticket is his pride. The music-lover had become more active, recognizing the irreplaceable authentic value of a live performance.

In no time this hidden surge for musical performances found expression in the formation of semi-professional chamber groups who would most often perform for themselves or for a limited circle of personal admirers and devotees. Concert halls and auditoriums at the American University of Beirut (AUB), Beirut College for Women (BCW), and L'Ecole Superieure des Lettres stepped up their public performances. AUB, incidentally, had a head start in this regard since piano recitals and musical performances were introduced to the public early in the 1920s. In fact, the introduction of formal instruction in music at AUB predated art instruction by over three decades. Taking advantage of the large number of gifted Russian refugees who had found their way to Beirut after World War I, AUB recruited Professor Arkadie Kouguell, at one time director of a conservatory in the Crimea, to establish the Institute of Music in 1929. Since his arrival in the early 1920s, Kouguell had been giving private lessons and organizing concerts at the University.

Music at the time, as elsewhere in the Arab world, was not as yet a scientifically or professionally cultivated art. Musical performers and those associated with the performing arts and other traditional elements of popular culture, were not highly regarded and did not rank high in social status. Exposure to European classical music was also minimal. Hence, the establishment of an institute for formal instruction in music was bound to be met with some reservation. Concerts and recitals were first subsidized. Otherwise, the public would have had no inducement to attend (Penrose 1941: 255). Gradually, however, the concerts began to draw an enthusiastic audience beyond the confines of Ras-Beirut. President Bayard Dodge noted the following in his annual report of 1928–29:

Gradually the music became so popular that Professor Kouguell was able to arrange for fortnightly concerts given by a symphony orchestra of thirty-five pieces, to audiences of five or six hundred people. Many high French officials and their wives encouraged the music and the students became enthusiastic. . . . In the symphony orchestra there are Russians, Armenians, French, Americans and members of other nationalities. Professor Kouguell has also organized a student orchestra (AUB Annual Report 1928–9: 21).

By 1928, the University was so encouraged by the public response that it sought government permission to launch a private conservatory of music under the leadership of Kouguell. The institute was a radical departure in more than one sense. What made it so remarkable was that it was the unlikely outcome of collaboration with the French. The diplomas were recognized by L'Ecole Normale des Music of Paris and, more surprising, the language of instruction was in French. At the turn of the twentieth century, it must be recalled, the scions of the founding fathers of Presbyterian missionaries were still harboring disparaging views about Jesuit cultural incursions into the Levant and propagating strategies for shielding native groups from such benighted manifestations of the so-called forces of "anti-Christ." The collaboration with the French, though short-lived, was very beneficent. By 1940, there were eighty-three registered students in the Institute, exclusive of large numbers taking courses as electives. Typically, students were drawn from the culturally mixed student body AUB enjoyed at the time who must have played a part in imparting this music appreciation to other parts of the Arab World.

Unfortunately, the Institute was suspended in 1947 when Kouguell chose to emigrate to America. By then, however, the Lebanese Conservatory of Music, established in 1924 as an autonomous body financed by the Ministry of Education, started to expand its resources to accommodate this growing demand for formal instruction in music. By the mid 1960s it had 500 students and 70 instructors and offered a curriculum of about 25 subjects (Taky Deen 1969: 218). The "Occidental" and "Oriental" conventional clusters gave way to a more integrated program. As in other dimensions of cultural life, the renaissance of music in the 1960s was reinforced largely through private initiative and the patronage of voluntary associations. *Les Jeunesse Musicales du Liban*, established in 1954, was one such organization that enjoyed the support of several foreign cultural missions in the country. The first generation of accomplished Lebanese concert pianists, vocalists, and other instrumentalists was largely an outcome of such ventures.

More perhaps than other modes of cultural expression, it was during the 1960s that theatre may be considered to have truly come of age. Of course theatrical performances appeared much earlier. In fact the first stage production, a play by Maroun Naccache, was performed in public in 1846. In subsequent decades works of noted literary figures like Nassif Yaziji, Farah Antoun, George Abyad, Najib Rihani, along with those of Egyptian playwrites (especially Yusuf Wahbé and Ahmad Shawki) were also staged. Translations or adaptations of foreign plays were also in vogue. It was not, however, until 1960 that theatre, as a movement and an art formcame into its own. All earlier productions were mostly adaptations of prominent authors like Mikhail Naimeh, Said Akl, Said Takkiyddine, Yusef Ghassoub and Toufiq Awwad which did not lend themselves easily to staging or acting.

According to Paul Shawool (1989), the turning point was Issam Mahfouz's *Zinzalakht* (The Neem Tree) in 1968. It marks the first attempt to create a theatrical language and a script receptive to the needs of stage and actors. What facilitated this transformation was that the text was in colloquial language and, hence, served as an inducement for popular actors to create portrayals that were close to the realities of everyday life. This innovative element in Issam Mahfouz's work, sparked off the creative and artistic talents of a growing circle of playwrights, poets, actors and producers like Onsi al Hajj, Raymond Jbara, Jalal Khoury, Shakib Khoury, Munir Abu Dibs, Nidal Ashqar, Antoine Courbage, and Antoine Multaqa. Individually and collectively this spirited group managed to produce a succession of plays, often polemical and controversial but always experimental and avant garde in form and substance. They also made recognizable efforts to organize workshops, study groups, institutes, and centers for instruction and founded associations to promote their careers and professional interests as performing artists (For further details see Said 1998: 21–47). When they were not putting on their own plays, they staged translations or adaptations of well-known plays and playwrights. They made deliberate efforts to break away from the stylistic syntax of classical prose and traditional theatre. By doing so they also gave vent to a new genre of satirical plays, particularly political humor, drawing-room and stand up comedy.

The entertaining sketches and performances of comedians like Nabih Aboul-Husen, Hasan Ala'Iddine "Shou-Shou" and Ziad al-Rahbani found particular appeal among an enthusiastic audience cutting across communal and class boundaries. So were the vaudevillian skits of "Abou Melhem" and "Abou Salim" aired nightly on national radio and television. They became almost unrivalled in their popularity and mass appeal. Albeit more lowbrow, the comic characterization of folkloric episodes in village and urban settings had an evocative and transcending impact. It also elevated this provincial art form into a noteworthy cultural export to neighboring states.

Much like the impetus resident foreign artists had in stimulating creative interest in music, photography, painting, and sculpture, here as well many of the budding generation of local playwrights and actors attribute their enthusiasm for the theatre to their encounters with foreign mentors. At the American University of Beirut, Professor Christopher Scaife a gifted actor and director, was a source of inspiration to a succession of theatre enthusiasts around the university community. Likewise, at the Centre Université d'Etudes Dramatique, George Shehadi, Jaques Metra and Anne-Marie Deshayes were instrumental in launching the careers of a sizeable number of actors. Alphonse Philipe as a stage-set designer was invaluable for the studios involved in experimental theatre.

The cultural rivalry between the Francophone and Anglo-Saxons was also intense here and did much to enrich the volume and diversity of performances. Around AUB alone more than a handful of organized group — Berytus Theatre Ensemble, British Council, New Theatre Group, the Phoenix Players, American Repertory Theatre (ART)- were active in staging play readings, classical and contemporary plays, musicals, operettas, variety shows to packed audiences in West Hall, Irwin Hall, Gulbenkian, Alumni Club or Beirut Theatre. Around USJ and L'Ecole Superieure Des Lettres an equal number of studios and workshops were also active. Most prominent were the Forums of Contemporary and Experimental Theatre organized by Antoine Multaqa, Munir Abu Dibs, Antoine Courbage, and Raymond Jbara. Armenians had also enough talent to organize their own ethnocentered theatre. The circle of Armenian Intellectuals, under the resourceful leadership of Wahran Papazian and Berge Vazalian staged some memorable productions.

The outcome of all this flurry of activities was a very vibrant theatre program; both high in quality and rich in diversity. Between 1964–75 Khalida Said (1998) lists an inventory of more than 100 commercial productions (nearly a dozen performances every season) in four languages and, hence, accessible to a wide range of theatergoers in various quarters of Beirut. The Baalback National Festival was also at its pinnacle at the time and thus offered local and foreign audiences another rich array of world-class performances.

An exposition of the performing arts in Lebanon is incomplete unless one recognizes the role of folkdance during the 1960s and how it became embedded into the national ethos and collective memory of society. The emergence and growth of folkdance as a popular art form was in part the enigmatic byproduct of the incursion of Russian artistic elements into this traditional Lebanese folk art. This fortuitous encounter dates back to 1956 when Igor Moisseev visited Lebanon with his popular Bolshoi Dance Company.

The two countries have, through the centuries, sustained distinct and separate cultural identities. Yet one can discern a common feature rooted in the symbiotic interplay between their traditional manifestations of country life and the popular arts, particularly folkdance. In both countries, this edifying interplay transcends the prosaic character of dance routines compelling as they may be. They are also emblematic of deeper and more complex sociocultural realities. The vibrant expressions of voices and melodies; the rhythmic cadence of syncopated movements, in which every muscle of their bodies bespoke of the dramas of everyday life and sacred rituals embedded in their collective memory. In Lebanon, as in Russia, folkdance, perhaps more than other collective artistic expressions, evokes and memorializes, indeed it celebrates, the wide gamut of human emotion — the bitter and the sweet, the joyful and the sorrowful; the lighthearted, festive dances for courtships and weddings, along with the more somber and cheerless chants, often posturing as dance, for burials, wakes, rituals of revenge and the calls to war. In a word, the joys of victory and the anguish of defeat.

At the time Moisseev visited Lebanon, Lebanese folklore was barely coming of age. Pioneering groups and dedicated artists, largely self-taught but inspired by the wealth and diversity of village life, were trying to forge a new vision of Lebanese folklore. Efforts were made to retain the authenticity of its folk heritage while grafting it to the imperatives of modernity. Foremost among the pioneers were the talented duo — Marwan and Wadia Jarrar — who founded a dance company for tutoring gifted young students. Their efforts were hailed at the time as a revivalist movement. In retrospect, they must also be credited for transforming folkdance into an edifying and enabling national pastime.

Lebanese audiences, from all walks of life, were enthralled, often spellbound, by the exuberant success of Moisseev's performances. They left an indelible and vibrant impression. It was, however, the timely patronage Mrs. Zalfa Chamoun bestowed on the burgeoning arts, the Baalbeck Festival in particular, which reinforced this enriching encounter with the Russian master and his renowned troupe. Her moral authority, as wife of the President of the Republic, lent her efforts added impetus and credibility.

The National Committee of UNESCO, at whose invitation Moisseev was in Lebanon, were soon exploring with their guests, and with the Soviet Cultural Mission, means by which Moisseev could assist in the development of Lebanese popular dance into a full-fledged art. The intention, of course, was to move the folklore, as was the case in Russia, from the village square to the limelights of national theatres.

Igor Moisseev agreed to engage in an exploratory tour of Lebanon (accompanied by the Jarrars) to study and observe the various *dabkeh* performances in their diverse natural settings: in the Beqa', North Lebanon, Mount Lebanon and the South. By the end of his study tour, the Russian master presented a comprehensive and probing report going beyond the description and analysis of salient dance techniques. He also explored some of the sociohistorical dimensions of folklore, the rigorous training and methodical discipline it necessitates, its cultural messages, and the national role it could serve as an expressive, cathartic, and healing art form. The report spared little: choreography, scenery, costumes, thematic inspiration and, finally, how to preserve the reawakened national spirit of folklore while striving to imbue it with universal dimensions.

In light of the Moisseev report, which was at the time subjected to careful scrutiny and debate, it was agreed, with the support of the Ministry of National Education, to send the Jarrars on an extended mission to Moscow. They were commissioned to work there and receive the necessary knowledge and training. Upon their return they were entrusted with the establishment of a much needed and desired national ballet company.

Only a year later, in the Baalbeck Festival of 1957, these cherished hopes were realized. The *Lebanese Nights* embellished its program and captivated the hearts of the throngs — both natives and foreign alike — who were privileged to watch it. From then on, the Folklore performances became the most eagerly awaited event. In a quick succession of varying styles, often venturesome and dazzling, it metamorphosed into an evolving genre of its own; a source of inspiration to multitudes in Lebanon and elsewhere in the world.

More important perhaps, the instant success of *Lebanese Nights* fired up the imagination of that talented coterie of impassioned artists and composers of the like of Rahbani brothers, Zacky Nassif, Tawfic el Bacha and gifted vocalists: Feirouz, Wadih Safi, Sabah, Romio Lahoud, Nasri Chamseddine, among others. All became national icons of sorts. Together, they helped in transforming folkdance into operettas, drama, and evocative theatrical performances of high quality.

The resurgence of folklore had a transforming impact on national culture and ordinary life, at all levels of society. Baalbeck had lost its monopoly long before the war interlude interrupted the International Festival. Even during the war, folklore traveled with the Lebanese wherever they fled or emigrated. Yet, wherever it went, it did not just nurture the longing for nostalgia but also their commitment to return to a sacred homeland, Baalbeck in particular.

Lebanon as a Playground

All metaphors, as analogies or popular figures of speech, involve some inevitable distortions of reality. They rarely tell the whole truth. Nevertheless, to label Lebanon as a "playground" is still, in my judgment, more germane and informative than some of the other hackneyed labels it has been tagged with over the years: both the redeeming ones which make it seem like a privileged and wondrous creation, a "Switzerland" or "Paris" of the Middle East, or the more pejorative, almost epitaph-like, slurs it has been maligned with lately; namely that it is no more than a congenitally flawed, artificial entity bent on putative self-destruction. A deranged oddity of this sort, the obituaries bemoan, is beyond understanding and beyond cure. Like a diseased organism, the most one can do is to "quarantine" or contain it lest it contaminate others.

As a metaphor, a "playground" conjures up images of an open, gregarious accommodating space, germane for felicitous inventiveness and experimentation but also vulnerable to all the vicissitudes of excessive passions, heedless narcissism, complacency, and indulgent egoism. In this sense it is a more neutral metaphor. It neither adulates nor abnegates. It allows us, instead, to allude to and illuminate certain inescapable realities, which cannot be wished away, whitewashed, or mystified. It is also a more inclusive metaphor, thus enabling one to incorporate its everyday discursive and reflexive manifestations, which pervade virtually all dimensions of society.

A "playground," incidentally, is more than just a heuristic and analytical tool. It also has cathartic and redemptive features. By eliciting those latent and hidden longings for play, conviviality, adventure, a "playground" may well serve as an expressive and transcending outlet. It brings out all the "Homo ludens" virtues of fair play, the exuberance of individual and competitive sports and differential rewards for harnessed and accomplished feats of excellence.[12] In this respect a "playground" becomes an ideal site for cultivating the virtues of civility and commitment to the courtesies of the rules of the game. The very survival after all of a playground, particularly since it is associated with spaces where children can indulge in play, is predicated on the premise of monitoring and controlling the hazards of reckless and foolhardy impulse. When uncontained, a "playground" could easily slip into a free-for-all, raucous, rough and tumble public ground. It is then that lines demarcating civil and the uncivil, couth and uncouth behavior, foul and fair play are blurred. Indeed, fair becomes foul and foul fair.

The curative and healing aspects of a playground are naturally more pertinent in times of collective unrest and postwar stress and uncertainties. A boisterous political culture suffused with factional and contentious rivalries can find more than just momentary release in such outlets. Some of the enabling features of a playground — i.e., those of fair play, teamwork, equal recognition, and the sheer exuberance of doing one's thing without encroaching on the rights and spaces of "others" — can all aid in the restoration of civility. At least they need not be dismissed and trivialized. Inordinate effort and resources, as will be argued later, have been squandered on strategies of political and administrative reform and the broader issues of regional conflict and infrastructural reconstruction. Important as these are, they overlook some of the more human and sociocultural issues of coping with pervasive fear and damaged national identities. It is also these areas which are amenable to individual intervention. Ordinary, and otherwise passive and lethargic, citizens are given opportunities to participate and become actively and meaningfully engaged in processes of reconstruction and rehabilitation.

Within this context, at least five features of a playground stand out, particularly those which have some bearing on Lebanon's seemingly lopsided character. Expressed differently, in all those features we find many of the enabling and disabling sources of the "playground"; i.e., those which account for Lebanon's "success story" and those which render it more vulnerable to internal and external contradictions.

1. *By virtue of its location, composition, and its historical role as a place of refuge for dissidents or a gateway for itinerant groups, Lebanon has always been a fairly open and free space.* Exit from and entry into society has been relatively easy. Indeed, some argue that Lebanon became much too open, too hospitable and, hence, too vulnerable to the vicissitudes of internal and regional disturbances. It availed itself to abuse by the very forces that sought it as a haven from repression or homelessness. A free press, uncensored media, absence of exchange controls, a "free zone" in Beirut's port, secret

bank account, liberal migration laws, receptivity to novelties and fads, progressive and permissive life styles all reinforce the discordant dualism inherent in its character as a free and open society. Hence its generative and positive attributes were often undermined by subversive elements and deplorable consequences. Lebanon became all too often no more than an expedient conduit, a transit point, for the trafficking and recycling of displaced groups, goods, capital, and ideas.

Naturally, such trafficking was not always of a desirable and lawful character. Inevitably, Lebanon became notorious for smuggling, arms-running, trading in drugs, black-marketing of illicit contraband products, and other nefarious activities. Perhaps more damaging was the abandon with which dissident groups exploited this freedom to launch vilifying press campaigns and plots against repressive regimes in the region. This only served to arouse the suspicion and retributive strategies of the targeted states or groups against Lebanon. On both counts Lebanon became unjustly victimized.

2. *As in a playground, the Lebanese displayed a proclivity for playfulness sparked by a mood of carefree and uncommitted activity.* They had a special fondness for humorous encounters. Here, as well, this pervasive playful mood was double-edged. While a source of unflagging resourcefulness, sustained by a sense of experimentation and adventure, when unrestrained it would quickly degenerate into restless expenditure of energy, mischievous activity, and anarchy. Much too often a heedless element of play and unplanned activity permeated every fabric of society. The laissez-faire ethos, in such a free-for-all milieu, was clearly a relief to an inept government and a welcome to those adept at exploiting it. Even the corrupt civil servant "became increasingly appreciated by the national and international business communities, since bribes now served to circumvent red tape and to effect short-cuts; which made conduct of business, in many ways, more 'efficient' in Lebanon than in even the most advanced countries" (Tabbarah 1977: 22).

There are other more grievous manifestations of this predisposition for unrestrained play. It is evident in the wasteful discrepancy between audacious and playful planning on the one hand and executive ineffectiveness on the other. This has plagued government bureaucracy for so long and has been a blatant source of administrative inefficiency and misuse of resources. Some of the schemes for development are often so adventurous in their visions that they remain unrealized blueprints; victims of reckless planning or short-sighted expediency. Examples of such disjunctions are legion.

The Litani River Authority of 1954, was supposed to irrigate 32,000 hectares in the South-Western regions of the Biqa'a valley. By 1975, twenty years after the establishment of the project and despite hundreds of millions of pounds already expended, the coveted waters of the Litani were still draining to the Mediterranean (Nasr 1978: 8). The Green Plan of 1964, successive urban planning schemes, and comprehensive master plans, rent and zoning laws, as well as educational and civil service reforms, to mention a few, are all grievous byproducts of this dissonance between exuberant planning and flawed implementation.

This is also apparent, as we have seen, in the political process, particularly electoral campaigns and contests for public office which were suffused with playful and festive elements. The whole style of daily politics is sustained by a large residue of political maneuverings as sources of animated exchanges bordering on public entertainment. Indeed, as one of the smallest nation states in the world, Lebanon has always been ravaged by an inordinate number of people who expend their energies and derive their sense of esteem from "playing" politics. This is, in itself, another reflection of the problematic and ungovernable character of the Lebanese polity. To many of these political actors, prominent and not-so-prominent figures who meddle in the political affairs of their society, the art of politics is often reduced to a self-indulgent game, a morbid form of public amusement and exhibitionism. So alluring is the game that successive generations of politicians have found it extremely difficult to redirect their energies into less flattering but more resourceful and creative pastimes. There is something akin to a compulsive addiction to playing politics. Like any other addictive or habit-forming activity, actors, it seems, suffer all the symptoms of withdrawal once they are compelled to abstain. Witness how difficult it is for political actors in Lebanon to retire from politics.

Even the character of fighting was not entirely free from manifestations of play. Combatants, during the early stages of the 1975 war, when bearing arms and combat still assumed redemptive and purgative features, went about their militant roles with considerable aplomb and savoir-faire. Indeed, any identification with the garb, demeanor, or life styles of fighters and militia groups became almost chic — a fashionable machismo. Belligerency, in fact, became so stylized that groups literally disfigured themselves to simulate such playful and alluring identities. As fighting escalated in magnitude into massive bombardment, random shelling, car bombs, ground troop movement, and aerial attacks, it acquired all the artifacts of a colorful and dazzling spectacle, a "danse macabre," and was often viewed as such by the entrapped nonbelligerent population.[13]

3. *A playground is, above all, a place that thrives on gamesmanship.* In an open, free, and competitive milieu, one sustained by the maximization of private initiative and free enterprise, there is a correspondingly high premium placed on individual success and socioeconomic mobility. Ruthless competition may propel the Lebanese to new heights, stretch their abilities to new thresholds. Yet it also generates a form of "social Darwinism" and heedless individualism impervious to any controls or ethical restraints. Symptoms of anomie become rampant. Everything and anything becomes accessible or feasible, by fair means if possible or foul means if necessary. It is here that benign play degenerates into malevolent and foul play.

At the height of Lebanon's golden/gilded ages (the second half of the 1960s), there were already a growing chorus of dissenting voices decrying the abuses and the desecration of the country's potential. To René Habachi, there was nothing new about the crisis. There have always been two Lebanons:

> The present crisis is a quarter of a century old. It is as old as independence, that is one generation. It is a chronic, latent, disease which has suddenly burst out from under the embers of people's souls. The old style Lebanese, those who wore Ottoman boots, took over a country which had entered the modern age, but they ruled it with the mentality of the Sultan. The level of development of the country, its openness to civilization and its geographic, economic and human resources fitted it to live within the democracy of science and knowledge. Instead they ruled it like someone exploiting a farm he had inherited from his father, with the right to bequeath it in turn to his son. In Lebanon, today, there are two Lebanons. . . . (quoted by Awwad 1996:137).

Gamesmanship after all involves, literally, the internalization of the necessary social skills — those of tact, deftness, acumen, quick-wittedness — for handling and rearranging situations to one's own advantage. It conjures up images of Byzantine maneuvering, manipulation, deals and quid-pro-quos. Everything, including the most cherished values and resources, becomes negotiable. Lebanese entrepreneurship, particularly in its reckless form of speculation and risk taking, seems guided more by Adam Smith's "invisible hand" than by rational long-term planning.

These too are not unmixed blessings. While they may account for much of the resourcefulness and enterprise associated with Lebanon's "success story," they also sanction the use of ploys and other ethically and intellectually dubious means to achieve desired ends. Clientelistic politics, the sur-

vival of subversive patronage, graft, nepotism, and corruption are all byproducts of such pervasive practices. Those who stand to benefit from the spoils
and excesses of this form of deranged "social Darwinism" will naturally resist
any system that undermines their jealously guarded privileges. Spokesmen of
the radical left, heralding revolutionary change as the one panacea to rescue
society from its own inbred foibles and moral weaknesses, admitted that even
an organized revolt has little hope for undoing the deep-seated structure of
vested privileges. Writing again in the late 1960s Gibran Majdalani has this
to say:

> The realisation of the aims of a real revolution conflicts with vested
> interests and with apparatuses which were set up to protect those in-
> terests. It is unreasonable to those who are profiting from the present
> state of affairs voluntarily to give up those things which give them their
> power and their material and political potentialities. Those who are
> 'eating the cheese' (as they say) in any system will oppose any attempt
> at radical change because change implies the liquidation of their privi-
> leges and positions of influence and the threatening of their interests.
> The form of opposition to which the leaders and protectors of any
> system will resort determines, in the last resort, the method of revo-
> lution (quoted by Awwad 1976: 138).

4. *The most edifying and enabling feature of a playground is, doubtlessly,
its convivial and gregarious character.* In part because of the survival of a
large residue of primordial and intimate social networks, the Lebanese have
long displayed a proclivity for festive, light-hearted, and fun-loving encounters. If one were to single out a national pastime, the preoccupation of society
with feasting, spontaneous social gatherings, and companionship is clearly
the most appealing and visible. Time and budget analysis reveals that an
inordinate amount of time and resources are devoted to ceremonial activities, social visitation, and frequent contacts with close circles of family and
friends. Such contacts are invaluable sources of social and psychological
support, particularly in times of public distress. As the public world becomes
more savage, menacing, and insecure, people are more inclined to seek and
find refuge and identity in the reassuring comforts of family and community.
So intense and encompassing are these attachments that the average Lebanese recognizes hardly any obligations and loyalties beyond them. Here lie
many of the roots of deficient civility and the erosion of the broader loyalties
to public welfare and national consciousness.

Once again, what enables at one level, disables at another. At the local

and communal level conviviality is a source of group solidarity and an ave-
nue for vital sociopsychological and economic supports. At the national and
public level, however, such solidarity could easily degenerate into parochial
and oppressive encounters. Compassion for and almost obsessive preoccupation with and concern for micro interests coexist with (indeed are a byproduct of) uninterest in or indifference toward others. Nowhere is this more
apparent than in the character and functioning of voluntary associations.
The concern for public welfare continues to be inspired and mobilized on
sectarian, communal, or factional grounds. Hence national and broader societal problems such as child and family welfare, mental health, orphanages,
the aged, delinquency, poverty, protection of the environment and habitat,
and concern for the threatened architectural, archaeological, and cultural
heritage are all articulated as parochial and segmented problems. Indeed,
the character of voluntary associations, their membership, financial resources, and organizational leadership continue to reflect sub-national loyalties. Even interest in competitive sports, normally the most benign and
affectively neutral and transcending of human encounters, have lately become bitter and acrimonious sectarian rivalries.

5. *Finally, Lebanon is recognized and treated as a "playground" by the
multitudes who perceive it and seek it as a popular resort.* The country's
captivating topography, scenic beauty, temperate climate, historic sites, colorful folklore, reinforced by an aggressive infrastructure of commercial, financial, medical, and cultural facilities, have made it a year-around tourist
attraction, a popular amusement center and summer resort.

As a national industry, tourism and related services have always served to
invigorate the Lebanese economy. By the early 1950s tourism was already
the most important invisible export; earning more than half of the value of
all exported merchandise (see Gates 1998: 117–80). Revenues from tourism
grew four times in the period 1968–74, to provide 10 percent of the gross
domestic product (Owen 1988: 37). By the outbreak of hostilities in 1975 it
was contributing significantly (at least $40 million annually) to GNP and
thus offsetting the unfavorable trade balance. It opened up society further
and enhanced the receptivity of isolated communities to diverse cultural
contacts.

There was, however, a darker side to tourism and Lebanon's image as a
resort center. It exacerbated further the lopsidedness of the Lebanese economy by rechanneling vital resources into the largely unproductive sectors of
the economy. The country was increasingly becoming a nation of services,

middlemen, agents, idle *rentiers* and hotel keepers. Popular resorts, invariably, became tempting spots for venial and not-so-venial attractions. Lebanon was hardly a paragon of virtue in this regard. It had its full share of houses of ill-repute, casinos, gambling parlors, nightclubs, discos, bars, escort bureaus, and other abodes of wickedness.

More damaging perhaps was its blemishing impact on the country's national character. As a "merchant republic" Lebanon became a country obsessed with and too eager to please and serve others, with all the cruel ironies that such ingratiation and servility often do to society's self-esteem. Artisans, villagers, and farmers abandoned some of their venerated crafts, vocations, and sources of traditional status to capitalize on the transient rewards of tourist-affiliated activities. Many became idle much of the year awaiting the alluring promises of a quick and sizeable windfall generated by the influx of vacationers during the brief summer months. Others wallowed in aimless indolence.

Sparked by the ethics of a mercantile culture, it is easy to see how tourism could deepen further the inauspicious consequences of rampant commercialism and the vulgarization of some of the cherished values and institutions. As a result the society embodied at times the most lurid features of a bazaar and an amusement park where the impulse for fun and profit remains unabashed. Practically everything and anything becomes for sale or is converted into a sleazy tourist attraction. Every entity and human capacity is conceived as a resource for the acquisition of profit or as a commodity to be exchanged for the highest bidder. This is most visible in the ruthless plunder of Lebanon's scenic natural habitat and dehumanization of much of its living space. Hardly anything is spared: shore lines, green belts, public parks and private backyards, suburban villas, historic sites and monuments are all giving way to more intensive forms of exploitation to enhance their fashionable attributes.

7 From Playground to Battleground: Preludes to Civil Strife

"When the ox falls butchers abound"
— Lebanese Proverb

"My friends, because my horse is stolen, you have hastened one and all to tell me my faults and shortcomings. But strange, not one word of reproach have you uttered about the man who stole my horse."
— Khalil Gibran, *The Forerunner* (1920).

"And each of the factions was able to enlist some outside power on its behalf. All this turned Lebanon into a miniature model of all the Middle East conflicts rather than, as it had been historically, a symbol of their resolution."
— Henry Kissinger, *Years of Renewal* (1999)

". . . . Reprisals as vital lymph. . . . they help maintain a high tension among our population and army. . . . The long chain of false incidents and hostilities we have invented. . . . The many clashes we have provoked.
— *Sharett's Diary* (1955)

Throughout its checkered history, Lebanon's enigmatic, Janus-like character has never ceased to baffle. It has been a source of bewilderment, as we have seen, to both its detractors and admirers. A few of those struck by its perplexities have been candid enough to caution against facile analysis and hasty inferences. Two veteran observers, separated by more than two decades of eventful history, advance almost the same sobering caveats. Writing in 1963, to account for the "seeming vitality and durability of the country's confessional democracy," J. C. Hurewitz prefaces his essay by stating that Lebanon by then was already an "oddity, not in the Arab lands alone, where representative government has almost vanished, but among the world's democracies. It beggars summary analysis" (Hurewitz 1963: 487).

Two decades later, William Quandt accounts for the trials and errors of American policy in Lebanon: "Lebanon is a harsh teacher. Those who try to ignore its complex realities, whether Israeli grand strategists, ill-informed optimists sitting in Washington, or ambitious Lebanese politicians usually end up paying a high price." (Quandt 1984: 237).

Lebanon's peculiarities, both enabling and disabling, have aroused the relentless curiosity of seasoned scholars, diplomats, and travelers. Leading humanists of all shades and persuasions have been equally perplexed. To many, in fact, Lebanon has been more than just a "harsh teacher." Successive Generations of writers, essayists, poets, artists, and intellectuals, who have at times evoked more poignant imagery than the predominantly dispassionate treatment of scholars, have discovered their voice and honed their literary imagination by elucidating its distinct features and multilayered history.

Two decades of free-floating hostility and treacherous bloodletting has inevitably transformed the nature and tone of their writing. It is in this existential sense that Lebanon has been much more than a scabrous and humbling tutor. Lebanon's literary output has always been imbued with a strong and enduring romantic tradition sustained by an idealization of the country's scenic beauty and captivating natural endowments. This idyllic pastoral image did not only find expression in nostalgic reveries, popular culture, artistic byproducts and artifacts. Much of the country's folklore, as well as its national icons, and historic identity, are also suffused with such imagery. Peasant village life, with its emblematic values of simplicity, integrity, genuine caring, and neighborliness, are treated as paragons of virtue. Indeed, in dark times such romanticization becomes understandably pronounced. It serves as final refuge and sources of reenchantment.

Lebanon's most prolific and creative talents have, off and on, continued to dip into this seemingly undepletable legacy as sources of renewed inspiration and national consciousness. Of course to Khalil Gibran, Mikhail Naimy, Amin Rihani, Charles Corm, and other successive generations of those who struggled with the pathos of exile and diaspora, such writing was elevated into an accomplished art form. It became the undisputed canon consecrated in national textbooks and high school anthologies. For a while, generations of students were exposed to little else.[1]

In post-independence, as Lebanon started to grapple with some of the unsettling manifestations of uneven development and socioeconomic transformations, a generation of writers broke away from such romanticized visions and started to expose (often dramatize) symptoms of injustice, confessionalism, corruption, and poverty. Even urbanization and city life were perceived as threats to the sublime authenticity inherent in pastoral Lebanon. Lebanon, in other words, was being "denatured," hence the longing to preserve, if not return, to such an idyllic or imagined past, became much more pronounced.[2]

By the 1950s and 1960s Lebanon was being "denatured" by a new set of threatening incursions and "borrowed" ideologies: Baathist, Socialist, Arabist, and Islamist. Of course, while such ideologies were not uniformly perceived as threatening or borrowed, they nevertheless altered the nature and character of the discourse. This was also happening at a time when Lebanon, and especially Beirut, was quickly becoming a vibrant cultural and intellectual epicenter, an open publishing house or forum for experimentation, and a permissive haven for political dissidents. The radicalization of Arab politics was bound to reverberate within such a setting. While welcomed by some, this political Arabization of Lebanon was dreaded by other Lebanese "Essentialists" and diehards who saw in it a precurser to the foreboding prospects of rendering their country more vulnerable to such zealous and impassioned radicalization. Christian minorities in particular harbored apprehensions of becoming increasingly marginalized, if not besieged, and outnumbered by their Muslim compatriots who entertained broader allegiances to pan-Arab nationalist sentiments.

Reactions to such apprehensions, at least intellectually, were manifold. Three are perhaps the most visible. First, the fear of being engulfed or marginalized led, naturally, to some extreme essentialist views often assuming (as in the writings of Said Akl, Charles Malik, Kamal al-Hajj, and their political offshoots) a regression into putative and self-defensive parochial forms of territorial and communal identities. Here, all forms of "Maronism" and "Lebanism" harked back to the historic mystique of their unique heritage in Mount Lebanon, pregnant with all symbolism and rituals of religious and communal solidarities. Second, and not necessarily essentialist, this re-imagining of the Lebanese identity began to assume a "folklarized" character, particularly in popular music, folk dance, musicals, and dramatic performances that reenacted village squabbles, heroic affrays, and brawls or else commemorated national and seasonal events. Presentations were always in colorful idiom employing vernacular and colloquial expressions and rendered romantically and lyrically. The Rahbbani-Feiruz duo emerged as mentors and role models to a nascent but talented coterie of popular artists. This "folklorization" of popular entertainment evolved into a transcending and homogenizing national pastime. It cut across ideological and communal divisions and served to coalesce the Lebanese. The products, in fact, became major cultural exports often overtaking the popularity of Egyptian productions. Thirdly, at the level of high culture, this same transcending feature was apparent in the experimental and inventive intellectual output of a growing circle of gifted writers. A decentered and avant-garde literary and aesthetic imagination in art, poetry, theatre found a receptive and engaging audience. The writers, at least initially, skirted ideological and polemical discourse. They also avoided the idealized and folklorized pastoral image of Lebanon so rampant at the time. Instead, their main concern was to carve a new role to safeguard uncensored venues through which their creative energies could best capture the spirits of the modern age.[3]

The outbreak of hostility in 1975 quickly changed the character and tone of writing. Of course the stunning defeat of the Arabs in 1967 and the deplorable plight of uprooted Palestinian refugees had already released a barrage of acrimonious and indignant writing decrying the complicity of the Arab regimes for the *Nakba*. To such disinherited liberals Beirut became the last sanctuary, the only cultivated outpost in a desolate wilderness. To Adonis, the disgraceful defeat was symptomatic of the "sterility of a senile and collapsing sand-culture" (al-Udhari 1986: 64). The war in Lebanon, particularly after the Israeli invasion and the siege of Beirut in 1982, provided another shameful context. Once the nerve center of Arab creativity and cosmopolitanism, Beirut was being overrun by shibboleth and banality. By then, as Alcalay put it, "what was cultivated reverts to wilderness: the desert finally overruns the city, paradoxically making an end to growth and a return to the primal place of purification" (Alcalay: 1993: 99).

When Beirut fell, its ugly fate, treacherous as it was, seemed deserving. At least this is how the outcome was viewed by those keen on establishing a link between the internal dislocations and the city's downfall. Rather than treating Lebanese as a victim of regional and global rivalries, they were much too eager to assign blame to its internal foibles. The country became, as it were, fair game for assault and heedless bashing, much like the fate of the aggrieved villager in Gibran's *The Forerunner* cited in the epigraph at the opening of this chapter.

This tension between the vibrant Beirut of old and its foreboding descent into anomie invited some of the most compelling and graphic queries. Some were perplexed by the dual and alternating character, the "flourishing/suffering" component of Beirut's composite profile. Cooke employed the "Bitch/Godess" metaphor to highlight the city's downfall from the "jewel of the Mediterranean" to a shameless center of debauchery and prostitution (Cooke 1988: 15–16). Alcalay speaks of the "Poetics of Disaster" to catalogue how a cultivated city is overrun by the wilderness of a desert culture (Alcalay 1993: 99). To Liza Manganoro (1998) it is akin to a "Hannibal Lecter war:

beauty and civility turned monster." Others, probed into the criminal/victim paradox to assign culpability and vindicate the blameless. Nizar Qabbani, the gifted Syrian poet, talked about the destruction of society from within. Shamefully he decried:

> *Our enemies did not cross our borders*
> *they crept through our weaknesses like ants.*
>
> (Qabbani 1986: 98).

The answer to Qabbani, such aspersions aside, remained ambivalent. While he confesses to the guilt of partaking in the process of violating Beirut, the city remains nonetheless a scapegoat:

> *Beirut, Queen of the world*
> *Who sold your bracelets inlaid with sapphire?*
> *Who seized your magic ring, and cut your golden nails?*
> *Who sacrificed the joy sleeping in your green eyes?*
> *Who slashed your face with a knife, and threw fire water on your luscious*
>   *lips?*
> *Who poisoned the water of the sea, and sprinkled hate on the pink*
>   *shores?*
> *We've come to apologize . . . to confess*
> *That we were the ones who, in tribal spirit, opened fire on you*
> *And we killed a woman . . . called Freedom*
> *Whence come your harshness, Beirut . . . you were once as gentle as a*
>   *houri?*
> *How did the gentle bird become a wild night cat?*
> *How did you forget God, and return to idols . . .*
>
> (Qabbani 1994: 498–99).

Poetic license aside, "how did the gentle bird become a wild night cat?" One might restate this by invoking a less poetic but more pedantic and heuristic metaphor? How did Lebanon's "playground" become a "battleground"?

This is not, clearly, so trifling a query. Those of us who had witnessed the early rounds of the war were baffled by what seemed to us then as a sudden outpouring of hordes of "wild cats" striking havoc in the streets of Beirut. Perhaps we had only seen the "gentle birds" and were amazed that they had turned into voracious wild cats overnight? Nor could we have imagined how these seemingly benign outbursts could beget such relentless outbreaks of murderous destructiveness and reckless brutalities.

Were they not there? How could we not have seen them? What kind and whose playground was it? At what point did the playground become a battleground? Were we not, as Qabbani is confessing, the ones who, incited by our own bigoted tribalism, had "sprinkled hate on its pink shores . . . and killed its freedom?" Or, and perhaps more likely, could it not be that some of the forces which were incensed by the "playground" had exacerbated its own abuse and demise, thereby expediting its transformation into a "battleground"? A proxy playground is more likely, after all, to beget its own proxy battleground.

The chapter, more explicitly, will address three related dimensions by way of elucidating the connection between the divisions within society and how they were being compounded by salient socioeconomic and political transformation and how, in turn, these find expression in social protest and varying forms of collective violence: (1) What dislocations and disparities, both vertically and horizontally, were exacerbated by the changes Lebanon was undergoing during its golden/gilded epoch? What social strata, communities, regions stood to benefit or suffer the most from these inequalities? (2) What were the issues and grievances that aroused public discontent and mobilized groups in movements of collective protest? What specific forms did such mobilization assume within the various communities? How and why do they differ? Was the protest consistent with the socioeconomic grievances or was it politically and ideologically mobilized by concerns unrelated to indigenous sources of unrest, perceptions of neglect, and relative deprivation? (3) Finally, when and why did grievances and social unrest take more belligerent manifestations? When and why, in other words, did civil violence begin to degenerate into incivility?

To answer these questions is, by any measure, a tall order. They have all been explored and fully documented, from various perspectives, by the prodigious volume of writing Lebanon continues to invite. The intention here is not to provide yet another such comprehensive analysis. Instead, the effort is much more succinct and eclectic — to focus on those features which can best elucidate some of the leading premises of this exploration; namely, surrogate victimization, the reassertion of communalism, and the drift into uncivil violence.

I have been suggesting all along that Lebanon's bloody history with collective strife is largely a reflection of the destabilizing interplay between internal divisions and external dislocations. The internal divisions are naturally a by-product of deep cultural cleavages inherent in sharp communal, confessional, and other primordial and segmental loyalties. Juxtaposed to these are the uneven socioeconomic and cultural transformations which have had a differential impact on the relative standing of the various strata and/or communities.

The external sources are also discordant and divisive in two respects: Unresolved regional conflict, incited by ideological rifts and personal rivalries, will always find receptive grounds among disenfranchised and neglected groups. These are often used as wedges or sources of political patronage or leverage. Impetuous ideological shifts in adjacent regimes, be they pan-Arabist, Ba'thist, Socialist, Islamist or the resurgence of Palestinian resistance reinforced communal and sectarian cleavages. They also served, as we shall see, as proxy platforms for the radicalization of discontent and social unrest. More penetrable, perhaps, are the global transformations engendered by the proliferation of long-distance interconnectedness, media technologies, and the diffusion of life styles, ideas, migrant labor and monolithic and irresistible marketing and consumerism. Here, as well, local groups markedly differ in their resistance or adaptation to such threatening incursions.

The discordant elements of these inside/outside dialectics have always accentuated the asymmetry within society and threatened its tenuous balance. Accordingly, successive governments, despite commendable efforts, have been in varying degrees ineffective in coping with the mounting tensions and imbalances generated by such inevitable dislocations. There is nothing unusual in this kind of problematic interplay. Lebanon, as we have been suggesting, has always fallen victim to some of its disruptive consequences. Three such defining elements stand out: The resilience and tenacity of Lebanon's primordialism, inveterate foreign incursions, and heightened belligerency. By elucidating first the origin, survival, and changing character of such cleavages, one can better gauge or assess their interplay with the other two defining elements; namely, foreign patronage and uncivil violence.

Radicalization of Discontent and Fear

Incipient and early symptoms of radicalization of grievances were doubtlessly associated with the tumultuous political changes in neighboring Arab states. A fateful watershed was 1963, when radical Ba'thist regimes had gained power in Iraq and Syria. Nasser's charisma, though tarnished by the collapse of the UAR, still retained much of its luster. Prominent Muslim leaders, partly to capture the appeals Nasser continued to inspire among disillusioned masses, were still paying homage by seeking his audience in deference to the hopes the Egyptian leader espoused on behalf of Arabism and Arab unity.

Except for the abortive coup of the Syrian Social Nationalist Party (SSNP) on New Year Eve of 1961, incidences of political unrest and collective protest until 1969 were infrequent, relatively nonbelligerent, and generally not symptomatic of internal socioeconomic disparities or grievances. It is interesting to observe that the highest incidence of political violations (about 22) during that 10-year interlude involved the suspension or confiscation of newspapers or the arrest of editors. Virtually all of these occurred between 1961 and 1963. By then Lebanon was already serving as a refuge for political, largely left-wing, dissidents fleeing oppressive regimes in Syria and Iraq. Its fairly open and liberal press became a vehicle for mobilizing dissent. Hence, the bulk of the charges and indictments against the press involved arresting or suspending newspapers and editors for publishing material deemed injurious to adjacent regimes or detrimental to relations with them. For example, *an-Nahar* was suspended for ten days on May 3, 1961 for publishing a cartoon depicting Lebanon as a Syrian Province. *Al-Hawadith* was suspended on July 22, 1963 for publishing an offending caricature of an Arab State. Newspapers and their editors were also targets of direct hostility. Seven of all fourteen explosions during the decade of the sixties were directed against their premises and headquarters. One of the two political assassinations during this same period was that of Kamel Mroueh (May 16, 1966), editor of *al-Hayat*.

Strikes were the second-largest category of political unrest. Almost half of the 20 recorded strikes were organized by students and dealt with or were incited by political regional issues. For example, American University of Beirut's (AUB) students called for a strike (December 18, 1960) in protest of the suspension of thirteen of their colleagues for participating in a demonstration commemorating the anniversary of Algeria's independence. Likewise, their strike of February 22, 1961 was to observe the UAR anniversary. As early as March 13, 1963, AUB students were already protesting violations of the sanctity of Palestinian camps. Only one student strike (organized by Lebanese University students on February 16, 1965) dealt with purely academic issues. Protesting students were demanding a single building to house all proposed five faculties.

The bulk of labor strikes involved government and public-sector employees such as dockyard workers, public school teachers, judicial assistants, and telephone operators in protest of low wages, poor work conditions, or dismissal for union organizing. IPC workers and Lebanese University teachers resorted to a hunger strike in protest of arbitrary dismissal. Student demonstrations were also generally benign and nonconfrontational during this period. Two were nonideological, calling for reform of school syllabi in Tyre or in support of teachers' demands for wage increases. The remaining five were political in character, such as those in support of Palestinian commandos or to protest the visit of the Sixth Fleet or a proposed visit of the American Ambassador (Dwight Porter) to Tyre on May 7, 1967.

The incidence and intensity of armed clashes were also infrequent in number and moderate in magnitude. Of the dozen reported by internal security, seven were tribal in character involving factional rivalries or local feuds in regions of the Beqa', Baalback, and Akkar. All the remaining five were political or ideological clashes. Of these only two — those between the Kataib and PPS in the wake of the latter's aborted coup — reflected internal political disputes. The rest were militant confrontations between Nasserites and their adversaries among Baathists and Communist coalitions. One in particular, a telling precursor of other such episodes, took place in Kahalé on March 5, 1961. A convoy to vehicles on route of Damascus to congratulate Nasser on the third anniversary of the UAR was attacked as it drove through the Maronite village.

All other manifestations of political unrest during the early 1960s were associated with fallouts from the aborted attempt of the PPS to seize power. Hence 1962 witnessed successive efforts by security forces to pursue, arrest, and disarm fugitives, to dissolve illegal political parties, and to deport dissident groups suspected of being involved in the coup.

The stunning defeat of the Arabs in the Six Day War of 1967 more, perhaps, than any other event was instrumental in reshaping the character and consequences of the local, regional, and global dialectics. Israel emerged as the dominant single power in the East Mediterranean. The U.S.-Egyptian power-balance, which had dominated the region, was profoundly redrawn. Since the U.S., unlike the role it played in the Suez Crisis of 1996, was not directly involved in the outcome of the fighting, it could now pose as a more neutral arbiter in the ensuing postwar debacle. Nasser's resounding defeat and the humiliation of the regular armies that the Egyptian and Syrian regimes had been building up for more than a decade, left a gaping sense of dishonor and bitterness. The resurgent popular enthusiasm, incited by Palestinian resistance as an emancipatory movement, received an added spur. To embittered masses, the purity and idealism of armed struggle as a purging and rejuvenating source of insurgency, seemed like a timely antidote to national defeat and humiliation.

The soul-searching weeks and months following the *nakba* witnessed a surge of popular support for the spirit of armed struggle and the sacred rights of return to one's homeland. While the Lebanese in general were unanimous in their support of such rights, they differed markedly on the issue of how armed resistance can be "regulated" without compromising the sovereignty and security of the state. Maronites, in particular, even at a time when the enthusiasm for emancipatory and nationalist consciousness was at its height, expressed serious reservations about Palestinian militancy. Indeed, the initial euphoria the movement inspired as a popular "street" phenomenon, must have provoked the added fears of the traditional Maronite establishment. No such hesitation, at least initially, was visible among large segments of the Muslim communities. As we shall see, it was not until late in the 1970s, when destabilizing consequences of Israeli reprisals became much too disruptive, that Shi'ites in the South started to veer away from the initial solidarity and support they had displayed for the guerrilla movement.

Within such a setting, the Palestinian issue was not only destined to wreak havoc on the country's political system, it was also instrumental in radicalizing sources of discontent and ultimately transforming the country into a proxy war zone. In the late 1960s, the government was already embroiled in a relentless series of Palestinian-related crises at the very time manifestations of socioeconomic unrest and mobilization were becoming more visible. From then on, as Helena Cobban has persuasively argued, the Palestinian and internal Lebanese issues became "inextricably intertwined" (Cobban 1985: 106). When radical students at the American University of Beirut were protesting tuition increases or Henry Kissinger's visit in connection with the proposed Arab-Israeli peace settlement, they employed Palestinian tactics. Indeed many of the students at the time were supporters of the newly emerged Rejection Front. Likewise, when factory workers were protesting inflation and cost of living increases, they too raised Palestinian rhetoric. Finally, Shi'ite villagers invoked Palestinian slogans to mobilize their outrage against the savage Israeli onslaughts in the South.

As will be shown later, the South and subsequently the southern urban fringe of Beirut proved to be a particularly propitious site for nurturing progressive and radical mobilization among ravaged shi'ites. Of course, symptoms of heightened politicization had appeared much earlier in the South. The Communist Party, for example, had by the early 1940s already made inroads in villages such as Bint Jbeil, Nabatieh, and Marjayoun (for further derails see Shararah 1996). The rising tide of Arab Nationalism, Socialism, and Ba'th, during the 1950s and 1960s, found receptive grounds for party recruits in the urban quarters of Sidon and Sour. Marouf Saad and Mussa al Sadr drew upon this same pool of disgruntled but listless masses to sustain their political leadership and nascent social movements late in the 1960s. (see Ajami 1986; Norton 1987; Halawi 1992). It was, however, the eman-cipatory ethos whipped up by Palestinian resistance movements that reso-nated most ardently with the profound feelings of neglect and dispossession Shi'ites were suffering at the time. At least initially their political strategies converged.

This interplay between growing internal tensions and outside pressures was, by the early 1970s, becoming more pointed, even contentious. Internal tensions were first apparent in the growing rifts within the ranks of Franjieh's government. It was more though than just a reflection of commonplace fractious and petulant cabinet politics. The President's feudal and cliente-tistic political leanings and predispositions made him, at times, unreceptive to some of the progressive and liberal reforms of his "youthful" cabinet.[4] Manifestations of economic prosperity, particularly the construction boom and increase in the growing imports of luxury products, were marred by rising inflation and heightened economic woes of the underclass.

On their own these would not have amounted to much had they not been exacerbated by mounting external pressures. Three, in particular, were becoming more grievous. First, adjacent Arab regimes, in the throes of 1967 *nakba*, were getting more boisterous and radicalized. Second, the fledgling PLO was still basking in the afterglow and idealism of an emancipatory movement. Hence, its appeals among disenfranchised strata, disgruntled pol-iticians and growing mass of agitated students were becoming more strident. Finally, and as usual, the most onerous pressures came from the South. Israeli reprisals to commando operations (always much more immense and disproportionate in scale) devastated the southern regions and heightened the exodus of villagers. Makeshift shelters in Beirut's urban fringe swelled with displaced refugees. Early in 1970, the official report of the regional governor estimated the number of refugees from southern borders at about 23,000. It is then that the gap between the privileged few and the masses became more stark.

It is not within the scope of this study to explore the full impact of the establishment of the state of Israel in 1948 on the destabilization of Lebanese society or its direct involvement in inciting and exacerbating the magnitude of hostility and warfare in the region. This has been ably and amply done elsewhere.[5] I only wish to underscore in passing the magnitude of Israel's avowed expansionist strategies, particularly how it managed to establish and stockpile one of the most sophisticated technologies of human destruction, reinforced by the glorification of terror and revenge as the moral and sacred values of its national identity. Aggression in Israel has always been rationalized as "reprisal operations" vital for the national security and survival of the state. In Israel virtually everything and anything is justified on the basis of Jewish survival and security. Israel's policies, from ethnic dominance and outright discrimination and violation of human rights of Arabs and other minorities to campaigns of terror and provoked aggression, are legitimized on such pretexts. Sharett, one of its many military heroes, was forthright and unequivocal in this regard. He felt no need to restrain or mince his words when he recorded the following in his Diary: "Reprisals are the vital lymph. . . . they help us maintain a high tension among our population and army. . . . the long chain of false incidents and hostilities we have invented. . . . the many clashes we have provoked (As cited in Rokach 1980: 7). He goes further to spell out the threefold purpose of such deliberate and unprovoked aggression — namely to push weak Arab states into confrontations, to demoralize their population, and to disperse Palestinians.

The very establishment of the state of Israel has been predicated and sustained by the victimization of others. It began its existence by cutting all links between northern Palestine and the rest of the Arab world, blocking economic and trade routes with Arab Africa, and devastating the economy of South Lebanon. Its expansionism has also involved ruthless measures for annexing and appropriating entire villages. In the process up to 1.2 million Palestinians have been uprooted, evicted, and displaced from their homes. In 1948 close to 900,000 Palestinians were living in the territory that became Israel. Of these, it is estimated that 750,000 were expelled (Masalla 1997: 21). In 1949, 17,000 bedouins from the Negev area were expelled to Egypt. Another 2,700, a year later, were uprooted to Gaza. During the 1967 war, 340,000 were uprooted. Another 12,500 were expelled shortly after by Israel (for these and other estimates see Harris 1956: 109; Zureik 1997: 24–30). The UN partition plan had allotted the Jewish state 5,500 square miles. By the end of 1955 it had expanded to about 8,000. After the 1967 war the number leaped to 30,000 (Petran 1987: 66).

Lebanon, of course, stands in stark contrast to virtually everything epitomized by Israel as a confessional, exclusionary, and highly militarized state. Lebanon's consociationalism condoned pluralism and was much more open and tolerant of coexistence between religious communities. As such, Lebanon was an irritant, especially to Israel. Michel Chiha was, perhaps, among the first Lebanese intellectuals to caution how Lebanon's very existence has always stood as a threat to Israel. (Chiha 1964: 124). At least, Israel's justification for its own exclusionary ethnicity — that coexistence between different confessional groups is impossible — becomes unsupportable.

Throughout its history, as we have seen, Lebanon served as a refuge and asylum to a wide spectrum of itinerant and dissident groups. Its fairly open liberal democracy, laissez faire economy and uncensored press were both envied and feared by all its neighboring monolithic regimes. Above all, Lebanon pursued a pacifist national security policy and was clearly the least militarized. Its essentially professional army of about 19,000 — with not more than 100 tanks and 150 artillery and anti-aircraft guns, an air force of 24 fighter aircraft, and a navy of 5 patrol boats — was symbolic and could not pose a threat to anyone (see Hanf 1993: 161).

In this regard, Lebanon is antithetical to Israel's glorification of military might or soldiering as a vector for national identity or political resocialization. Prewar Lebanon had no mandatory program of conscription or military service. Members of the military claimed little status or social prestige and clearly not role models for aspiring adolescents or enterprising college graduates eager to entertain unconventional career options. A military career has never been highly coveted. Indeed, the bulk of the volunteers were drawn from the least privileged strata of society.

So enamored were some Lebanese with their country's neutrality and pacifist overtures that Lebanon's "weakness" was, at times, transformed into "strength"; a ploy for diplomatic posturing and preserving the country's defenseless borders. During much of its checkered history, the diplomatic guarantees for Lebanon's neutrality appeared to work. At least until the mid-1960s, Israel's border with Lebanon was its most peaceful, because it regarded Lebanon as its least hostile neighbor. The Arab states also respected Lebanon's decision not to participate militarily in the struggle against Israel. This is at least what came to pass at the 1964 summit conference of the Arab League in Cairo. The Khartoum summit, three years later, had also reconfirmed this by deciding that Palestinian guerrilla activities could be launched only from Jordan, Syria, and Egypt. Lebanon was expressly excluded.

Israel's expansionist strategies and deliberate efforts to destabilize and provoke confrontations with vulnerable and bickering confrontation states changed all this. Lebanon was inescapably drawn into the fray. The Cairo Accord of 1969 had of course stipulated general guidelines and spelled out strict limits on military operations. It required, for example, that PLO military command should "co-ordinate" with the Lebanese Army "without compromising the overall sovereignty of Lebanon." The guidelines, like all their subsequent attempts to impose any restraints on their freedom of operations, were at best rhetorical. Given the nascent emancipatory mood, Palestinians felt, as Helena Cobban (1985:109) put it "exuberantly free to express their nationalist sentiments." A collision course with the Lebanese Army or security forces became inevitable.

The first such episode occurred in 1964 when the Deuxième Bureau arrested guerrillas before they could infiltrate into Israel. One of the suspects (Jalal Ka'wash, a resident of Ein el-Hilweh camp near Sidon) died under detention. Security forces claimed that Ka'wash had committed suicide. Palestinians and the growing mass of Lebanese sympathizers rejected, of course, such allegations. Government was accused of torturing detainees and a string of boisterous demonstrations were staged in protest. Shortly after Yassir Arafat and some of his closest associates were held for forty days on the grounds they had provoked confrontations between Lebanon and Israel because of unrestrained Fatah activities. From 1965 on, such contentious and explosive episodes became more frequent and volatile. There is no need here to provide another chronicle of the pattern and escalation of such belligerent encounters.[6] Two overriding realities, however, need to be emphasized. The efforts of Palestinians to extend and consolidate the base of their operations in Lebanon, and the spiraling character and magnitude of Israel's reprisals.

Once again the Six-Day War stands out as a critical threshold. Until then the bulk of operations of Fatah within Lebanon consisted of transporting guerrilla commandos through on route from Syria to Israel. After 1968, when Palestinian resistance broke down in the occupied territories, the PLO shifted the base of their operations to southeast Lebanon. Because of the influx of armed Palestinians into the Arkoub district, the area swiftly acquired the label of "Fatah Land." The adjoining mountain tracks, through which reinforcements and supplies filtered, was dubbed "the Arafat Trail" in a reference to the notorious "Ho-chi-Minh Trail." The cycle of violence, from then on, became relentless.

As usual, Israeli reprisals, provoked or otherwise, were always infinitely more savaging in their impact. When commandos shelled a Kibbutz close to the border, Israel retaliated by devastating entire villages with heavy artillery. On December 28 1968, guerrillas lobbed rockets at an Israeli plane on a runway in Athens. The Israelis responded by landing commando units at Beirut's International Airport, blew up oil-tanks and destroyed virtually the entire fleet of Middle East Airlines planes on the airport tarmac.

Of course in this, as in other subsequent reprisals, the intention was to compel the indisposed and reluctant Lebanese government to clamp down on the growing freedom of Palestinians to mount terrorist attacks from Lebanon. The outcome was always the opposite. By their indiscriminate assault on civil targets and innocent villages, Israeli incursions only served to arouse public uproar, stir up waves of solidarity with the Palestinians, and provoke a chain of cabinet crises.

In the spring of 1969 the Lebanese army tried, but without success, to force the Palestinians to withdraw from the border villages so as not to give Israel further pretexts for retaliations. Doubtlessly the Palestinians' resistance was made possible by the timely support they received from Syrian-backed Saiqa troops. In repeated clashes with the Lebanese Army they prevailed and were able to secure their hold on refugee camps. More compelling, the alliance between the Palestinians (particularly Habach's Popular Front) and the Lebanese left proved astonishingly effective in soliciting the political support of recalcitrant Muslim politicians. It must be noted here that Kamal Jumblat, as Minister of Interior during the final months of Charles Hilu's troubled presidency, announced in December 1969, that the Parti Populaire Syrien (PPS), the Community Party, the Arab Nationalist Movement (ANM), the Ba'th Socialist Party, and the Armenian Tashnak and Hentshak, could resume operations. All these suspended parties became hefty fodder for mobilization.

It was also then that the popularity of the Palestinian resistance, as a source for reclaiming damaged national identities and correcting social injustices, was growing. At a time when other Pan-Arab, ideological and party loyalties were being undermined, the idealism inherent in selfless nationalist struggle and sacrifice emerged as a source of collective euphoria. Most striking was the transformation in the standing and public image of the refugee. The camp subculture, which in the past had festered with muted hostility and bitterness, received a rehabilitative jolt. The lethargic youth of the camps, who more perhaps than other hapless refugees had suffered all the pathos and indignities of dereliction and marginalization, now found themselves catapulted into enviable role models. Once meek and fearful, treated with a mixture of contempt and pity, they now brandished their newfound powers with assertiveness, often bordering on arrogance.

Since refugee camps dotted strategic locations and points of intersection along the urban sprawl, they could easily disrupt daily routines and become sources of fear, lawlessness. and public disorder. This they did, often with abandon and total disregard for the havoc they wreaked on the host country which had been very sympathetic and accommodating in nurturing the aspirations as well as the organizational and logistical demands of a revolutionary movement. Their violations were abusive and intimidating. They imposed roadblocks, detained, abducted, and kidnapped arbitrarily on the pretexts that suspects posed a threat to the ideals of the revolution. They occupied, seized, appropriated property, illegally levied impositions, and breached ordinary human rights of innocent citizens.

Carefree and peripatetic Lebanese, averse to such treatment by legitimate forces of law and order, were more than incensed that they had to succumb to the intimidations of Palestinian refugees. Maronites, in particular, and other communities already outraged by the stipulations of the Cairo Accord, felt all the more infuriated and deceived. If the state could not ensure the security of its own citizens, they felt justified to take over such responsibilities, let alone safeguarding their country's violated integrity and national sovereignty. Much like the Palestinians, they were left with no choice but to shape their destiny with their own hands. In no time private militias and paramilitary organizations became, as we shall see, a regular appendage to political aspirants and communal leaders.

During 1971 and 1972, violations committed by Palestinian organizations, as reported by the Lebanese Army Intelligence Unit, reached as high as 787 episodes. As shown in table 7.1, carrying arms and explosives, kidnapping civilians and imposing checkpoints and roadblocks, witnessed the sharpest increases.

Late in the 1960s the incidence and form of violence started to change. Parallel to, perhaps associated with the above, the pattern of violence contrary to what Winslow asserts was becoming more focused and directed rather than random and sporadic (see Winslow 1996: 172). For example tribal clashes, common in the early sixties, disappeared by the late sixties. All armed clashes between civilians and security forces were either a by-product of attempts by security forces to impose controls on Palestinian commandos or a direct response to protests against such restrictions. Such confrontations were also not confined to Beirut and its suburbs but extended to other regions.

Armed clashes between security forces and Palestinian commandos reached their peak by the late sixties. In 1969 alone, 33 such confrontations occurred. The clashes, if measured by the growing incidence of casualties, were definitely becoming much more belligerent. They also displayed evidence of outside incitement and provocation. Even seemingly peaceful demonstrations protesting government restrictions on guerrilla operations were deflected into violent confrontations. On April 23 and 24 simultaneous demonstrations in Tripoli, Saida, Baalback, Sour, Mt. Hermon, and Nabatieh resulted in more than fifteen casualties and many injuries. Funeral proces-

TABLE 7.1 Violations Committed by Palestinian Organizations 1971–1972

Type of Violation	1971	1972	Total
Carrying unlicensed Weapons and Explosives	44	85	129
Shooting and gun fire on different occasions	49	54	103
Attacks and Threats to kill civilians	30	30	69
Rocket attacks on Israel from Lebanese Territory	30	34	64
Infiltration into restricted military areas	30	31	61
Attacks on Army and Internal Security	23	30	53
Training and arming of Lebanese Citizens	28	23	51
Arrests and Kidnapping of Civilians	17	33	50
Public display of Weapons	20	23	43
Armed Robberies	27	9	36
Shooting at Lebanese Military Targets	8	18	26
Establishing Checkpoints and searching cars	3	16	19
Premeditated Killing of Civilians and Military	9	9	18
Refusal to stop at army checkpoints	9	4	13
Occupying houses by force	5	7	12
Unlicensed buildings	6	4	10
Collecting contributions by force	7	2	9
Attacks on Lebanese government authorities	—	8	8
Bombing and use of explosive devices	—	—	3
TOTAL	345	442	787

Source: Lebanese Army Intelligence Report, dated 3–7–1973

sions of fallen victims always provoked added violence and heightened public tension. A state of emergency was imposed, schools suspended, and public demonstrations prohibited. On May 5, 1969 more than 200 Ba'athists were deported because of their presumed guilt in participating in the disturbances. Infighting between and among the various splinter commando organizations started to surface.

By 1973 the more radical wings of the PLO began to display their powers with greater aplomb and bravado; thereby disclosing the impotence and vulnerability of the government. The political disarray in Lebanon, particularly at a time when border villages in the South were relatively quiet and the economy was fairly prosperous, must have become apparent to Israel. On April 10, 1973 without any overt provocation, Israeli commandos conducted their second adventurous raid into Lebanon during which three prominent Palestinian leaders were assassinated. This embarrassing assault, much more than the relentless ground invasions the Israeli Army had already launched in 1972, provoked a flurry of incriminations, mayhem, street agitation and, as expected, a succession of government crises.

Outraged Palestinians displayed their fury with greater arrogance and disregard of state security and low and order. They were not only avenging their fallen leaders but also becoming increasingly apprehensive about the dread of being "liquidated." The inaction of the Lebanese Army, the silence of their Arab "brethren," and the complicity of foreign powers only served to compound their fears of that impending threat. By then, particularly after the Black September in Jordan (1970), Lebanon was the only site from which they could operate (protected by Cairo Accord and the Melkart Protocol) with some measure of freedom and autonomy.[7]

Palestinians were naturally keen on consolidating their position in Lebanon, which had become their last remaining stronghold. Their defeat in Jordan coincided with two other changes. The Assad regime in Syria was subjecting the PLO to more stringent controls and Sadat in Egypt was already embarking on his policy of reconciliation with Israel. In Lebanon, on the other hand, the sociopolitical setting seemed considerably more favorable. The emancipatory activism heralded by Palestinians was receptive, as we have seen, to the emergent spirit of dissent taking root among at least three rather vociferous segments of society: the displaced and unemployed, a radicalized student movement, and those spirited portions of the middle-class and intelligentsia, who were driven by public and social consciousness but barred from full political participation in the political system.

Indeed, Lebanon at the time was not only the Palestinian's bastion of last resort, it was an ideal terrain for the kind of base support the PLO was trying to cultivate. Their notorious camps, situated at strategic locations in nearly all major cities, were granted by the Cairo Accord's quasi-extraterritorial rights. Because of the sympathies, reliable allies, and public enthusiasm they managed to cultivate among segments of the society, they were able to translate this into more substantial autonomy and freedom of operations. Lebanon's fairly advanced and open communication and diplomatic networks were also exploited effectively. Even Edward Said, who normally is not very charitable in his assessment of Lebanon's political culture, described Beirut as a "substitute for Palestine" and went further to single out the Lebanese period in the history of the Palestine national movement as the "first truly independent period of Palestinian national history" (Said 1983: 5–8).

To consolidate their position, the PLO reached out to align itself with those strident segments of society. More decisive, they were able to extend their cover of the Cairo Accord to other radical groups. In effect, this meant that all militia organizations in Lebanon could now employ the same pretext to arm themselves. From then on, as Kamal Salibi put it, Lebanon was thus "transformed into a powder keg with a fuse attached" (1976: 69). Such dreaded portents of militancy were, in fact, visible in the steady escalation of clashes between Palestinians and the Lebanese Army. What was more ominous, they unleashed a campaign of terror of its own.

The first serious clash between Palestinians and armed Christian militias took place in March 1970 in the Maronite village of Kahhalè on the main highway to Damascus. The episode, clearly an outcome of the highly charged atmosphere, came to epitomize many other such seemingly unprovoked confrontations. A Palestinian convoy, escorting the body of a fallen guerrilla killed by hashish smugglers, was caught in a traffic jam as they drove through the village. Somehow, a clash ensued with the villagers and the army, leaving two dead and a score of wounded on both sides. On its return trip from Damascus the convoy fired into the air as it drove through the village. The firing, intended as a gesture of defiance, was mistaken for an attack by the vigilant villagers. After the first episode, rumors were rife that such an attack was imminent. The watchful villagers shot back, killing ten Palestinians. Heavy fighting broke out between Palestinian and Kata'ib commandos which, for the first time, was extended to involve the Tel al-Za'tar camp and the predominantly Maronite suburb of Dekwaneh. It was then that Bashir Gemayyel the younger son of the veteran Kata'ib leader, was kidnapped and held in Tel al-Za'tar. Though released after a ten-hour captivity, the episode provoked a week of heavy fighting. It ended with the intervention of the Egyptian and Libyan envoy but left in its trail a mood of deep suspicion and hostility.[8]

Two critical byproducts are worth noting. First, the radicalization and growing militancy of the Palestinians was beginning to create internal divisions and widen rifts within society. Second, there was a profound change in the character and magnitude of violence. Fairly restrained and ordinary forms of collective protest often turned into contentious confrontations. Street demonstrations, personal squabbles, and clan feuds were deflected into confessional and communal hostility. As early as March 1970, evidence of sharp polarization among the governing elite became more visible. While the Kata'ib and their traditional allies were demanding that Palestinians observe restrictions demanded by the Cairo Accord, many of the Sunni Muslim leaders, along with Kamal Jumblat and his left-wing coalitions, were reluctant to impose any such restraints on commando activities. The Kata'ib were legitimately alarmed by the heightened militarization of Palestinians. Successive consignments of heavy armaments, via Libya, Syria, and Iraq, had, in effect, transformed refugee camps into full-fledged military bases. With the tacit support of the Lebanese Security Forces and the Deuxième Bureau, the Kata'ib stepped up the level of confrontation with the Commandos.

I dwell briefly on this episode because, in several recognizable features, it prefigured what was to become a recurrent scenario: A volatile political setting provokes a confrontation which almost always is followed by contradictory accounts as to how and why the fighting started. In this case, Palestinians claimed they were victims of a deliberate ambush while the Kata'ib argued that they had simply fired back in self-defense. Those uninvolved in the fighting attribute the episodes to mysterious or unidentified parties (agents provocateurs). If groups from among the fighters are held suspect, they are dismissed as "uncontrolled" or "unrestrained" elements. Either way, casualties on either side provoke a round of bloodier and more widespread fighting. Foreign intervention manages to arrange a cease-fire which turns out to be no more than a brief respite for combatants to brace themselves for another round of vengeful bloodletting.

From then on the incidence and intensity of tension and violence, at virtually all levels of society, rose sharply. As Palestinians sustained their guerrilla operations, Israeli reprisals became more savage, thereby pressuring the Lebanese Army to clamp down on them. As early as 1965, incidents between the Lebanese Army and the guerrillas were already becoming frequent. From the very beginning the resources of the army and security forces, let alone their will to do so, seemed much too deficient to monitor the long Syrian–Lebanese borders or to impose effective controls on their operations within the camps or across the southern borders. Even restrictions demanded by the Cairo Accord could not be enforced, given the sharp schisms and rifts within the movement. For example, the government in May 1970 had prohibited the PLO from firing rockets from Lebanese Territory or from bearing arms in towns and villages. Fatah and Saiqa complied with such expectations. The Popular Front, however, which had rejected the Cairo Accord, refused to comply. More grievous, even if the Lebanese government was willing and able to rightfully protect its sovereignty, it was restrained by the mounting pressures from Arab states with radical and more conservative regimes alike.

The test of wills between the army and the Palestinians did not always end up in favor of the former. President Franjieh's resolute determination was tested early in his term (October 5, 1970) before he even had formed his first cabinet. A plane with a contingent of Arab Liberation Front guerrillas from Baghdad landed at Beirut airport. The Cairo Accord prohibits air entry. Guerrillas are allowed to travel only by overland routes through Syria. Accordingly, they were not permitted to disembark. After some heady and tense negotiations, the plane was forced to return to Baghdad. It was clear though that in such ensuing encounters the government might be hard pressed to uphold its legitimate rights. Indeed, all subsequent attempts to tame Palestinians (by force or through diplomatic accords), proved inconclusive. All military confrontations and showdowns between them became humiliating as the failure of the Lebanese Army was more demonstrable.

As several observers have recognized, Lebanon was trapped between two inherently contradictory logics: the natural rights of Palestinian struggle could not be reconciled with the concerns for sovereignty of the Lebanese state. Any attempt to accommodate the two, as John Cooley (1979) put it, is as futile as squaring the circle.

As state powers continued to erode, the incidence and magnitude of unrest was bound to deteriorate further. As noted earlier episodes of major conflict were already increasing in the early seventies. After the Yom Kippur war of 1973 and the stunning Israeli raid on Beirut, the number increased to 23. By 1975 it leaped to 83, and by the outbreak of hostilities it escalated further to 171 (see Winslow 1996: 175–78 for further substantiation). Even manifestations of seemingly benign socioeconomic tensions grew fiercer and more unmanageable. Students went on strike over issues of tuition, while academic programs were deflected into sporadic agitation and aimless turmoil.

In December 1973, radical students with the tacit support of the Rejection Front, organized a strike to protest the first visit in Henry Kissinger's shuttle diplomacy on behalf of the flawed Arab-Israeli peace process. A strike in Tripoli by students protesting the high cost of living escalated into a bloody confrontation with the police. Like other such episodes, the event sparked off a quick succession of violent street demonstrations. Kissinger's second visit (February 1974) provoked more combative and radical flare-ups. The student strike organized for that purpose was transformed into sporadic rioting and bloody clashes with security forces. The same disruptive fate befell other student protests. For example, the general strike they called for reforming and upgrading the academic standards of the Lebanese University also ended up in bloody clashes with security forces.

Similarly, labor protest over wages, cost of living, working conditions, and amendments in labor legislation were politicized and derailed into confrontation with security forces. Most symptomatic of the change in the character of violence was the appearance of acts of terror largely unrelated to internal tension. Associated with this was the proliferation of clandestine organizations and undercover splinter groups who often claimed responsibility for the terror. For example, on October 18, 1973, explosions off the Lebanese coast damaged the underwater cable network between Beirut and Marseille, thereby cutting off communications with Europe and the U.S. On the same day, a group of gunmen, members of a so-called Arab Communist Organization, raided the Bank of America and held customers and staff hostage. They demanded, among other things, the payment of $10 million in support of the Arab war effort.

In the fall of 1974, as the security situation deteriorated further, public disorder became more rampant. Bomb explosions, vandalism, robberies, abductions became almost daily events. Most striking were the abductions and political assassinations of Arab rather than Lebanese political figures. For example, all five successful or attempted assassinations that took place in 1972 involved dissident Arab politicians (e.g. Umar Suhayri, Tunisian opposition leader; Muhammad Umran, former Syrian Deputy Premier) or Palestinian activists (e.g Ghassan Kanafani, leader of PELP; Anis Sayegh, director of Palestine Research Center; or Bassam Abu Sharif, Sayegh's Successor). Gangs of local thugs and their henchmen rose to assert control over urban quarters and remote regions, thereby challenging state authority and the powers of traditional political *zu'ama*. In Tripoli, for example, Ahmad al Qaddour took control of the city's old quarter and terrorized the entire city. Likewise in Akkar, the Ba'rinis in al-Funaydiq challenged the powers of the traditional feudal clan. Other such factional rivalries erupted elsewhere and sparked off a succession of armed clashes and street brawls, particularly in Beirut and Saida. In July 1974, a series of squabbles flared up between smugglers, and this escalated into armed confrontations between the hostile suburbs of Beirut; namely, Tel-al-Za'tar and Dekwaneh.

The most disruptive, of course, were the escalating clashes between the Palestinians and the army and, eventually, between the Palestinians and Christian militias. After the 1973 October war, the PLO was under pressure to suspend their commando operations. They sustained nonetheless their militant struggle within the occupied territories. This only served to compound Israel's massive reprisals thereby heightening tension in the southern villages and Beirut's teeming suburbs, where most of the uprooted refugees ended. As the pressure mounted — both because of the ferociousness of Israeli reprisals and the anarchy incited by the unrestrained behavior of dissident Palestinian groups and their radical allies—political polarization within society became sharper and more boisterous. The Kata'ib and Chamoun's National Liberation Party called for a referendum on the presence of Palestinians in Lebanon. Muslims and their left coalitions denounced the government, particularly the repressive strategies of the army, in foiling the Palestinian struggle.

Increasingly, Lebanon found itself caught between two treacherous options: Destroy the armed presence of PLO and risk the grim prospects of Christian–Muslim confrontations. Entrust the army with the task of defending the South and suffer the inevitable humiliations of a military showdown with Israel. Typically, Lebanon opted for inaction and played for time. Time, however, was hardly a bearer of good tidings. As usual, external events aggravated the magnitude of internal disarray and conflict. Though Lebanon did not participate in the Yom Kippur war of 1973, it paid heavily. Its radar installations in Baruq, which Lebanon had placed at the disposal of Syria, were destroyed. Israel also resumed its merciless incursions into the South thereby abetting another influx of embittered refugees into Beirut. More taxing, as Syria's disengagement agreement with Israel took effect, Lebanon was to bear from then on the bulk of the beleaguering fallout of the Arab–Israeli conflict.

The Arab league conference in Rabat, convened in October 1974 to allay differences between contentious Arab states, did just the opposite. Like most other such summits the disagreements became sharper. The Rabat summit recognized the PLO as the sole legitimate representative of the Palestine people. It also resolved that no further separate accords were to be concluded with Israel. Sadat, however, went ahead and signed another disengagement agreement with Israel (the infamous Sinai II). This outraged both Syria and the Rejection Front. Lebanon was destined to become, once again, the hapless proxy victim and surrogate battlefield for resolving Intra-Arab rivalries over the Palestinian crisis. By the time Presidents Assad and Franjieh met in Chtaura (January 7, 1975), to contain the gathering storm in Lebanon, the tension was already getting out of hand.

Israel is always more than ready to up the ante. A massive attack by Israeli troops devastated the border village of Kfar Chouba. Shortly after, separate units within the Rejection Front—the Iraqi-sponsored ALF and the Popular Front—attacked the Lebanese Army at different points, including the military barracks in Tyre. Typically, Arafat blamed a dissident PFLP faction for the incident. The Kata'ib lambasted the PLO for its failure to control recalcitrant and fractious elements and, hence, held it accountable for deepening anarchy and the sources of polarization and communal hostility in the country.

Both belligerent groups were seething with hostility and fear: Palestinians were dreading the portents of another "Black September" in Lebanon; the Christian parties were perhaps more terrified by the prospects of a shift in the locus of power toward the Palestinians and their leftist allies. Like combatants in a mortal showdown, the conflict started to degenerate into a fateful life and death struggle. The conflict over "divisible" socioeconomic and political rivalries were deflected into belligerent and deadly struggles over the "indivisible" issues underlying primordialism, national sovereignty, collective identity, and communal loyalties. The inflammable tinder needed just a flint. Anything, in fact, could have sparked off the fire. The spark, as usual, needed little by way of provocation.

Outbreak of Violence: Early Rounds

Chronicles of Lebanon's protracted hostilities often single out distinctive violent episodes such as the fishermen's strike in Saida in February 1975 and/or the Ain al-Rummaneh bus incident of April 1975 as flash points; the forerunners of the menacing cruelties of armed conflict. One observer goes as far as to dub the bus incident as the "Sarajevo" of the Lebanese civil war to draw analogies to comparable incidents associated with the onset of World War I (Khalidi 1979: 47). Dramatic as such claims are, they are not altogether inappropriate. Given the critical issues underlying these events and the momentous, bloody forces they unleashed.

The fishermen's strike is practically a textbook case of a genuine protest movement being transformed into a violent confrontation. Struggling underprivileged fishermen of Sidon and other coastal towns had called for peaceful demonstrations to mobilize opposition against the licensing of a large enterprise (Proteine Company) to mechanize Lebanon's fishing industry. The fishermen perceived such threatening prospects as monopolistic incursions by foreign capitalists attempting to undermine their traditional sources of livelihood. Much like other deprived groups in the country, they were already bitter about the government's neglect and failure to resist or contain the devastations wrought by Israeli incursions into the South. That Proteine was formed by a joint Kuwaiti and Lebanese capital under the chairmanship of none other than Camille Chamoun deepened their bitterness and sense of injustice. The popular media depicted the crisis, with all the hackneyed Marxist clichés, as a confrontation between "small fish and the devouring sharks." At the time, around 40 percent of Sidon's population and nearly half of its fishermen were of Palestinian origin. The inhabitants and much of the city's political cultures displayed progressive leanings and were sympathetic to Palestinian resistance and other radical and populist movements.

For some obscure reason, the peaceful demonstration degenerated into a riot during which Marouf Saad, Sidon's most popular leader, was killed. In this, as in subsequent confrontations between government troops and protesters, the intervention of the army in suppressing popular uprisings, given its impotence in protecting the country's defenseless borders, generated acrimonious parliamentary debates and precipitated a succession of cabinet crises. In addition, the disruptive episodes reawakened communal hostility and suspicion and sharpened the incipient polarization within society.

Challenging or questioning the role or sovereignty of the army, almost always invites divisive reactions. The Muslim establishment, with its radical and Palestinian allies, hastened to denounce the army as a fascist, exclusive instrument of Maronite power and supremacy. They decried its role in suppressing liberties and legitimate grievances of dispossessed groups while failing to protect defenseless villagers from Israeli raids. They called for the dismissal of its commander-in-chief and an overhaul of the army structure to permit a more equitable participation of non-Christian recruits and officers. Maronite factions, and their Christian supporters in East Beirut, responded by organizing their own demonstrations in support of the army. They proclaimed March 5 as "Army Day," denounced efforts to undermine its sovereignty, and cautioned against the growing intervention of Palestinians in Lebanon's domestic affairs.

In short, the Sidon episodes and the violent convulsions they unleashed gave vent to many of the unresolved issues which were to precipitate and sustain subsequent rounds of civil strife: regional and sectarian socioeconomic disparities, Israeli incursions and the radicalization of Palestinian refugees, Muslim demands for a more equitable share of power and political participation, state impotence, and the role of the army in maintaining internal security.

The havoc provoked by the Sidon disturbances had hardly been contained when another seemingly spontaneous incident, bloodier and much more grievous in magnitude and consequences, was thrust on an already charged political situation. As Pierre Gemayyel, leader of Kata'ib, was attending (April 13, 1975) a new Maronite church in Ain al-Rummaneh, the Christian suburb of east Beirut, a car with unidentified assailants and concealed license plate broke through a Kata'ib security line and fired at the Sunday church congregation. Four men, including two of Gemayyel's personal bodyguards, were killed. Later in the afternoon of the same day a bus with twenty-eight passengers, mostly Palestinian commandos returning to their camp of Tel-al-Za'tar from a parade in one of the Muslim quarters of West Beirut, somehow drove back through the same anxiety-ridden area. Outraged Christian militias were in no mood but to assume that the armed Palestinians in the bus were coming back to provoke another confrontation. In vengeance, they ambushed the bus and massacred all its passengers.

The reactions, both politically and militarily, were instantaneous and sweeping. That same evening leaders of the National Movement (a coalition of Arab Nationalists, leftists, and other radical Muslim factions and parties under the leadership of Kamal Jumblat) met and called for the dissolution of the Kata'ib party and the expulsion of its two ministers from the cabinet. At the same time, PLO leader Yassir Arafat appealed to Arab heads of state to intervene and foil what he termed a conspiracy to disrupt Lebanese–Palestinian relations.

The conflict, given the intensity of recriminations and reawakened communal hostility on both sides, could not have remained a nonbelligerent political discord. It quickly touched off waves of violence. Armed clashes between the Kata'ib and Palestinian commandos erupted virtually everywhere around Beirut. Fierce fighting with rockets and artillery raged for three days. Much of the fighting assumed first the form of shelling and counter-shelling between the Kata'ib forces, perched on the Ashrafieh heights of the Christian quarter in East Beirut and Palestinians in the outlying refugee camps in Tel-al-Za'tar. As the fighting intensified, it soon engulfed adjacent quarters and neighborhoods and displayed sectarian and communal manifestations. Armed Palestinians from Bourj-al-Barajina camp, reinforced by Shi'ites, Communists, and other dissidents, terrorized the predominantly Christian suburbs of al-Shayyah and Haret Huryak. Shops and homes were plundered. Cars parked along the streets were blown up. Business enterprises with known religious affiliations or identities were dynamited. Gangs and unidentified elements took to the streets. They blocked roads and alleyways and committed wanton acts of crime. For the first time passageways of the southern outskirts of Beirut became unsafe.

By the time Mahmoud Riad, Secretary General of the Arab League, arrived in Beirut to mediate a truce, the fighting had already claimed the lives of about 350 persons. No sooner was a cease-fire secured (April 16, 1975) and life returned to normal, when snipers appeared in downtown Beirut and parts of Tripoli. Business life in both cities came to a sudden halt. As in the Sidon episodes, mysterious "third parties" were held responsible for inciting the violence; with each side attributing the mischievous elements to their adversaries. Typically, the Kata'ib and their allies were inclined to accuse the "borrowed ideologies" of radical extremists and saboteurs of "rejectionist" Arab regimes. Palestinians and the National Movement blamed Maronite "Isolationists" and state agents; part of what was perceived as an international conspiracy to liquidate the resistance as a movement.

As in the Sidon episodes, the bus incident precipitated a government crisis, polarized and deepened hostility between the major antagonists and escalated the level of terror and fear. It also unleashed new forms of violence disclosing, thereby, the communal character of enmity: i.e., targeted kidnapping of sectarian groups, sniping and artillery barrages between neighborhoods and strategically located suburbs. Likewise, the Ain al-Rummaneh episode revealed the volatility of the issues underlying the conflict: Palestinian presence, socioeconomic disparities, and the call for political reforms, the role of the army in maintaining security, and overarching polemics over Lebanon's sovereignty and its national identity. Indeed, the security and reform issues became interlocked.

Existing political parties — i.e., the Kata'ib, Chamoun's National Liberation Party (PNL), Kamal Jumblat's PSP, The Syrian Nationalist's PPS — all stepped up their mobilization by launching recruitment, training and paramilitary campaigns. Maronites in particular, already outraged by an assassination attempt on Camille Chamoun and the kidnapping of Bashir Gemayel, felt ostensibly the most threatened and ardent to arm itself. Chamoun built up a "Tiger Militia" under the leadership of his son Danny. The Franjieh's in Zghorta did likewise under the command of Tony, Suleiman's older son and heir apparent to assume the clan's leadership. Reminiscent of the mobilizing role the Maronite clergy had played during the peasant uprisings and other episodes of communal strife in the nineteenth century, they were more than just covertly active in inciting and organizing armed struggle. Then, as now, they were directly involved in recruiting; in providing material support, and in offering shelter and refuge in times of public distress. More important, they gave moral and spiritual legitimization to acts of violence. No sooner, for example, had the fighting broken out in 1975 than the Maronite monastic orders, under the leadership of Sharbel Kassis, stepped promptly into the fray. Sunni Muslim, Shi'ite, and Druze clerics and religious leaders were equally involved in mobilizing their own communities.

Precipitously many of the original nonsectarian sources of unrest receded and the conflict began to acquire a life of its own and was deflected into directions unrelated to the initial sources of hostility. The fighting also became bloodier and more belligerent as it evolved into a struggle over the "indivisible" and more contentious principles of communal identity, cultural heritage, national sovereignty, pluralism, and sectarian coexistence.

8   Scares and Scars of War

> "Violence, Unlike Achilles' lance, does not heal the wounds that it inflicts."
> — John Keane, *Reflections on Violence* (1996)

> "The animus was always the same: Whether nation, province, or city, whether religion, class or culture — the more one loved one's own, the more one was entitled to hate the other. . . . Through the centuries politicians had exploited this human trait. In the knowledge that hatred can be cultivated with a purpose, they constructed enemies in order to bolster domestic concord."
> — Peter Gay, *The Cultivation of Hatred* (1993)

For almost two decades, Lebanon was besieged and beleaguered by every possible form of brutality and collective terror known to human history: from the cruelties of factional and religious bigotry to the massive devastations wrought by private militias and state-sponsored armies. They have all generated an endless carnage of innocent victims and an immeasurable toll in human suffering. Even by the most moderate of estimates, the magnitude of such damage to human life and property is staggering. About 170,000 people have perished; twice as many were wounded or disabled; close to two thirds of the population experienced some form of dislocation or uprootedness from their homes and communities. By the fall of 1982, UN experts estimated that the country had sustained $12 to 15 billion in damages, i.e., $2 billion per year. Today, more than one third of the population is considered to be below the poverty line as a result of war and displacement, (for these and other related estimates, see Hanf 1993: 339–57; Labaki and Abu Rjeily 1993).

For a small, dense, closely-knit society of about 3.5 million, such devastations are, understandably, very menacing. More damaging, perhaps, are some of the sociopsychological and moral concomitants of protracted hostility. The scars and scares of war have left a heavy psychic toll which displays itself in pervasive post-stress symptoms and nagging feelings of despair and hopelessness. In a culture generally averse to psychoanalytic counseling and therapy, these and other psychic disorders and fears are more debilitating. They are bound to remain masked and unrecognized and, hence, unattended to.

The demoralizing consequences of the war are also visible in symptoms of vulgarization and impoverishment of public life and erosion of civility. The routinization of violence, chaos, and fear only compounded the frayed fabrics of the social order. It drew seemingly nonviolent groups into the vortex of bellicose conflict and sowed a legacy of hate and bitterness. It is in this fundamental sense that Lebanon's pluralism, radicalization of its communities, and consequent collective violence have become pathological and uncivil. Rather than being a source of enrichment, variety, and cultural diversity, the modicum of pluralism the country once enjoyed is now generating large residues of paranoia, hostility, and differential bonding.

It is also in this sense that enmity today, although the outward manifestations of violence have ceased, is deeper, assumes different forms, and is more pervasive than it used to be at the initial stages of hostility. This is why the almost myopic concern with exploring the etiology of violence is not just short-sighted. It has become counter-productive.

Unfortunately, much of literature on civil strife, as I have been repeatedly suggesting, continues to be concerned with its inception or origins. Consistent with the overwhelming bias inherent in most of the leading perspectives on collective violence, explorations of episodes of political unrest in Lebanon, as elsewhere, have also been skewed in that direction. Hence we know too much already about the preconditions, changing political settings (both regional and global), economic disparities, and cultural and psychological circumstances which motivated and predisposed groups to resort to collective protest.

Instructive as such analyses have been, they tell us little about the forces which sustained and escalated violence. Nor do they disclose the changing forms of violence. More striking, perhaps, they do not help in understanding how seemingly ordinary citizens get entrapped in it and how traumatized groups come to cope with chronic hostility and fear. Likewise, this obsession with the origin of violence tells us comparatively little about the impact of the war on collective memory, on changes in group loyalties, collective psychology, perceptions, and changing attitudes toward the "other."

At least in the case of Lebanon this obdurate exercise has become rather futile; at best a laborious elaboration of the obvious. For example, it is not very uncommon that a fragile, pluralistic society caught up in regional and superpower rivalries should display a high propensity for violence. The lack of political integration in such fragmented political cultures, has been cited over and over again as a major cause, indeed a prerequisite for political unrest. One could, likewise, write volumes about the destabilizing impact of internal socioeconomic disparities, the presence of Syrians, Palestinians, Israelis, or the unresolved regional and global rivalries without adding much to what we know already. It is hoped that the evidence provided thus far, both historical and recent, is sufficient to dispel the need for further substantiation of such uncontested realities.

What is, however, in need of elucidation is the persistence, growing intensity, shifting targets of hostility, and the way violence acquired a momentum and a life of its own unrelated to the initial sources of conflict. Most atrocious in the case of Lebanon was the way violence splintered further as intercommunal rivalries degenerated into fratricidal bloodletting. The ecology of violence, reinforced by the demonization of the "other," provided the sources for heightened vengeance and entrapment into relentless cycles of retributive in-fighting. Hence, much of the conventional characterization of the initial stages of civil unrest (i.e. "Christian versus Muslim," "right versus left") became readily outmoded as internecine violence and factional turf wars became bloodier and more rampant.

First, and perhaps most compelling, there is a need to elucidate how some of the menacing cruelties of the war were normalized and domesticated. I will here argue that by "sanitizing" the war and transforming it into an ordinary routine, terrorized groups were able to survive its ravages. By doing so, however, they also allowed it to become more protracted and diffused.

Second it is equally interesting to show how the war managed to reshuffle the country's social geography and impose its grotesque and ferocious logic on private and public space. Here again, by seeking shelter in communal solidarities, traumatized groups were able to find temporary relief from the atrocities of war. What enabled them, however, to survive its immediate horrors rendered them more vulnerable to other more menacing long-term consequences. By distancing themselves from the demonized "other," they could of course release their guilt-free aggression with impunity, but they also made themselves easier and more accessible targets to focused and directed acts of hostility. Casualties on both sides mounted. More damaging, the prospects for reconciliation and peaceful coexistence became unlikely.

Finally, and more intriguing, various communities displayed strikingly different predispositions and evolved different adaptive strategies to cope with the cruelties of protracted strife. Hence an anomalous disparity became visible: communities which were victims of a larger magnitude of trauma were not necessarily those which also displayed greater stress and posttraumatic symptoms. An effort will be made to account for this disjunction. How is it, in other words, that some of the more traumatized groups were able to put up with the adversities of war without the accompanying syndromes of distress and demoralization? Such resilience, incidentally, may also give us a clue as to the persistence of violence. This is another seemingly anomalous situation the Lebanese were entrapped in. The more adept they became at adjusting to, or coping with, the cruelties of strife, the more opportunities the war had to reproduce and sustain itself. Once again, the enabling and disabling features became inexorably locked together.

The Domestication of Violence

In some remarkable respects one might well argue that wars in Lebanon, despite some of their appalling manifestations, displayed comparatively little of the bizarre and grotesque cruelties associated with so-called "primitive" and/or "modern" forms of extreme violence, namely; the systematic rape of women by militias, the ritual torture and mutilation of victims, the practice of forcing family members of a family group at knife or gunpoint to kill each other (for further such details, see Wilson 1992). Other than episodic massacres and vengeful acts of collective retribution (Sabra and Chatila, Tal-el-Za'atar, Damour, etc.), there was little to compare to the planned and organized cruelty on a mass scale typical of extermination campaigns and pogroms.

The incivility of collective violence in Lebanon was, nonetheless, visible in some equally grotesque pathologies, particularly those which domesticated killing by rendering it a normal, everyday routine; sanitized *ahdath* (events) bereft of any remorse or moral calculation. A few of these pathologies merit highlighting here.

Collective violence assumed all the aberrant manifestations and cruelties of relentless hostility. Unlike the other comparable encounters with civil strife, which are often swift, decisive, and localized, and where a sizeable part of the population could remain sheltered from its traumatizing impact, the Lebanese experience has been much more protracted and diffuse. The savagery of violence was also compounded by its randomness. In this sense, there is hardly a Lebanese today who was exempt from these atrocities either directly or vicariously as a mediated experience. Violence and terror touched virtually everyone.

Fear, the compulsion for survival, and efforts to ward off and protect oneself against random violence had a leveling, almost homogenizing, impact throughout the social fabric. Status, class differences, and all other manifestations of privilege, prestige, social distinctions, which once stratified and differentiated groups and hierarchies in society, somehow melted away. At least for the moment, as people fell hostage to the same contingent but enveloping forces of terror and cruelty, they were made oblivious of all distinctions; class or otherwise. Other than those who had access to instruments of violence, no one could claim any special privilege or regard. As Mai Ghoussoub poignantly put it, when people are suddenly thrown together into anguished corridors and damp cellars, their status, as well as their bodies, is squeezed:

> The Civil war that sprang upon the country very soon engulfed the neighbourhood in which Farid's second home was located. The stagnant, cozy routines of its inhabitants were so abruptly disrupted, and their streets turned so easily into an apocalyptic battlefield, that it was as if it had all happened under the spell of some magician's wand. The settled little hierarchies of these petty bourgeois clerks, these shopkeepers and their families, were suddenly huddled into anguished corridors and damp cellars, in which their status was squeezed as well a their bodies. The powerful and the less powerful, the compassionate and the unfeeling, the arrogant and the timid were brought to one same, common level in their struggle for survival. Nothing of what had once been mattered any longer, in the apocalyptic fires that governed their fate at this moment. They all feared the streets, and submitted willingly to the chaos of control by trigger-happy fighters (Ghoussoub 1998: 66).

Equally unsettling, the war had no predictable or coherent logic to it. It was everywhere and nowhere. It was everywhere because it could not be confined to one specific area or a few combatants. It was nowhere because it was unidentified or linked to one concrete cause. Recurring cycles or episodes of violence erupted, faded, and resurfaced for no recognized or coherent reason.

The warring communities had also locked themselves into a dependent relationship with violence and chronic conflict. It was in this sense that violence became both protracted and insoluble. It was a form of self-entrapment that blocked all avenues of creative peaceful change. It was also sustained by a pervasive feeling of helplessness — a demoralized and obsessive dependency on external patrons and foreign brokers. It was then that violence started to assume a "tunnel vision" effect; i.e., a tendency to focus, almost obsessively, on one's involvement in the conflict to the exclusion of any other relevant course of action. In acute cases, every action, every statement, and every institution acquired value and meaning in relation to the conflict itself. So much so, in fact, that some observers at the time went so far as to suggest that in Lebanon violence and chronic fear became an intrinsic part of society's ethos and mythology. It became an absorbing and full-time concern that overshadowed many other societal, communal, and individual interests (Azar 1984: 4). It may sound like a cliché, but violence became a way of life; the only way the Lebanese could make a statement or assert their beings and damaged identities. Without access to instruments of violence, one ran the risk of being voiceless and powerless. The meek inherited nothing. This is perhaps one of the most anguishing legacies of the arrogance and incivility of violence.

Abhorrent as it was, the fighting went on largely because it was, in a sense, normalized and routinized. In the words of Judith Shklar (1982) it was transformed into an "ordinary vice;" something that, although horrible, was expectable. The grotesque became mundane, a recurrent every-day routine. The dreadful and outrageous were no longer dreaded. Ordinary and otherwise God-fearing citizens could easily find themselves engaged in events or condoning acts which had once provoked their scorn and disgust. In effect, an atrocious raging war became, innocuously, *ahdath*. This "sanitized" label was used casually and with cold indifference; a true wimp of a word to describe such a dreadful and menacing pathology. But then it also permitted its hapless victims to "survive" its ravages.

This is precisely what had transpired in Lebanon: a gradual pernicious process whereby some of the appalling features of protracted violence were normalized and domesticated. Killing became inconsequential. Indeed, groups engaged in such cruelties felt that they had received some kind of cultural sanction or moral legitimization for their grotesque deeds. Those witnessing these horrors were also able, by distancing themselves from their gruesome manifestations, to immunize themselves against the pervasive barbarism. Witnessing and coping with the dreaded daily routines of war became also remorseless and guilt-free.

The manifestations of such normalization are legion. In the early stages of the war, when bearing arms and combat assumed redemptive and purgative features, any identification with the garb, demeanor, or life style of fighters and militia groups became almost chic — a fashionable mode of empowerment and of enhancing one's machismo. Belligerency, in fact, was so stylized that groups literally disfigured themselves to ape such identities. Bit by bit, even the most grotesque attributes of the war became accepted as normal appendages to rampant chaos and fear. Literary accounts and personal diaries, often in highly evocative tones, recorded such pathologies with abandon. The daily body count was greeted with the same matter-of-factness, almost the equivalent, of a weather forecast. Fallen bodies, kidnapped victims, and other casualties of indiscriminate violence became, as it were, the barometer by which a besieged society measured its temporal daily cycles.

The most dismaying no doubt is when those grotesque features of war begin to envelop the lives of innocent children. All their daily routines and conventional modes of behavior — their schooling, eating and sleeping habits, playgrounds, encounters with others, perceptions, daydreams and nightmares, their heroes and role models — were inexorably wrapped up in the omnipresence of death, terror, and trauma. Even their games, their language became all warlike in tone and substance. Their makeshift toys, much like their fairly tales and legends, mimicked the cruelties of war. They collected cartridges, empty shells, and bullets. They played war by simulating their own gang fights. They acquired sophisticated knowledge of the artifacts of destruction just as earlier generations took delight in identifying wild flowers, birds, and butterflies.

There is hardly an aspect of Lebanese children's lives, and this is certainly more so for adolescents who were involuntarily drawn into the fray of battle, that is exempt from such harrowing encounters. They have all been homogenized by the menacing cruelties of indiscriminate killing and perpetual anxieties over the loss of parents and family members. These and other such threats, deprivations, and indignities continue to consume their psychic energies and traumatize their daily life. Successive generations of adolescents have, in fact, known little else.

Norbert Elias's notion of the "sanitization of violence" could be of relevance here. It will most certainly help us in understanding not only how violence is camouflaged, even stylized so that it no longer seemed offensive, but also how in the process it becomes protracted and insoluble (Elias 1988). During certain interludes, these same horrors were not only bereft of any moral outrage, but also managed to become sources of fascination and venues for public amusement and entertainment. The war, in other words, began to acquire some of the trappings of a spectacle, not unlike the morbid fascination frenzied spectators encounter in the stylized rituals of a Spanish bullfight! (Marvin 1986: 133–34). In this recent book *On Killing* Dave Grossman argues that a continuous presence of images of violence threatens to blur the line between entertainment and the conditioning of fighters and soldiers. He refers to a "stage of desensitization at which the infliction of pain and suffering has become a source of entertainment. . . . we are learning to kill and we are learning to like it." (Grossman 1998: 311).

Mai Ghoussoub (1998) recounts the transformation of Said, a cheerful, gentle and spirited grocer's son, the neighborhood's most beloved boy, who was metamorphosed overnight into a calloused and heartless killer. Said, the pride of his doting parents, was slated to fulfill his father's ambitions by pursuing his studies at the Ecole Hôteliére. Instead, he was so enamored, almost entranced and bewitched, by the machismo and charisma of the militiamen, that he could not resist the temptations of becoming one himself, to the chagrin of his dismayed parents. This is how Ghoussoub depicts the episode signaling this anguishing transformation:

> . . . despite his mother's warnings and lamentations, he watches the groups of militiamen who have settled in at the entrance of the building facing his. They have all that he does not. And they are free of all that he has. The sad, heavy, constant presence of his parents worrying about him. Asking him to hide and keep a low profile, to smile, like his father, at every potential customer on the street. The militiamen are dressed in a relaxed but manly way. They sit on their chairs with their heads slightly tilted back, their feet stretched way in front; cigarettes hanging constantly from the corners of their mouths, they smoke and laugh and play cards just there on the pavement, next to the door of the building. When a jeep stops with a great sudden screech of its brakes, two lithe and powerful young men jump out of it, adjust the position of their kalashnikovs on their shoulder and give big, generous handshakes to each one of the militiamen that Said sees from his balcony. To Said these men are beautiful. The glamour that emanates from them fills his heart with dreams. He would like to belong to these men, to be as attractive as they are, to feel as young and powerful as they feel, instead of totting in his miserable little apartment (Ghoussoub 1998: 81).

This facile, almost effortless and light-hearted socialization of innocent adolescents into militancy is another disheartening legacy of the arrogance and incivility of collective violence. Said's case is far from anomalous. Legions of such recruits, often from privileged families, stable and entrenched middle-class groups, became willing volunteers to join the ranks of militias as regular fighters or subsidiary recruits. If one were to believe autobiographical accounts and obituaries of fallen fighters (often doctored to heighten notions of self-sacrifice, daring, and fearlessness) they were all lionized into heroes. On the whole though, particularly during the early rounds of fighting, one saw evidence of over-zealous fighters buoyed by the bravados of their savagery and warmongering. This is again a reminder that killing is not a byproduct of some crazed deranged monster-like creatures driven by the frenzy of atavistic and irresistible compulsion for aggression. Rather, it is more often the outcome of ordinary people being induced by like-minded peers or the aura of bearing arms in defense of threatened values.

This is precisely what Primo Levi had in mind when he cautioned: "Monsters exist, but there are very few of them to present any real danger. Those who are dangerous are the ordinary men" (Levi 1987: 73). More anguishing is to bear witness to how ties of trust, intimacy, benevolence, and caring among neighbors were readily deflected and deformed into enmity. Once embroiled in such structured and heightened enmity one is compelled to take revenge for his group even though he might bear no particular grudge against those he is driven to kill. Here, as well, entrapped combatants flung themselves, often irrationally, into a relentless war of gangfights linked to one concrete cause. Recurring cycles or episodes of violence erupted, faded, and resurfaced for no recognized or coherent reason.

Multiple and Shifting Targets of Hostility.

Unlike other comparable experiences with protracted collective violence, hostilities were not confined to a limited and well-defined number of combatants and adversaries. By the spring of 1984, there were no fewer than 186 warring factions — splinter groups with different backgrounds, ideologies, sponsors, grievances, visions, and justifications as to why they had resorted to armed struggle.

This bewildering plurality of adversaries and shifting targets of hostility has rendered the Lebanese experience all the more gripping and pathological. For example, from 1978 to 1982, the interlude falling between the two Israeli invasions, the country was besieged and beleaguered by every conceivable form of collective violence and terror. The sheer volume and magnitude of such incidents peaked in comparison to all other "rounds" or phases of the war. Keeping track of who is fighting whom, the swift oscillation in proxies and sponsors, the targets of hostility and the motives propelling and sustaining the violence, is a dizzying and perplexing task.

Virtually no area in the country was spared the ravages of war. All traditional battlegrounds were ablaze. East Beirut was still under siege from relentless Syrian bombardments. Many residents had no choice but to seek shelter, much as they resented it, in West Beirut. Though at the time the neighborhoods of West Beirut were still riven with turf battles between the Mourabitoun and other Sunni Muslim rivals, the area was considerably safer than the heavy and devastating artillery the Syrian army was lobbing on Achrafieh. Both suburbs of Beirut were embroiled in intra-communal turf wars. After Bashir Gemayyel had, in the spring of 1977, gained effective control of the Lebanese Forces (a coalition of all Maronite militias comprising the Phalange, Tanzim, Tigers, and Guardina of the Cedars), he proceeded to consolidate his powers by subduing his potential rivals. Hence there were repeated incursions into the strategic coastal enclaves of Dany Chamoun's Tigers, particularly the military installations at Safra and Amsheit. These were finally overrun (on July 7, 1980), after bloody and fierce assaults that wiped out more than 150 innocent civilians. Christian militias were also engaged in intermittent clashes with Armenian leftists and the Syrian National Party (PPS).

On the southern fringe, confrontations between Amal and the Communist Action Group were already degenerating into open shootouts, a preamble to the more contentious struggles between Amal (Syrian proxy) and Hizbollah (Iran proxy). Further north, Franjieh militias were still trying to thwart the encroachment of Gemayyel's Lebanese Forces into their traditional fiefdom. In June of 1978 Bashir's commandos made that fateful crossover which ended in the tragic massacre at Ihden where more than 40 members of the Franjieh clan were murdered, among them Tony (the heir apparent to the clan's leadership) along with his wife and child.

In Tripoli, Sunni centrists, supported by the Syrians, Sunni radicals, the PLO and Muslim fundamentalists, were engaged in pitched battles. In the central Beqa', Bashir Gemayyel had hoped to link up with Zahlé, the area's largest Christian enclave. Armed and assisted openly by the Israelis, he was overzealous in his foray. The Syrians, refusing to allow such an affront to their hegemony in so strategic a region, besieged the town and after three months drove Bashir out of the Beqa'.

The Palestinians and Shi'ites were also embroiled in their own pernicious strife between and among their various factions. In addition to the ongoing rivalry between pro-Syrian Amal and pro-Iranian Hizbullah, the latter were split further between those loyal to indigenous leaders like Sheikh Fadlallah and those affiliated to Iranian clerics in the Beqa'. The infighting within the various Palestinian factions was also unabated. Pro-Iraqi and pro-Syrian groups sought to resolve their regional and ideological rivalries in Lebanon. So did Arafat loyalists and those opposed to him.

This became much more pronounced in the wake of mounting public discontent with the PLO's disgraceful conduct during the Israeli invasion of 1982. Syria deployed several of its local proxies to undermine Arafat. It bolstered the "Palestine Salvation Front" with the military units of Abu Musa, the dissident Fatah rebel. Along with Syria's Sa'iqa and the Yarmouk brigade, they battled Arafat's forces from mid-1983 onward. In Tripoli they were joined by the local 'Alawi militias and other Syrian client groups such as the Ba'th and the Syrian Nationalists (SSNP).

Marginal ethnic groups like Armenians and Kurds, as if drawn into the vortex of belligerency by contagion, also found alibis to redress their differences by resorting to arms.

The most beleaguered region was, of course, the South. Added to the inveterate splits between the traditional Zuáma and scions of feudal and neofeudal families, the South was splintered further by the volatile and vacillating hostility between and among the various Shi'ite and Palestinian factions, exacerbated by the presence of the Israeli-backed Saad Haddad's South Lebanese Army (SLA). The major breach between Amal and Hizbullah, fueled by their Syrian/Iranian patronage, was also compounded by the emergent hostility between Palestinians and Shi'ite villagers. Embittered by the havoc and terror Palestinians were spawning in the South, some of the Shi'ites of Jabal Amil were drawn into the SLA.

So multiple, so various and so explosive are the sources of belligerency that South Lebanon is doubtless today the world's most perennial war zone and killing field; a peerless example of "low intensity conflict" that never goes away. Given the mounting casualties, the prefix "low" does not do justice to the magnitude of cruelties the southerners are subjected to. Its hapless victims live in constant fear of being killed or displaced without anticipating or recognizing the identity of their victimizers. Villagers are not only terrorized by the turf wars of warring factions, they are also the surrogate victims of state-sponsored armies. Indeed, villagers in the South could well be bombarded by at least six different sources: Israelis, Syrians, Palestinians, the so-called Republic of Free Lebanon (SAL), UNIFEL and the Lebanese Army, if and when it ventured South.

Is this not the ultimate in incivility, a feature that compounds the futility and impunity of violence? Innocent citizens are victimized without being cognizant of the source or identity of their victimizers. In this regard it might be argued that Palestinians, Jews, Armenians, Kurds, Corsicans, Ulster Catholics, Basques, Bosnians, Serbs, Croats, and other victims of collective suffering are, perhaps, more privileged. They can, at least, identify and mobilize their outrage against those who might be held accountable for their suffering. The Lebanese are still unable, as a result, to vindicate their collective grievance. They have been homogenized by fear, terror and grief, but remain divided and powerless in identifying and coping with the sources of their anguish. Hence, they are gripped by a crushing sense of impotence and entropy. They are bitter but cannot direct or mobilize their fury and rage toward recognized targets.

The Reterritorialization of Identities

Another striking and unsettling feature of protracted and displaced hostility is the way the Lebanese had been caught up, since the outbreak of fighting in 1975, in an unrelenting process of redefining their territorial identities. Indeed, as the fighting blanketed virtually all regions in the country, few were spared the anguish of uprootedness from their spatial moorings. The magnitude of such displacement is greater than commonly recognized. Recent estimates suggest that more than half, possibly two thirds, of the population has been subjected to some transient or permanent form of uprootedness from their homes and communities. (see Labaki and Abou Rjeily 1993).

Throughout the war, in other words, the majority of the Lebanese were entrapped in a curious predicament: that painful task of negotiating, constructing, and reconfirming a fluid and unsettled pattern of spatial identities. No sooner had they suffered the travails of dislocation by taking refuge in one community, than they were again uprooted and compelled to negotiate yet another spatial identity or face the added humiliation of reentry into their profoundly transformed communities. They became, so to speak, homeless in their own homes, or furtive fugitives and outcasts in their own communities.

The sociopsychological consequences of being dislodged from one's familiar and reliable landmarks, those of home and neighborhood, can be quite shattering. Like other displaced groups, the Lebanese became disoriented and distressed because the terrain had changed and because there was no longer a neighborhood for them to live in and rely upon. "When the landscape goes," says Erikson "it destroys the past for those who are left:

people have no sense of belonging anywhere" (Erikson 1976). They lose the sense of control over their lives, their freedom and independence, their moorings to place and locality and, more damaging, a sense of who they are.

Those bereft of place become homeless in at least three existential senses: they suffer the angst of being dislodged from their most enduring attachments and familiar places; they also suffer banishment and the stigma of being outcasts in their neighborhoods and homes; and finally, much like the truly exiled, they are impelled by an urge to reassemble a damaged identity and a broken history. Imagining the old places, with all their nostalgic longings, serves as their only reprieve from the uncertainties and anxieties of the present.

The effusive war literature, particularly the generation of so-called "decentrist" woman writers and other disinherited liberals, is clearly symptomatic of efforts to grapple with such damaged identities. A growing number of such exiled and uprooted writers felt homeless in their own homes. Much like the earlier generation of exiled Lebanese and Syrian poets (e.g. Gibran and Rihani), who had transformed the anguish of their uprootedness into inventive literary movements (the Pen Bond and the Andalousian Group), they too found shelter in a "poetics of disaster." (See Alcalay 1993: 99). But this brief, blissful interlude turned much too afflictive as the tensions between the vibrant Beirut of old and its descent into anomie became more flagrant. Khalil Hawi's suicide on the eve of the Israeli invasion is seen now as a grim icon, a requiem for that dark abyss in Arab cultural history (see Ajami 1998; Alcalay 1993).

Curiously, the women of the "Beirut Decentrists" found some redemption in the war. The chaos, anarchy, meaninglessness, and the ultimate collapse of society gave women, paradoxically, a liberating place and a new voice (for an elaboration of these see, Cooke 1988; Alcalay 1993; Manganaro 1998). Oddly, as society was unraveling itself and the country was being stripped of its identity, women were discovering venues for validating and asserting their own identities. Incidentally, this transformative, redemptive role did not mean that women were in effect challenging patriarchy or that they were partaking in efforts to restore civility in society. As Miriam Cooke put it:.

Their concern was not to gain acceptance into a predominantly male preserve but rather to register a voice. These voices were rarely heard in what has been termed the public domain. Their content was deemed irrelevant. How could the expression of private experience become acceptable outside its immediate confines? How could the apparently mutually exclusive domains of private and public, of self and other, be reconciled? Boundaries had to be challenged and shown to be fluid, elusive. Such a radical reassessment and construction of social and literary order could not be achieved spontaneously. . . .

The Lebanese war provided the context. Violence in this case represented universal loss of power, but it also undermined the private/public dichotomy, revealing the private to be public, and the personal to be universal. Private space became everyone's space and it was appropriated literarily in a collective endeavor to express and thereby understand the reign of unreason (Cooke 1988:87).

But even as "voice" or mere writing, the works of women remained marginal and frivolous. The writers themselves harbor few illusions in this regard other than seeing their personal struggles to forge new identities or reconstruct more coherent selves being closely tied to the enveloping malaise surrounding them. Cooke again provides evidence from the works of Ghada Al-Samman, Etél Adnan, Claire Gebeyli, Hoda el-Námani and Hanan al-Shaykh in support of this:

By the late 1970s, the Beirut Decentrists were using language to create a new reality. Their writings were becoming transformative, even prescriptive. As self-censorship gave way to uninhibited expressions of self-assertion, the hold of the oppressive male critic was shaken. It was only with the breakdown of Lebanon's identity as an independent patriarchal polity that women began to assert their female identity publicly. . . . As the violence persisted and men fought senseless battles or fled, women came to realize that the society of which they were also members was collapsing; unravelling seams revealed the need for collective responsibility, but also for responsibility for the self. The individual had to become aware to survive. The time that was right for assertion of female identity coincided with the disintegration of the country's identity (Cooke 1988: 11–12).

This poignant predicament, i.e. where the horrors of war are transformed into redemptive features, is most eloquently expressed in Hanan al-Shaykh's novel, *The Story of Zahra*. The torrents of war do not only render all conventions irrelevant and sweep away the hollowness of daily routine and restore normality. They accomplish much more: they became sources of illumination and self-discovery. Indeed, given the catalogue of horrors Zahra was subjected to in her "normal" life (i.e. intimate violence, incest, rape, arranged marriage, divorce), the war seemed more than just a blissful anti-dote and return to normality. In her own words, it made her "more alive and more tranquil."

> This war has made beauty, money, terror and convention all equally irrelevant. It begins to occur to me that the war, with its miseries and destructiveness, has been necessary for me to start to return to being normal and human.
>
> The war, which makes one expect the worst at any moment, has led me into accepting this new element in my life. Let it happen, let us witness it, let us open ourselves to accept the unknown, no matter what it may bring, disasters or surprises. The war has been essential. It has swept away the hollowness concealed by routines. It has made me ever more alive, ever more tranquil (al-Shaykh 1986: 138).

Equally devastating has been the gradual destruction of Beirut's and, to a large extent, the country's common spaces. The first to go was Beirut's Central Business District, which had served historically as the undisputed focal meeting place. Beirut without its *Burj*, as the city center is popularly labeled, was unimaginable. Virtually all the vital public functions were centralized there: the parliament, municipal headquarters, financial and banking institutions, religious edifices, transportation terminals, traditional souks, shopping malls, and theaters kept the prewar Burj in a constant state of activity. There, people of every walk of life and social standing came together.

With decentralization, other urban districts and regions in the country served as supplementary meeting grounds for common activities. They, too, drew together, albeit on seasonal and interim bases, groups from a wide cross-section of society, thereby nurturing outlets germane for coexistence and plural lifestyles. Altogether, there were very few exclusive spaces beyond the reach of others. The social tissue, like all seemingly localized spaces, was fluid and permeable.

Alas, the war destroyed virtually all such common spaces, just as it dis-mantled many of the intermediary and peripheral heterogeneous neighbor-hoods, which had mushroomed with increasing urbanization in cities like Tripoli, Sidon, and Zahleh. The war did not only destroy common spaces. It also encouraged the formation of separate, exclusive, and self-sufficient spaces. Hence, the Christians of East Beirut had no compelling urge to cross over to West Beirut for its cultural and popular entertainment. Likewise, one can understand the reluctance of Muslims and other residents of West Beirut to visit resorts and similarly alluring spots of the Christian suburbs. With internecine conflict, quarters within urban districts, just like towns and villages, were often splintered into smaller and more compact enclosures. Spaces within which people circulated and interacted shrunk still further. The sociopsychological predispositions underlying this urge to huddle in insulated spaces is not too difficult to trace or account for.

This compulsion to huddle in compact, homogeneous enclosures further "balkanized" Lebanon's social geography. There is a curious and painful irony here. Despite the many differences that divide the Lebanese, they are all in sense homogenized by fear, grief, and trauma. Fear is the tie that binds and holds them together — three primal fears, in fact: the fear of being marginalized, assimilated, or exiled. But it is also those fears which keep the Lebanese apart. This "geography of fear" is not sustained by walls or artificial barriers as one observes in other comparable instances of ghettoization of minorities and ethnic groups. Rather, it is sustained by the psychology of dread, hostile bonding, and ideologies of enmity. Massive population shifts, particularly since they are accompanied by the reintegration of displaced groups into more homogeneous, self-contained, and exclusive spaces, have also reinforced communal solidarity. Consequently, territorial and confessional identities, more so perhaps than at any other time, are beginning to converge. For example, 44 percent of all villages and towns before the outbreaks of hostilities included inhabitants of more than one sect. The sharp sectarian redistribution, as Salim Nasr (1993) has shown, has reshuffled this mixed composition. While the proportion of Christians living in the southern regions of Mount Lebanon (i.e. Shouf, Aley, Upper Metn) was 55 percent in 1975, it shrunk to about 5 percent by the late 1980s. The same is true of West Beirut and its suburbs. Likewise, the proportion of Muslims living in the eastern suburbs of Beirut has also been reduced from 40 percent to about 5 percent over the same period (Nasr 1993).

Within urban areas, such territorial solidarities assume all the trappings and mythology of aggressive and defensive "urban '*asabiyyas*" which exist, Seurat (1985) tells us, only through its opposition to other quarters. In this sense, the stronger the identification with one's quarter, the deeper the enmity and rejection of the other. Seurat's study also suggests that, once such a process is under way, a mythology of the quarter can develop. In it, the quarter is seen not only as the location where a beleaguered community fights for its survival, but also as a territorial base from which the community may set out to create a utopia, a world where one may live a "pure" and "authentic" life, in conformity with the community's traditions and values. The neighborhood community may even be invested with a redemptive role and mission (such as the defense of Sunni Islam in the case of Bab Tebbane in Tripoli which Seurat was studying). Hence, the dialectics between identity and politics may be better appreciated. Politics implies negotiation, compromise, and living side by side with "the other." Heightened feelings of identity, however, may lead one to a refusal to compromise, if negotiation comes to be perceived as containing the seeds of treachery that may undermine the traditions, values and "honor" of one's community. In such a context, violence and polarization become inevitable: precisely the phenomena that have plagued Lebanon for so long.

The Spaces of War

Another graphic and poignant consequence of protracted and displaced strife is the way the spaces of war, and their concomitant geographies of fear, started to assert their ferocious logic on public and private spaces. Much of Lebanon's geography and landscape took on the grotesque nomenclature of the war. Equally telling is the ingenuity of its besieged hostages in accommodating this menacing turnover in their spatial surroundings.

Public thoroughfares, crossroads, bridges, hilltops, and other strategic intersections which served as links between communities were the first to be converted. They became treacherous barriers denying any crossover. The infamous "Green Line" (which acquired its notorious label when shrubs and bushes sprouted from its tarmac after years of neglect) was none other than the major thruway (the old Damascus Road) which connected Beirut to its hinterland and beyond. Likewise, major squares, traffic terminals, and pedestrian shopping arcades became desolate "no-man's lands," *al Mahawir al-taqlidiyya* (traditional lines of confrontation) or *khutut al tamas* (lines of confrontation).

While prominent public spaces lost their identity, other rather ordinary crossings, junctures, hilltops, even shops, became dreaded landmarks. The war produced its own lexicon and iconography of places. In an evocative, often searing memoir of her encounters with civil strife in Beirut, Jean Said Makdisi (1990) provides an amusing but instructive "Glossary of Terms Used in Times of Crisis." Schoolboys, oblivious to the location of some of their country's national treasures, became more attuned to and dazzled by *Galerie Sim'an, Sodeco, al-Matahen, Hayy al-Buseinat, al-Laylaki, Barbir, Bourj al-Murr, Fattal, Mar Mikhail, Khaldeh triangle,* etc. By virtue of their contingent location these, and other such inconsequential places and spaces, became fearsome points of reference and lines of demarcation — part of the deadly logistics of contested space.

When the hostility shifted to internecine confrontations, as it repeatedly did, it assumed the manifestations of factional localized "turf wars" between militias vying to eliminate adversaries or extend the bases of operations. Negotiating one's safe havens within this labyrinthine maze of embattled quarters and dense pockets of shifting allegiances became more cumbersome. Here as well, unknown passageways and winding alleys, because they provided relatively safe access to rerouted roads, acquired a new image and notoriety. Overnight, a road became a barricade or a "flying road-block;" a walled garden became a blockaded stronghold; a street corner turned into a check point. Private space was not spared these tempestuous turnovers in land use. Indeed, the distinctions between private and public space were blurred and lost much of their conventional usage. Just as basements, rooftops, and strategic openings in private homes became part of the logistics of combat, roadways were also "domesticated" as family possessions, discarded furniture and bulky items spilled into the public domain to improvise barricades. Balconies, verandahs, walk-ups, doorways, and all the other open airy and buoyant places the Lebanese craved and exploited with such ingenuity became dreaded spaces to be bolted and shielded. Conversely, dingy basements, tightly sealed corridors, attics and other normally neglected spaces became more coveted simply because they were out of the trajectory of snipers and shellfire. They became places of refuge. (For further details, see: Sarkis 1993; Yahya 1993; Khalaf 1995).

The symbolic meanings and uses of a "house," "home," or "dwelling" space, as Maha Yahya (1993) has demonstrated, were also overhauled. The most compelling, of course is the way the family unit and its private space have been broadened to accommodate other functions, as disengaged and unemployed household members converted or relocated their business premises to their homes. The thriving informal war economy reinforced such efforts and rendered them more effective.

As land turns over, so do our perceptions and commitments to it. Such changes are visible not only in the way the Lebanese are confirming their spatial moorings and the language they employ in asserting their retribalized identities but also in the way their images of the "other," those who intrude on their spaces and beyond, have been profoundly transformed.

Such transformations are, doubtless, a reflection of their attachments and devotions to the places they occupy. The war has had in this regard two diametrically opposed reactions. On the one hand, displaced Christians who have been relocated among their co-religionists in integrated communities have become more spatially anchored. On the other hand, uprooted refugees, largely Shi'ites and other disenfranchised groups, have had a markedly tenuous attachment to the spaces they are compelled to occupy. At both ends, the habitat suffers. As we have seen, the out-migration of Christians has been disproportionately higher than other groups. It is estimated that today they make up not more than 35–38 percent of the total Lebanese population. They have not only shrunk demographically, but also spatially. Salim Nasr (1993) suggests that by the mid-1980s more than 80 percent of the Christians were concentrated in a surface area of about 17 percent of the country. Such contraction was bound to dramatically change their perception and uses of space. Feeling more entrapped and hemmed in within compressed areas, they have become predisposed toward more intensive forms of land utilization. Hence, the eastern suburbs and the lush slopes of the northern mountain ridge are now dense with high rises and other strictly city-like constructions.

While the countryside is being urbanized, the cities and sprawling suburbs are being ruralized. Both are perverse. Dislocated groups that converge on squatted settlements in the city center and urban fringe are generally strangers to city life. On the whole, they are dislodged, dispossessed and unanchored groups, traumatized by fear and raging with feelings of bitterness and betrayal. They are, so to speak, *in* but not *of* the city. Hence, they have no attachments to, or appreciation of, the areas they found themselves in, and are not likely to display any interest in safeguarding or enriching its character. To many, in fact, their makeshift settlements are merely places to occupy and amenities to exploit.

Altogether, and perhaps most unsettling, is the way the tempo of war imposed its own perilous time frames, dictating traffic flows, spaces to be used or avoided. Time, space, movement and interaction all became enveloped with contingency and uncertainty. Nothing was taken for granted anymore. People lived, so to speak, situationally. Short-term expediency replaced long-term planning. Everything had to be negotiated on the spur of the moment. The day-to-day routines, which once structured the use of space and time, played havoc with their lives. Deficient communication, irregular and congested traffic rendered all forms of social interaction fortuitous and unpredictable. One was expected to accomplish much of one's daily activities at unexpected hours depending on the merciless whims of fighters or the capricious cycles of violence. Beirutis became, as a result, astonishingly adept at making instant adaptations to such jarring modulations and precipitous shifts in the use of time and space.

The street was suddenly deserted. Beirutis have broken all records for getting out of the way on time. It is incredible to see how quickly a street swarming with people can be transformed into ghostly emptiness. Shopkeepers close their doors and pull down their iron shutters, mothers scoop up their children and run, vendors scuttle away with their carts, and after an even more than usually furious beeping of horns, the traffic jam evaporates in no time at all.

As suddenly as the commotion started, it stopped, and as suddenly as Hamra was emptied, it filled up again; within a few minutes life went on as though nothing had happened (Makdisi 1990:86).

A War System

The resilience of the Lebanese and their adaptive strategies to cope with the cruelties of war would not alone have created the circumstances that allowed the war to go on for so long. What abetted and reinforced the war's duration was that it had evolved an elaborate subculture of its own and became something akin to a "war system." Foremost, the void created by the collapse of state authority (particularly between 1975 and 1990), enabled the war to generate and institutionalize its own groups and networks with its particular structures and interrelated web of rules and obligations. Individuals and agencies that provided access to amenities, vital resources, information, smuggled goods, black markets, and war booty, found new shortcuts and other venues for empowerment and enhanced status. Some were propelled into folk heroes. Others, almost overnight, became acclaimed public figures with no legitimate claims for their prominence other than the access they provided for such ephemeral but coveted goods and services. These and the burgeoning informal, parallel, war economy, with its extortionist and protection rackets, its underclass of new warlords and war profiteers and other well-placed individuals, were understandably reluctant to put an end to a situation that had become their lifeline for power and privilege. They all had a vested interest in maintaining the status-quo of belligerency.

The "war-booty" was a bountiful windfall to large segments of society and not restricted to those directly involved in combat. Given its disguised and clandestine character, it is extremely difficult to ascertain its full magnitude.

It was though, by any criteria, immense. Nor was it an ephemeral or transient feature. It played a major role in reshuffling the conventional socioeconomic strata in society. Indeed during the first two years of the war the fighting for control of Beirut's central business district must have precipitated what some claim to be "the greatest redistribution of wealth in modern Lebanon's history" (Hanf 1993: 329).

Like other nefarious exploits, this "war system" was not entirely indigenous. Regional and global sponsors of local militias funneled in inordinate sums of money. Foreign remittances also poured in large reserves to bolster the war efforts of their respective communities. Most dramatic, however, was the new social stratum of war profiteers, contraband traders, and large-scale looters which flaunted its new wealth and privileges with unrestrained exuberance and abandon.

There is also evidence that the looting of souks, vandalizing of private estates and residential quarters, and the extensive bank robberies were not all the work of amateurs. Much of it was accomplished with the technical assistance of professional pillagers, and safecrackers from Europe, possibly supplied by the Mafia (see, for further details, Randal 1984: 98–100; Petran 1987: 231–32; Winslow 1996: 212–19). Zuhair Muhsin, the leader of Sa'iqa (Syrian-sponsored Palestinian militia) was derisively nicknamed the "Persian" for the quantities of valuable Persian carpets his men looted as they vandalized privileged residential quarters in Beirut.

The string of clandestine and makeshift ports stretching from Junieh to Tripoli, in addition to those appropriated from the state, generated untold revenues for the Lebanese Forces. The Gemayyel militias alone, by barring the government from levying custom duties from Pier Five at Beirut's port, managed to siphon off, it is estimated, more than five billion LP during the first seven to eight years of the war (Winslow 1996: 217). Traffic in hashish and other drugs through the Biqa' Valley was also rampant during this period. The Syrian-Franjieh coalition walked away with the lion's share of such nefarious but lucrative ventures. The Syrian Army in Shtura and Akkar was also involved in protection rackets for the trafficking of consumer durables and other products (Harris 1997: 212). Indeed, the scandalous and extensive corruption and involvement of Syrian soldiers and officers in unscrupulous and self-aggrandizing schemes and activities was a source of embarrassment to the Syrian regime. Efforts were made in fact to rotate those on duty, or to restrict their term, to foil or curtail such opportunities. The magnitude of such complicity was still immense: bribery, sale of arms to local Lebanese militias, cultivation, smuggling and drug trafficking, widespread smuggling of goods from Lebanon to Syria. Rifat Assad alone, the President's notorious brother, was involved it is reported, in deals worth billions of Syrian pounds (see, *Le Monde* 1984; Avi-Ran 1991: 195, 207).

Incidentally, the Israeli Army fared no better in this regard. The Israelis, too, displayed many of the malevolent symptoms of wanton greed, arrogance, and profligacy typical of any conquering army. Ironically, they came in as peacekeepers. Their 1982 invasion, dubbed as "Operation Peace for Galilee," had little to do with peace-keeping or peace-making. They besieged and bombarded the residential quarters of West Beirut and its dense suburbs, destroyed its infrastructure, and generated the heaviest toll of casualties throughout the war. An estimated 17,000 were killed and 30,000 wounded, mostly innocent citizens (See Labaki and Abou Rjeili 1993: 27; Hanf 1993: 341). As if the massive destruction and legacy of hate and bitterness they left behind was not enough. They also hauled away a hefty reward. Apart from the 520 tons of arms and material, ordinary Israeli soldiers were taken it seems by the manifestations of wealth and the life style of the Lebanese bourgeoisie. Quarters under their control were looted. Nothing was spared: private cars, telephones, telex machines, gadgets and appliances, even wooden school benches! (For further substantiation see Randal 1984: 266–67).

The Magnitude of Trauma and Stress

Since Lebanon was, for nearly two decades, besieged by every conceivable form of collective terror, it is pertinent to assess the impact of these beleaguering encounters on those entrapped in them. As we have seen, the magnitude of damage to human life and property and the psychological and moral consequences of relentless violence have been, by any measure, immense — especially since they involved a comparatively small and fractured society with a bewildering plurality and shifting targets of hostility.

The results of an empirical survey, undertaken in 1983 to probe some of the salient sociopsychological effects of the war, provided a few explicit and systematic measures of such unsettling realities. The sample was extracted from a universe of mostly middle- and upper-middle-class professionals, semi-professionals, businessmen, bankers, university and college professors and instructors, government employees, journalists, and the like residing in three different communities in Beirut. Close to 900 heads of households responded to the questionnaire. Matters such as the changing attitudes and perceptions of the respondents, their everyday experiences during the war, and their encounters with various forms of traumatization, deprivation, and displacement were explored. The survey also enabled us to assess symptoms of stress, particularly some of the psychological and behavioral disorders induced by the traumas of war.

As shown in table 8.1, close to 75 percent of the respondents had experienced some form of deprivation and 66 percent were compelled to take refuge in shelters. By deprivation is meant being denied water, electricity, and other basic amenities. A fairly large portion, about 55 percent, also suffered property damage and more than 40 percent were displaced from their homes or communities. More traumatizing, 36 percent indicated that they had lost a family member or close relative and slightly more (38%), a close friend or acquaintance. Equally anguishing, one-fourth of the sample reported that they had directly witnessed a war-induced death.

The extent of humiliation, of being insulted, intimidated, or harassed by armed men at check points or street crossings was also fairly high. Close to a third of the respondents suffered such indignities. Also a fairly large portion (21%) had their houses broken into or occupied (19%). While only five

TABLE 8.1 Magnitude of Traumatization
% of Total Respondents

	Respondent	Family/ Relatives	Close Friend	Witnessed	Average
Deprivation	74%	53%	58%	36%	55%
Refuge in Shelter	66	50	59	34	52
Property damage	54	42	51	27	43
Displacement	41	37	42	22	35
Death	0	36	38	25	33
Humiliation	33	27	29	26	29
Injury	8	26	32	23	22
House broken into	21	24	22	9	19
House/Property Occupied	19	23	23	12	19
Insult/Harassment	19	18	20	20	19
Imposture	17	20	19	11	17
Car stolen	12	26	20	7	16
Kidnapped	5	21	30	10	16
Assault	4	14	21	22	15
Threats	14	16	18	12	15
Disability	3	10	21	16	12
Detention	6	13	19	7	11

percent of the respondents reported being kidnapped, the proportion leapt to 21 percent among other family members and 30 percent among friends. A slightly higher number suffered injury that required hospitalization; 26 percent among family and relatives and 32 percent among friends. Also 10 percent of the respondent's family and relatives suffered a permanent disability as did 21 percent of their friends.

Though not directly related to the conduct of fighting, car thefts, like other symptoms of the breakdown in law and order and public insecurity, became rampant. Twelve percent were victims of such offenses. It was considerably higher for other family members (26%) and friends (20%). About the same number were victims of imposture, detention, and threats.

The psychological concomitants of trauma, particularly as they manifest themselves in emotional and psychosomatic disorders, behavioral and associational problems, were also quite pervasive. No one, as shown in table 8.2, was spared these stressful and crippling trials. This is, after all, another poignant attribute of all uncivil wars; namely the futility of violence and the legacy of senseless destruction, repressed feelings of guilt, shame, trauma and fear they leave in their trail. The scars and scares of war have a way of resurfacing, often with greater intensity and trauma. They rarely go away. The violated are doomed to be haunted by the ghosts of violence. Most stressful, as reported by respondents, were symptoms of restlessness and instability, inability to concentrate, sleep disorders, depression and other behavioral problems associated with over-reacting, such as excessive smoking. About 49 to 54 percent of the respondents suffered these symptoms from time to time.

The moderate symptoms of stress converged on problems like feelings of desperation, obsessive worry, and eating or psychosomatic disorders. The quality of their social relations, particularly their interactions with family, friends, and colleagues at work were also adversely affected. More than 38 percent cited these as sources of unnecessary tension and friction. The family in particular, especially since it is embedded in a kinship culture sustained by a large residue of close and intimate ties and obligations, was a surrogate victim of such displaced tension. Much of the unappeased hostility and daily frustrations induced by protracted violence is apt to be released in such settings on vulnerable and accessible family members.

Tension within the family was compounded by two seemingly divergent sources of strain. Heads of households and other adult members of the family (particularly males) who had to interrupt their employment, were compelled to become house bound. Hence they were "wasting" inordinate chunks of

TABLE 8.2 Induced Stress and Psychological Disorder
(% of total respondents)

	Never	Occasionally	Often	Index
Psychological Disorders				
Restlessness/ Instability	18.6%	52.0%	14.7%	81.4%
Sleep-disorders	20.2	54.0	10.0	74.0
Depression	21.6	47.0	9.0	65.0
Desperation	32.3	37.6	8.6	54.8
Worry, unjustified fears	28.0	39.0	7.6	54.2
Psychosomatic problems	34.7	30.2	7.8	45.8
Loss of will	39.4	30.7	4.6	40.0
Thoughts of death	45.2	23.6	3.4	30.4
Self-blame	53.0	17.3	2.3	22.0
Behavioral Changes				
Over-reacting	22.6	44.0	14.2	72.4
Over-smoking	38.0	24.8	19.0	62.8
Instability to concentrate	26.2	49.0	5.0	59.0
Over-eating	38.5	30.8	7.0	44.8
Over-drinking	49.5	20.6	4.0	28.6
Unlawful predispositions	53.2	17.0	2.5	22.0
Aggressive tendencies	56.3	13.2	2.6	18.4
Associational and Interaction Problems				
With friends	35.7	38.6	2.7	44.0
With family	30.7	35.5	3.2	42.0
With colleagues	34.8	36.5	4.2	35.0
With spouse	33.9	20.0	2.2	24.6
Sexual	54.5	16.7	1.1	19.0

idle and uncommitted time at home. Such involuntary confinement at home, let alone the demoralization that accompanies such symptoms of disengagement and entropy, became an inescapable source of family discord.

Conversely, families suffered from the other extreme: the involuntary absence of men from home. In addition to those involved in the war, many had to seek employment opportunities outside Lebanon and, hence, suffer

TABLE 8.3 Magnitude of Stressful Disorders

Acute Problems	Moderate Stress	Mild Stress
Restlessness (81%)	Desperation (55%)	Over-drinking (27%)
Sleep disorders (74%)	Excessive worry (52%)	Problems with spouse (24%)
Over-reaction (72%)	Psychosomatic (46%)	Self-blame (22%)
Depression (65%)	Over-eating (45%)	Unlawful (22%)
	Problems with friends	
Over-smoking (63%)	(44%)	Sexual (19%)
Lack of Concentration	Problems with family	
(59%)	(42%)	Aggression (18%)
Problems with colleagues		Preoccupation with death
(40%)	Suicidal (5%)	(30%)

the travails of diaspora and extended periods of isolation from home. Both intimacy within and distance from the family were excessive and unwanted. The former exacerbated the intensity of family squabbles and rendered the already beleaguered family setting more vulnerable and testy. The latter did much to "feminize" the household. The absence of men and heads of household for extended interludes undermined patriarchal authority and, more damaging, denied children their conventional male role models. Some of the sociopsychological implications of such disjunctive or defective socialization are grievous.

The results of the survey disclose another seemingly anomalous feature. There was no direct relationship between the magnitude of traumatization and symptoms of stress and psychological disorder. In other words groups who had suffered a larger share of trauma were not necessary those who also displayed greater symptoms of stress. Two factors could readily account for this disparity. First, at the time the survey was conducted, shortly after the Israeli invasion of 1982, Christian respondents and residents of the Eastern suburbs of Beirut who had exhibited such tendencies were inclined then to view the conduct of the war in more positive terms. Since they felt that the fortunes of war were still in their favor, the trials they had suffered were partly assuaged or redeemed. Christians were not as yet afflicted with feelings of *ihbat* (a sense of being defeated or demoralized) they would come to be beset with later. Second, Christian groups had also displayed greater readiness for communal solidarity and mobilization in hard times. Voluntary groups, such as church and neighborhood associations, were active in pro-

viding the needed services and support for welfare and relief. Such mobilization might have redressed some of the sources of tension.

Postwar Barbarism

Postwar interludes, particularly those marked by diffuse and protracted
civil strife, anarchy, and disorder, normally generate moods of restraint. People are more inclined to curb their conventional impulses and become more
self-controlled in the interest of reappraising and redirecting their future
options. Rather than freeing them from their prewar excesses, the war in
Lebanon paradoxically induced the opposite reactions. It unleashed appetites and inflamed people with insatiable desires for acquisitiveness, lawlessness, and unearned privileges.

Some of these excesses are so egregious that they assume at times all the
barbarous symptoms of the not-so-moral substitutes of war. They generate
circumstances under which aggressive emotions could liberate themselves
from conventional and civilized constraints. Indeed, most of the conventional restraints that normally moderate people's rapacious and impulsive
behavior were neutralized. Boisterous and disorderly behavior was routinized. Some, such as ravaging the country's natural habitat, violation of zoning and building ordinances, embezzlement, fraud, corruption, deficient
civic and public consciousness — most visible in the preponderance of low
crimes and misdemeanors — are all deeply embedded in the cultural ethos
of laissez-faire, excessive economic liberalism, and political clientelism.

For example, mercantilism and its concomitant bourgeois values were
always given a free rein in Lebanon. The outcome of such excessive commercialization was already painfully obvious in the prewar years. With staggering increases in land values, commercial traffic in real estate (particularly
during the 1960s when the magnitude of urbanization and construction
industry were at its peak) became one of the most lucrative sources of private
wealth. Hence, the ruthless plundering of the country's scenic habitat and
the dehumanization of its living space became starkly visible. In the late
1960s, at the height presumably of Beirut's splendor and golden age, the
seasoned world traveler John Gunther was so dismayed by what he saw that
he prefaced his chapter on the "Pearl of the Middle East," this way:

> Beirut commits treason against itself. This ancient city, the capital of
> Lebanon, blessed with a sublime physical location and endowed with

a beauty of surroundings unmatched in the world, is a dog-eared shamble — dirtier, just plain dirtier, than any other city of consequence I have ever seen.

In the best quarter of the town, directly adjacent to a brand-new hotel gleaming with lacy marble, there exists a network of grisly small alleys which, so far as I could tell, are never swept at all. Day after day I would see — and learned to know — the same debris: bent chunks of corrugated iron, broken boulders or cement, rags, rotten vegetables, and paper cartons bursting with decayed merchandise. Much of the detritus seems to be of a kind that goes with a rich community, not a poor one. The cool and sparkling Mediterranean across the boulevard looks enticing for a swim, until you see that the water is full of orange peel, oil slick, blobs of toilet paper, and assorted slimy objects (Gunther 1969: 281).

With the absence of government authority, such excesses became more rampant. What had not been ravaged by war was eaten up by greedy developers and impetuous consumers. Hardly anything was spared. The once pristine coastline was littered with tawdry tourist attractions, kitschy resorts, and private marinas as much as by the proliferation of slums and other unlawful makeshift shoddy tenements. The same ravenous defoliation blighted the already shrinking greenbelts, public parks, and terraced orchards. Even sidewalks and private backyards were stripped and defiled. As a result, Beirut today suffers, perhaps, from one of the lowest proportions of open space per capita in the world. The entire metropolitan area of the city claims no more than 600,000 square meters of open space. A UN report stipulates that for an environment to qualify as a healthy one, each person requires approximately 40 square meters of space. Beirut's is as low as 0.8 per person (for these and other estimates see Safe 2000).

Rampant commercialism, greed, and enfeebled state authority could not, on their own, have produced as much damage. These now are being exacerbated by the pathos of a ravenous postwar mentality. Those who had so long fell victim to the atrocities of human suffering become insensitive to these seemingly benign and inconsequential concerns or transgressions. Obsessed with survival and harassed by all the futilities of an ugly and unfinished war, it is understandable how those moral and aesthetic restraints which normally control public behavior become dispensable virtues. They all seem much too remote when pitted against the postwar profligate mood that is

overwhelming large portions of society. Victims of collective suffering normally have other, more basic, things on their mind. They rage with bitterness
and long to make up for lost time and opportunity. The environment becomes an accessible surrogate target on which to vent their wrath. In a
culture infused with a residue of unappeased hostility and mercantilism,
violating the habitat is also very lucrative. Both greed and hostility find an
expedient proxy victim. The abandon with which ordinary citizens litter and
defile the environment and the total disregard they evince for safeguarding
its ecological well-being is much too alarming. This is further exacerbated
by a notoriously high incidence of excessive quarrying, deforestation, traffic
congestion, reckless driving, air and noise pollution, and hazardous motor-
ways which violate minimum safety requirements, let alone the conventional
etiquettes and proprieties of public driving.

The sharp increase in traffic violations and fatal car accidents in recent
years attests to this. Both the incidence of traffic violations and the impound-
ing or seizing of cars for legal custody — because of forged papers or license
plates, lack of inspection or proper registration — have been persistently increasing. From 21,692 seized cars and 192,487 violations in 1993, the number has almost doubled by 1999.

Traffic accidents have also witnessed a corresponding increase. They were
naturally low during the war years. For example records of the Information
Division of the Internal Security registered not more than six injuries and
twenty deaths induced by collisions and car accidents in 1987. The figures
increased to 21 and 56 in 1988. From 1993 and on, however, and with the
cessation of hostilities, the number of such casualties increased sharply and
persistently. From 274 deaths and 2,042 injuries in 1993, the incidence
increased correspondingly to 331 and 4,210 in 1999.

Perhaps access to new highways and the recent introduction of radar and
new technologies for monitoring roadways may, in part, account for this
increase. Clearly though not all, particularly since the increase in violations
and other manifestation of reckless driving were visible before such facilities
became readily available.

This almost innate cultural disposition to violate or depart from normative
expectations is apparent in the preponderance of non-traffic related violations. These, too, have been persistently increasing: from about 10,000 in
1993, 14,000 in 1996 and 18,000 in 1999. The Bureau of Internal Security
normally categorizes as "ordinary violations" such infractions as the infringement of protective regulations safeguarding forests, public gardens, sand
dunes, archaeological and tourist sites, as well as building and zoning ordinances. Also included are the transgressions of the rules governing hunt-

ing, fishing, quarrying, and municipal and public health requirements. These like all other contraventions of regulations on the use of public utilities, particularly water, electricity, and telephones, become readily abused proxy victims of deflected rage and hostility.

Recently the press has begun to devote some attention to such violations, particularly flagrant instances of environmental abuse, corruption, and the misuse of public funds by high government officials. Many of the other "ordinary" violations, however remain undetected, and the fines are too low to dissuade violators, even if they are apprehended.

If smoking in public spaces were ever to be prohibited by decree, the Lebanese would almost certainly brush the injunction aside like all other restrictions on their impulses and extravagant appetites. Lebanon today is a haven for indulgent smokers. Anyone can indulge, virtually anywhere and to their lungs' dismay, unhampered by any prohibition or public disapproval. Indeed, the incidence of smoking is perhaps one of the highest in the world. Studies conducted by WHO and the Ministry of Health reveal that 66 percent of the adult male population are smokers, as are 47 percent of women. By contrast, in most developing countries the percentage of women smokers never exceeds the single digits. For example it is not more than 2.3 percent in Egypt and 7.1 percent in Jordan.

The incidence of smoking is bad enough. More egregious, however, is the bravado with which smokers flaunt their addictive habits. They do so with total disregard for its public health menaces or rights of nonsmokers for fresh air.

For a country beleaguered by formidable expenditure on rehabilitation and reconstruction, the magnitude of what is being wasted on smoking and all its seamy side effects and byproducts is immense. According to the Ministry of Health, a total of $400 million a year is spent on healthcare for those suffering from smoking-related illness. Another $100 million is spent every year on cigarette promotion. The most scintillating ads are for tobacco. Liquor, Lingerie, and cellular telephones are a poor second. Public highways and desolate country roads are decked with imposing billboards beckoning one to Malboro country. Even politicians and public figures (presumably the country's most illustrious role models) cannot part with their cigarettes even when they make TV appearances.

With smoking such a part of everyday life, all attempts to launch a comprehensive country-wide tobacco control strategy or plan of action to curb some of the adverse derivatives of smoking have been abortive so far. Even the laws passed in 1995 banning smoking in hospitals, infirmaries, pharmacies, theatres, public transportation terminals, health clubs, schools, universities, elevators, etc. are ignored and unenforced. A proposal for a law banning all tobacco advertisements on television, radio, and print media failed to be endorsed by the Council of Ministers. In this and other regards, Lebanon is today where the United States used to be more than fifty years ago. Given the mood of popular intransigence, the public is not likely to entertain any restrictions on their indulgent disposition to pollute their surroundings.

In such a free-for-all context, any concern for the aesthetic, human, or cultural dimensions of living space is bound to be dismissed as superfluous or guileless. As a result, it is of little concern whether our public spaces are ugly, whether they debase their inhabitants, whether they are aesthetically, spiritually, or physically tolerable, or whether they provide people with opportunities for authentic individuality, privacy, and edifying human encounters. What counts is that the unconditional access to land must satisfy two overriding claims: the insatiable appetite for profit among the bourgeoisie and the vengeful feeling of entitlements to unearned privileges among the disenfranchised.

By the time authorities step in to restrain or recover such violations, as was to happen repeatedly in the prewar years, the efforts were always too little, too late. By then, officials could only confirm the infringements and incorporate them into the legitimate zoning ordinances.

Retribalization

As the scares and the scars of war became more savaging and cruel, it is understandable that traumatized groups should seek refuge in their most trusted and deeply embedded primordial ties and loyalties, particularly those which coalesce around the family, sect, and community. Even in times of relative harmony and stability, kinship and communal groupings were always effective as mediating sources of sociopsychological support and political mobilization.

As we have seen, the cruelties of protracted and diffused hostility had drastically rearranged the country's social geography. Massive population shifts, particularly since they involved the reintegration of displaced groups into homogeneous and exclusive communities, rendered territorial identities sharper and more spatially anchored. It is in this sense that "retribalization" became more pervasive. The term, as suggested earlier, is employed here loosely to refer to the reinforcement of kinship, confessional, and communal loyalties — especially since they also converged on tightly-knit spatial enclosures. Lebanon, in other words, is being retribalized precisely because in each of the three basic groupings (i.e. family, community, and sect) loyalties and obligations and the density of social interaction which binds groups together are increasingly becoming sources of intense solidarity. A word about each is in order.

Familism

The Lebanese family has always been a resilient institution. Despite the inevitable decline in the sense of kinship the family experienced in the prewar years — generated by increasing urbanization, mobility, and secularization — it continued to have a social and psychological reality that pervaded virtually all aspects of society. As repeated studies have demonstrated, there was hardly a dimension of one's life which was untouched by the survival of family loyalty and its associated norms and agencies. To a considerable extent, a person's status, occupation, politics, personal values, living conditions and life style were largely defined by kinship affiliation. So intense and encompassing were these attachments that the average Lebanese continued to seek and find refuge and identity within close family circles. This was most apparent in the emergence and survival of family associations — perhaps unique to Lebanon. Even when other secular and civic voluntary associations were available, the family was always sought as a mediating agency to offer people access to a variety of welfare and socioeconomic services (Khalaf 1971).

The war years have shored up the family's prominence. A significantly larger number of people found themselves, willingly or otherwise, enfolded within the family. By their own testimonies, they were drawn closer to members of their immediate and extended family than they had been before the war. They were also expending more effort, resources, and sentiments on family obligations and interests. As a result, the traditional boundaries of the family expanded even further to assume added economic, social, and recreational functions.

For example the concept of kin, *ahl* or *'ayleh*, became more encompassing and extended beyond the limited confines of a nuclear family. Only 12 percent of the respondents perceived the boundaries of their family to be limited to spouses and children. Almost 40 percent extended their definition to include both parents. Another 22 percent stretched it further to include paternal and maternal uncles. The remaining 27 percent extended the boundaries even further to encompass all relatives. The family was not only becoming more encompassing. It was also becoming more intimate and affectionate, reinforced by repeated visits and mutual help. Close to 60 percent evaluated their family relations in such highly positive terms. The remaining 38 percent considered them as moderately so. Only 2 percent admitted that their family relations were distant, cold and had no sign of any mutual help or support.

As shown in table 8.4, more than 58 percent of the respondents to the 1983 survey referred to above reported that their ties and relationships with their immediate families had been strengthened by the war. The incidence fell to about 23 percent for relatives and dropped to as low as 18.8 percent for colleagues. The respondents were also asked to indicate, on the conventional 5-point scale, the degree of their involvement in domestic and family affairs. More concretely an effort was made to assess the extent to which such family concerns were becoming more, remaining the same, or becoming less important since the outbreak of civil hostilities. Here as well, and for understandable reasons, more than 60 percent of the respondents indicated that they had become more preoccupied with domestic and family affairs. Thirty-eight percent felt that there was no change in such relations during the war, and only 2 percent reported that domestic and family-centered interests became less important for them.

Given the large-scale devastation of state and other secular agencies and institutions, the family was one of the few remaining social edifices in which people could seek and find refuge in its reassuring domesticity and privacy. It became, to borrow Christopher Lasch's apt title, a "haven in a heartless world" (Lasch 1979). Whether the family will be able to withstand such mounting pressure remains to be seen. What is clear though is that during

TABLE 8.4 Impact of the War on the nature and Identity of Social Relations

	Immediate family	Relatives	Friends	Colleagues
Strengthened	58.2%	22.9%	27.6%	18.8%
About the same	39.4	65.4	57.5	68.6
Weakened	2.4	11.7	14.9	12.6
Total	100.0	100.0	100.0	100.0

the war it had to reinvent and extend itself to assume added functions. For example, beyond absorbing a larger share of the leisure, recreational, welfare, and benevolent needs of its members, it also served as an economic and commercial base. Many, particularly lawyers, craftsmen, retailers, and agents, were forced to convert their homes into offices for business operations. Housewives, too, were known to have used their homes to conduct a variety of transactions and to sell clothing, accessories, and other such items.

Communalism

The manifestations of "retribalization" were also resurfacing at the communal level with, perhaps, greater intensity. Since the boundaries and horizons within which groups circulated were becoming more constricted, it is natural that these tightly knit localities should become breeding grounds for heightening communal and territorial identities. Inevitably, such bonding in exclusive spaces was bound to generate deeper commitments toward one's community and corresponding distance from others. In-group/out-group sentiments became sharper. Segmental and parochial loyalties also became more pronounced. So did the sociocultural, psychological, and ideological cleavages. In this sense the community, locality, neighborhood, or quarter was no longer simply a space to occupy or a place to live in and identify with. It became an ideology — an orientation or a frame of reference through which groups interact and perceive others. It is then, as we suggested earlier, that the community is transferred into a form of communalism.

Two unsettling, often pathological, features of such retribalization are worth highlighting again. More and more communities began to assume some of the egregious attributes of "closed" and "total" entities. The two are naturally related. Comparatively mixed, hybrid, and open communities were becoming more homogeneous and closed to outsiders. Such polarization was bound to engender and sustain the growth of almost totally self-sufficient communities and neighborhoods.

Since early in the initial stages of the war the traditional city center and its adjoining residential quarters witnessed some of the fiercest rounds of fighting and destruction, the episodes were accompanied by a quickening succession of massive population shifts and decentralization. In no time business establishments and virtually all the major public and private institutions — including universities, schools, banks, embassies, travel agencies, and the like — took measures to establish headquarters or branch offices in more than one district. This clearly facilitated the proliferation of self-sufficient urban enclaves. Before the war, people by necessity were compelled to traverse communal boundaries to attend to some of their public services and amenities. Gradually the urge to cross over became superfluous and undesirable. As a result, a rather substantial number of Lebanese were living, working, shopping, and meeting their recreational, cultural, medical, and educational needs within constricted communal circles. More compelling, generations of children and adolescents grew up thinking that their social world could not extend beyond the confines of the ever smaller communities within which they were entrapped.

Some of the sociopsychological and political implications of such reversion to "enclosed" communities are grievous. The psychological barriers and accompanying sociocultural differences are becoming deeper and more ingrown. More and more Lebanese have been forced over the past two decades to restructure and redefine their lives into smaller circles. What is rather unsettling in all this is that they don't seem to particularly resent such restrictions.

A few results of our empirical survey, particularly those which reinforce the proclivity of groups to seek shelter in cloistered spatial enclosures and their corresponding inclination to maintain distance from other communities, are worth noting. Around 70 percent of the respondents indicated that their daily movements are restricted to the area or neighborhood they live in. Surprisingly, a slightly larger number desire to live, work and confine their movements to such restricted areas. Only 22 percent were moving at the time, albeit furtively, between different sectors of the city.

The religious composition of the three broad communities from which the samples were drawn (Ras-Beirut, Basta, and Achrafieh), must have, no doubt, enhanced their receptivity to sustain and encourage feelings of communal solidarity and to entertain unfriendly and hostile feelings toward other groups. The sectarian composition of our respondents corresponds to the religious profile we generally associate with those urban districts. As shown in table 8.5, Ras Beirut is the only fairly mixed district. The majority (40%) are Orthodox, followed by Sunnis and Protestants. The rest are almost equally distributed among Maronites, Catholics, Shi'ites, and Druze, with a few Armenians and other Christian minorities. On the whole, however, Ras Beirut is more than two-thirds Christian and around 27 percent Muslim. On the other hand, Basta is almost exclusively Muslim in composition, just as Achrafieh is also exclusively Christian. The proportion of Maronites, Catholics, and Protestants is as negligible in Basta as is the proportion of

TABLE 8.5 Religious Composition of the Three Communities

	Ras Beirut	Basta	Achrafieh	Total
Maronites	9.1%	2%	40%	17.2%
Catholics	7.3	2	13.5	7.6
Orthodox	40.0	7.8	30.8	26.2
Protestants	15.4	0	1.9	5.8
Armenians	1.8	2	5.7	3.2
Sunnis	17.3	60.8	3.8	27.3
Shi'ites	5.5	15.6	3.8	8.3
Druze	3.6	9.8	0	4.4
Percent	100.0	100.0	100.0	100.0
N	110	51	52	213

Sunnis, Shi'ites, and Druze in Achrafieh. The only exception is perhaps the Orthodox. It is the only sect which is represented in the three communities, although to a much lesser degree in Basta.

It is natural that residents of such closely knit and homogenous communities should begin to display particular attitudes toward other sectarian groups. The war, judging by some of our preliminary results, has apparently sharpened such sentiments. The respondents were asked: "How do you evaluate your present feelings and opinions toward the groups listed below? Do you feel closer to them now than before the war, or do you have unchanged feelings, or do you feel more distant?"

The results, as summarized in table 8.6, reveal some obvious and expected tendencies that reflect the roles the various communities played during the war at the time of the survey and the consequent social distance between them.

If we take the sample as a whole, 39 and 38 percent have grown more distant from the Kurds and Druze respectively and harbor hostility toward them. Next come Maronites (29%), Shi'ites (26%) and Sunnites (23%), followed by Syriacs (18%) and Armenians (17%). The rest, namely Catholics, Christian minorites, Orthodox, and Protestants evoke little or no hostility or negative feelings. Conversely, the respondents feel closer to Maronites (22%), Orthodox (19%) and Sunnites and Shi'ites (15%). Groups that elicit least sympathy are Druze (8%), Syriacs (8%), Armenians (5%) and Kurds (1.6%).

TABLE 8.6 Enmity and Social Distance

	Closer	Unchanged	More Distant
Maronites	22.0%	40.0%	29.0%
Orthodox	19.0	62.0	8.0
Catholics	10.0	71.0	7.0
Protestants	7.0	73.0	8.0
Xian Minorities	8.0	72.0	7.0
Sunnites	15.0	50.0	23.0
Shi'ites	15.0	47.0	26.0
Druze	8.0	44.0	38.0
Kurds	1.6	45.0	39.0
Armenians	5.0	64.0	17.0
Syriacs	8.0	60.0	18.0

Distant From		Closer To	
Kurds	39%	Maronites	22%
Druze	38	Orthodox	19
Maronites	29	Shi'ites/Sunnites	15
Shi'ites	26		
Sunnites	23		

It is interesting to note that, with the exception of the Druze, attitudes toward belligerent sects (Maronites, Sunnis, Shi'ites) invite both extremes. Nearly the same proportion who indicate that they have grown closer to a particular sect also display enmity and distance toward them. They are equally admired and admonished. It is also interesting in this regard, to observe that attitudes toward nonbelligerent groups or those who were not directly involved in the fighting, (i.e. Protestants, Christian minorities, Catholics, and Greek Orthodox) remained largely unchanged.

A few other, albeit self-evident, variations are also worth noting. Ras Beiruties on the whole feel far closer toward Maronites (32%) and Orthodox (23%) than they do toward Sunnis (16%) and Shi'ites (15%). The Druze received the lowest score (5%). They have grown distant from the Druze (56%) and then almost equally from Shi'ites (30%), Sunnis (26%), and Maronites (24%).

The Basta residents feel closer toward Shi'ites (27%) and to a slightly lesser degree, Sunnis, Druze and Orthodox (23%). The bulk of their resentment is directed toward the Maronites.

The Achrafieh residents are naturally closest to Maronites (51%), followed by Orthodox (35%) and Catholics (27%). Their resentment is directed toward the Druze (57%) and to a much lesser degree, Shi'ites (30%) and Sunnis (22%).

Communities in Lebanon were becoming more "closed" in still another and, perhaps, more vital and disturbing sense. A few of these communities were beginning to evince features akin to a total, even "totalitarian" character in several significant respects. I borrow the term here employed by Erving Goffman (1961) in his analysis of total institutions such as prisons, hospitals, monasteries, mental asylums, and the like.

1. *Because of the massive population shifts and decentralization, accompanied by the fear and terror of intercommunal hostilities, communities became increasingly self-sufficient.* A full range of human activities has developed within each of those communities.

2. *As a result, even where entry and exit into and from these communities remained largely voluntary, an increasing number of people were reluctant to cross over.* The boundaries, incidentally, are not merely spatial. Sometimes an imaginary "green line," a bridge, a road network, might well serve as the delimiting borders. More important, the barriers became psychological, cultural, and ideological. Hence, there emerges within each of those communities a distinct atmosphere of a cultural, social, and intellectual world closed to "outsiders." It is for this reason that the social distance and the barriers between the various communities grew sharper. The barriers are often dramatized by deliberately exaggerating differences. Such dramatization serves to rationalize and justify the maintenance of distance. It also mitigates part of the associated feelings of guilt for indulging in avoidance.

The same kinds of barriers that have polarized Beirut into "East" and "West" started to appear elsewhere. As we have seen, Residents of "East" Beirut depict the Western suburbs as an insecure, chaotic, disorderly mass of alien, unattached, and unanchored groups aroused by borrowed ideologies and an insatiable appetite for lawlessness and boorish decadence. In turn, residents of Western Beirut depict the Eastern suburbs as a self-enclosed "ghetto" dominated by the overpowering control and hegemony of a one-party system where strangers are suspect and treated with contempt. In short, both communities are cordoned off and viewed with considerable fear and foreboding. Each has vowed to rid or liberate society from the despicable evil inherent in the other!

3. A *total institution, often in subtle and unobtrusive ways, involves an effort to remake or resocialize individuals and groups within it.* This, by necessity, requires that prior values, ideas and patterns of behavior be dislodged and then be replaced by new ones. To varying degrees such manifestations of resocialization became visible at the early stages of the war. The various communities and warring factions, supported by an extremely well developed and sophisticated media — with their own broadcasting stations, newspapers, periodicals, pamphlets, slogans, symbols, and motifs — competed in gaining access to potential recruits, clients, and converts. Each developed its own ethnocentric interpretation of the war, its own version of the social and political history of Lebanon, and proposed diametrically opposed views and programs for the socioeconomic and political reconstruction of the country. The differences do not stop here. They have pervaded virtually every dimension of everyday life: the national figures and popular heroes they identify with, their life style, public and private concerns, and their perceptions of the basic issues in society are being drastically reshaped and redefined.

As a result, there are very few national symbols or fundamental issues with which all the Lebanese can identify. It is facts of this sort that prompt me to argue that Lebanon's pluralism, particularly if those same parochial loyalties and sentiments are maintained, remains more of a divisive force than a viable source of organic solidarity and national unity.

4. *Finally, one can also discern signs of total control.* Individuals and groups, particularly in areas where private militias and political groups enjoy a large measure of hegemony, are subjected to increasing forms of social controls — ranging from direct measures of conscription, taxation, impositions, censure to the more subtle forms of intervention in individual freedom and modes of expression and mobility. Some of these measures became so pervasive at different interludes of the war that at times nothing was held to be morally or legally exempt from the scope and unlimited extension of the group in power.

Confessionalism

Finally, symptoms of retribalization were doubtlessly most visible in the reassertion of religious and confessional consciousness. What makes this particularly interesting is that religious and confessional loyalties manifest a few paradoxical and seemingly inconsistent features that reveal the sharp distinctions between them. Clearly religiosity and confessionalism are not and need not be conterminous. Indeed results of the 1982–83 empirical survey revealed some sharp distinctions between the two.

Curiously, as respondents indicated that their religiosity was declining (as measured by the degree of changes in the intensity of their spiritual beliefs, religious commitments, and observation of rituals, practices, and duties of their faith), their confessional and sectarian identities however were becoming sharper. When the respondents were asked whether the war has had an impact on the religious practices and activities, the majority (85%) admitted that they had not changed in this regard.

One could infer from such findings that the Lebanese are not taking recourse in religion in an effort to find some spiritual comfort or solace to allay their rampant fear and anxiety. To a large extent this kind of refuge is better sought and served in the family and community. Religion is therefore clearly serving some other secular — indeed socioeconomic and ideological — function.

Some of the results clearly support such an inference. It is, in a way, revealing that when it comes to matters that reflect their religious tolerance and their willingness to associate and live with other sectarian or religious groups — such as the schooling of their children, their attitudes toward interconfessional marriages and their residential preferences — confessional considerations begin to assume prominence.

When asked, for example, whether they would agree to send their children to a school affiliated with a sect other than their own, close to 30 percent of the respondents answered in the negative — i.e. a preference to educate their children in schools with similar sectarian background. Their attitudes toward mixed sectarian or religious marriages — for both males and females — reveal much of the same sentiments. Close to 28 percent disapprove of such religiously mixed marriages for males and 32 percent for females. Similar predispositions were expressed regarding their preferences to live in a locality that has a majority of people from their own sect. Around 21 percent were sympathetic with such a prospect.

Altogether, a surprisingly large proportion of what presumably is a literate, cosmopolitan, and sophisticated sample of professionals, university and college teachers, intellectuals, journalists, and the like displayed strong confessional biases, and a distance from and intolerance toward other groups. This was apparent, in their disapproval of interconfessional marriages, their preference for parochial schooling for their children, and their reluctance to associate and live with other sectarian and religious groups. More poignant, perhaps, it was also becoming increasingly visible in this rather narcissistic preoccupation with one's community, with its corresponding exclusionary sentiments and phobic proclivities toward others. This heightened confessional consciousness, understandable in times of sectarian hostility and fear, started to assume fanatic and militant expressions of devotion to and glorification of one's group. The relative ease with which the various communities were politically resocialized into militancy was largely an expression of such aroused sectarian consciousness.

9   From Shakib Efendi to Ta'if

"In cases where conflict is primarily of an ethnic, communal
character in contrast to those provoked by economic and/or
political issues, the likelihood of a negotiated non-belligerent
resolution becomes very slim. Indeed, all communal wars end in
blood. There must be a victor and a vanquished before
combatants begin to consider negotiation."
— Jay Kaplan, "Victors and Vanquished: Their Post-War Relations" (1988)

"The history we leave behind is painful and hard. We must not
forget it but we must not be controlled by it."
— William J. Clinton, "Speech in Vietnam" (November 19, 2000)

This study is predicated on the overarching premise that
much of the *displaced* and *protracted* character of collective strife that has
beleaguered Lebanon at various interludes could well be a reflection of two
other constant features of its fractious political history; namely the radicalization of communal solidarities and the unsettling, often insidious, character
of foreign intervention. By probing further into the nature of this interplay
one, it is hoped, can better understand when, how and why social strife
becomes more belligerent and assumes some of the menacing cruelties of
uncivil violence.

Hopefully the evidence provided thus far has shown how some of the
socioeconomic disparities, both vertical and horizontal, are often linked to
the uneven and asymmetrical developments generated by Western contacts.
Naturally, many of the unsettling manifestations of such contacts were unintended consequences. All cross-cultural encounters affect recipient groups
differently. For example, Christian communities, particularly during the second half of the nineteenth century, were much more receptive to the secular,
liberal, and technological changes associated with Western incursions in
Mount Lebanon. Hence the disproportionate socioeconomic standing and
privileges they enjoyed were, to a large extent, a reflection of such predis-

positions. For a variety of considerations, they were in a position that allowed them to take fuller advantage of the opportunities generated by such encounters.

Clearly, not all the internal disparities should be attributed to foreign intervention. Nor were they exclusively generated by unplanned and fortuitous circumstances. Foreign powers, by virtue of their preferential and shifting patronage of different communities, must have also contributed to the accentuation of such gaps and dislocations. This is most visible in their direct involvement, often as principal architects of covenants and pacts or in negotiating terms of settlements on behalf of their client groups or protégés. Such willful and deliberate involvement carries their intervention to its ultimate degree. Without exception all pacts in Lebanon, particularly those coming in the wake of armed struggle, were brokered by foreign governments either unilaterally or through their trusted local or regional allies.

Despite sharp differences in their visions, all the foreign powers involved in the various settlement schemes ended up, willfully or otherwise, by consolidating the confessional foundation of the political order. I wish to argue here that the schemes which were fairly successfully (particularly the *Règlement Organique* of 1861 and the *Mithaq* of 1943), had recognized the realities of confessional affiliation but sought to secularize sectarianism in such a manner as to encourage harmonious coexistence between the various confessional groups. In short, they made efforts to transform some of its divisive and pathological features into a more enabling and constructive system.

The *Mithaq*, in particular, managed to contain sources of division by meeting or bypassing those critical differences over the "indivisible" issues of political identity, secularization, and power sharing. Even in the absence of national consciousness over such issues, the collective struggle for independence allowed the various communities to transcend or suspend the atavistic passions aroused by these differences. The conventional forms of mitigating conflict through avoidance or "mutual lies," as they are dubbed by the local political culture, were workable. In other words, as long as the Lebanese continued to skirt over these issues — both the discourse over the issues of destiny (*qadayah al-masir*) and those concerned with mundane matters of everyday life (*qadayah al hayatiyyah*) — their accommodation to the sources and manifestations of divisions became less contentious or problematic. Such accommodation was also rendered more feasible when external powers refrained from exacerbating those differences.

By the mid 1970s it was increasingly apparent that the unsettling consequences of this precarious inside-outside dialectics were becoming more unmanageable.

All five, despite their mixed record, offered Lebanon at various stages in its political history opportunities to experiment with different forms of representative government. More vital, perhaps, they all dealt with the nagging issues of confessional balance, the country's national identity, and its foreign policy in a changing regional and global setting.

The intention of this chapter is to elaborate on these realities by reviewing the record of five such critical landmarks in the political history of Lebanon: the partition scheme of 1843, the *Règlement Organique* of 1861, the creation of the state of Greater Lebanon in 1920, the National Covenant of 1943, and the Ta'if Accord of 1989. The first two came in the wake of bitter communal hostility. The third marked the collapse of the Ottoman Empire following its defeat in 1919. The National Pact (*Mithaq*) of 1943 ushered in Lebanon's independence from the French Mandate. Finally, the Ta'if Accord, still struggling to consolidate itself, put an end to fifteen years of collective strife and proposed reforms that laid the foundation for national reconciliation, the restoration of state autonomy and independence.

The Partition Scheme of 1843

The *Règlement Shakib Efendi* of 1843, as the plan is dubbed by historians of the period, was largely a reaction to problems of Ottoman centralization and growing sectarian tensions in Mount Lebanon. As we have seen, European intervention — particularly on behalf of France and Britain — prevented the Ottoman government from imposing direct control over Lebanon. The efforts, however, failed to reconcile the Druze and Maronites. The five powers, eager to contain the mounting tension between them, agreed in 1843 to a scheme of partitioning Lebanon into two administrative districts: a northern district under a Christian *qa'immaqam* ("sub-governor"), and a southern under a Druze *qa'immaqam*. Each was expected to rule over his coreligionists while being responsible to the local Ottoman governor residing in Beirut. Interestingly, even then the Beirut–Damascus road was seen as a natural divide or demarcation line.

Like other subsequent schemes, it took considerable diplomatic jockeying to bring it about. In fact it was the byproduct of a compromise arrangement between the Ottoman and French proposals, masterminded by an eminent diplomat; Prince Metternich. The French, backed by the Austrians, were hoping to restore the Shihabi Emirate. The Ottomans, along with the Russians, were insisting on the integration of Lebanon into the Ottoman Empire. Hence, they were naturally averse to any scheme that would have promised Mount Lebanon any measure of autonomy.

The double *qa'immaqamiyyah*, like all other partition schemes, was destined to fail. Indeed, it brought forth precisely the opposite of what it was intended to accomplish. Rather than mitigating the sources of religious and confessional cleavages, it ended up by deepening them. According to the partition plan, each sub-governor was to exercise authority over his own coreligionists. The religious composition of the two districts was, however, heterogeneous. Hence, this created the problem of how to treat subjects who belonged to one religious community, but happened to reside under the political authority of another. This was particularly acute in mixed regions like the Matn, Shuf and the Gharb.

To overcome the jurisdictional problems created by the mixed districts, the Porte decided to limit the authority of each *qaimmaqam* to his own territory. By doing so Christians in the Druze districts were denied the right of appealing to a Christian authority in judicial and personal status matters (Kerr 1959: 6–7). As usual, each of the European powers intervened on behalf of their protégés. France, as the protector of Maronites and Catholics opposed the Ottoman plan. Instead, it encouraged the church to remove Maronites from the jurisdiction of the Druze *qa'immaqam* and to place them directly under the Christian one. Britain, eager to safeguard the prerogatives of the Druze feudal sheikhs, was naturally more receptive to the revised scheme. In the meantime, Russia maintained that the Greek Orthodox community of 20,500 was populous enough to justify the creation of a special *qa'immaqamiyyah* (for further details, see Salibi 1965: 63–66).

In the face of such disparate expectations, an arrangement was arrived at whereby Christian and Druze *wakils* would be entrusted with judicial authority over their coreligionists in the mixed districts. Mixed cases, involving Christians and Druze, would be heard jointly by the two *wakils*, who were also empowered, it must be recalled, to collect taxes, each from his own sect, on behalf of the feudal chief.

The outbreak of hostilities in the spring of 1845, barely two years in the life of the partition, finally convinced the Ottomans of the inadequacies inherent in the double *qa'immaqamiyyah*. They were reluctant, however, to resort to a thorough reorganization of Mount Lebanon. Instead, they modified the existing arrangement by settling the jurisdictional problems of Christians living in Druze districts. As shown earlier, the Règlement not only reinforced the confessional proclivities of Mount Lebanon but also enhanced the social and political privileges of its feudal structure. The articles of the Règlement were quite explicit in this regard. The sub-governor was to be appointed from the feudal families. The choice was to be restricted to only two families: Abillama for the Maronites, Arslan for the Druze. After consultations with the *a'yan* and the clergy, an elected council of twelve members (two from each of the major six religious communities) was to be selected at large from the people without restriction to birth and status. Yet the Christian clergy had the strongest voice in determining the election, while the Muslim members were appointed by the *wali* of Saida (Harik 1968: 273). Furthermore, in the event that any vacancies were to arise in the council, the heads of the religious sects were to appoint the new members.

Feudal families throughout Lebanon had recognized Shakib Efendi's Règlement as a direct threat to their status and traditional privileges and did their utmost to resist its application. Shortly after his departure, both Christian and Druze feudal sheikhs began "to resort to the old ways and revive old fiscal abuses, much to the distress of the peasants" (Salibi 1965: 73). The abuses, exacerbated by the dislocations generated by the disruptive impact of European industrialization on the local economy, finally culminated in a fresh outbreak of sectarian hostilities.

The Règlement Organique of 1861

As we have seen, the massacres of 1860 were so devastating that they drew the attention of the international community, France in particular, which as a leading Roman Catholic power had for a long time considered itself the protector of the Maronites as fellow Roman Catholics. To ward off European intervention, the Ottomans were eager to dismiss the crisis as a purely internal affair. Accordingly, Khurshid Pasha, the governor of Beirut, succeeded in drawing up a peace settlement between the warring factions, which, among other things, gave the Ottomans increased control over the country. The crisis was almost settled when, only three days after the Druze-Christian peace convention in Lebanon was signed, the Christian quarter in Damascus was, without provocation, attacked and set on fire, resulting in the loss of 11,000 lives. Foreign intervention became unavoidable and imminent.

Through French initiative, major powers — Great Britain, Austria, Russia, and Turkey — convened and decided on intervention. An international commission was set up to fix responsibility, determine guilt, estimate indemnity and suggest reforms for the reorganization of Lebanon.

The political settlement was complex and problematic. Internal divisions and a growing polarization between the two communities were compounded by the divergent plans and intentions of foreign powers. France advocated restoration of an autonomous Maronite principality much like the Shihabi Emirate of the pre-1840 model. Russia mildly supported the French proposal while it was bitterly opposed by Britain, Austria, and Turkey. Britain, it seems, had designs to transform all Syria into a vice-royalty similar to the Egyptian Khedivate, or to partition Mount Lebanon into three *qa'mmaqamiyyah*: Maronite, Druze, and Greek Orthodox. After eight months of extended discussion, agreement was reached on June 9, 1861 on a new organic statute (*Règlement Organique*) which reconstituted Lebanon as an Ottoman province or *mutasarrifyyah* (plenipotentiarate) under the guarantee of the six signatory powers.

At least on paper the Règlement called for some radical reorganization of the country's political, administrative, and institutional structures, along with its geographic boundaries: A Catholic Christian governor (an Ottoman subject but non-Lebanese), designated by the Porte with the approval of the signatory powers, was now to govern Lebanon. He was to be assisted by a central Administrative Council of twelve elected members representing the various confessional groups. Distribution of seats within the Council was purely on a confessional basis; i.e., each of the major six sects (Maronite, Greek Orthodox, Catholic, Druze, Shi'te, and Sunni Muslim) claimed two seats.

The provisions of the Règlement also called for a new geographic delimitation of Lebanon. The country was now stripped of its three major coastal cities (Beirut, Tripoli, and Sidon) and its fertile regions of al-Biqa' and Wadi al-Taym, and divided into seven districts (*qada*), each under a Qa'immaqam with further divisions into small counties (*mudiriyyat*).

All members of the Administrative Council, judiciary councils, and smaller counties were to be, according to article 11, "nominated and chosen, after agreement with the notables, by the leaders of the respective communities and appointed by the government." Likewise, the administration of local justice involving minor cases was left in the hands of government appointed or popularly elected sheikhs. Ecclesiastical jurisdiction over cases in which only clergy were involved was maintained.

Other than the geographic rearrangement of Lebanon's boundaries and the formal abolition of feudalism, which continued to survive in other forms, the Règlement did not involve a radical redefinition or a qualitative transformation of the social order as in often suggested. In fact, it reinforced the provisions of Shakib Efendi's Règlement of 1845. This is apparent in its explicit avowal of confessionalism as a basis for distributing seats within the Administrative Council. The architects of the Règlement had no other option at the time. Given the mutual confessional bitterness and suspicion, generated by decades of civil unrest, they sought to maintain a modicum of harmony among the various sects. Accordingly, the most they could do was to fashion an arrangement, which from then on was to become not only the *sine qua non* of Lebanon's political culture, but also its Achilles' heel. They saw to it that no one sect was placed in a position of dominance over another. Hence, in its original form, the Règlement favored straightforward sectarian representation over a more territorial, proportional, or "democratic" representation.

This disregard of the proportional principle of representation was not enthusiastically received by the Maronites, and was a source of unrest and agitation during the formative years of the Mutessarifate. By a twist of historical irony, the Maronites themselves subsequently became resentful or hostile when other sects, particularly Sunnis and Shi'ites, made similar claims for numerical representation. Since they were then the most populous group in the mountain, the Maronites favored a system of representation consonant with their numerical or territorial distribution. It must be recalled that in the 1860s they formed close to 60 percent of the Mountain's population (Akarli 1993:10). By contrast, although Shi'ites once had substantial pockets in the central and southern regions of the Mountain, their numbers diminished significantly by the mid nineteenth century. Largely because of the suppression they were subjected to by the Sunni potentates of Saida and Tripoli, they dispersed to regroup in less hostile regions. In the 1860s they constituted less than 6 percent of the Mountain's population (see, among others Hourani 1986).

The designation of an Armenian Catholic (Dawud Pasha) as the first *Mutesarrif* was intended as a compromise appointment. By 1864 it was apparent that the Règlement needed drastic revisions, if the growing tension between the *Mutesarrif* and the Maronite community of the North were to be mitigated and controlled. Once again, the signatory powers intervened, each advancing a proposal intended to give its favored protégé or client group added advantage. The French sought a reconsideration of the confessional formula and proposed the allotment of seats in the Administrative Council on a territorial basis giving one seat for each of the seven districts. By outwardly opting for more "democratic" representation, the French were hoping to give the Maronites a guaranteed opportunity for increasing their seats on the council.

The British and the Russians were not eager to endorse the French scheme. The former, because under a territorial representation the most that their Druze clients could gain was only one seat in their stronghold of the shuf; the latter, because their Greek Orthodox clients were also not likely to gain more than one seat in the Kura district.

Strong opposition and months of debate persuaded the French to modify their principle of territorial divisions and to accommodate a greater measure of sectarian representation. The final formula that emerged embodied both these principles and proved instrumental in shaping the political life of Lebanon. The council was now to be composed of twelve members: four Maronites, three Druze, two Greek Orthodox, one Greek Catholic, and one from each of the Sunni and Shi'i communities.

This compromise arrangement was acceptable to both the signatory powers (particularly France, Russia, and England) and their confessional protégés in the Mountain. It maintained a delicate balance between the Uniate, Muslim, and Druze representatives, and gave the Greek Orthodox, in the event of a sectarian split, the decisive votes; something Russia was angling for. Confessionalism, in short, became firmly rooted into Lebanon's political system.

The Règlement Organique had recognized the confessional and pluralistic realities of Mount Lebanon but carefully worked out a formula that avoided the political subordination of one sect to another. In doing so it restrained the outward expression of confessional violence and managed to ensure a modicum of sectarian coexistence. In no sense, however, should this be taken to mean that confessional loyalties had been diluted. In fact, religious sentiments came to assume a more intense role in sustaining identity and communal solidarity. Other than the growing disparities in wealth and life style, which accentuated the differences between the various communities, there were at least three major manifestations of the persistence and growing dominance of confessionalism.

First, both in its original and revised forms, the Règlement Organique had, by institutionalizing confessional representation on the Administrative Council, confirmed the sectarian foundation of society. More important, perhaps, the broad religious conflict was compounded by a more diffuse, often pernicious, intersectarian rivalry, as each sect sought a greater share of power and privilege. Indeed some of the governors of the *mutasarrifiyya* openly admitted and took special pride in inciting such discord. Wasa Pasha, the third governor (1883–92), was unrestrained in making such a confession in one of his letters to the Porte: "Since it would be politically expedient to have the religious heads of the Maronite community at logger-heads, I paid due attention to this important matter and managed to bring about a degree of discord and mutual aversion among them." (Akarli 1993:50). Such conflict, however, rarely degenerated into belligerent hostility or assumed manifestations of collective violence.

Secondly, the Maronite community in the North continued to hark back for the communal consciousness awakened earlier during the century. In a sense, the Maronites never ceased to recognize Mount Lebanon as their national home. Accordingly, they longed for a greater measure of autonomy and independence. There were several episodes which attempted to re-awaken such communal sentiments. Yusuf Karam himself, after his exile, made several attempts, in 1873, 1874, 1875, and 1877, to liberate the Mountain. Of course Karam was not acting alone. French political circles and the Maronite clergy were encouraging the resurgence of such sentiments.

Thirdly, the forces of secularization, which often accompany urbanization, growing literacy and exposure to alternate sources of socialization, did not detract from the dominance of the church and growing influence of prelates. It should be remarked here that both Catholic and Ottoman theories of government legitimized and reinforced the exertion of such an influence.

The church was not only gaining increasing recognition as the protector and promoter of Christian autonomy in the Mountain, but was also reinforcing and extending the multifaceted roles it had initiated earlier. Church-affiliated schools and colleges of the various monastic orders became more widespread. Enterprising monks sustained their agricultural and industrial activities, and maintained their position as a major source of employment. The ubiquitous village priests dominated the everyday life of their communities as much as they did at the turn of the century. In short, the church continued to satisfy much of the spiritual, welfare and benevolent needs of Mount Lebanon.

It is in this fundamental sense that sectarian loyalties, along with those of kinship and communal attachments, survived as sources of social and cultural integration, satisfying much of the unmet needs of various groups. This is reflected in the type of benevolent and welfare agencies that emerged at the time. For example, of the 100 recorded voluntary associations established between 1860 and 1919, 53 were family associations, 42 religious and 5 communal. None, whatsoever, were secular in character (Khalaf 1987: 161–184). In other words, the extension of state services and public welfare activities did not undermine the nature and intensity of confessional allegiances.

Indeed, the *mutasarrifiyya* evolved into a sort of "confessional sectocracy." In the words of an astute observer of the period, it was altogether a "feeble but embryonic nation-state" or at least a felicitous experiment in nation and state-building (Akarli 1993: 1–3). Though the country's economic development became more subordinate to European market forces and was marked by a massive demographic hemorrhage in its manpower resources, on the whole this special political arrangement managed to contain external sources of instability and usher Lebanon into its longest interlude of guarded coexistence. Except for the minor revisions introduced in 1864, the Règlement remained in effect until the State of Greater Lebanon was declared in 1920.

Perhaps because the Ottomans were keen to woo the Lebanese away from the growing appeals of French influence, they encouraged the development of basic integrative political institutions germane for organized political participation and self-government. The special internationally guaranteed status the Mountain enjoyed at the time, embedded in capitulatory and other concessionary protocols, was also helpful in enabling the Lebanese to develop and consolidate their own political identity. In time this salutary measure of autonomy, and the presence of a fairly independent-minded and recalcitrant local political elite, allowed the Lebanese to extricate themselves from the troubles the Ottomans were ultimately beset with. Once again, Akarli is unequivocal in his overall assessment: "the Ottoman evidence suggests that whereas European intervention in the affairs of the Mountain was often self-interested, sectarian, and divisive, the Ottomans perforce worked hard, until 1912–13, to build a stable governmental order which would help reconcile the moral and material differences among Lebanon's different regions, sects, and dominant social classes" (Akarli 1993: 189).

The State of Greater Lebanon 1920

Though, outwardly, the creation of Greater Lebanon in 1920 appeared to have sustained this relatively blissful interlude, this new entity was not born in harmony. Indeed, to some observers it was a "schizophrenic birth," an ironical outgrowth of French-British diplomatic rivalries each, in turn, exploiting internal sectarian parochialism (see Hudson 1968: 37–39; Petran 1987: 29).

The fascinating and labyrinthian story of how France established its mandate over Lebanon has been told and retold elsewhere. What needs to be emphasized here is, once again, the impact of this inside-outside dialectics on exacerbating sectarian hostility. Though 1920 marks the creation of the political state of modern Lebanon with its internationally recognized borders, it also heralds an epoch of mounting tension. Despite its remarkable durability the creation of this entity has had grave consequences for upsetting the precarious demographic and sectarian balance, and therefore has become a perpetual source of confessional suspicion and ill-feeling. As we have seen, a growing segment of the Maronite community was never too happy with what it regarded as a truncated Mount Lebanon and harked back to the days of the Emirate. Without the coastal cities and the fertile hinterland, the *Mutesarrifiyya* became too dwarfed and vulnerable. France, ever so ready to rush to the rescue of its reliable ally, took measures to annex parts of Ottoman Syria to the autonomous province of Mount Lebanon.

Like most other arrangements, the creation of Greater Lebanon was replete with discord at virtually all levels: French-British rivalry, differences within and among the French, between various communities, and even among the Maronites themselves. It must be recalled that much of the diplomatic discourse was taking place in the wake of the Arab Rebellion of 1916 and the aborted Cherifian government of 1918.

Shortly after World War I, the standing of the French in geographical Syria was being undermined. British troops were in control of the coastal areas and much of the other strategic regions. The French had hoped to convince Amir Faisal to accept a French mandate over his envisioned state. These and related developments were, naturally, a source of considerable anxiety within Mount Lebanon. Faisal was in no position to look with favor at any autonomous entity in Lebanon, let alone the prospects of territorial enlargements entertained by the so-called "Kiyanists" who perceived "Greater Lebanon" as the natural geographical and historical boundaries. To them, a Lebanon without access to the agricultural resources of the Biqa' or the port of Beirut is detrimental to its economic viability and autonomy. The "Kiyanists" were also keen to preserve some of the liberal attributes of the *mutasarrifiyya*; namely parliamentary democracy, protection of minority rights, self-rule, independence and other civil and secular liberties. They were also willing to accept support from the French government for the "cultural and political progress . . . and the security it would provide against any infringements upon the country's independence" (for further details see, al-Khuri 1960: 1: 269–271; Haffar 1961: 207–300; Zamir 1985: 53–54).

The Arab Revolt of 1916 and the brief Cherifian interlude of 1918 had inspired genuine Arab nationalist sentiments and strong antipathy at French sponsorship of an "artificial" Greater Lebanon. If foreign protection was deemed inevitable at the time, there was clear preference for the British, particularly among Muslims, Druze, and Greek Orthodox. Indeed, the King-Crane Commission, based on the plebiscite they conducted in the summer of 1919, had recommended the creation of an autonomous Lebanon but only within a larger Syrian entity. Of course, the King-Crane recommendations were ignored.

French diplomatic circles were not, it seems, of the same mind. Even those who were in support of breaking up the French-mandated territory in the Levant into a patchwork of ethnic states (to prevent the consolidation of a large anti-French Syrian Arab unity) were apprehensive about such prospects (see Zamir 1985). The Maronites themselves were also divided. The diehards among them continued to hope for greater alignment with France to protect the Christian entity against ascendant Pan Arab and Muslim sentiments. Some, particularly Patriarch Huwayyik and the delegation he headed to the Paris Peace Conference in 1919, were in support of a French mandate over Lebanon, but wished to curb its excesses in undermining the sovereignty and independence of the future state. Some of the ardent members of the Huwayyik delegation were clearly more concerned about preserving the Christian identity of Lebanon. "They undermined the differences between the Western-Oriented Lebanese and the mostly Bedouin and culturally backward Arabs," and described at length the atrocities inflicted upon Christians during the war for their loyalty to France. The delegation also appealed to France's responsibility in protecting Christians against Muslims (Akarli 1993: 176–77). Others, led by Emile Edde, Lebanon's President (1936–1941), saw in the territorial reduction of Lebanon, given the anticipated demographic changes in favor of Muslims, a more homogeneous and cohesive Christian entity.

Ultimately, a more reconciliatory and flexible school of thought came to prevail, one more receptive to the need of incorporating non-Christian minorities in an essentially Christian Lebanon. Thanks to the foresight of Michel Chiha and his enlightened circle of intellectual, business, and political associates, who articulated a vision of Lebanon more open to European and Western contacts without necessarily undermining the nascent Arabist and nationalist sentiments coveted by Muslim and Christian secularists. It was largely the ideas of this circle along with thoughtful Sunnites, equally mindful of the legitimate fears of Christians being engulfed in an avalanche of Arabism, which were incorporated into the constitution of 1926 and the National Covenant of 1943. External events, once again, facilitated the workings of this more consociational resolution of the discord. France's political demise after World War II tilted in favor of the Constitutional Bloc of Bishara al Khoury which was more receptive to such an accommodationist view.

The National Covenant of 1943

The National Covenant of 1943 (*Mithaq al Watani*), an unwritten pact brokered by the British to secure the country's independence from France, also evolved into a pragmatic political strategy to alleviate the tensions engendered by the issues of confessional coexistence and national identity. Essentially a gentlemen's agreement between the two leading spokesmen of their respective communities, the *Mithaq* provided a consensual basis for articulating the character of Lebanon's polity and the distribution of power in the country. Briefly, it stipulated four basic tenets: (1) The independence, neutrality and sovereignty of Lebanon; and called upon Christians to forego seeking Western protection (particularly French) in return for Muslim renunciation of attempts to align Lebanon with Syria or other forms of Arab union. (2) Lebanon was a country with an Arab "face" while retaining its separate and special identity. In other words, despite its Arabism, Lebanon should not cut off its cultural and spiritual ties with the West. (3) Lebanon was to cooperate with all Arab states provided that they recognize its sovereignty and independence. (4) Finally, it called for a reinterpretation of the constitutional provisions for an "equitable" distribution of seats in the executive and legislative bodies to approximate more closely the proportional sectarian representation.

Although the *Mithaq* was far from perfect, critics have been too excessive in attributing many of the country's frailties to it. Over the years it has served as a convenient scapegoat to account for virtually all the pitfalls inherent in its testy political culture: Immobilism, consecration of confessionalism, inhibiting the emergence of organized political parties, the exclusion of extremists and other ideological groups from the arena of legitimate political behavior, have, among other pathologies, been attributed to the *Mithaq*. (see Hudson 1968: 44–45; Saab 1966: 276; Maksoud 1966: 241). For nearly three decades though, both as a solemn pact and a pragmatic instrument of political management, it was effective in accommodating the inbred mutual suspicions between religious groups whose political orientations and frames of reference were basically different. What the architects of the *Mithaq* sought to do was to mute or neutralize those differences and thus forestall the emotional and confessional upsurges associated with them. To a considerable degree, at least if measured by the low incidence of collective political violence, this was realized.

In this sense the *Mithaq* was more than just an "expedient deal among a few politicians" (Binder 1966: 319). It was something akin to a "social contract." Like all other contracts or covenants, it exacted a price: the renunciation of some of the politically charged claims or sentiments of each of the major religious groups for the sake of national concord and amity. This was vividly apparent by the way the crisis of representation was resolved. The ratio agreed upon, 6:5 in favor of Christians, did not reflect demographic realities of the time. Rather it evinced a sentiment of "noblesse oblige" among Muslims or, more concretely, a concession on their part to preserve this skewed margin in favor of Christians in order to allay their fears as an endangered minority about to be engulfed in an overwhelming Muslim region.

At the same time, the *Mithaq* promoted political balance and did not detract much from the actual power of the other sects. For example, the electoral system, based on the quota principle and multi-sect constituency, promoted a greater measure of nonsectarian alignment of leaders in the parliament and, in doing so, reduced sectarian tensions. The results of the national elections of 1972, the last such regular elections held before the outbreak of hostilities in 1975, clearly demonstrate the redistributive potential of this ingenious arrangement. At least thirteen Christian deputies were elected to parliament under the sponsorship or cooptation of Muslim leaders, while only five Muslims gained entry to the national assembly under the sponsorship of Christian leaders. Such gains clearly tilted the actual distribution of parliamentarians in favor of Muslim representatives (Harik 1987: 194–95). The office of Prime Minister also witnessed appreciable enhancement in its power and public stature. Sunni Muslim premiers have traditionally suffered from this "second fiddle," subservient status. They repeatedly complained that their tenure in office is often at the whim and mercy of a Maronite President. "By 1974, however, the office had gained so much power that it was nearly equal in importance to the presidency. Indeed, a major problem of the Lebanese state since the 1960 was what it had become a two-headed institution, with each head having veto power over the other" (Harik 1987: 196).

More fundamental perhaps, as Albert Hourani has propounded repeatedly, the *Mithaq* reconciled two distinct visions or ideologies of Lebanon which had been tenuously held together since the creation of Greater Lebanon in 1920.

On the one hand, there was the idea of Mount Lebanon: a society rural, homogeneous, embodied in an institution, the Maronite church, with a self-image . . . and with a vision of an independent and predominantly Christian political community. On the other, there were the urban communities of Beirut and other coastal cities, mainly Sunni Muslim but with Orthodox and other Christian elements, and with a different idea: that of a trading community open to the world, and serving as a point of transit and exchange, and therefore a community where populations mingled and coexisted peacefully; of a society which needed government and law, but preferred a weak government to which the leaders of its constituent groups had access and which they could control (Hourani 1988: 7–8).

Hourani traces the theoretical basis of this vision and its embodiment in the *Mithaq* to, of course, the writings of Michel Chiha, in which we can see the marriage of the two ideologies; the mountain and the city:

Lebanon the mountain of refuge and Lebanon the meeting place, rooted in its own traditions but open to the world, with bilingualism or trilingualism as a necessity of its life; possessing stable institutions which correspond with its deep realities, an assembly in which the spokesmen of the various communities can meet and talk together, tolerant laws, no political domination of one group by another, but kind of spiritual domination of those who think of Lebanon as part of the Mediterranean world (Chiha 1949).

Chiha's optimistic vision notwithstanding, the marriage was strenuous from its very inception. It was, after all, an arranged liaison, a contract; not a romantic bond. With all the bona fides of its architects and the noblesse oblige of the consenting parties, the *Mithaq* could not have possibly survived the multilayered pressures (local, regional, and international) it was burdened with. It was a partial covenant. It did not fully express the changing demographic and communal realities of the time. With the creation of Greater Lebanon, Christians as a whole were no longer in a majority, though arguably the Maronites were still the largest single community. The annexation of the coast and the Biqa' also ushered in an unsettling variety of political cultures and disparate ideologies.

Incidentally, it is these "New Phoenician" voices which captured the attention of the American Legation offices in Beirut at the time; particularly

those of Chiha, Gabriel Menassa, Alfred Kettaneh, and their extended network of family circles and close associates of the commercial and political
elite. As staunch advocates of free trade, they were opposed to any form of
central planning and protectionism, shunned industrialization, jealously
guarded the sources of their new wealth and lived by the edict: "import or
die." Writing to the Secretary of State, on August 19 1947, Lowell Pinkerton
of the U.S. Legation had this to say:

> The ancient commercial craft of the Phoenicians is still very evident
> . . . perhaps it will prevail more modern counsels, or be more effec-
> tively supplemented by expert foreign advice. In any case, here are
> vigorous exponents of the capitalist system who now look only to the
> United States for ideas and encouragement (Gendzier 1990: 35).

Chiha himself, incidentally, was fully aware that his vision was far from
an exemplar of stability and harmony. His liberal image of Beirut as a cosmopolitan city-state coexisting with the more archaic tribal and primordial
loyalties of those of the mountain and hinterland was, to say the least, a
cumbersome and problematic vision. This was compounded, particularly
after 1920, by the impassioned claims of the rival ideological currents taking
root in the coastal cities. The "Lebanism" of the Christians was pitted against
the "Arabism" of the Sunni Muslims with reverberations among the Shiites
and Druze of the hinterland. No wonder that during the 1930s the neighborhoods of Beirut were periodically "the scene of violent clashes between
Christian and Muslim gangs, one side brandishing the banner of Lebanism,
the other of Arabism" (Salibi 1988: 180).

That the Mithaq managed to hold such a potentially violent society together for more than three decades is a tribute to both its architects and the
so-called "fathers of independence"—a generation of visionaries but also
moderate and reasonable leaders.

The shortcomings of the Mithaq, then, are not inherent in its basic philosophy or modus vivendi to arrive at a consensual compromise between
communities seeking to contain potentially explosive issues of sovereignty,
representation, and peaceful coexistence. The Mithaq was also addressing
perhaps the more delicate problems associated with the "fears" of the Christians and the "demands" and "grievances" of the Muslims. Like most pacts
it involved mutual renunciation. As we have seen, the Christians undertook
to renounce their traditional alliances with the West and France in particular, while the Muslims promised to abandon their pan-Arabist aspirations.

In effect both communities were to turn away from the larger world to help galvanize their loyalties to Lebanon. George Naccache's pungent aphorism notwithstanding—"deux négations ne font pas une nation"—this double renunciation seemed both feasible and appropriate at the time.

The Ta'if Accord of 1989

The Ta'if Accord is often heralded as an innovative and remarkable pact marking the threshold of a new republic. It is credited for putting an end to nearly two decades of protracted violence and for laying the foundation for reconciling differences over the three implacable sources of long standing discord and hostility, namely: political reforms, national identity, and state sovereignty. To Latif Abul-Husen the Accord is seen as a "breakthrough," a quest not only for the termination of conflict but also for the establishment of permanent peace. Until then, he maintains, peace remained elusive since all earlier attempts at resolving the conflict were no more than stopgap measures that failed to produce any substantial results. He goes further to assert that Ta'if succeeded because it "brought the conflict down to a legal and manageable level . . . by establishing a workable and effective conflict resolution" (Abul-Husen 1999: chap-6).

Even those who recognize its precarious birth, its inherent shortcomings, and its falling short in meeting the desired expectations of the actors and groups involved still see it as a document of "immense historical significance." To Paul Salem it is "the first general, written agreement among a broad spectrum of parties, militias and leaders on fundamental political issues . . . and it does provide the first real chance for the winding down of war and the re-establishment of a workable state and a relatively fair political system." By virtue alone of the reforms it managed to introduce into the Lebanese Constitution, particularly with regard to power-sharing, Ta'if is seen, regardless of its ultimate success or failure, as ushering a new and radical turn in Lebanon's modern political history (Salem 1991: 75–77). To Richard Norton Ta'if's uniqueness is attributed to one significant feature: "it was the byproduct of elected officials who were not, in most cases, belligerents in the war" (Norton 1991: 461).

These and other such optimistic assessments of Tai'f's virtues notwithstanding, I wish to advance here a more moderate and realistic view of its avowed promises and accomplishments. Foremost, Ta'if does not constitute a paradigm shift or a radical departure from earlier attempts at political

reform or conflict resolution. Indeed, it embraces some of the deeply ingrained traditions and defining elements that have long sustained its political
culture: its consociative attributes, and the ethos of no victor and no vanquished. More grievous, the hailed Accord did not put an end to the fighting.
Rather, it sparked off another more devastating outburst of internecine carnage and generated a heavy residue of renewed feelings of marginalization
and intercommunal hostility and paranoia. Even if one were to recognize
that Ta'if may represent a "radical turn" in the evolution of Lebanon's protracted crisis, it is a doubtful whether it has or could bring about any tangible
political progress or restructuring in basic loyalties or perceptions.

Like virtually all its predecessors it came in the wake of a treacherous and
relentless war and involved the same disparate and conflicted set of local,
regional and global actors. The setting and atmosphere that enveloped the
negotiations had an air of urgency and drama, suffused with pregnant expectations mixed with feelings of apprehension and uncertainty as to the
final product. That product, again like many of its illustrious forerunners,
was almost faultless as a written document. All its avowed assertions, whether
expressed as anticipated hopes or explicit stipulations, display genuine concern to introduce desired political reforms and constitutional amendments.
These are often enshrined in terms of lofty and uncontested national goals
such as the abolishment of political confessionalism and the establishment
of universal social and economic justice, reclaiming state authority, sovereignty, independence and territorial integrity. The Accord also addresses
boldly the two critical issues of ending the war: disbanding the militias and
scaling down Syrian presence in the country.

It had a difficult, almost cesarean, birth. Credit goes, of course, to the
determination and skills of the midwife(ves). Saudi Arabia, which hosted
the conference at Ta'if, was at the time in a propitious diplomatic position
to act as the main sponsor. Of course the Saudis were not a new player in
Lebanon's troubled waters. Throughout the war they had stepped in on
repeated occasions to mediate between and among the local and regional
combatants.

It was in Riyadh during the first Arab League summit (October 17–18,
1976) that the Arab Deterrent Force (ADF) was created. As contributor to
ADF, the Saudis took part in the Beit Eddin conference, convened to mitigate the mounting tensions between Syria and the Lebanese Christians.
Also, after the Arab summit in Tunis (November 20–22, 1979) Saudi Arabia
was part of the quadripartite Arab Vigilance Committee established to implement the resolutions. Most crucial perhaps when general Awn declared

his so-called "War of Liberation" against Syria (mid March 1989), this disastrous turn of events, sparked off by this new spectacle of senseless cruelty,
gave added credence to another beneficent Saudi diplomatic intervention.
At the Casablanca summit (May 25–26, 1989), the Arab League Committee
of six was reactivated. It was then that the Tripartite High Commission,
composed of King Hassan of Morocco, President Chadli Benjedid of Algeria,
and King Fahd of Saudi Arabia, was entrusted with the task of resolving
Lebanon's protracted crisis. The triumvirate, with the astute assistance of
Lakhdar Ibrahimi, the Assistant Secretary General of the Arab League, was
specifically charged with the mandate of overseeing the impending presidential elections and envisioned reforms.

Syria, it must be noted, was visibly excluded from the Commission. More
injurious, the first report of the Commission (issued at the end of July 1989)
was highly critical of Syria, singling it out as detrimental to the restoration
of Lebanese sovereignty (for these and other related details, see Maila 1994;
Norton 1991; Salem 1991).

Saudi Arabia's diplomatic intervention was more than just an expression
of its longstanding investment in Arab peace and the reconciliatory role it
is often called upon to play in containing the ruinous fallouts of bickering
Arab regimes. Unsettling regional and global transformations, some with
immense historic implications, rendered Saudi mediation efforts all the
more compelling. Indeed, no other power at the time was better equipped
to play that role. After the Cold War, with the bitter superpower rivalry
between the Soviet Union and the U.S. now ended, a U.S. brokered solution
through a trusted ally became feasible. Saudi Arabia, given her phobic proclivities about some of her conventional enemies, particularly ascendant
Shi'ism, fractious Palestinians, and Islamic extremism, was more than eager
to step in. Some of the local combatants also welcomed, declared or otherwise, this shift away from the Syrians and toward the Saudis.

It was against this background, made all the more compelling by, perhaps,
the most tumultuous years in Lebanon's fractious political history, that the
urge to meet at Ta'if must be viewed. Even against the gruesome backdrop
of the previous fifteen years of reckless bloodletting, those of 1988–90 seem
all the more menacing. They were dense with the havoc of bewildering
succession of disruptive and terrifying events: a constitutional crisis of unprecedented dimensions in which two governments contested the legitimacy
of the other but with no president; recurrent crises of presidential succession;
reawakened fears of partition; the specter of Syria's tightening grip over the
country; and, most devastating, the bitter residues of three fractious wars

between factional leaders vying to extend their hegemony over the marginalized and threatened Christian community.

The grim story and catalogue of events surrounding those years have been
told and retold elsewhere. I only wish here to highlight briefly some of their
distinctive implications for a better understanding of the prospects of conflict
resolution engendered by Ta'if.

Between September 22, 1988 and November 24, 1989, Lebanon knew
three presidents: the tumultuous term of Amin Gemayyel, the brief and
tragic tenure of Rene Mouawad, and the inauguration of Elias Hrawi. Minutes before the expiration of his official tenure in office (on September 22,
1988), President Amin Gemayyel, in view of the failure of the parliament
to elect a successor, exercised his last prerogative as president and appointed,
albeit reluctantly, General Awn to head a bi-sectarian interim government
composed of six military officers — three Christian and three Muslims. The
confessionally balanced cabinet was intended as a caretaker government
until a new President was elected. This unprecedented move unleashed a
flurry of fateful repercussions. Gemayyel's appointment of a Maronite as a
Prime Minister, a post reserved by the *Mithaq* and by political convention
to the Sunnis, outraged the Sunni Muslim establishment and their allies on
the National Movement and Reformist Camp. Shortly after the announce-
ment of the new cabinet, the three Muslim officers declined to serve. Awn
was left heading a cabinet with two other Christian colleagues.

Salim al-Hoss, the incumbent Prime Minister since Rashid Karami was
assassinated in 1987, refused to recognize Awn's government. With popular
Muslim support reinforced by Syria's blessings, Hoss continued to head his
cabinet from West Beirut. For the next year, the country was, in effect, run
by two rival governments: one in West Beirut presided over by Hoss and the
other in in Ba'abda, led by Awn.

This tenuous division of powers soon started to unravel. It quickly became
apparent that Awn had greater political ambitious in mind. He not only
denied the legitimacy of Hoss's government but went even further to claim
that his Council of Ministers was also constitutionally entrusted with all the
powers of the president as long as the post remained vacant. Hence, he saw
no urgency in holding presidential elections. He embarked instead on an
adventurous scheme to extend and consolidate his powers.

The rivalry between the two governments spilled over to other contentious militia groups and paramilitary organizations eager to exploit the power
vacuum. The Lebanese Forces (LF) took over President Gemayyel's party
bases in his hometown and adjoining regions. Hizbollah and Amal clashed
in the southern suburbs of Beirut. More decisive, Awn launched his first

offensive (mid February of 1989) against the LF in his campaign to consolidate his hold over the Christian enclave. The pitched street battles, lasting
hardly a week, left about 80 dead and more than 200 wounded. After a few
initial successes, Awn found himself unable to subdue Ja'ja. He reluctantly
accepted a cease-fire brokered by the Papal Nuncio and the Maronite Pa-
triach. Awn had, however, succeeded in recapturing Beirut's port. Buoyed
by this victory he launched his second assault, hardly a month later, by
imposing a sea blockade on all illegal ports in the country. Since many of
these ports were controlled by other militias and were a source of immense
revenues, it sparked off the violent opposition of virtually all the militias and
their accessories: the Shi'ite Amal, the Druze PSP, and the Christian Marada
of Suleiman Franjieh. More disconcerting, it provoked the indignation of
their Syrian Patrons.

It was at this point that the confrontation started to assume more war-like
and belligerent manifestations. In-fighting and localized turf wars were suspended to confront bigger enemies beyond. The conventional embattled
war zones and demarcation line, dormant for a while, were reawakened.
The dreaded din of artillery exchanges across the "Green Line," dividing
East and West Beirut, resumed its vengeful cycles. So did the cycle of broken
cease-fires.

Syria's direct involvement brought another unlikely regional actor, Iraq,
into the fray. Like other such proxy interventions, it was bound to escalate
the level of hostility. On March 14, 1989 Awn declared his "war of liberation" to expel Syrian forces from Lebanon. Clearly Awn, even in alliance
with the LF, was no match for Syria's military presence in the country. His
defiant call to war, often attributed to his impulsive and impetuous behavior,
might have been intended to draw regional and international attention. By
"arousing national sentiments and challenging Syria's presence in Lebanon,
he wanted to force the great powers to pay more attention to the fate of his
country" (Laurent 1991: 96).

International attention was late and timid. The war raged for six months
with no apparent victor or vanquished. The cost was massive: more than
1,000 casualties, 5,000 wounded and $1.2 billion in damages to homes and
infrastructure. It was estimated that more than 1 million Beirutis had to flee
the city to escape the relentless volleys of artillery fire between the two sectors
of the city. Syrian gunners on the western flanks responded it seems with
greater savagery, inflicting thereby greater damage on residents in the east.
(For these and other vivid details see Fisk 1990: 629–43; Salem 1991:67;
Norton 1991: 465–66).

As usual, innocent civilians and bystanders, were disproportionately victimized. But the country was also a surrogate victim, as in other such seemingly internal wars, of more pernicious regional and international rivalries. France, the traditional ally of the Francophone and Francophile Christians of Lebanon, was naturally inclined to support Awn's efforts in restoring his country's sovereignty and independence. The U.S., however, the more potent broker in the region, was reluctant to be embroiled again in Lebanon's quagmire before a definite settlement of the Arab-Israeli conflict.

The intensity of the suffering finally, induced international concern. A diplomatic exit, the congruence of regional and international power brokers, became feasible. The U.S. and Saudi Arabia were to endorse an Arab League initiative in which the Lebanese parliament would convene at Ta'if (Saudi Arabia) to discuss and approve what appeared to be a plausible middle-course for all concerned: Awn was to halt his "war of liberation," Syria would agree to a timetable for its withdrawal, and the Lebanese parliamentarians would agree on the desired political reforms, particularly the contested issues of power-sharing, sovereignty, and national identity.

After eight weeks of heated, often contentious, debate, agreement was finally reached (October 22, 1989) on a draft document. Considering the polemical baggage of dogmatic mindsets the conferees carried with them, let alone the polarized sentiments and aspirations of their own constituencies, it is remarkable that an agreement could have been achieved at all. Each of the two broad coalitions came to Ta'if with diametrically opposed, often irreconcilable, views regarding the three fundamental issues under debate: political reforms, state sovereignty, and national identity (For an informed analysis of these differences, see Abul-Husen 1998).

On political reforms the most striking feature of the Accord was its attempt to provide a more balanced confessional redistribution of power. Accordingly, it endorsed the transfer of some of the executive powers of the president, traditionally reserved for a Maronite, to the Chamber of Deputies and the Council of Ministers. The ministerial portfolios were also equally divided between the two main religious communities.

The speaker of the Chamber of Deputies, a post customarily reserved for a Shi'i Muslim, was to be elected for a four rather than one-year term. The number of seats were also increased from 99 to 108 and were divided equally between the two confessional groups. Likewise, the powers of the Sunni prime minister were elevated. His nomination by the president requires now consultation with the speaker who becomes the real custodian of executive powers. With a few minor exceptions, such as the accreditation of ambassadors and the granting of pardons, the autonomous powers of the president are shifted to the cabinet. In effect, as one observer puts it, the president is "stripped of most of his executive powers and is reduced to a largely ceremonial figure who reigns but does not rule. He remains the head of the state and symbol of its unity, but he can only exert executive authority through the cooperation of the Council of Ministers" (Salem 1991:78).

In addressing the entrenched and testy issue of sectarianism, Ta'if simply reiterates the call for its elimination made by earlier covenants and proposed pacts. Here again, this is expressed as a "fundamental national objective" and a phased plan is provided for at least abolishing political sectarianism. The proposed plan stipulates measures of how to rely on merit, capability, and specialization in public jobs (excluding top level positions) as a substitute for sectarian quotas. It also goes as far as to call for the deletion of the mention of sect and denomination on the identity card.

The issue of national identity and sovereignty are addressed in the preamble as a set of general principles. The Accord opens up by stating that "Lebanon is a sovereign, free, independent country and final homeland for its citizens." Then it goes on to assert that it is Arab in belonging and identity. It is an active and founding member of the Arab league and is committed to the League's charters.

Sovereignty is considered in the context of three testy and controversial issues: the Israeli occupation of parts of southern Lebanon, the abusive powers of the militias in undermining state sovereignty, and, most thorny, the scaling down of Syrian presence in the country. With regard to the first, the Accord simply urges the implementation of UN Resolution 424, of March 1978, and other Security Council Resolutions concerned with the withdrawal of Israeli troops from southern Lebanon. Likewise, the Accord stipulates that all militias and paramilitary organizations are to be disbanded within six months after the approval of the Accord's charter. It does not, however, indicate how this is to be done, or how to reabsorb the tens of thousands of trained fighters into the institutions and agencies of civil society.

The contentious issue of Syria's presence and the timing of its phased withdrawal is dealt with in two ways. First, it is invoked in the context of how the state is to spread its authority over all the Lebanese territories. "In view of the fraternal relations binding Syria to Lebanon, the Syrian forces shall thankfully assist the forces of the legitimate Lebanese government to spread the authority of the state within a set period of no more than two years." In the interim, the Accord would have been ratified, a president elected, a cabinet formed and the political reforms approved. It is only at the end of this period that the two governments "shall decide to redeploy the Syrian forces in the Beqa' region." Secondly, Syria's presence is addressed in the final article of the Accord under the rubric of the distinctive relations between the two countries which derive their "strengths from the roots of blood relationships, history and joint fraternal interests. . . ." The last clause of the Accord ends with the following protective and patronizing high note:

> Consequently, Lebanon should not allow itself to become a pathway or a base for any force, state, or organization seeking to undermine its security or Syria's security. Syria, which is eager for Lebanon's security, independence, and unity, and for harmony among its citizens, should not permit any act that poses a threat to Lebanon's security, independence, and sovereignty.

Awn was naturally very critical of the Accord. Even before the delegates had convened at Ta'if, he made efforts to foil the meeting by insisting on Syrian withdrawal as a precondition. When that failed, he resorted to all the intimidating, often insidious gambits against the deputies who participated, or those who were favorably predisposed toward it. Even those who had not openly declared their opposition to Ta'if were considered traitors and a threat to the country's sovereignty and well-being. Not even the Maronite Patriarch, Nasrallah Sfeir, was spared. He was so harassed at his official residence in Bkirki that he sought refuge in Diman, the Syrian–controlled region in the North.

To forestall parliamentary approval of the Accord, Awn tried to dissolve the parliament. However, it still managed to meet in Qulay'at (November 5, 1989) when the Accord was formally approved and René Mouawad was elected President. Mouawad's term was tragically cut short seventeen days later when he was assassinated by a remote-controlled bomb as his motorcade drove through Beirut. His brutal cold-blooded assassination, like so many others, remains unsolved, or at least the identity of the murderer has never been revealed. Elias Hrawi, a favored Syrian candidate, was elected to succeed him.

Awn's vehement condemnation of the Accord was based on at least two grounds. First, the withdrawal of Syrians, his most passionate demand, even in principle, remained nebulous. Only a "redeployment" of the forces to the Biqa' was to take place two years after the ratification of the Accord. No explicit timetable was given as to further withdrawal other than the indefinite reference that such withdrawals would be "negotiated at the appropriate time

by the governments of Syria and Lebanon." Second, Awn was equally adamant in his opposition to the alleged political reforms because they involved
no more than the shift of the executive powers of the President to the Prime
Minister. This, in his view, would further undermine the already marginalized political standing of the Christian community.

In the fall of 1989, shortly after the ratification of the Accord, the alliance
between Awn and the LF, tenuously held together during the "war of liberation," started to dissolve. The fierce intra-Maronite rivalry between Awn
and Ja'ja' soon erupted into open warfare. When Awn declared his intention
(January 30, 1990) to "unify the gun under one control," it became apparent
that the much-dreaded military confrontation between Awn's army and the
LF commanded by Ja'ja was bound to be a particularly menacing example
of the normally atrocious and anguishing fratricidal warfare.

Fighting erupted suddenly in pitched street battles in densely populated
quarters that took much of the resident population off-guard. The suicidal
war pitted two combatants seething with mutual enmity, each yielding considerable destructive power but with neither in a position to achieve a decisive victory. The army under Awn was highly motivated, fairly well-trained
and equipped. So were the LF under the supervision of Fuad Malik, an ex-
army officer.

At a more ideological level, the confrontation was also pitting two different visions of Lebanon and the place of the Christian community within it.
Awn was articulating a more unified vision where the state will restore its
total authority and sovereignty and territorial integrity. Ja'ja, on the other
hand, envisioned the establishment of a federal system with a strong and
cohesive Christian state or canton. He also did not exclude the possibility
of a loose association with other confessional mini-states in a system of semi-
independent cantons (for further details, see Laurent 1991: 88–101). Either
way, the stakes were very high since at the time the confrontation was, in
effect, a showdown over the leadership of the Christian community.

Like all other seemingly internal wars, the changing course of battle,
brought in some very improbable shifts in the pattern of regional and global
alliances. For example, when the LF forces proved more resilient than Awn
had expected, Syria, normally his most accursed nemesis, rushed in to assist
him. This obviously outraged Iraq, which prodded Saddam Hussein and his
Foreign Minister, Tariq Aziz, to undertake a diplomatic initiative, along with
France and the Vatican, to arrange for a cease-fire. After an uneasy lull of a
few months, fighting broke out again with greater ferocity. Barely four
months old, the war generated a massive toll in human and material destruc-

tion: there were about 1,000 casualties and 2,500 injuries (for estimates see Abul-Husen 1998: Norton 1991: 467).

Despite the war's damage, and much like other instances of internal strife, it never ended or was permitted to end in a decisive victory of one adversary over the other. Awn was neither victorious nor defeated. Despite the popularity he continued to enjoy in parts of the Christian enclave, he was unable to transform the groundswell of enthusiasm he elicited among ordinary citizens for political activism into concrete political gains. He became increasingly isolated both internally and externally and lost much of the sympathy of his former supporters, particularly Iraq, France, and the Vatican.

As in other such local squabbles, an expected shift in the regional and global setting had a decisive impact in redirecting its course. The Gulf crisis allowed Syria to exploit this sudden diversion in diplomatic attention and its enhanced standing in Washington to exacerbate Awn's ultimate demise. Indeed by then the U.S. was already calling for the removal of Awn as the only solution to the Lebanese crisis (Friedman 1991). A joint Syrian-Lebanese military assault (October 13, 1991) on Ba'abda and the Metn region bombed Awn out of his headquarters in the Presidential Palace. He had no choice but to flee to the adjoining French Embassy where he sought political asylum and eventual exile in France.

As mentioned earlier, it was against this background, made all the more pressing by the ruinous hemorrhaging of the Lebanese economy, its crumbling services, and the relentless exodus of (mostly Christian) young professionals and skilled groups, that Ta'if must be viewed. As Joseph Maila (1994) persuasively argues, the urge to meet at Ta'if could well be seen as the immediate result or convergence of three fateful failures: the failure of General Awn's war of liberation against Syria; the failure of Syria to impose a solution acceptable to all the factions and communities in Lebanon; and finally, the failure of all internationally mediated efforts.

Despite its shortcomings one must recognize a few of its distinctive features. Foremost, and unlike earlier efforts of conflict resolution, those who convened at Ta'if were elected parliamentarians, not warlords or those who were directly involved in the fighting. For example, the short-lived Tripartite Agreement mediated by Syria in 1985 brought together the heads of the three most belligerent militia organizations. Elie Hobeika, Walid Jumblat and Nebih Berri. It barely survived two weeks. It was cut short by the mutiny of Samir Ja'ja' against Hobeika and his removal from the leadership of the LF.

Another enlightened feature of Ta'if was its recognition of the inextricable link between the intensity of internal rivalries and unresolved external conflict. Rather than treating the crisis as a reflection of exclusively internal dislocations it pronounced its regional and international dimensions. Though not very committal or definitive it at least promised the provision of Arab guarantees for safeguarding Lebanon's sovereignty and territorial integrity. Groups who are inimical to Syria's growing dominance in the country felt a measure of reassurance that they need not face Syria's intransigence alone.

Equally enlightening is the way Ta'if enshrined intercommunal consensus to sustain its solemn pact of communal coexistence (*al aysh al-mushtarak*) and safeguard the strained features of power-sharing and distributive justice as the defining elements of its political culture. This is at least a tacit recognition on the part of the architects of the Accord that nearly two decades of civil strife had done little by way of undermining the intensity of communal and sectarian loyalties in society. Ta'if, in other words, has judiciously opted to embrace, as Joseph Maila has argued, the "consensual, sectarian logic and accepted its dictates." This, once again, renders Lebanon "more of a contractual, consociative country than one based on a constitution. According to this tradition, the formal, legal framework is always subordinate to pragmatic, consensual approach to mitigating conflict within the country, and to managing national and communal strains" (Maila 1994:31).

Such auspicious features notwithstanding, Ta'if's record for nearly a decade now does not provide an encouraging outlook regarding its future prospects either as a peace-making venture or as a covenant for achieving a more balanced and harmonious intercommunal coexistence. Since its inception, in fact, the Accord has been a source of heated controversy. Some observers continue to maintain that its flaws are congenital. Others suggest that these inborn defects were compounded by the setting and the history surrounding the three-week diplomatic bonanza at Ta'if. It was clear that some of the conferees were acting under duress. Although they were freely elected participants, the charged atmosphere imposed constraints on how far they could have ranged beyond some of the pre-prepared texts and agendas. They were left with a very limited margin to maneuver or to work out alternative schemes and proposals.

Even these who found no fault with the text still had misgivings about its lofty overtones, rendering it altogether more "declarative than definitive (Maila: 1994:37). Hence, at the operational level virtually all the concrete proposals for reform have either been "violated or derailed" (el-Khazen 1999:2). Political deconfessionalization, let alone the aspired hope of transforming Lebanon into a truly secular society, has yet to be achieved. Some, particularly a few of the noted architects of the Accord, see no resemblance between the initial text and the one groping to be implemented (al-Husseini 1994; Mansour 1993). For example, the government's efforts to decentralize have come repeatedly under fire in parliament. The government in fact has been abrogating to itself the right to redraw the country's administrative districts, doing so by decree, and thus bypassing parliament. The proposed plan, another radical departure from Ta'if, would do away with the *qada* system and create, instead, thirty-two smaller units. Areas which historically have been the basis for a coherent and meaningful territorial identity (e.g. Iqlim al-Kharoub in the Chouf or Hammana of Babda) are now splintered arbitrarily into fragmented units.

Most grievous perhaps is the pronounced and uneven shift in the relative political standing of the various communities. Ta'if's political reforms, particularly in laying the foundation for a more balanced system of power-sharing of sectarian representation, were expected to redress some of the internal gaps and disparities. As we have seen, the transfer of executive powers of the President to the Chamber of Deputies and the Cabinet rendered the position of a Maronite president more ceremonial and symbolic in character. The political standing of the Maronites has been unevenly undermined in other more disparaging respects.

The size of the electoral district, a hotly contested issue at the moment, has direct bearing on the hegemony and scope of political influence the various communities can yield. The electoral laws of 1992 and 1996, by rearranging the size of electoral constituencies, contributed in no small measure to curtailing the impact of Christian voters on the election of Christian deputies. The post-Ta'if electoral laws were such that they assigned large districts in predominantly Muslim regions where Christians are in the majority. This, in effect, meant that more Christian deputies were elected by Muslim votes than Muslim deputies elected by Christian votes. In his methodical analysis of the conduct and outcome of the two post-Ta'if elections (1992 and 1996), Farid el-Khazin substantiates such anomalies. In both elections, for example, Greek Orthodox and Greek Catholic voters had little or no impact on choosing any of their deputies in their respective constituencies. This was not true, however, of Muslim representatives who were brought to parliament by the votes of their co-religionists (el-Khazen 1998:27).

Such manifestations of political dispossession and disinheritance, particularly among the Maronites, have been spilling over to other dimensions of the political system, which serve to heighten further the feelings of marginalization and disenchantment (*ihbat*). Christian representatives on the Executive, in successive cabinets, have also been of lesser stature and credibility in comparison to those of Muslims. On the whole, the three leading Muslim communities continue to be represented by their most established and credible political leaders. Rafic Hariri for the Sunnis, Nabih Berri for the Shi'a, and Walid Jumblatt for the Druze all enjoy a wellspring of popular support and almost uncontested power base which wields considerable bargaining strength on behalf of their constituencies. In stark contrast, Christian communities, with rare exceptions, are bereft of such consequential public spokesmen. Those who command such standing are either excluded from public office or are in voluntary or, more likely, involuntary exile.

The collective fears and anxieties of Christians are exacerbated by two other momentous problems with dire consequences for intercommunal balance and harmony: The return of the displaced and the specter of naturalization. Ta'if makes a passing and declarative reference to the former: "The problem of the Lebanese evacuees shall be solved fundamentally, and the right of every Lebanese evicted since 1975 to return to the place from which he has been evicted shall be established. Legislation to guarantee this right and to insure the means of reconstruction shall be issued."

The problem of the displaced and the prospects for their return is a complex issue fraught with an interrelated set of economic, sociocultural, and psychological implications. In sheer magnitude it is immense. Close to 827,000 (about one-third of the country's resident population) were displaced between 1975 and 1989. Christians, however, bore a disproportionate burden of its misfortunes. The same source (Labaki and Abu Rjeily 1998) reveals that of those, 670,000 are Christians and only 157,500 are Muslims, roughly a ratio of 7 to 1. Also 70 percent of those who have not as yet reclaimed their homes and property are Christians. This is notably true of Areas like Aley and Chouf where displaced Christian families continue to harbor misgivings about their return.

The measures the government have taken thus far are not only fickle. They have also been mired in charges and counter charges of corruption, favoritism, and mismanagement of resources. The special fund established in 1993, attached to the Prime Minister's Office and administered by the Ministry of the Displace, has drained more than $600,000 million. I say drained, because close to 80 percent of the fund's budget has been squandered on indemnifying squatters to reclaim the houses and premises they have illegally occupied in Beirut and elsewhere.

The problem of naturalization, though not attributed to Ta'if, has also aroused the apprehensions of Christians since this, too, carries with it the dread of their demographic marginalization. The naturalization decree (ratified by the parliament on June 20, 1994), has reawakened their fears, particularly since the religious breakdown of those who were recently naturalized is skewed heavily in favor of Muslims: About 80 percent compared to only 20 percent Christians (el-Khazin 1999: 7–8). The problem is compounded by two further unsettling considerations: A large proportion of those granted citizenship (about 40,000) were UNRWA-registered Palestinian refugees. More disruptive, efforts were made to register the new citizens in selected mixed villages and towns to tilt the demographic profile of these electoral constituencies in favor of known pro-government candidates (for further details, see Atallah 1997).

It might be too soon to pass judgment on the ultimate future of Ta'if. If howerver, the first decade of its life is any measure, and if one were to judge its prospects in light of its own declared intentions, the outlook is far from promising.

Any cursory review of the swift and arresting succession of events heralding the onset of Ta'if attests to the compelling transformations it managed to unfold. In hindsight, they stand out as a stark threshold in the country's recent political history. As in earlier such episodes, unforeseen regional and international changes had a momentous impact on the course of internal events. The gulf war, this time, acted as the catalyst.

Syria quickly seized the day. Exploiting the diplomatic rewards of its membership in the anti-Iraqi coalition, it proceeded adroitly to implement Ta'if's edicts in ways consistent with its own interests. Since it was in full military and political control, with Awn out of the way, it met little resistance in consolidating its hegemony over a war-weary and fragmented country. Militias were disbanded, arms were confiscated, passageways and road blocks were cleared, an armistice was declared, and deputies were appointed, thereby imparting the impression of "normalization." Damascus went further to sign (on May 22, 1991) The Treaty of Brotherhood, Cooperation, and Coordination followed, a few months later, by the Pact of Defense and Security. A Lebanese-Syrian Upper Council was also established to "decide upon general cooperation and coordination policies between the two countries" (for further details see Maila 1994). Most disquieting, the Tripartite Arab High Commission was nullified; hence rendering Lebanon all the more subservient to Syria's political dictates.

In a word, Ta'if has once again confirmed, if reconfirmation is needed, that indelible feature of Lebanon's political culture; namely, that its ultimate political destiny is largely shaped outside its borders.

By de-escalating the rhetoric of war, Ta'if did in effect put an end to outward violence. It also managed to restore a measure of peaceful coexistence thereby permitting the reappearance of civility in everyday life. But this was accomplished at a prohibitive price. Lebanon had had to forfeit much of its national sovereignty and political autonomy. It is ironical that at a time when other repressed groups throughout the world are liberating themselves from the repressive yokes of their servility, Lebanon is now being engulfed by all the disheartening manifestations of mounting disempowerment and subjugation Equally grievous is the pronounced shift in the relative political standing of various communities. The guns might have been muted but deep-seated hostility and paranoia are far from being quelled. This is most visible in the redrawing of the country's social geography and other symptoms of retribalization. Unappeased hostility and fear predispose threatened and marginalized groups to find refuge in cloistered spatial localities and, hence, become distant from or indifferent to other communities. Coexistence, let alone the professed goals of national reconciliation, become all the more elusive.

10   Prospects For Civility

"Differences are held in suspension in successful communities of difference — what civic nations are when they succeed — and that entails a certain amount of studied historical absentmindedness. Injuries too well remembered cannot heal."
— Benjamin Barber, *Jihad vs. McWorld* (1996).

"While olive trees are essential to our very being, an attachment to one's olive trees, when taken into excess, can lead us into forging identities, bonds and communities based on the exclusion of others."
— Thomas Friedman, *The Lexus and the Olive Tree* (2000).

"The quality of our political and economic activity and our national culture is intimately connected to the strength and validity of our associations. Ideally, civil society is a setting of settings: all are included, none is preferred."
— Michael Walzer, *The Idea of Civil Society* (1991).

Lebanon today is at another fateful crossroads in its political and sociocultural history. At the risk of some oversimplification, the country continues to be imperiled by a set of overwhelming predicaments and unsettling transformations. At least three stand out by virtue of the ominous implications they have for the prospects of forging a viable political culture of tolerance and peaceful coexistence.

First, Lebanon is in the throes of postwar reconstruction and rehabilitation. Given the magnitude and scale of devastation, the country will almost certainly require massive efforts in virtually all dimensions of society to spearhead its swift recovery and sustained development. Processes of postwar reconstruction, even under normal circumstances, are usually cumbersome. In Lebanon, they are bound to be more problematic because of the distinctive character of some of the residues of collective terror and strife with which the country was besieged for so long. Among such disheartening consequences, two are particularly poignant and of relevance to the concerns of our final chapter. Both were alluded to earlier but need to be underscored here: the salient symptoms of retribalization apparent in reawakened communal identities and the urge to seek shelter in cloistered spatial communities and a pervasive mood of lethargy, indifference, and weariness, which borders, at times, on collective amnesia. Both are understandable reactions that enable traumatized groups to survive the cruelties of protracted strife. Both, however, could be disabling, as the Lebanese are now considering less belligerent strategies for peaceful coexistence.

Second, Lebanon is grappling with all the short-term imperatives of reconstruction and long-term need for sustainable development and security, and it has had to do so in a turbulent region with a multitude of unresolved conflicts. Also the country remains largely impotent to act on issues destined to shape its political future. Ordinary Lebanese citizens, much like their political representatives, are still disempowered or not yet in a position to have a decisive impact on matters that directly affect their country's political destiny or national sovereignty. As we have seen, Lebanon's entry or exit from war, its involvement in the peace process, the outlines of its foreign policy; even the character of its electoral laws and local municipal elections, are still largely shaped outside its borders.

Impotent as the country might seem at the moment to neutralize or ward off such external pressures, there are measures and programs, already proved effective elsewhere, which can be experimented with. These will at least fortify Lebanon's immunity against the disruptive consequences of such destabilizing forces. Such efforts can do much to reduce the country's chronic vulnerability to these pressures while enhancing opportunities for empowerment and self-determination. As will be argued, any form of voluntarism that can provide venues for participation in public space and while nurturing some of the attributes of civility and collective consciousness will be welcome. Likewise, more accessible opportunities to participate in civic and welfare associations, competitive sports, rehabilitative ecological, environmental, public-health, and heritage programs can also be invaluable as strategies for healing symptoms of fear, paranoia, and transcending parochialism. More substantive perhaps are the nascent prospects for public intervention in areas like urban planning, design, architecture, archaeological heritage, and landscaping.

Finally, Lebanon as of late is also embroiled, willingly or otherwise, in all the unsettling forces of postmodernity and globalism: a magnified importance of mass media, popular arts, and entertainment in the framing of everyday life, an intensification of consumerism, the demise of political participation and collective consciousness for public issues, and their replacement by local and parochial concerns for nostalgia and heritage.

Unfortunately, many of the public manifestations of nostalgia so rampant today in Lebanon have scant, if any, concern with what Christopher Lasch (1988) has called a conversational relationship with the past. Instead, they assume either the construction and embellishment of grandiose and monumental national symbols, or the search for roots, the longing to preserve or invent often contrived or apocryphal forms of local and communal identities. More disheartening, this valorization of or escape into the past, particularly at the popular cultural level, has taken on some of the garish symptoms of commodification of heritage into kitsch and the vulgarization of traditional folklore and indigenous artifacts.

Memory, Space, and Identity

Within this context, issues of collective memory, contested space, and efforts to forge new cultural identities begin to assume critical dimensions. How much and what of the past needs to be retained or restored? By whom and for whom? Commonplace as these questions might seem, they have invited little agreement among scholars. Indeed, the views and perspectives of those who have recently addressed them vary markedly.

As pointed out earlier, to Ernest Gellner collective forgetfulness, anonymity, and shared amnesia are dreaded conditions resisted in all social orders (Gellner 1988). Perhaps conditions of anonymity, he argues, are inevitable in times of turmoil and upheaval. But once the unrest subsides, internal cleavages and segmental loyalties resurface.

D. MacCannell (1989) goes further to assert that the ultimate triumph of modernity over other sociocultural arrangements is epitomized not by the disappearance of premodern elements, but by their reconstruction and artificial preservation in modern society. Similarly, Jedlowski (1990) also maintains that a sense of personal identity can only be achieved on the basis of personal memory.

Benjamin Barber, however, argues that successful civic nations always entail a certain amount of "studied historical absentmindedness. Injuries too well remembered," he tells us, "cannot heal." (Barber 1996: 167). What Barber is implying here, of course, is that if the memories of the war and its atrocities are kept alive, they will continue to reawaken fear and paranoia, particularly among those embittered by it. Without an opportunity to forget, there can never be a chance for harmony and genuine coexistence.

Both manifestations — the longing to obliterate, mystify, and distance oneself from the fearsome recollections of an ugly and unfinished war, or efforts to preserve or commemorate them — coexist today in Lebanon. Retribalization and the reassertion of communal and territorial identities, as perhaps the most prevalent and defining elements in postwar Lebanon, in fact incorporate both these features. The convergence of spatial and communal identities serves, in other words, both the need to search for roots and the desire to rediscover, or invent, a state of bliss that has been lost; it also serves as a means of escape from the trials and tribulations of war.

Expressed more concretely, this impulse to seek refuge in cloistered spatial communities is sustained by two seemingly opposed forms of self-preservation: to remember and to forget. The former is increasingly sought in efforts to anchor oneself in one's community or in reviving and reinventing its communal solidarities and threatened heritage. The latter is more likely to assume escapist and nostalgic predispositions to return to a past imbued with questionable authenticity.

Either way, concerted efforts need to be made to reinvigorate or generate meaningful public spaces in order to diminish fear and transcend parochialism and the compulsion to withdraw into the compact enclosures of family, community, and sect. These are also, to a considerable extent, apolitical tasks; or at least ventures that retain appreciable residues of voluntary and participatory action unrestrained by political considerations.

More than in any other time in recent history, architects, urban planners, landscape designers and other environmental professionals and habitat advocates in Lebanon now have a rare opportunity to step in and assert and validate the reconstructive and radical visions of their profession. With all the disheartening manifestations of the war, we catch Lebanon at a critical and propitious threshold in its urban history. The massive reconstruction underway, particularly in the historic core of Beirut's Central Business District, has provoked a rare mood of nascent and growing public awareness of spatial and environmental issues. Perhaps for the first time growing segments of the Lebanese are becoming increasingly conscious and verbal about what is being done to the spaces around them.[1]

If there are visible symptoms of a "culture of disappearance" evident in the growing encroachment of global capital and state authority into the private realm and heedless reconstruction schemes, elements which are destroying or defacing the country's distinctive architectural, landscape, and urban heritage, there is also a burgeoning "culture of resistance." Such a culture is contesting and repelling this encroachment and dreaded annihilation, as well as the fear of being engulfed by the overwhelming forces of globalization.[2]

Within this setting, urbanists and others have considerable latitude for advancing strategies to awaken and mobilize silenced, lethargic, and disengaged segments of the society to become more vigilant and actively engaged in pacifying some of the forces ravaging their habitat and living space. It is my view that in this ameliorative interlude of postwar reconstruction, such involvement can do much in healing and transcending sources of fear and division in society. Also through such involvement, an aroused public can begin to assist in transforming "spaces" into "places." After all, the way spaces are used in a reflection of people's identities and commitments to them. The more we live in a particular place — as we become part of it, so to speak — the more inclined we are to care for it. It is in this sense that "spaces" are converted to "places."

As concerned citizens, it is of vital interest to us to be involved in safeguarding, repairing, and enriching our experience of space. Indeed, these are basic human rights, almost universal needs. If they are abused, we all are diminished. Consider what happens when a country's most precious heritage either is maligned or becomes beyond the reach of its citizens. This is precisely what has been happening to many Lebanese. Their country's scenic geography, its pluralistic and open institutions, which were once sources of national pride and inspiration, things around which they wove dreams that made them a bit different from others, have either become inaccessible to them, or worse, are being redefined as worthless. At best, they have been reduced to mere "spaces" for commercial speculation.

Some of the most unsettling transformations in postwar Lebanon converge on the contingent interplay between collective memory, a virtual obsession with heritage (*tourath*), the redefinition of spatial localities, and efforts to forge new cultural identities. This ongoing dialectics between memory, space, and identity are naturally interrelated. All three are in a state of flux and are being contested.

Clearly, not all these transformations are byproducts of civil strife. Many, particularly those associated with rampant globalism, mass consumerism, and popular culture were not there during the war. But they have in the interim made their inroads into virtually all dimensions of public life much too visibly. How this interplay between memory, space, and identity will be resolved is not a trifling matter. It will most certainly prefigure much of the emerging contours and future image of Lebanon's urban setting and spatial environment.

In preceding discussions we explored some of the striking spatial transformations, specially the way the country's social geography was redefined by protracted strife and concomitant displacement and population shifts. Two other related issues will be addressed here: First, an attempt is made to identify and account for how various communities are responding to the forces which are undermining their local heritage and identities. As will become apparent, various communities are evolving different strategies for resisting such threatening incursions on their local identities. Secondly, and at a broader level, we will consider the most likely set of actors or technologies particularly predisposed to play the role of pacifying or healing the country's fractured social fabric. This will also lead us to consider what and how much of the old heritage should be restored and rehabilitated.

The Cultures of Disappearance and Resistance

All wars, civil or otherwise, are atrocious. Lebanon's encounters with civil strife, we have been suggesting, are particularly galling because their horrors were not anchored in any recognizable or coherent set of causes. Nor did they resolve the issues that had sparked the initial hostilities. It is in this poignant sense that the war was altogether a wasteful and futile encounter with collective violence.

The muted anguish and unresolved hostilities of the war are now being compounded by all the ambivalences and uncertainties of postwar reconstruction and the encroachment of conglomerate global capital as it contests the efforts of indigenous and local groups in reclaiming and reinventing their threatened spatial identities. What we are in fact witnessing at the moment is a multilayered negotiation or competition for the representation and ultimate control of Beirut's spatial and collective identity. Much of Beirut's future image will be largely an outcome of such discrepant claims and representations. This is also largely true of other areas now in the throes of massive reconstruction. The contesting groups (i.e., funding and state agencies, planners, property owners and shareholders, advocacy groups, voluntary associations, and the concerned public), by virtue of their distinct composition and objectives, vary markedly in their proposed visions and strategies.

The ongoing competition and the public debate it has incited has also served to accentuate the fears of the public, particularly since the struggle is now intimately aligned with the intrusions of global capital, mass culture, and consumerism. Hence the fears of disappearance, erasure, marginalization, and displacement are becoming acute.

The overriding reactions have much in common, in fact, with the three neurophysiological responses to fear and anxiety, namely: "freeze," "flight" and "fight." While the first two normally involve efforts to disengage and distance oneself from the sources of fear, the third is more combative since it involves a measure of direct involvement, negotiation, and/or resisting the threats of erasure.[3] All three, in varying proportions, are visible today in Lebanon.

The first, freeze, perhaps the most common, is a relic of the war. To survive all its cruelties, the Lebanese became deadened and numbed. Like other victims of collective suffering, they became as we have seen desensitized and overwhelmed by muted anguish and pain. During the war, such callousness (often masquerading as resilience) served them well. It allowed them not only to survive but also to inflict and rationalize cruelties on the "other." By distancing themselves, or cutting themselves off, from the "other," the Lebanese routinized the brutality of embattled communities. Violence became morally indifferent. People could engage in guilt-free violence and kill with impunity precisely because they had restricted contact with their defiled victims.

There is a painful irony in this mode of response. That which enabled embattled groups and communities to survive the atrocities of strife is clearly disabling them now as they are considering options for rearranging and sharing common spaces and forging unified national identities. We must here recall Collins's aphorism that "the point is not to learn to live with the demons, but to take away their powers" (Collins 1974: 416). The issue, here as well, converges on who is to mobilize or speak on behalf of those who have been rendered "frozen," namely, disengaged, inactive, and bereft of speech.

There is, after all, something in the character of intense pain, Elaine Scarry tells us, which is "language destroying." "As the content of one's world disintegrates, so the content of one's language disintegrates. . . . world, self, and voice are lost, or nearly lost, through the intense pain." (Scarry 1985: 35). This is also a reflection of the fact that people in pain are ordinarily bereft of the resources of speech. It is not surprising that the language for pain should in such instances often be evoked by those who are not themselves in pain, but by those who speak on behalf of those who are. Richard Rorty expresses the same thought. He, too, tells us that "victims of cruelty, people who are suffering, do not have much in the way of language. That is why there is no such thing as the "voice of the oppressed" or the "language of the victims." The language the victims once used is not working anymore, and they are suffering too much to put new words together. So the job of putting their situation into language is going to have to be done for them by somebody else" (Rorty 1989).

"Flight," second more interesting and complex response, is not purely escape, but involves an effort to distance oneself from the atrocious residues of protracted strife and the disenchanting barbarism of postwar times. This nostalgic retreat is a search for "re-enchantment" evident in the revival of heritage or the imagined nirvana of an idyllic past. Three manifestations of such escapist venues are becoming increasingly visible in various dimensions of daily life and popular culture: The first, and perhaps most obvious, the reassertion of communal solidarities and other forms of retribalization, was discussed earlier. Two other escapist venues deserve some elaboration here. — nostalgia and the proliferation of kitsch.

Escape into the past has obviously a nostalgic tinge to it, but such a retreat need not be seen as pathological or delusionary. It could well serve, as Bryan Turner has argued, as a redemptive form of heightened sensitivity, sympathetic awareness of human problems and, hence, it could be "ethically uplifting." In this sense it is less a "flight" and more of a catharsis for human suffering (Turner 1987: 149).

There is much in the vulgarization of traditional forms of cultural expression and the commodification of kitsch and sleazy consumerism, so rampant in postwar Lebanon, which needs to be curtailed and challenged. This nostalgic longing, among a growing segment of disenchanted intellectuals, is at least a form of resistance or refusal to partake in the process of debasement of aesthetic standards or the erosion of bona fide items of cultural heritage. Impotent as such efforts may seem, they express a profound disgust with the trivialization of culture so visible in the emptiness of consumerism and the nihilism of the industry of popular culture. They are also an outcry against the loss of personal autonomy and authenticity. Even the little commonplace, mundane things and routines of daily life — street smells and sounds and other familiar icons and landmarks of place — let alone historic sites and architectural edifices, are allowed to atrophy or be effaced.

Here again this nostalgic impulse is beginning to assume some redemptive and engaging expressions. A variety of grassroots movements, citizen and advocacy groups, and voluntary associations have been established recently to address problems related to the preservation and protection of the built environment. Earlier special-interest groups have had to redefine their objectives and mandates to legitimize and formalize their new interests. A succession of workshops, seminars, and international conferences have been hosted to draw on the experience of other comparable instances of postwar reconstruction. Periodicals and special issues of noted journals, most prominently perhaps the feature page on "heritage" by the Beirut daily *An-Nahar*, are devoting increasing coverage to matters related to space, environment, and architectural legacy.

At the level of popular culture, this resistance to the threat of disappearance is seen in the revival of folk arts, music, and lore, flea markets, artisan shops, and other such exhibits and galleries. Personal memoirs, autobiographies, nostalgic recollections of one's early childhood, and life in gregarious and convivial quarters and neighborhoods of old Beirut are now popular narrative genres. So are pictorial glossy anthologies of Beirut's urban history, old postcards, maps, and other such collectibles. They are all a thriving business. Even the media and advertising industries are exploiting such imagery and nostalgic longing to market their products.

The other mode of retreat or escape from the ugly memories of the war and the drabness or anxieties of the postwar era is the proliferation of kitsch. While kitsch, as an expression of the appeal of popular arts and entertainment whose objective is to "astonish, scintillate, arouse, and stir the passions," is not normally perceived as a mode of escape, its rampant allures in Lebanon are symptomatic of the need to forget and, hence, it feeds on collective amnesia and the pervasive desire for popular distractions (for further details, see Calinescu 1987: 238). It is clearly not as benign or frivolous as it may appear. At least it should not be dismissed lightly. It has implications for the readiness of the public to be drawn in and become actively and creatively engaged in the processes of reconstruction and safeguarding the edifying beauty of their natural habitat and human-created environment.

It is not difficult to account for the allure of kitsch in postwar Lebanon: the need to forget and escape the atrocities and futility of a senseless war; the mindless hedonism and narcissism associated with an urge to make up for lost time; the dullness and trivialization of everyday life; the cultural predispositions of the Lebanese for gregariousness, conviviality, and fun-loving amusement. All of these have contributed to its appeal. So has the ready access to high technology and "infotainment." Lebanon is not spared the scintillations of such global incursions. Indeed, bourgeois decadence, mediocrity, and conspicuous consumption have compounded the public seductions of kitsch.

The fundamental allures of kitsch are inherent in its ability to offer effortless and easy access to the distractions of global entertainment. It is compatible with the public mood of lethargy, disengagement, and uninterest. It is also in this sense that kitsch becomes a form of "false consciousness" and ideological diversion; a novel opiate for aroused and unanchored masses. To the rest, particularly the large segments who have been uprooted from their familiar moorings, kitsch feeds on their hunger for nostalgia. Altogether, it is a form of collective deception since it is sustained by the demand for spurious replicas or the reproduction of objects and art forms whose original aesthetic meanings have been compromised. As Calinescu puts it, kitsch becomes "the aesthetics of deception; for it centers around such questions as imitation, forgery, counterfeit. It is basically a form of lying. Beauty turns out to be easy to fabricate (Colinescu 1987: 228).

In Lebanon, the pathologies of kitsch display more ominous byproducts. These pathologies not only debase the aesthetic quality of high culture but also vulgarize folk art and architecture. National symbols, historic monuments, and cherished landmarks become marketable souvenirs or vacuous media images. This frenzy for the prostitution of cherished cultural artifacts and the consumption of pseudo-art cannot be attributed merely to the impulse for status seeking and conspicuous consumption, potent as these predispositions are in Lebanon today. What constitutes the essence of kitsch, as Adorno (1973) among others reminds us, is its promise of "easy catharsis." The object of kitsch, after all, is not to please, charm, or refine our tastes and sensibilities. Rather, it promises easy and effortless access to cheap entertainment and scintillating distractions.

Here again, there are vital implications for urbanists, architects, and other cultural producers, who must restrain and redirect the distracting allures of kitsch toward more redemptive and creative venues. This is not an easy task. Above all, it involves the incorporation or reconciliation of two seemingly opposing options: to tame the excesses of kitsch, while acting as sentinels who can arouse the disengaged and disinterested by infusing their world with some rejuvenated concern for edifying and embellishing the aesthetic quality of their environment.

Providing outlets for the release of such creative energies should not be belittled or trivialized. As Nietzsche was keen or reminding us, an aesthetic solution through artistic creation could well serve as a powerful expression for releasing individuals from the constraints of nihilism and resentment. "It is in art that we appear to realize fully our abilities and potential to break through the limitations of our own circumstances" (G. Stauth and B. S. Turner 1988: 517).

By far the most promising in this regard are the strategies various communities have begun to employ in order to resist threats to their local heritage and identity. Here responses to fear and uncertainty — whether generated by internal displacement, global capital, or mass culture and consumerism — have reawakened and mobilized local groups to reclaim their contested spaces and eroded cultural identities. The emergent spaces reveal more than just residues or pockets of resistance. There are encouraging signs of so-called "third spaces," found in hybridized cultures that have a mixed degree of tolerance.

This is, after all, what Bennett implied by "cultures of resistance," i.e., how a "local spatial system retains many of its traditional institutions and utilizes these to manipulate and control the extreme forces" (Bennett, as cited in Milnar 1996: 80). Hence, many of the public spaces, more the work of spontaneity than design, are in fact spaces of bargaining and negotiation for national memory and indigenous reemergence. More so than in other such instances of "glocalization," in Lebanon local groups are becoming increasingly globalized and, conversely, global incursions are becoming increasingly localized. In other words, we see symptoms of "inward shifts" where loyalties are redirected toward renewed localism and subnational groups and institutions. We also see "outward shifts," where loyalties and interests are being extended to transnational entities (DiMuccio and Rosenau 1996:80).

This is, incidentally, a far cry from the portraits one can extract from recent writings on the spatial and cultural implications of this global/local dialectics. For example, in his polemical but engaging work on the interplay between "jihad" and "McWorld, Benjamin Barber pits McWorld, as the universe of manufactured needs, mass consumption, and mass infotainment against *jihad* the Arabic word meaning holy war, as a shorthand for the belligerent politics of religious, tribal, and other forms of bigotry (Barber 1996). The former is driven by the cash nexus of greedy capitalists and the bland preferences of mass consumers. The latter is propelled by fierce tribal loyalties, rooted in exclusionary and parochial hatreds. McWorld, with all its promises of a world homogenized by global consumerism, is rapidly dissolving local cultural identities. Jihad, by re-creating parochial loyalties, is fragmenting the world by creating tighter and smaller enclosures. Both are a threat to civil liberties, tolerance, and genuine coexistence. "Jihad pursues a bloody politics of identity, McWorld a bloodless economics of profit. Belonging by default to McWorld, everyone is a consumer; seeking a repository for identity, everyone belongs to some tribe. But no one is a citizen" (Barber 1996: 8).

We see little of such sharp dichotomies and diametrical representations in postwar Lebanon. While many of the emergent spatial enclaves are cog-

nizant and jealous of their indigenous identities, they are not averse to ex-
perimenting with more global and ephemeral encounters and cultural products. Likewise, global expectations are being reshaped and rearranged to
accommodate local needs and preferences. Expressed in the language of
globalization and post-modernity, the so-called "world without borders," is
not a prerequisite for global encounters. At least this is not what has been
transpiring in Lebanon. Indeed, as Martin Albrow argues, one of the key
effects of globalization on locality is that people "can reside in one place
and have their meaningful social relations almost entirely outside it and
across the globe." This, Albrow goes on to say, "means that people use the
locality as site and resource for social activities in widely different ways according to the extension of their sociosphere" (Albrow 1997: 53).

Recent case studies of three distinct sites in Beirut (Ain al-Mryseh, Gemmayzeh, and the "Elisar" project in Beirut's southern suburb) provide instructive and vivid support of how local groups and communities have been
able to resist, avert, and rearrange the powers of global agendas. Indeed, in
all three instances, globalization has contributed to the strengthening and
consolidation of local ties and, thereby, has reinforced the claims of Persky
and Weiwel regarding the "growing localness of the global city" and the
globalization of urban structures.

'Ayn al-Mryseh, arguably one of the oldest neighborhoods of Beirut, hud-
dles on a picturesque cove on the waterfront of the western flank of the city
center. It adjoins the hotel district devastated during the war. In the prewar
period, 'Ayn al-Mryseh, like the rest of Ras Beirut, was a mixed neighborhood
with fairly open and liberal lifestyles. Indigenous groups, mostly Sunni,
Druze, Shi'a, Greek Orthodox, along with Armenians and Kurds, lived side
by side. The location of the American Embassy and the American University
of Beirut also drew a rather large portion of foreign residents — diplomats,
intellectuals, journalists, artists, and other itinerant groups. The neighborhood's politics were progressive; its culture cosmopolitan and pluralistic. By
virtue of its proximity to the city center and seaport, its inhabitants were
mostly merchants, retailers, and clerks in the burgeoning tourist sector of
hotels, nightclubs, bars, and sidewalk cafes. The bulk of its indigenous population worked at the port or were fishermen, serving as the mainstay of the
neighborhood and its defining character.

The war, more so than in other neighborhoods of Beirut, profoundly
changed its character. Because of heavy internecine fighting, Christians and
Sunnis were compelled to leave, along with, of course, most of the foreign
residents. They were replaced by displaced Shi'a, arriving mostly from the
South and from Beirut's suburbs.

The massive reconstruction of Beirut's center and adjoining hotel and resort district has enhanced the economic prospects of the neighborhood. Real estate and land values have increased sharply. Traditional property holders and homeowners could not resist the tempting offers of conglomerate capital in collusion with local entrepreneurs. Hence, many of the edifying suburban villas and red-tiled roofs which once graced the shoreline have given way to high-rise office buildings and smart, exclusive resorts.

The influx of foreign capital is not only transforming the city's skyline, but also undermining its moral character and public image. The social fabric is becoming more fractious; its culture more raucous, strident, and kitschy. Shi'ite squatters, awaiting gentrification and other speculative projects, resist eviction from the premises they unlawfully occupy. Hence, fashionable hotels and global resorts stand next to dilapidated homes and squalid backyards. The most jarring event, perhaps, was the invasion of the Hard Rock Café, less than fifty yards away from two of the neighborhood's most imposing landmarks: the mosque and Gamal Abdul-Nasser's monument.

Armed with a city zoning law that bans the location of entertainment functions too close to religious establishments, the neighborhood association organized a protest movement to resist such intrusion. Its mobilization, however, failed to relocate the "offensive" café. Now, the muezzin's righteous calls to prayer are competing with the impertinent din of loud music just one block away.

The fishermen did not fare any better in their opposition to the construction of *Ahlam*, a towering forty-floor high-rise comprising an upscale residential complex with a direct underground passage to the Mediterranean and private landings for yachts and speedboats. *Ahlam's* site is none other than the traditional cove, a miniature harbor, that the fishermen of 'Ayn al-Mryseh have used for centuries to tend to their time-honored trade and only source of livelihood.

The Mosque Association and that of the Revival of Heritage of 'Ayn al-Mryseh came to the assistance of the fishermen by lobbying the authorities and mobilizing the support of local politicians to thwart the project. The outcome, after nearly three years of embittered negotiation, was naturally in favor of *Ahlam*. As compensation, the fishermen have been offered an alternative site as a fishing harbor (three miles farther south) which they refuse to recognize or use.

As this local–global tug-of-war has continued, two rather interesting groups or strategies for coping with global intrusions have recently emerged within the neighborhood. Both seem likely to prefigure or presage the direction 'Ayn al-Mryseh is bound to take in the future. First, a growing number of young fishermen, enticed by the new and appealing jobs the global-resort sector is generating, no longer seem as virulent in their opposition. Indeed, quite a few, to the chagrin of the older generation, are beginning to break away and accept new jobs. A second group, largely members of the Association for the Revival of Heritage, have opted for a more nostalgic and retreatist response. Recognizing that they can do little to contain or tame the forces of global capital, they have taken shelter in preserving and rediscovering the threatened legacy of their history and culture. This is evident in a couple of makeshift "museums" and galleries established to collect and display items emblematic of its colorful past (Swalha 1997).

Gemmayzeh, at least spatially, is 'Ayn al-Mryseh's counterpart on the eastern flank of Beirut's city center. It also adjoins the port with its outlying resort attractions, warehouses, and traffic terminals. Much like 'Ayn al-Mryseh, the neighborhood emerged as the city's population started to spill beyond the confines of its medieval walls during the second half of the nineteenth century. Both also harbor strong communal loyalties and pride in their unique history and collective identity.

But this is where all similarities end. While 'Ayn al-Mryseh was confessionally mixed and socially heterogeneous, Gemmayzeh was predominantly an enclave of the Greek Orthodox and Maronite communities. It also remained as such: fairly prosperous Greek Orthodox propertied families were "invaded" by successive inflows of more modest Maronite craftsmen, retail, and small-scale merchants. This symbiotic association between the two rather distinct socioeconomic strata has been one of the defining elements of the neighborhood.

Although located on the demarcating lines separating East and West Beirut, Gemmayzeh was spared the devastations other comparable communities witnessed during repeated rounds of civil strife. Nor was it beleaguered by any dislocations or permanent displacements of its indigenous inhabitants. Except for two moderate high-rise apartments, at its remote eastern limits, its skyline has remained largely intact.

As the city center is being virtually reconstructed from scratch, Gemmayzeh is simply remaking and embellishing its original identity. Through APSAD (Association for the Protection of Sites and Ancient Dwellings) and other voluntary associations, efforts are being made to preserve the architectural character of the neighborhood. Plans are being finalized for a joint project with the European Commission to paint and beautify the facades of all buildings originally earmarked for restoration.

The neighborhood is experiencing more than just a cosmetic facelift. Voluntary associations, youth clubs, and local businessmen are collaborating in efforts to revitalize its image and cultural identity as the "Montmartre" of Beirut. This is in fact how some of the young generation speak of Gemmayzeh. A seasonal festival, Daraj al-Fann (Stairway of the Arts), now attracts a devoted following. So do the rehabilitated craft shops, sidewalk cafes, and upscale boutiques.

The neighborhood, finally, does not seem reticent or furtive about pronouncing its Christian character. Festive decorations during Christmas, graffiti of crosses and other religious emblems, adorn walls and windows. During the Pope's historic visit, his posters were decked with white and yellow ribbons. His only competitor was the equally imposing portrait of the late Bashir Gemayel, the neighborhood's deceased leader.

Altogether, postwar Gemmayzeh does not feel any threat to its identity or future prospects. In fact, the destruction and long term reconstruction of the city center is largely viewed with indifference and disregard, mixed with some derision and sarcasm. Indeed, Beirut's center is often contemptuously dismissed as "Solidere."[4]

While 'Ayn al-Mryseh and Gemmayzeh are neighborhoods rich in history and uncontested collective memory, the Elisar Project is an attempt to forge an identity for a suburban slum with no history to speak of other than the besmirched and defiled image of a squalid space. It is, to borrow Benjamin's apt label, Beirut's "site of dereliction," an eyesore defamed with every slur possible. Indeed, the neutral expression, *dahiya al janubiyya* (literally, the southern suburb) has been debased to become a synonym for degradation, squalor, anarchy, squatters, illegality, and aberrant behavior.

Late in the 1960s, as successive waves of displaced Shi'ite refugees were fleeing the chronically embattled villages in southern Lebanon, the *dahiya* quickly acquired the label of Lebanon's "Misery belt": a ghetto seething with feelings of neglect and abandonment and, hence, accessible to political dissent, mobilization, and violence. This constructed global image, spawned and reinforced by the international media, belies, of course, much of the reality of the suburb. It is not so monolithic in its composition or misery. Nor is it a hotbed of dissidents and marginalized groups eager to wreak vengeance on a neglectful government and an indifferent public. As an open, coveted space, though, it has always managed to attract a much larger share of the dispossessed than other marginal and impoverished suburbs. During the war, its demographic and sectarian composition was sharply altered as other displaced groups — predominantly from the Beqa' and the

South — sought it for shelter. Initially, for example, the Shi'ite–Maronite balance was slightly tilted in favor of the latter. Today, approximately 80 percent of the southern suburb's inhabitants are Shi'ites (for further details see el-Kak 1998).

The political mobilization of the *dahiya* began before the war. First, the relatively moderate Amal Movement, inspired by the late Imam Musa al-Sadr, gained considerable popularity. Early in 1980 it was joined by Hizbullah and other more radical "Islamic" factions. Hizbullah, by virtue of its aggressive outreach programs of social, educational, and medical welfare, has been able to gain great inroads and consolidate its virtual hegemony over the area. It is, however, still rivaled by other, lesser political factions in the production and management of urban services. Today, this plethora of political actors has to reckon with the growing efforts of the government to regain its legitimate presence.

It was largely part of such efforts, and to allay Rafik Hariri's public image as some-one obsessively and exclusively interested in the rehabilitation of downtown Beirut, that the Elisar Project was launched in 1992.[5] Conceived as an infrastructure rehabilitation works, it evolved by 1994 into a real estate company legitimized by the same law that established Solidere. Amal and Hizbullah immediately challenged and contested its formation as a private company. The ensuing power struggle resulted in some significant modification whereby the company was transformed into a public establishment with the state becoming, in effect, the major actor in the reorganization of the project. More important, perhaps, Amal and Hizbullah gained their own representatives on Elisar's board.

Despite the sharp antagonisms among the three major rivals (Hariri, Amal, and Hizbullah), the project was uniformly conceived and perceived as a scheme for development and modernization. The vision and underlying ideology of the overall design comply with other such urban "utopias" intended to introduce a hygienic element of "cleansing" and relocation through social housing and supportive rehabilitative strategies.

The Social Technologies of Pacification

Lebanon's troubled history with pluralism leaves little room for further experimentation. Of all encounters with many of its varied forms — coexistence, guarded contact, compromise, and integration — the political management of separate, exclusive, and self-contained entities has always been the most costly and short-lived. Expressed more concretely: if at times it has been difficult for the Lebanese to live together, it is extremely unlikely that they can live apart. The calls for cantonization, federalism, or other partitioning and dismantlement schemes, like earlier such experiments, are by-products of xenophobic fears and vengeful impulses. They were impelled by a merging of parochial interests and short-term political expediency, not by genuine efforts to coalesce identities.

Even the reluctance of certain displaced communities to return to their original towns and villages does not seem today as resolute or intransigent as it did a few years back. Though such wavering in some instances, particularly in regions like Beirut's suburbs, Aley, and the Chouf, is understandable given the residues of fear and distrust still visible in these areas, they are clearly exceptions. These, like all the other symptoms of retribalization, cannot and should not be made to become once again sources of socioeconomic and political mobilization. Nor can they inspire any cultural rejuvenation. Like all other monolithic and cloistered communities, they can only inculcate further dogmatism and intolerance. More disquieting, they are inclined to stifle cultural and intellectual experimentation and generate obfuscating milieux germane for the spiritless, joyless lifestyles symptomatic of all closed and homogenized societies. Pluralism is, after all, an antidote to collective amnesia.

Another veritable reality also affirms itself. As a fragmented, diminutive state entrapped in a turbulent region, Lebanon will always be made more vulnerable by forces beyond its borders. This is the fate of many such tiny republics. Hence, Lebanon is destined to remain at the mercy of its neighbors' good will and the compassion of international organizations. Much can be done, however, by the Lebanese themselves to merit and consolidate such redemptive concerns. Furthermore, tasks of reconstituting or reconstructing a society are much too vital to be left to local politicians and embattled groups or to the impervious whims of officious international organizations. The former are much too vengeful, and the latter are too distant and often obsessed with intricate diplomatic haggling over matters such as bilateral or multilateral agreements, constitutional reforms, demilitarization, peace keeping, border controls, and the like.

The Lebanese can at least begin by putting their internal house in order. There are measures and programs, already proved effective elsewhere, which can be experimented with to fortify their immunity against the disruptive consequences of external destabilizing forces. Such efforts can do much to reduce the country's chronic vulnerability to these pressures, particularly if

directed toward two basic objectives: to broaden and incorporate the participation of seemingly indifferent and lethargic groups in society, and to consider alternative dimensions thus far overlooked or dismissed as irrelevant.

I take my cue here from two seemingly incongruent sources almost a
century apart: a classic nineteenth century liberal (Spencer 1898) and a post-
modernist (Rabinow 1989). In addressing exigent public issues and pressing
problems, Herbert Spencer implored us to recall the analogy of the bent
iron plate. In trying to flatten the wrought-iron plate, it is futile, Spencer
pointed out, to hammer directly on the buckled area; we only make matters
worse. To be effective, our hammering must be around, not directly on, the
projected part.

The implications of such strategies are obvious. Rather than focusing
almost obsessively on issues directly concerned with peace accords, conflict
resolution, political and constitutional reforms, and the like, we could reach
out to other seemingly irrelevant components or areas. For example, urban
planning, architectural design, the rejuvenation of popular culture and the
performing arts, curricular reform, competitive sports, and the wider participation of indigenous groups in local rehabilitation projects — thus far overlooked because of excessive reliance on regional and international initiatives
for conflict resolution — can do much in pacifying and healing sources of
division and thereby expedite the transformation of the salient geography of
fear into a culture of tolerance (see Khalaf 1993; Khalaf and Khoury 1993).

Paul Rabinow's (1989) analysis of the sociocultural history of France between 1830 and 1930 offers equally instructive hints. He delineates the con-
stellation of thought, action, and passion underlying what he terms the "social technologies of pacification" as tools for reforming and controlling the
inherent antagonisms between space and society, and between forms and
norms that France was undergoing during that eventful century. Rabinow
identifies a set of actors — ranging from aristocratic dandies, governors, and
philanthropists, to architects, intellectuals, and urban reformers — who were
all infused with this passion to "pacify the pathos" and, consequently, articulated a set of pragmatic solutions to public problems in times of crisis (e.g.
wars, epidemics, strikes, etc.). Despite their divergent backgrounds, they
shared two common perspectives: bitterness about the institutional and cultural crisis of their society, and an unshaken faith in the production and
regulation of a peaceful and productive social order.

One can easily glean from Rabinow's analysis several persuasive examples
of such successful consolidation. Urban designers, architects, intellectuals,
humanists of all shades and persuasions, along with other outraged but

muted groups, are particularly qualified to play this role in Lebanon. Will-fully or otherwise, they have thus far been shunted aside and trivialized. They have to shed their timidity and reclaim the credibility of their professions and legitimate interests. By mobilizing aesthetic sensibilities and other artistic energies and popular cultural expressions in everyday life, they can do much to arouse the public to redeem its maligned heritage. More important, they can prod the Lebanese to turn outward and transcend the parochial identities to connect with others. City life, after all, is an ideal environment for acting out and working out personal and social conflicts.

As suggested earlier, these enabling forms of voluntarism and mobilization — competitive sports, performing arts, reviving interest in national theatre, museums, and efforts to rehabilitate the country's neglected landmarks and historic sites — can do much in this regard. Recent such instances of public mobilization are legion. They are also beginning to spill over to other areas of the public sphere.

Most visible, perhaps, are environmental campaigns to clean up beaches, river basins, natural preserves, and increase public awareness about toxic waste and industrial pollution. Equally strident are the calls made to protect local agricultural produce and to regulate unfair competition from foreign and migrant labor. The Association of Agricultural Products, Importers and Traders recently has been urging the government to adopt protective measures and tax exemptions on local produce and to prohibit the entry and dumping of foreign products. Even students have staged public demonstrations in support of such efforts.

Most vociferous, doubtlessly, are the activities launched by students affiliated with the Free National Movement (FNM) headed by exiled General Michel Awn. Evocative banners and leaflets were very explicit in their outcries: "Lebanese production, Lebanese workers, equals more money" . . . "where do labor leaders stand on the illegal competition of over 1 million Syrian laborers who are taking the livelihood of impoverished Lebanese workers?" A spokesperson for the group saw the protest as more than just a futile symbolic gesture at a time, as he put it, when Lebanon is "reeling under the worst economic crisis since the turn-of-the-century famine." He went further to express his dismay at the presence of more than a million untaxed foreign workers. He also called upon the government to stem the relentless hemorrhage of the country's young talented professional and skilled manpower (Daily Star, May 11, 2000: 3).

Women activists have been audible in lobbying to garner support for the amendments of discriminatory laws against women or those which violate international conventions. The National Boy Scouts Association, one of the rare nonsectarian and nonpolitical movements in the country, has also taken steps lately to reactivate and extend its prewar programs. Equally compelling is the emergence of new organizations such as the Youth Association for Social Awareness (YASA). In cooperation with the Internal Security Forces and Civil Defence, they have been hosting a series of workshops and meetings across the country to raise awareness of the hazards of speeding and reckless driving.

These and other such forms of public mobilization are clearly redemptive in more than just mundane and cathartic terms. They can be effective outlets for releasing groups from constricted and "total" sociocultural settings and, hence, serve as transcending and liberating encounters. Though still formative in some instances, they do evince encouraging manifestations of remedial and emancipatory public action. At the least such outlets will draw participants closer to the distant "others" and render them less indifferent to them.

It is pertinent to note that the sources of inspiration, initiative, leadership, and frames of reference of many of these movements are not exclusively indigenous in character. Indeed, many of the active participants are drawn from itinerant groups and "returnees" who had spent varying interludes of time outside the country.

One can advance a few added considerations by way of justifying why such groups are ideally suited today to act as the focus for the mobilization of a political culture of tolerance, civility, and coexistence. Hence, they are better equipped to articulate this new language and vision on behalf of their besieged compatriots. First, a disproportionate number of such groups have been, for much of the duration of the war, in diaspora. Every culture has its own diaspora. Lebanon's trials with exile and dispersal have been quite acute. They were, however, also enabling. Mavericks, as histories of itinerant populations tell us, rarely stay at home. Just like the traditional Lebanese *makari* (peddler), who always wandered beyond the narrow confines of his bounded village and came back with tales, goods, tidbits, of the world beyond, we have today the making of a growing generation of global multiculturalists. Both established and younger cohorts of gifted professionals and entrepreneurs have been deepening and extending their skills and experiences abroad. Many are rightfully disillusioned, perhaps bitter, but have not been rendered speechless by the harrowing events. They only experienced the war vicariously, from a distance. Hence, they have not been as numbed or cynical. Nor do they harbor deep-seated hostility toward other groups.

Second, though exiled, they have not severed their ties or nostalgia to their native culture. They bring in comparative vision, not the alien constructs of "foreign experts" imposed on unfamiliar and unreceptive milieux. Finally, by virtue of such multicultural sympathies, they are less likely to perceive their projects as efforts for privileging or empowering one group or community in opposition to another. Hence, they are more predisposed to transcend their parochialism as an antidote for doing away with the geography of fear and its demarcating lines and enclosures.

Pacifying Lebanon's pathos, though intricate, is not insurmountable. Much can be done to prepare for this blissful eventuality. Foremost, the Lebanese must be made to realize that massive postwar reconstruction and development can and must be accomplished without added damage to the environment. Given its size, Lebanon clearly can ill afford any further environmental abuse. Spare and menaced, the country's dazzling landscape is, after all, its distinctive legacy, a source of national pride and resourcefulness. Indeed other than the ingenuity of its human resources, the good will of its neighbors, and gratuitous guarantees of geopolitics, the country has little else to sustain its vulnerable existence. In an existential sense, there are two inescapable realities that homogenize the Lebanese today: geography and fear. We have no choice but to invoke the captivating beauty of the country's habitat as an antidote to fear.

Here as well, much can be done to stop the defoliation of open spaces and reconnect disinherited and denationalized groups with their country's national treasures and collective memory. Likewise, much can be done to assuage those roused with fear that they need not be fully appreciative of the "others" to be able to live with them. Some of the liveliest cities in the world are, after all, those that managed to live with tolerable conflict among their diverse communities. Many in such places express violent aversions toward those with whom they do not identify. Yet they recognize such differences as a given, something they must live with (Fischer 1982, 206). Louis Wirth, in his classic essay "Urbanism as a Way of Life," expressed this same reality when he declared that "the juxtaposition of divergent personalities and mode of life tends to produce a relativistic perspective and a sense of toleration of differences" (Wirth 1938, 155).

Likewise, the Lebanese must also be reassured that their territorial commitments are understandable and legitimate under the circumstances. But so is their need to break away. Being spatially anchored, as we have repeatedly observed, reinforces their need for shelter, security, and solidarity. Like other territorialized groups, they become obsessed with boundary delineation and safeguarding their community against trespassers and interlopers. The need for wonder, exhilaration, exposure to new sensations, world views, and the evaluation of our appreciative sympathies — which are all enhanced through connectedness with strangers — are also equally vital for our sustenance. Witness the euphoria of kids in an urban playground as they cut themselves off in play from the ties of family and home, or the excitement of visitors in a bustling city street. The village *makari*, in admittedly a much different time and place, played much the same role. He, too, broke away, crossed barriers, and was a cultural broker of sorts precisely because he exposed himself to new sensations and contacts. He had no aversion to strangers. He wandered away but always managed to return home. We need to revive and extend the ethos of the *makari* as the prototype of an idyllic national character. With all his folk eccentricities, he epitomizes some of the enabling virtues of a "traveler" and not a "potentate."

Edward Said employs this polar imagery to construct two archetypes for elucidating the interplay between identity, authority, and freedom in an academic environment. In the ideal academy, Said tells us, "we should regard knowledge as something for which to risk identity, and we should think of academic freedom as an invitation to give up on identity in the hope of understanding and perhaps even assuming more than one. We must always view the academy as a place to voyage in, owning none of it but at home everywhere in it" (Said 1991, 18). Are these not also the attributes or paradigms we should seek in restoring a city or the places and institutions within it to render them more permeable for this kind of voyaging?

> The image of traveler depends not on power, but on motion, on a willingness to go into different worlds, use different idioms, and understand a variety of disguises, masks, and rhetorics, Travelers must suspend the claim of customary routine in order to live in new rhythms and rituals. Most of all, most unlike the potentate who must guard only one place and defend its frontiers, the traveler *crosses over*, traverses territory, and abandons fixed positions, all the time (Said 1991, 18).

Ideally, this could well serve as the leitmotif of those entrusted with educational reform, cultural rehabilitation and political resocialization, i.e. to create the conditions germane for this transformation of "potentates" into "travelers." When we are implored to find some way of making "ghettos" and all other cloistered spaces more respectable, we are in effect making a plea to keep them open to facilitate the voyaging, traversing, and crossing over. They should be, in other words designed in such a way that people can move on when the need for communal support and shelter is no longer essential. Any form of confinement, in the long run, becomes a deprivation. Conversely, open urban spaces can also be rendered more congenial to cushion groups against the tempestuousness of city life.

The image of the Lebanese as a spatially anchored creature, compulsively huddling and defending his domains (i.e. the compact enclosures of family and neighborhood) against potential trespassers, needs to be modified. He is also (or at least was until the war terrorized his public spaces) a creature of the outdoors. Design can do much to restore the conviviality of such open spaces. Street life is emblematic of urban provocation and arousal precisely because one lets go, so to speak, and drops one's conventional reserves toward others. As Richard Sennett puts it, as "one goes to the edge of oneself, he sees, talks and thinks about what is outside. . . . By turning outward, he is aroused by the presence of strangers and arouses them." Sympathy in such instances becomes a condition of "mutual concern and arousal as one loses the power of self-definition." It is also in such instances that "differences" are reinforced without sustaining "indifference" to others (Sennett 1990, 149).

Prospects for Restoration of Civility

The Lebanese at the moment, and for understandable reasons, seem bent on "retribalizing" their communal and spatial identities. This is not, as we have seen, unusual. In times of disaster, even in cultures aversive to propinquity, traumatized groups are inclined to reconnect with family, home, and community for security and shelter. Pathological as they now seem, such territorial solidarities need not continue to be sources of paranoia and hostility. If stripped of their bigotry and excesses they could be extended and enriched to incorporate more secular and plural identities. Thomas Friedman, in more graphic terms, is making the same plea when he implores us to avoid the excesses of strong attachments to one's roots. Essential as these tribal loyalties to one's "olive trees" are, "when taken to an excess, can lead us into forging identities, bonds and communities based on the exclusion of others" (Friedman 2000: 32). There is still a faint hope, given the tenacious survival of religiously mixed communities, that the country might still evade this fateful crossover into that barbarous logic of enclosure and intolerance to differences.

Even in times of fierce fighting, when all crossings between the two halves of Beirut were either cut off or became hazardous, people continued tenaciously to cross over. Hence, differences between the two sides were "staved off," as Jean Makdisi put it, "by those sullen people who stubbornly cross over, day after day by the thousands, some to go work, others to visit friends and relatives, and *many just to make a point*" (Makdisi 1990: 77; emphasis added). A more telling indicator of the resistance to succumb to pressures of partition are the marked differences in real estate prices. Land values in religiously mixed areas, regardless of their aesthetic or urban quality, continue to be higher than in exclusive or homogeneous areas. So is the volume of construction activity and other manifestations of economic enterprise. That proverbial "invisible hand" of the market appears to be sending the Lebanese a prophetic an astute message; namely, that a mixed and heterogeneous political culture is at least more economically viable.

Lebanon's experience, treacherous and perplexing as it has been, is not all that unique. In considering the preferred setting, the most supportive environment for what Michael Walzer calls the "good life," he arrives (after reviewing predominant socialist and capitalist ideologies in the nineteenth and twentieth centuries) at a similar conclusion. To "live well," he tells us, "is to participate with other men and women in remembering, cultivating and passing on a national heritage" and that such a "good life" can only be realized in a civil society. "The realm of fragmentation and struggle but also of concrete and authentic solidarities where we fulfill E. M. Foster's injunction of *only connect*, become social or communal men and women" (Walzer 1991, 298).

Walzer goes on to assert:

> The picture here is of people freely associating and communicating with one another, forming and reforming groups of all sorts, not for the sake of any particular formation — family, tribe, nation, religion, commune, brotherhood or sisterhood, interest group or ideological movement — but for the sake of sociability itself. For we are by nature social, before we are political or economic beings, . . . What is true is that the quality of our political and economic activity and of our national culture is intimately connected to the strength and vitality of our associations. Ideally, civil society is a setting of settings: all are included, none is preferred (Walzer 1991, 298).

Other equally sobering voices (e.g. Dahrendorf 1990; Konrad 1984; Havel 1985) have also been making similar appeals for the restoration of civil society. All three remind us that the task of reconstruction will require more than political reform, physical rehabilitation, and economic development. More compelling and problematic is the need to restructure basic loyalties. By its very nature, this is bound to be a long and fragile process. Dahrendorf is, perhaps, most assertive: "It takes six months to create new political institutions; to write a constitution and electoral laws. It may take six years to create a halfway viable economy. It will probably take sixty years to create a civil society. Autonomous institutions are the hardest things to bring about" (Dahrendorf 1990: 42). In almost identical terms, all three caution us that the reproduction of loyalty, civility, political competence, and trust in authority are never the work of the state alone, and the effort to go it alone — one meaning of totalitarianism — is doomed to failure.

Three parting thoughts: now that the prospects for recovering a free and autonomous Lebanon seem imminent (indeed that recovery is heralded as a momentous milestone presaging a new order), we must bear in mind, lest we get disillusioned again, that cities, civilizations, and citizenship share a linguistic and historical root. Where communities, cities, nations — great or small — are not hospitable to the multiplicity of groups, voices, and the interplay of viewpoints, civil society will always suffer. Second, creating such a political culture of tolerance demands, among other things, that every Lebanese today should change his perception of the "other." Only by doing so can we begin to transform the geography of fear into genuine but guarded forms of coexistence. Third, pathological as they may seem at times, communal solidarities need not continue to be sources of paranoia and hostility. They could be extended and enriched to incorporate other more secular and civic identities. If stripped of their bigotry and intolerance, they could also become the bases for more equitable and judicious forms of power-sharing and the articulation of new cultural identities. Here lies the hope, the only hope perhaps, for an optimal restructuring of Lebanon's pluralism.

This is not another elusive pipe dream. Just as enmity has been socially constructed and culturally sanctioned, it can also be unlearned. Group loyalties can, after all, be restructured. Under the spur of visionary and enlightened leadership, groups through a revitalized voluntary sector can at least be resocialized to perceive differences as manifestations of cultural diversity and enrichment; not as dreaded symptoms of distrust, fear, and exclusion.

Notes

1. On Proxy Wars and Surrogate Victims

1. These and other such expressions are all titles of books or articles written on Lebanon. See for example, Barakat 1977; Binder 1966; Gordon 1980; Hudson 1968; Meo 1965; Shills 1966.

2. The writings of the so-called "founding fathers" of the Lebanese Republic and some of their chauvinistic philosophers abound with such idyllic expressions. See, for example, Al-Hajj 1961; Chiha 1966; Habachi 1960; Malik 1974. President Amin Gemayyel during his blustering term in office (1982–1988) repeatedly invoked in several of his speeches the notion of *'unfuwan* — a distinguishing trait or state of mind which combines attributes such as vigor, aggressiveness resourcefulness and sense of pride. In his view, it was *'unfuwan* that accounts for the resilience and steadfastness of the Lebanese in resisting the persisting hardships and threats to their national sovereignty. It is also *'unfuwan* that will ultimately redeem them in regenerating and reconstructing Lebanon's enfeebled institutions.

3. For an elaboration of Lebanon's precarious and problematic foreign policy and its implications for exacerbating the inside-outside dialectics see, among others, the following: Azar 1984; Buheiry 1989; Gerges 1994, 1997; Hitti 1989; Salem 1993 and 1994; Stookey 1979.

4. Public opinion in Lebanon, incidentally, was not particularly pleased by the analogy. Religious figures were particularly incensed that Lebanon should be treated as a paragon for the ethnic cleansing and bloody confrontations accompanying the dismemberment of the Soviet Union (See Al-Nahar, April 26, 1994).

5. For a sample of these and other related views see: Farsoun and Wingarter 1981:

93–106; Fisk 1990; Gilmour 1983: 86–96; Hudson 1978: 261–278; Petran 1987: 142–84; Randal 1984: 61–108; Sirriyyeh 1967: 73–89.
6. See Nawaf Salam's (1979) exhaustive annotated bibliography of references and sources.
7. The Recent book of Irene Gendzier (1997) and earlier essays of 1988, 1989, and 1990 are very instructive and enlightening.

2. The Radicalization of Communal Loyalties

1. There has been a profusion of writing recently exploring various dimensions of the globalization of ethnic and communal violence. Interested readers may wish to consult the following: Barber 1996; Brezezinski 1993; Esman and Rabinovich 1988; Geyer 1985; Hanf 1995; Ignatieff 1994; Kakar 1996; Kelly 1994; Moynihan 1993; Wriston 1992.
2. For a representative cross-section of the literature see Almond and Coleman 1960; Almond and Powell 1966; Apter 1965; Eisenstadt 1966; Lerner 1962; Pye 1966; Shils 1965;
3. Substantive and persuasive evidence can be extracted from a score of studies in support of such views. See, among others, Chevallier 1971; Harik 1968; Khalaf 1979; Picard 1996; Salibi 1965.

3. The Drift into Incivility

1. The assassination attempt on Schlomo Argov, the Israeli Ambassador, was incidentally the works of Abu Nidal the most bitter rival of the PLO.
2. For further documentation see Winslow 1996
3. For a probing analysis of this violent legacy and its implications for present-day belligerent identity and communal strugglers, see Regina Schwartz 1997.

5. Civil Strife of 1958: Revolt and Counter Revolt

1. The war, incidentally, goes under a variety of labels; reflecting the wide range of perceptions it provoked among participants and observers. The following stand out: "insurgency," "rebellion," "insurrection," "sedition," "armed resistance," "disturbances," "cauldron." In addition, there are more sensational terms, such as "Revolt of the Pashas" and "Midsummer Madness."
2. Since its inception the 1958 crisis has generated an endless stream of writing; both by local and foreign scholars. In addition to sources cited here, interested readers may wish to consult Nawaf Salam (1979) for an exhaustive annotated bibliography of references and sources pertinent to various dimensions of the crisis. The role of the U.S. and its intervention, largely ignored in this discussion, has also been the object of extensive writing and speculation. Declassified

documents have recently renewed interest in reexamining U.S. perceptions and policy. See, in particular, the instructive essays and book Irene Gendzier has recently published (1988 1989 1990 and 1997).

3. Items were extracted for chronologies in *Middle East Journal* (Vol. 11, 12, 13), *Middle Eastern Affairs* (Vols. 8, 9, 10). Interested readers may wish to consult United National Observation Group in Lebanon (UNOGIL), *Report* (N.Y. Security Council Document S/4040 1958), Annex C, and speeches and replies by Dr. Charles Malik and Mr. Lutfi before Security Council (June 6 and 10, 1958) in Qubain (1961: 181–224).

4. Ibid.

5. Since its establishment in 1878, the Maqassed had been one of the most viable Sunni Muslim benevolent associations with extensive cultural, educational, and welfare activities. The Salam family, particularly Saeb, has skillfully patronized the association to extend the popular base of his political clientage.

6. For texts of Dr. Charles Malik and Mr. Umar Lutfi, UAR's delegate to the U.N., U.N. resolutions and other supportive evidence, see Qubain 1961: 181–235; Agwani 1963: 335–340.

7. Malki was a prominent Ba'thist and assistant to Syrian Chief of Staff. For an account of the "Malki affair," see Seale 1965: 238–246.

8. Mughabghab was eventually assassinated on a visit to the Chuf on July 27 1959.

6. *Lebanon's Golden/Gilded Age: 1943–1975*

1. Examples of such writing one legion. The following are just a few readers may wish to consult: Ajami 1988; Barakat 1977; Kliot 1987; Mackey 1989; Odeh 1985; Rabinovich 1985; Randal 1984; Rouleau 1975; Shmesh 1986.

2. For a critical assessment of this notion and its advocates, see Nabih Faris (1960).

3. The prerequisites Professor Issawi considers include factors such as size of territory and population; a high per capita income; an equal distribution of wealth; a large proportion of the population engaged in industry and services; a high degree of national, linguistic, and religious homogeneity; widespread education and a capacity for voluntary cooperative action (see Issawi 1964: 279).

4. The "New Phoenicians" is the self-assigned label of a close circle of liberal-minded and mostly Christian bourgeoisie, who were instrumental in shaping the economic and political future of Lebanon shortly after independence. The most ideological and most prominent mentor of the groups is, of course, Michel Chiha (President Khoury's brother-in-law) who evolved into something of a public intellectual, the regime's gadfly, testing platform and moral conscience. Other influential members of the circle included Gabriel Menassa, Henri Pharaon, Alfred Kettaneh and Philip Taqla (for further details see Gates 1998: 82–89).

5. Fuad Shihab's close circle of advisors was a more mixed and heterogeneous

group of military and civilians, Lebanese and French professionals and techno-crats: Louise-Joseph Lebret (Jesuit priest), Jean Lay (military engineer), Elias Sarkis, Georges Haimari, Shafik Muharram. Like those of Khoury-Chiha they were also committed, albeit a bit more moderately, to the ideals of liberal democracy (see Winslow 1996: 137).

6. For a systematic and well-documented elaboration of some of these abusive feature, see Baalbaki 1973; Lebanese Communist Party 1973; Nasr 1978.

7. A 1974 survey of the largest industrial firms of the eastern suburbs of Beirut, showed that 28 percent of the wage earners were employed for less than one year. An equal proportion had worked in the same enterprise for more than five years, and the remaining 44 percent between one to five years (Nasr 1978: 11).

8. I can name only a few here in passing: Asad Rustum, Constantine Zurayk, Zeine Zeine and Nabih Fares in History, Jibrail Jabbur, Anis Frayha and Kamal Yazigi in Arabic; Charles Malik in Philosophy; Said Hamadeh and Husni Saw-waf in Business Administration; Albert Badre and George Hakim in Economics; Habib Kurani, George Shahla and Jibrail Katul in Education; Nikula Shahine in Physics; Aziz Abdul-Karim and Adib Sarkis in Chemisty; Philip Ashkar, Henry Badeer, Dikran Berberian, Hrant Chaglassian, George Fawaz, Sami Haddad, Amin Khairallah, Mustafa Khalidi, Nimeh Nucho, Philip Sahyoun and Hovesp Yenikomashian in Medicine; Charles Abou-Chaar and Amin Haddad in Pharmacy.

9. The interested reader should consult the invaluable work of Suha Tamim (ed.), *A Bibliography of AUB Faculty Publications, 1866–1966* (Beirut 1967).

10. The following is a partial list just by way of indicating the magnitude of those who were actively engaged in producing the research output emanating from this group of scholars. The names were extracted from journals like *Travaux de Jours*, *Mélange*, *Annales*, and *Proche Orient*, where many of their publications appeared: Selim Abou, Tanios Abou-Rejeily, Robert Abourached, Omar Ad-dada, Michel Akl, Richard Alouche, Jean Baz, Munir Chamoun, René Cha-mussy, Waddah Charara, Abdullah Dagher, Farid Jabre, Antoine Fakhoury, Joseph Maila, Antoine Mourani, Antoine Messarra, Albert Nader, Pierre Nas-rallah, Moussa Prince, Najib Sadaka, Elie Safa, Subhi al-Saleh, Bahij Tab-barah, Mohsen Slim, Paul Tannous, Joseph Zaarour, Afif Zienaty.

11. No listing can be exhaustive but the following is sufficient to delineate the magnitude of this group: Abbas, Afifi, Alami, Ali, Asfur, Attallah, Awad, Azzam, Baramki, Bulus, Butrus, Dabbagh, Dajani, Durr, Fakhri, Fanus, Farah, Fulay-han, Halasa, Hanania, Hanna, Hijab, Husayni, Inglessis, Juzi, Katul, Ka'war, Khalidi, Khamis, Kurban, Malak, Muwafi, Najm, Nasr, Rizk, Salti, Sayegh, Shibre, Siksik, Suwaydan, Tarazi, Tuqan, Umar, Yaqub, Yashruti, Zahlan, Zayid, Ziadeh, Zuwiyyah.

12. For further elaboration, the interested reader may consult the following: Hui-zinga (1949), Illich (1980) and Peattie (1998).

13. I borrow the expression from Miriam Cooke (1988: 15) who, in exploring the literary output and background of a nucleus of women writers in Lebanon during the war, titles her first chapter as "Dance Macabre." So does, incidentally, Theodor Hanf (1993) in cataloguing the various stages and rounds of fighting.

7. From Playground to Battleground: Preludes to Civil Strife

1. In addition to Gebran, Naimy, and Rihani the following are part of that illustrious core: Maroun Abboud, Amin Nakhlé, Elia Abou-Madi, Elias Abou-Chabaki, Fawzi Malouf, Said Akl, Charles Malik, Fuad Bustani, among others. For an elaboration of the contributions of this circle — many of whom were influenced by Gibran and the so-called "Mahjar" poets — who broke away from the neoclassic traditions of Arab poetry and become part of a loose coalition of "Lebanese Romantic Literature", see al Eid 1979.
2. Most prominent among this group, at least if measured by the circulation and public recognition of their output, are the following: Ilyas Abou Chabaka, al-Akhtal al-Saghir, Omar Fakhoury, Ilya Abou Madi, Khalil Takieyddin, Amin Nakhlé
3. The circle grew appreciably in size. The following are its critical core: Yusuf al-Khal, Adonis (Ali Ahmad Said), Onsi al-Hajj, Fuad Rifka, Shawki Abu Shakra, Khalil Hawi, Talal Haydar, Issam Mahfouz, Ibrahim Jabra, Etel Adnan, Nadia Tueni.
4. Reference to "Youthful" cabinet.
5. Literature on the implications of the Arab-Israeli conflict and its destabilizing impact and accounts of the direct involvement of Israel in the wars in Lebanon are extensive. The following are instructive for the kind of arguments advanced here: Bulloch 1977, 1983; Evron 1987; Gammer 1984; Goria 1985; Haley and Snider 1979; Harkabi 1977; Herzog 1975; Hirst 1977; Khalidi 1978; Picard 1995; Rabinovich 1984; Schiff 1974; Schiff and Ya'ari 1984; Terrill 1987; Yaniv 1987.
6. No need to provide another chronicle of the pattern and escalation of such belligerent encounters. Any of the following can be consulted: Cobban 1985: 101–121; *Fiches du Monde Arabe* (Beirut and Laranka); Goria 1985: 88–172; Petran 1987; Salibi 1976; Winslow 1996: 131–161.
7. Full texts of the Cairo Accord and Melkart Protocols can be consulted in Chamoun 1963: 175–84.
8. Bashir Gemayyel, the younger son of the Kata'ib leader, was barely twenty years of age at the time. Like other cohorts of his, he was apolitical, rather carefree and sport-loving young student. The episode was a critical turning point in his political re-socialization.

10. Prospects for Civility

1. A critical core of established architects and urbanists, particularly those who had taken part in prewar construction (Assem Salam, Henri Eddeh, Pierre el-Khoury, Jad Tabet), have been very active in launching campaigns to disclose the foibles and shortcomings of Solidere and associated projects and schemes. These critical mentors have been recently joined by a growing number of fairly young, mostly Western-trained architects and urbanists. On their own or through APSAD (Association for the Protection Sites and Ancient Dwellings) and the revived Order of Engineers and Architects, they too have added their dissenting voices and proposed more viable alternatives. Hashim Sarkis, Habib Debs, Joe Nasr, Maha Yahya, Joumana Ghandour Atallah, Oussama Kabbani come to mind.

2. For further consideration of the local as "sites of resistance" to such threats of disappearance see, Dirlik (1996).

3. An edited volume by Nan Ellin (1997) contains meaningful theoretical and empirical evidence and instructive case studies substantiating the interplay between architecture, urban design, and fear.

4. For further elaboration see D. Genberg, "The Mutagenic Maquette of Beirut: A real-estate company's claim to a city", unpublished paper, CBR, American University of Beirut 1997.

5. Incidentally, Elisar derives its name from an ancient legend of a Phoenician queen who escaped Tyre to establish the city of Carthage. Prime Minister Hariri, a Sunni from Saida, suggested the name to commemorate this prehistoric myth. Nabih Berri, leaders of Hizbullah, and other Shi'ite notables were of course delighted to adopt the name to reassert, thereby, Shi'ite control over the southern suburb.

Bibliography

Abou, Selim. 1980. "The Myth and Reality of Migration." *Cultures* Vol. 7, No. 2.

Abraham, A. J. 1981. *Lebanon at Mid-Century: Maronite-Druze Relations in Lebanon, 1840–60.* Washington: University Presses of America.

Abul-Husn, Latif. 1998. *The Lebanese Conflict.* Boulder: Lynne Rienner.

Adorno, Theodor. 1973. *Philosophy of Modern Music.* NewYork: Seabury Press.

Agwani, M.S. 1963. "The Lebanese Crisis of 1958 in Retrospect." *International Studies* 4(4) (April: 329–348.

———. 1965. *The Lebanese Crisis, 1985.* N.Y.: Asia Publishing House.

Ajami, Fouad. 1986. *The Vanished Imam: Musa Al Sadr and The Shia of Lebanon.* Ithaca: Cornell University Press.

———. 1998. *Dream Palaces of the Arabs.* New York: Pantheon Books.

Akarli, Engin. 1993. *The Long Peace, 1861–1920.* Berkeley: University of California Press.

Albrow, Martin. 1977. "Travelling Beyond Local Cultures." In John Eade, ed. *Living the Global City.* London/N.Y.: Routledge: 37–55.

Alcalay, Ammiel. 1993. *After Jews and Arabs: Remaking Levantine Culture.* Minneapolis: University of Minnesota Press.

Alin, Erik G. 1994. *The United States and the 1958 Lebanon Crisis.* New York. and London: University Press of America.

Almond, G. and J. S. Coleman, eds. 1960. *The Politics of the Developing Areas.* Princeton: Princeton University Press.

Almond, G. and G. B. Powell, eds. 1966. *Comparative Politics: A Development Approach.* Boston: Little, Brown.

Antonius, George. 1938. *The Arab Awakening.* London: Hamiltion.

Aowad, Ibrahim. 1933. *Le Droit Privé des Maronites an Temps des Emirs Chihab.* Paris: Librarie Orientaliste.

Apter, D.E. 1965. *The Politics of Modernization*. Chicago: University of Chicgo Press.

Arendt, Hannah. 1958. *The Human Condition*. Garden City, N.Y.: Doubleday.

Al-Aswad, Ibrahim. 1925. *Tanwir al Athhan Fi Tarikh Lubnan*. Beirut: Saint Georgeous Press.

Atallah, Tony George. 1997. "Al-Mujannasun Fi Lubnan Ma Ba'd al Harb: Haqa'iq wa Arqam." The Naturalized in Lebanon: Facts and Figures *Al-Abhath* 45: 97–111.

Atiyah, Najla. 1973. *The Attitude of The Sunnis Toward The State of Lebanon*. London: Unpublished Ph. D. Dissertation.

Avi-Ran, Reuven. 1991. *The Syrian Involvement in Lebanon Since 1975*. Boulder: Westview Press.

Awad, Fuad. 1991. "Economics of Coincidence and Disaster in Lebanon." *The Beirut Review*, no. 2 (Fall: 82–95.

Awwad, Tawfik Yusuf. 1976. *Death in Beirut*. London: Heinemann.

Azar, Edward. 1984. *The Emergence of a New Lebanon: Fantasy or Reality*. New York: Praeger.

Baalbaki, A. 1973. *"Situation de L'agriculture Libanaise et Limites de L'intervention de l'état sur son Development."* Unpublished Ph. D University of. Paris

Badre, Albert. 1972. "The Economic Development of Lebanon." In C. A. Cooper and S. S. Alexander, eds. *Economic Development and Population Growth in the Middle East*. New York: Elsevier.

Baer, Gabriel. 1982. *Fellah and Townsmen in the Middle East*. London: Frank Cass.

Barakat, Halim 1977. *Lebanon in Strife: Student Preldues to Civil War*. Austin: University of Texas Press.

Barber, Benjamin. 1996. *Jihad vs. McWorld*. New York: Ballantine Books.

Bertrand, J. P., A. Boudjikanian, and W. Picadov, 1979. *"L'Industrie Libanaise et les Marchés Arabes du Golfe."* Beirut: CERMOC.

———. 1978. *"Etat et Perspectives de L'Industrie au Liban."* Beirut: CERMOC.

Binder, Leonard. 1966. "Political Change in Lebanon." In Leonard Binder, ed. *Politics in Lebanon*. New York: Wiley: 283–327.

Bell, J. Bowyer. 1987. *The Gun in Politics*. New Brunswick: Transaction.

Brezinski, Zbigniew. 1993. *Out of Control: Global Turmoil on The End of the Twenty-First Century*. New York: Scribner's.

Britt, George. 1953. "Lebanon's Popular Revolution." *The Middle East Journal* 7(1) (Winter): 1–17.

Brown, Robert Mc Afee. 1987. *Religion and Violence*. Philadelphia: The Westminister Press.

Buheiry, Marwan. 1989. "External Intervention and International Wars in Lebanon: 1770–1982." In Lawrence Conrad, ed.,*The Formation and Perception of the Modern Arab World: Studies by Marwan Buheiry*. Princeton, N.J.: Darwin Press.

Bulloch, John. 1977. *Death of a Country: The Civil War in Lebanon*. London: Weidenfeld and Nicolson.

———. 1983. *Final Conflict: The war in Lebanon.* London: Century Publishers.

Burckhardt, John L. 1822. *Travels in Syria and the Holy Land.* London: J. Murray.

Bustani, Emile. 1961. *March Arabesque.* London: Robert Hale Ld.

Calinescu, Matei. 1987. *Five Faces of Modernity.* Durham: Duke University Press.

Camara, Dom Helder. 1971. *Spiral of Violence.* Dimension Books.

Camus, Albert. 1956. *The Rebel.* New York: Vintage

Carrère d'Encausse, Hélène. 1993. *End of the Soviet Empire: The Triumph of the Nations.* Translated by Franklin Philip. New York: Basic Books.

Carroll, Bernice A. 1980. "Victory and Defeat: The Mystique of Dominance." In Stuart Albert and Edward Luck, eds. *On the Endings of War.* Port Washington, New York,: Kennikat Press: 47–71.

Carswell, John. 1989. "The Lebanese Vision: A History of Painting." In The British Lebanese Association, ed., *Lebanon: The Artist's View.* London: Quarlet Books: 15–19.

Chamoun, Camille. 1963. *Crise au Moyen-Orient.* Paris: Gallimard.

Chevallier, Dominique. 1968. "Western Development and Eastern Crisis in the Mid-Nineteenth Century: Syria Confronted with the European Economy." In Polk and Chambers, eds. *The Beginning of Modernization in the Middle East.* Chicago: University of Chicago Press.

———. 1971. *La Societé du Mont Liban a l'époque de la Revolution Industrielle en Europe.* Paris: Librarie Orientaliste Paul Geuther.

Chiha, Michel. 1964. *Visage et Présence du Liban.* Beirut: Michel Chiha Foundation.

———. 1966. *Lebanon at Home and Abroad.* Beirut: Cenacle Libanais.

Churchill, Charles H. 1853. *Mount Lebanon: A Ten Years' Residence From 1842–1852.* London: Saunders and Otley.

———. 1962. *The Druzes and the Maronites Under the Turkish Rule, 1840–60.* London: Spottiswoode and Company.

Cobban, Helena. 1985. *The Making of Modern Lebanon.* Boulder: Westview Press.

Colburn, Forrest, ed. 1989. *Everyday Forms of Peasant Resistance.* New York: M. E. Sharpe

Collins, Randall. 1974. "The Three Faces of Cruelty: Towards a Comparative Study of violence." *Theory and Society,* vol 1: 415–440.

Cooke, Miriam. 1988. *War's Other Voices: Women Writers on The Lebanese Civil War.* Cambridge and New York: Cambridge University Press.

Cooley, John. 1979. "The United States." In Haley and Snider, eds., *Lebanon in Crisis:* Participants and Issues. Syracuse: Syracuse: University Press.

Corm, Georges. 1988. "Myths and Realities of the Lebanese Conflict." In N. Shehadi and D. Haffar Mills, eds. *Lebanon: A History of Conflict and Consensus.* London: I. B. Tauris: 258–274.

———. 1989. "The Toll of Common Places." *The European Journal of International Affairs* 5 (Summer): 121–135.

Dahrendorf, Ralf. 1990. "Has the East Joined the West?" *New Perspective Quarterly* 7(2) (Spring): 41–43.

Davis, Natalie Z. 1975. *Society and Culture in Early Modern France*. Stanford University Press.

Daww, Istifan. 1911. *Hadiqat al-Jinan fi Tarikh Lubnan*. Batrun: al-Jamiah Press.

DiMuccio, R. B. A. and J. Roseanu. 1996. "Turbulence and Sovereignty in World Politics: Explaining the Relocation of Legitimacy in the 1990s and Beyond." In Z. Mlinar, ed. *Globalization and Territorial Identities*. England: Avebury

Direction Centrale de la Stastistique. 1972. *La Population Active au Liban*. Beirut.

Dirlik, Arif. 1996. "The Global in the Local." In Rob Wilson and Wimal Dissanayake, eds. *Global Local: Cultural Productions and the Transnational Imagination*. Durham: Duke University Press: 21–45.

Dubar, Claude and Salim Nasr. 1976. *Les Classess Sociales au Liban*. Paris: Presses de la Foundation Nationale des Sciences Politiques.

Ducruet, Jean. S.J. 1995. *Livre D'or: 1913–1993*. Beyrouth: Université Saint-Joseph de Beyrouth.

al-Eid, Yumna. 1979. *al Dalala al-Ijtima'iyya li-Harakat al-Adab al-Rumantiqiyya fi Lubnan*. Social Indicators for the Romantic Literary Movement in Lebanon.

Eisenstadt, S. N. 1966. *Modernization: Protest and Change*. Englewood Cliffs, N.J: Prentice-Hall.

Elias, Norbert. 1988. "Violence and Civilization: The State Monopoly of Physical Violence and Its Infringement." In John Keane, ed. *Civil Society and the State*. London and New York: Verso: 197–216.

Ellin, Nan. 1997. *Architecture of Fear*. New York: Princeton Architectural Press.

Emerson, R. 1960. *From Empire to Nation: The Rise of Self-Assertion of Asian and African Peoples*. Cambridge: Harvard University Press.

Entelis, John. 1974. *Pluralism and Party Transformation in Lebanon: al-Kata'ib, 1936–1970*. Leiden: Brill.

Erikson, Kay. 1976. *Everything in Its Path: Destruction of the Community in the Buffalo Creek Flood*. New York: Simon and Schuster.

Esman, M. J. and I. Rabinovich. 1988. *Ethnicity, Pluralism, and the State in the Middle East*. Ithaca: Cornell University Press.

Evron, Yair. 1987. *War and Intervention in Lebanon: The Israeli–Syrian Deterrence Dialogue*. London: Croom Helm.

Fani, Michel. 1995. *Liban — 1880–1914 L'Atelier Photographique de Ghazir*. Paris: Editions de L'Escalier.

Fanon, Frantz. 1961. *The Wretched of the Earth*. New York: Grove Press

Farah, Caesar. 1967. "The Lebanese Insurgence of 1840 and the Powers." *The Journal of Asian History* 1: 105–32.

Faris, Fuad. 1976. "The Civil War in Lebanon." *Race and Class* 18 (August): 173–184.

Faris, Hani. 1992. "The Failure of Peacemaking in Lebanon, 1975–1989." In Deirdre Collings, ed. *Peace for Lebanon*. Boulder: Lynne Rienner: 17–30.

Faris, Nabih Amin. 1960. "Lebanon, Land of Light." In James Kritzech and R. Bayly Winder, eds, *The World of Islam: Studies in Honor of Philip K. Hitti*. London: Macmillan: 336–50.

Farouk-Sluglett, M. and P. Sluglett. 1982. "Aspects of the Changing Nature of Lebanese Confessional Politics: Al-Murabitun, 1958–1979." In *Liban Remises en Cause. Peuples Mediterranéens* (July–September): 59–73.

Farsoun, Samih K. and Rex B. Wingerter. 1981. "Palestinians in Lebanon," *SAIS Review* 2 (Winter): 93–106.

Fattouh, Bassam Ahmad. 1998. *Emerging Lebanon: A New Role for the Future*. Oxford: Center for Lebanese Studies.

Fawaz, Leila Tarazi. 1983. *Merchants and Migrants in Nineteenth-Century Lebanon*. Cambridge: Harvard University Press.

———. 1994. *An Occasion for War: Civil Conflict in Lebanon and Damascus in 1860*. London: I.B. Tauris.

Fischer, Claude. 1982. *To Dwell Among Friends: Personal Networks in Town and City*. Chicago: University of Chicago Press.

Fisk, Robert. 1990 *Pity the Nation: The Abduction of Lebanon*. New York: Atheneum.

Friedman, Thomas. 1991. "U.S. Calls Removal of Aoun Only Solution for Lebanon." *New York Times*. October, 28.

———. 1984. *From Beirut to Jerusalem*. New York: Simon and Schuster.

———. 2000. *The Lexus and The Olive Tree*. New York: Anchor Books.

Fukuyama, Francis. 1989. "The End of History." *The National Interest*, no. 16. (Summer).

———. 1998. "Women and the Evolution of World Politics." *Foreign Affairs* 77(5) (September/October): 24–40.

Gammer, Moshe. 1984. "The War in Lebanon: The Course of Hostilities." In Colin Legum et al, eds. *Middle East Contemporary Survey* 6 (1981–82). New York and London: 128–57.

Gates, Carolyn L. 1998. *The Merchant Republic of Lebanon: Rise of an Open Economy*. London: I. B. Tauris.

Gay, Peter. 1993. *The Cultivation of Hatred*. New York: Norton.

Gellner, Ernest. 1988. *Culture, Identity and Politics*. London: Cambridge University Press.

———. 1997. *Nationalism*. New York: New York University Press.

Genberg, Daniel. 1997. "The Mutagenic Maquette of Beirut: A Real-Estate Company's Claim to a City." Unpublished paper, CBR, American University of Beirut.

Gendzier, Irene. L. 1988. "The Declassified Lebanon 1948–1958: Elements of Continuity and Contrast in US Policy Toward Lebanon." In N. Shehadi and D. Haffar-Mills, eds. *Lebanon a History of Conflict and Consensus*. London: I. B. Tauris: 187–209.

———. 1989. "The United States, The USSR and The Arab World in NSC Reports of the 1950s." *Arab American Affairs* no. 28. (Spring): 22–29.

———. 1990a. "The U.S. Perception of the Lebanese Civil War According to Declassified Documents: A Preliminary Account." In Riva S. Simon, ed., *The Middle East and North Africa.* New York: Columbia University Press: 328–344.

———. 1990b. "No Forum for the Lebanese People." *Middle East Report.* (January–February): 34–36.

———. 1997. *Notes from the Minefield : United States Intervention in Lebanon and the Middle East, 1945–1958.* New York: Columbia University Press.

Gerges, Fawaz. 1994. *The Superpowers of the Middle East: Regional and International Politics, 1955–67.* Boulder: Westview Press.

———. 1997. "Lebanon" In Yezid Sayigh and Avi Shlaim, eds. *The Cold War and the Middle East.* Oxford: Clarendon Press: 77–101.

Geyer, Georgie Anne. 1985. "Our Disintegrating World: The Menace of Global Anarchy." *Encyclopaedia Britannica, Book of the Year,* 1985. Chicago: University of Chicago Press: 11–25.

Ghoussoub, Mai. 1998. *Leaving Beirut.* London: Saqi Books.

Gibb, H.A.R. and Bowen, H. 1957. *Islamic Society and the West.* London: Oxford University Press.

Gide, Andre. 1950. *Littérature Engagée.* Paris: Gallimard.

Gillian, James. 1996. *Violence.* New York: Vintage Books.

Girard, René. 1977. *Violence and the Sacred.* Baltimore: Johns Hopkins University Press.

Goodman, Paul. 1964. *Utopian Essays and Practical Proposals.* New York: Vintage.

Gordon, David 1988.*Lebanon: The Fragmented Nation.* London: Croom Helm.

Goria, Wade. 1985. *Sovereignty and Leadership in Lebanon, 1945–1976.* London Ithaca Press.

Grossman, David. 1998. *On Killing.* New York: Diane Publishing Co.

Group for the Advancement of Psychiatry, Committee of International Relations. *Us and Them: The Psychology of Ethnonationalism.* New York: Brunner/Mazel 1987.

Gulick, John. 1967. *Tripoli: A Modern Arab City.* Cambridge: Harvard University Press.

Gunther, John. 1969. *Twelve Cities.* New York, Harper and Row.

Guys, Henri. 1850. *Beyrouth et le Liban.* Paris: Imprimerie de W. Ramquet el Fie.

Habachi, René 1960. *Hadharatuna 'ala al Muftarak* (Our Culture on a Crossroad). Beirut:: Cenacle Lebanais.

Haffar, Ahmad. 1961. "France in the Establishment of Greater Lebanon." Ph. D dissertation, Princeton University.

al-Hajj, Kamal Yusuf. 1961. *Al-Ta'ifiya al-Banna'a: Aw Falsafat al-Mithaq al-Watani.* Beirut: Matba'at al-Rahbaniya al-Lubnaniya.

a-Halabi, Antun. 1927. *Hurub Ibrahim Basha al-Misri fi Suriyah wal Anadul.* 2 volumes, Asad Rustum and Bulus Qar'ali. Heliopallis: Syrian Press.

Halawi, Majed. 1992. *A Lebanon Defied: Musa al-Sadr and the Shi'a Community.* Boulder: Westview Press.

Haley, Edward and L.W. Snider. 1979. *Lebanon in Crisis: Participants and Issues.* Syracuse University Press.

Hanf, Theodor. 1993. *Coexistence in Wartime Lebanon.* London: I. B. Tauris.

———. 1995. "Ethnurgy: On the Analytical use and Normative Abuse of the Concept of 'Ethnic Identity.' " In Keebet von Benda-Bechman and M. Yerkuyten, eds. *Nationalism, Ethnicity and Cultural Identity in Europe.* The Netherlands: Utrecht University 40–51.

Hamacher, Werner. 1997. "One Too Many Multiculturalisms." In Hent de Vries and Samuel Weber, eds. *Violence, Identity and Self Determination.* Stanford: Stanford University Press: 284–325.

Harik, Iliya. 1965. "The Iqta' System in Lebanon: A Comparative Political View." *The Middle East Journal* (Autumn) 19 (4): 405–21.

———. 1968. *Politics and Change in a Traditional Society: Lebanon 1711–1845.* Princeton: Princeton University Press.

———. 1987. "Communalism and National Cooperation in Lebanon." In Barbara Freyer-Stowasser, ed. *The Islamic Impulse.* London: Croom Helm

Harkabi, Yehoshafet. 1977. *Arab Strategies and Israel's Response.* New York: Free Press.

Harris, William. 1997. *Faces of Lebanon: Sects, Wars and Global Extensions.* Princeton: Markus Wiener Publishers.

Harris, Wilson. 1956. "Taking Root." In E. H. Hutchison, ed. *Violent Trance.* New York: Devin-Adair.

Al-Hattuni, Mansur. 1884. *Nadbhah Tarikhiyah fi al-Muqata'ah al-Kisrwaniyah.* Beirut: n.p.

Havel, Vaclav. 1985. *The Power of the Powerless: Citizens Against the State.* Armonk, N.Y.: M. E. Sharpe.

Herzog, Chaim. 1975. *The War of Atonement.* Boston: Little, Brown.

Hirst, David. 1977. *The Gun and The Olive Branch: The Roots of Violence in The Middle East.* London

Hitti, Nassif. 1989. "The Foreign Policy of Lebanon: Lessons and Prospects for the Forgotten Dimension." *Papers on Lebanon.* Oxford: Center for Lebanese Studies.

Hitti, Philip. 1957. *Lebanon in History.* London: Macmillan and Company.

Hobsbawn, Eric. 1985. *Bandits.* Harmondsworth: Penguin Books.

Horowitz, Donald L. 1985. *Ethnic Groups in Conflict.* Berkeley: University of California Press.

Hottinger, Arnold. 1961. "Zu'ama and Parties in the Lebanese Crisis of 1958." In *Middle East Journal* 15(2) (Spring): 127–40.

Hourani, A.H. 1962. "Historians of Lebanon." In B. Lewis and P. M. Holt, eds. *Historians of the Middle East*. London: Oxford University Press: 226–45.

———. 1966. "Lebanon: The Development of a Political Society." In Leonard Binder, ed. *Politics in Lebanon*. New York: Wiley: 13–29.

———. 1976. "Ideologies of the Mountain and the City." In Roger Owen, ed. *Essays on the Crisis in Lebanon*. London: Ithaca Press: 33–41.

———. 1986. "From Jabal 'Amil to Persia." *Bulletin of the School of Oriental and African Studies* 49: 133–140.

———. 1988. "Visions of Lebanon." In Halim Barakat, ed. *Toward a Viable Lebanon*. London: Croom Helm: 3–14.

Hudson, Michael. 1968. *The Precarious Republic*. New York: Random House.

———. 1976. "The Lebanese Crisis: The Limits of Consociational Democracy." *Journal of Palestine Studies* 5(3/4): 104–22.

———. 1978. "The Palestinian Factor in the Lebanese Civil War." *Middle East Journal* 32 (Summer): 261–78.

Huizinga, John. 1949. *Homo Ludens*. London: Routledge.

Huntington, Samuel. 1993. "The Clash of Civilizations?" *Foreign Affairs* 72 (Summer): 22–49.

———. 1996. *The Clash of Civilizations And the Remarking of World Order*. New York: Simon and Schuster.

Hüppauf, Bernd-Rudiger 1997. *War, Violence, and the Modern Condition*. Berlin: Walter De Gruyter.

Hurewitz, J.C. 1963. "Lebanese Democracy in Its International Setting." *The Middle East Journal* 17(5) (Late Autumn): 487–506.

al-Husseini, Hussein. 1994. "What is Being Implemented Is Neither the Ta'if Agreement nor the Constitution." *An Nahar*, November 7.

Ignatieff, Michael. 1994. *Blood and Belonging: Journeys Into the New Nationalism*. New York: Farrar, Strauss and Giroux.

Ikle, Fred Charles. 1971. *Every War Must End*. New York: Columbia University Press.

Illich, Ivan. 1980. *Tools for Conviviality*. New York: Harper and Row.

Issawi, Charles. 1964. "Economic Development and Liberalism in Lebanon." *The Middle East Journal* 18 (3) (Summer): 279-292.

———. 1966. "Economic Development and Political Liberalism in Lebanon." In Leonard Binder, ed. *Politics in Lebanon*. New York: Wiley: 69–83.

———. 1967. "British Consular Views on Syria's Economy in the 1850s–1860s." *American University of Beirut Festival Book*. Festschrift. Beirut: American University of Beirut: 103–20.

James, William. 1902. *The Varieties of Religious Experience: A Study in Human Nature*. New York: Modern Library.

Jedlowski, P. 1990. "Simmel on Memory." In M. Kaern, B. S. Philips and R. S. Cohen, eds. *George Simmel and Contemporary Sociology*. Dordrecht: Kluwer.

Jessup, Henry H. 1910. *Fifty-Three years in Syria*. New York: Fleming Revell.

Jouplain, M. 1908. *La Question Du Liban, Etude d'Histoire Diplomatique et de Droit Internationale*. Paris: A. Rousseam.

Jumblat, Kamal. 1959. *Haqiqat al-Thawrah al-Lubnaniyah*. The Truth About the Lebanese Revolution. Beirut: Dar al-Nashr al-'Arabiyah.

———. 1960. *Fi Majra al-Siyasa al-Lubnaniyya*. On the Course of Lebanese Politics. Beirut: Dar al-Tali'ah.

el-Kak, Mona Harb. 1998. "Transforming the Site of Dereliction Into the Urban Culture of Modernity: Beirut's Southern Suburb and Elisar Project." In P. Rowe and H. Sarkis., eds., *Projecting Beirut*. Munich: Prestel: 173–181.

Kakar, Sudhir. 1996. *The Colors of Violence*. Chicago: University of Chicago Press.

Kanovsky, E. 1983/4. "The Economy of Lebanon: Postwar Prospects." *Middle East Review* 16(2) (Winter).

Kaplan, Jay. 1980. "Victors and Vanquished: Their Postwar Relations." In Stuart Albert and Edward Luck, eds., *On the Endings of War*. Post Washington, N.Y.: Kennikat: 72–117.

Karami, Nadia and Nawaf Salam 1959. *Waqi al-Thawrah al-Lubnaniyah*. The Reality of the Lebanese Revolution. Beirut: No Publisher.

Keane, John. 1996. *Reflections on Violence*. London/New York: Vesco.

Keen, Sam. 1986. *Faces of the Enemy: Reflections on the Hostile Imagination*. New York: Harper and Row.

Kelman, H. 1987. "On the Sources of Attachment to the Nation." Paper presented at the meeting of the International Society of Political Psychology. San Francisco, July 6.

Kelly, Kevin. 1994. *Out of control: The Rise of Neo-Biological Civilization*. Reading, Mass.: Addison-Wesley.

Kerr, Malcolm. 1959. *Lebanon in the Last Days of Feudalism, 1840–1868*. Beirut: Catholic Press.

Khal, Helen. 1987. *The Women Artist in Lebanon*. Beirut: Institute for Women's Studies in the Arab World.

Khalaf, Samir. 1979. *Persistence and Change in 19 th-Century Lebanon*. Beirut: American University of Beirut.

———. 1980. "Lebanon's Parliamentary Elite." In Landau, Ozbudun and Tachau, eds. *Electoral Politics in the Middle East: Issues, Voters and Elites*. Stanford: Hoover Institution, Stanford University: 243–71.

———. 1987. "The Background and Causes of Lebanese/Syrian Immigration to the United States Before World War I." In Eric J. Hooglund, ed. *Crossing the Waters*. Washington, D.C.: Smithsonian Institution Press: 17–36.

——— and G. Denoeux. 1988. "Urban Networks and Political Conflict in Lebanon." In N. Shehadi and D. Haffar Mills, eds. *Lebanon: a History of Conflict and Consensus*. London: I. B. Tauris: 181–200.

————. 1991. "Ties That Bind: Sectarian Loyalties and the Revival of Pluralism in Lebanon." *The Beirut Review* 1(1) (Spring): 12–61.

————. 1993. "Culture, Collective Memory and the Rehabilitation of Civility." Deirdre Collins, ed., *Peace for Lebanon: From War to Reconstruction*. Boulder: Lynne Rienner: 273–86.

———— with Philip S. Khoury. 1993. *Recovering Beirut: Urban Design and Post-War Reconstruction*. Leiden: E.J. Brill.

————. 1995. "Communal Strife in Global politics." In M. Esman and S. Telhami, eds., International Organization and Ethnic Conflict. Ithaca: Cornell University Press: 101–25.

Al-Khalidi, 'Anbara Salam. 1978. *Jawla fi al-Dhikrayat Bayna Lubnan wa Filastin*. (A Trip Through Memories Between Lebanon and Palestine). Beirut: Dar al-Nahar.

Khatir, Lahd. 1967. *'Ahad al-Mutesarrifiyyin Fi Lubnan*. Beirut: Lebanese University Publications.

El-Khazen, Farid. 1998. *Lebanon's First Postwar Parliamentary Elections: An Imposed Choice*. Oxford: Center for Lebanese Studies.

————. 1999. "Shrinking Margins: The Christians in Postwar Lebanon." In Barbara Reberson, ed. *The Breakdown of The State of Lebanon 1967–1976*. London: I. B. Tauris, in Press.

————. 2000. *The Breakdown of the State in Lebanon 1967–76*. London, N.Y.: I. B. Tauris.

al-Khuri, Bishara. 1960. *Haqa'iq Lubnaniya*. Lebanese Realities. Harissa, Lebanon.

Kissinger, Henry. 1999. *Years of Renewal*. New York: Simon and Schuster.

Kliot, 1987. "The Collapse of the Lebanese State." *Middle Eastern Studies* 23 (January).

Korbani, Agnes G. 1991. *U.S. Intervention in Lebanon, 1958 and 1982*. New York: Praeger.

Konrad, George. 1984. *Antipolitics*. New York: Harcourt Brace Jovanovitch.

Labaki, Boutros. 1971. *Some Salient Aspects of the Lebanese Economy*. Beirut Mimeograph

————. 1981. "Structuration Conmunautaire, Rapport de Force Entre Minorites el Guerres au Liban." *Guerres Mondiales et Conflit Contemporaines*, no. 151: 43–70.

————. 1993. "Development Policy in Lebanon Between Past and Future." *The Beirut Review* no. 6 (Fall): 97–111.

———— and Khalil Abou Rjeily. 1993. *Bilan des Guerres du Liban, 1975–1990*. Paris: Editions L'Harmattan.

Laing, R. D. 1967. *The Politics of the Family*. New York: Vintage.

de Lamartime, Alphonse. 1835. *Souvenirs, Impressions, Pensées et Paysages Pendant un Voyage on Orient, 1832–1833*. Paris: Macketice et Cie-Furne.

Lasch, Christopher. 1979. *Haven in a Heartless World: The Family Besieged*. New York: Norton.

———. 1988. "The Communitarian Critique of Liberalism." In C. E. Reynolds and R. V. Norman, eds. *Community in America: The Challenge of Habits of the Heart*. Berkeley: University of California Press.

Laurent, Annie, 1987. *Les Guerres Secretes au Liban*. Paris: Gallimard

———. 1991. "A War Between Brothers: The Army-Lebanese Forces Showdown in East Beirut." *The Beirut Review* no.1: 88–101.

Lebanese Communist Party. 1973. *The Agrarian Question in Lebanon in the Light of Marxism*. Beirut: Lebanese Communist Party.

Lerner, D. 1962. *Passing of Traditional Society: The Modernization of the Middle East*. Glencoe: The Free Press.

Levi, Primo. 1987. *Moments of Reprieve*. London: Abacus.

Mack, John.1979. Foreword to: *Cyprus: War and Adaptation, A Psychoanalytic History of Two Ethnic Groups in Conflict*, V. E. Volkan, ed.. Charlottesville: University of Virginia Press.

———. 1988. "The Enemy System." *The Lancet*. January.

Mackey, Sandra 1989. *Lebanon: Death of a Nation*. Chicago: Congdon and Weed.

MacCannell, D. 1989. *The Tourist: A New Theory of the Leisure Class*. New York: Schoken.

Maila, Joseph. 1994. "The Ta'if Accord: An Evaluation." In Deirdre Collings, ed. *Peace for Lebanon: From War to Reconstruction*. Boulder: Lynne Rienner: 31–44.

Makdisi, Jean Said. 1990. *Beirut Fragments*. New York: Persea Books.

Makdisi, Ussama. 2000. *The Culture of Sectarianism*. Berkeley: University of California Press.

Maksoud, Clovis. 1966. "Lebanon and Arab Nationalism." In Leonard Binder, ed. *Politics in Lebanon*. New York: John Wiley.

Malik, Charles. 1974. *Lubnan fi Thatehi* (Lebanon per se). Beirut: Badran Establishment.

el-Maqdisi, Jurjus al-Khuri. 1921. *'Azam Harb fi al-Tarikh*. Beirut

Manganaro, E. S. 1998. *Bearing Witness: Recent Literature from Lebananon*. Rutherford, N.J.: Fairleigh Dickinson University Press.

Mansour, Albert. 1993. *alInqilab 'ala al Taif*. Coup Against Ta'if. Beirut: Dar al-Jadid

Marvin, Garry. 1986. "Honor, Integrity and the Problem of Violence in the Spanish Bullfight." In David Riches, ed. *The Anthropology of Violence*. Oxford: Basil Blackwell: 118–35.

Masalla, Nur. 1997. *Maximum Land and Minimum Arabs: Israel, Transfer and Palestinians 1949–96*. Beirut: Institute of Palestine Studies.

Melikian, L.H. and L. N. Diab. 1974 "Stability and Change in Group Affiliations of University Students in the Middle East." *The Journal of Social Psychology* 93: 13–21.

Melko, Matthew. 1990. *Peace in our Time*. New York: Paragon House.

Meo, Leila. 1965. *Lebanon, Improbable Nation: A Study in Political Development*. Bloomington: Indiana University Press.

Messarra, Antoine, N. 1988. "The Challenge of Coexistence." Oxford: Center for Lebanese Studies.

The Middle East Journal. 1957, 1958, 1959. Chronologies in Vols. 11, 12, and 13.

Middle Eastern Affairs. 1957, 1958, 1959. Chronologies in Vols. 7, 8, 9.

Mideast Mirror. 1958

Midlarsky, Manus. 1992. *The Internationalization of Communal Conflict*. N.Y.: Routledge.

Milnar, Z, ed. 1996. *Globalization and Territorial Identities*. England: Avebury.

Le Monde. 1984

Moore, Barrington. 1966. *Social Origins of Dictatorship and Democracy*. Boston: Beacon Press.

Mousnier, Roland. 1970. *Peasant Uprisings in Seventeenth Century France, Russia and China*. New York: Harper.

Moynihan, Daniel Patrick. 1993. *Pandaemonium: Ethnicity in International Politics*. New York: Oxford University Press.

Mueller, John. 1989. *Retreat from Doomsday: The Absolescence of Major War*. New York: Basic Books.

Murphy, Robert 1964. *Diplomat Among Warriors*. New York: Doubleday.

Al-Nahar 1994. April 26.

Nasr, Salim. 1978. "The Crisis of Lebanese Capitalism." *MERIP Reports*. December No. 73: 3–13.

Norton, Augustus Richard. 1987. *Amal and The Shi'a: The Struggle for the Soul of Lebanon*. Austin: University of Texas Press.

———. 1991. "Lebanon After Ta'if: Is the Civil War Over?" *The Middle East Journal*, 45(1) Winter: 456–73.

———. 1999. *Hizbollah of Lebanon: From Political Realism to Mundane Politics*. New York: Council of Foreign Relations.

Odeh, B. J. 1985. *Lebanon: Dynamics of Conflict*. London: Zed Books.

Ortega y Gasset, Jose. 1932. *The Revolt of the Masses*. Authorized translation from the Spanish.

Owen, Roger. 1988. "The Economic History of Lebanon, 1943–1974: Its Salient Features." In Halim Barakat, ed. *Toward a Viable Lebanon*. London: Croom Helm: 27–41.

Peattie, Lisa. 1998. "Convivial Cities". In Mike Douglass and John Friedmann, eds. *Cities for Citizens*. New York: Wiley: 245–53.

Penderhughes, C. A. 1979. "Differential Bonding: Toward a Psychophysical Theory of Stereotyping." *American Journal of Psychiatry* 136 (1) (January): 33–37.

Penrose, Stephen 1941. *That They May Have Life*. Princeton: Princeton University Press.

Perlmann, M. 1958. "Midsummer Madness." *Middle Eastern Affairs* 9 (August–September): 246–61.

Petran, Tabitha. 1987 *The Struggle Over Lebanon.* New York: Monthly Review.

Picard, Elizabeth. 1996. *Lebanon: A Shattered Country.* New York: Holmes and Meier.

Poliak, A. N. 1939. *Feudalism: Egypt, Syria, Palestine and the Lebanon.* London: The Royal Asiatic Society.

Polk, William. 1963. *The Opening of South Lebanon, 1788–1849: A Study of the Impact of the West on the Middle East.* Cambridge: Harvard University Press.

Porath, Yehoshua. 1965. "The Peasant Revolt of 1851–61 in Kisrwan. "*Asian and African Studies* 1: 77–157.

Poujade, Eugene. 1867. *Le Liban et la Syrie, 1845–1860.* Paris: Librarie Nouvelle.

Pye, L. 1966. *Aspects of Political Development.* Boston: Little, Brown.

Quabbani, Nizar. 1986. "Footnotes to the Book of the Setback." In Abdallah Al-Udhari, ed. and tras. *Modern Poetry of the Arab World.* Harmondsworth: Penguin: 96–98.

———. 1994. "Beirut O Queen of the World." *The Literary Review* 37 (3): 498–502.

Quandt, William, B. 1984. "Reagan's Lebanon Policy: Trial and Error." *The Middle East Journal* 30(2) (Spring): 237–54.

Qubain, Fahim. 1961. *Crisis in Lebanon.* Washington, D.C.: The Middle East Institute.

Qurtas, Wadad 1983. *Dhikrayat.* Memoirs. Beirut.

Rabinovich, Itamer. 1985. *The War for Lebannon, 1970–1983.* Ithaca: Cornell University Press.

Rabinow, Paul. 1989. *French Modern.* Cambridge: MIT Press.

Randal, Jonathan, C. 1984. *Going all The Way.* New York: Vintage.

Ricoeur, Paul. 1967. *The Symbolism of Evil.* New York: Harper and Row.

Riyashi, Iskandar. 1953 *Qabl Wa-Ba'd.* Before and After. Beirut: al-Arfan Press.

Rokach, Livia 1980. *Israel's Sacred Terrorism.* Belmont, Mass: Association of Arab-American University Graduates.

Rorty, Richard. 1989. *Contingency, Irony and Solidarity.* Cambridge: Cambridge University Press.

Rouleau, Eric. 1975. "Clashes of Private Armies in Lebanon's Civil War." Series of three articles from *Le Monde* reprinted in *Manchester Guardian Weekly.* October 4, 11, 19.

Rule, James. 1988. *Theories of Civil Violence.* Berkeley: University of California Press.

Rupesinghe, Kumar. 1992. "The Disappearing Boundaries Between Internal and External Conflicts." In K. Rupesinghe, ed. *Internal Conflict and Governance.* New York: St. Martin's Press.

Rutgers University. 1990. "Conference on How Civil Wars End." Proceeding, March 2–4.

Saab, Hassan. 1966. "The Rationalist School in Lebanese Politics." In Leonard Binder, ed. *Politics in Lebanon*. New York: Wiley.

Saba, Paul. 1976. "The Creation of the Lebanese Economy: Economic Growth in the 19th and early 20th Centuries." In Roger Owen, ed., *Essays on the Crisis in Lebanon*. London: Ithaca Press, pp. 1–22.

Sa'd, Ma'ruf. 1959. *Indama Qawamna*. When We Resisted. Beirut: Dar al 'Iln Lil Malayin.

Safa, Elie. 1960. *L'Emigration Libanaise*. Beirut: University of Saint Joseph.

Safe, Joe. 2000. "The State of Human Rights in Lebanon, 1999." Beirut: Foundation for Human and Humanitarian Rights.

Said, Edward. 1983. "Palestinians in the Aftermath of Beirut." *Journal of Palestine Studies* 12(2).

———. 1989. Foreword to *Little Mountain* by Elias Khoury. Minneapolis: University of Minnesota Press.

———. 1991. "Identity, Authority, and Freedom: The Potentate and the Traveler." *Transition*, no. 54: 2–18.

Said, Khalida. 1998. *Al Harkah al Masrahiyya fi Lubnan, 1960–75*. The Theatre Movement in Lebanon. Arayya: Catholic Press.

Salam, Nawaf. 1979. *L'Insurrection De 1958 Au Liban*. Doctoral Dissertation, University of Paris.

Salame, Ghassam. 1988. "Is a Lebanese Foreign Policy Possible?" In Halim Barakat, ed., *Toward a Viable Lebanon*. Georgetown University: Center for Contemporary Arab Studies.

Salem, Paul. 1991. "Two Years of Living Dangerously: General Awn and Lebanon's Second Republic." *The Beirut Review* 1(1) (Spring): 62–87.

———. 1993. "Superpowers and Small States: An Overview of American-Lebanese Relations." *Beirut Review* 5. (Spring).

———. 1994 "Reflections on Lebanon's Foreign Policy." In Deirdre Collins, ed. *Peace for Lebanon? From War to Reconstruction*. Boulder: Lynne Rienner.

Saliba, Najib. 1981. "Emigration From Syria: *Arab Studies Quarterly* 3(1).

Salibi, Kamal. 1958. " The Lebanese Crisis in Perspective." *The World Today* 14(9) (September): 369–80.

———. 1959. *Maronite Historians of Medieval Lebanon*. Beirut: Catholic Press.

———. 1965. *The Modern History of Lebanon*. London: Weidenfeld and Nicolson.

———. 1966. "Lebanon Under Fuad Chehab: 1958–1964." *Middle East Studies* 2(3) (April): 211–26

———. 1976. *Crossroads to Civil War*. New York: Caravan Books.

———. 1988. *A Home of Many Mansions*. London: I. B. Tauris.

Sarkis, Hashin. 1993. "Territorial Claims: Architecture and Postwar Attitudes Toward the Environment." In Samilr Khalaf and Philip S. Khoury, eds. *Recovering Beirut*. Leiden: E. J. Brill.

Sartre, J. P. 1964. *Nausea*. New York: New Directions.

Scarry, Elaine. 1985. *The Body in Pain: The Making and Unmaking of the World*. New York: Oxford University Press.

Scheltema, J. F. 1920. *The Lebanon in Turmoil in 1860*. New Haven: Yale University Press.

Schiff, Ze'er. 1974. *October Earthquake: Yom Kippur, 1973*. Tel Aviv: University Publishers Projects.

———— and Ehud Ya'ari. 1984. *Israel's Lebanon War*. New York: Simon and Schuster.

Schmookler, A. B. 1988. *Out of Weakness*. New York: Bantam Books.

Schwartz, Regina. 1997. *The Curse of Cain: The Violent Legacy of Monotheism*. Chicago and London: University of Chicago Press.

Scott, James C. 1985. *Weapons of the Weak: Everyday Forms of Peasant Resistance*. New Haven: Yale University Press.

Scruton, Roger. 1987 *A Land Held Hostage*. London: The Claridge Press.

Seale, Patrick. 1965. *The Struggle for Syria*. London: Oxford University Press.

Sennett, Richard. 1990. *The Conscience of the Eye*. New York: Alfred Knopf.

Seurat, Michel.1985. "Le Quartier de Bab Tebane à Tripoli (Liban): Etude d'une Asabiyya Urbaine." In *C.E.R.M.O.C., Mouvements Communautaires et Espaces Urbains au Machreq*. Beirut: C.E.R.M.O.C.: 45–86.

Shararah, Waddah. 1996. *Dawlat Hizbollah. Lubnan Mujtama'n Islamiyyan*. Beirut: Dar al-Nahar.

Shawool, Paul. 1989. *Arab Modern Theatre*. London: El-Rayyes Books Ltd.

al-Shaykh, Hanan. 1986. *The Story of Zahra*. London: Pan Books.

Al-Shidyaq, Tannus. 1970. *Akhbar al-Ayan Fi Jabal Lubnan*. Beirut: Universite Libanaise.

Shihab, Amir Haidar. 1933. *Lubnan Fi 'Ahd al-Umara al-Shihabiyyin*, A.J. Rustum and F. E. Bustani, eds. Beirut: Catholic Press.

Shils, E. 1965. *Political Development in the New States*. The Hague: Mouton

————. 1966. "The Prospect for Lebanese Civility." In Leonard Binder. ed, *Politics in Lebanon*. New York: Wiley: 1–12

Shklar, Judith. 1982. *Ordinary Vices*. Cambridge: Harvard University Press.

Shmesh, Moshe. 1986. "The Lebanon Crisis, 1975–1985: A Reassessment." *The Jerusalem Quarterly*. no. 37: 77–94.

Showeiri, Joseph. 1973. *Al-Hizb al-Qawmi al-Ijtima'I*. The Syrian National Socialist Party A translation and a critique of Labib Zuwiyya. Beirut: Ibn Khaldoun Press.

Singer, M. and A. Wildavsky, A. 1993. *The Real World Zones: Zones of Peace/Zones of Turmoil*. N.J. Chatham.

Sirriyyeh, Hussein. 1976. "The Palestinian Armed Presence in Lebanon Since 1967." In Roger Owen, ed. *Essays on the Crisis in Lebanon*. London: Ithaca Press.

Smilianskaya, I.M. 1972. *Al-Harakat al-Fullahiyyah fi Lubnan*. Beirut: Dar al-Farabi Press.

al-Solh, Munah. 1984. "Kiyan Mu'allaq Bayna Thaqafatayn Siyasiyyatayn." Beirut :al-Safeer, May 14

al-Solh, Sami. 1960. *Mudhakkirat*. Memoirs. Beirut: n. p.

Sorel, Georges. 1961. *Reflections on Violence*. New York: Peter Smith.

Spencer, Herbert. 1898. *The Principles of Sociology*. New York: D. Appleton.

Stauth, G. and Turner, B. S. 1988. "Nostalgia, Postmodernism and the Critique of Mass Culture." In *Theory, Culture and Society* 5: 2–3.

Stewart, Desmond. 1959 *Turmoil in Beirut*. London: Allan Wingate.

Staokes, Frank. 1975. "The Civil War in Lebanon." *World Today* 32(1): January 8–17.

Stookey, Robert. 1979. "The United States." In Haley and Snider, eds. *Lebanon in Crisis*. Syracuse, New York: Syracuse University Press.

Storr, Anthony. 1968. *Human Aggression*. New York: Bantam

Suleiman, Michael. 1967. *Political Parties in Lebanon*. Ithaca: Cornell University Press.

Swalha, Aseel. 1997. "Globalization: Community Responses to Global Initiative in Ayn al-Mryseh." Unpublished Paper.

Tabbarah, Riad. 1977. "Rural Development and Urbanization in Lebanon." *Population Bulletin of the United Nations*. Beirut: ECWA No. 4: 3–25.

Taky Deen, Diana. 1969. "Music in Lebanon." Beirut College for Women, ed. *Cultural Resources in Lebanon*. Beirut: Librairie du Liban.

Tamim, Suha. 1967. A *Bibliography of AUB Faculty Publications, 1866–1966*. Beirut: American University of Beirut.

Temperley, H.W.V. 1964. *England and the Near East, the Crimea*. London: Archon.

Terill, Andrew. 1987. "Low Intensity Conflict in Southern Lebanon: Lessons and Dynamics of the Israeli–Shi'ite War." *Conflict Quarterly* 7(3): 22–35.

Thayer, Charles. 1959. *Diplomat*. New York: Harper.

Tibawi, A. L. 1969. A *Modern History of Syria*. New York: St. Martins Press.

Thomson, Willam. 1886. *The Land and The Book; or Biblical Illustrations Drawn from the Manners, Customs, Scenes, and Scenery of the Holy Land*. Two Vols. New York.

Tilly, Charles. 1978. *From Mobilization to Revolution*. New York: Random House.

Toubi, Jamal 1980. "Social Dynamics in War-Torn Lebanon." *The Jerusalem Quarterly* no. 17 (Fall): 83–109.

Touraine, Alain. 1981. *The Voice of the Eye*. Cambridge: Cambridge University Press.

Tueni, Ghassan. 1958. *Al-Ayyam al 'Asibah*. Days of Crisis. Beirut: Dar al-Nahhar.

———. 1985. *Une Guerre Pour Les Autres*. Paris: J. C. Lattés

———. 1995. "Asrar al. Mehnah wa Asrarun Ukhrah" (Professional and Other Secrets). Beirut: Dar an Nahar.

Turner, Bryan. 1987. "A Note on Nostalgia." In *Theory, Culture and Society* Vol. 4. 1.

Al-Udhari, Abdullah. 1986. *Modern Poetry of the Arab World*. Harmondsworth: Penguin.

UNESCO 1985. UNESCO Statistical Yearbook.

Volkan, V. D. 1979. *Cyprus-War and Adaptation: A Psychoanalytic History of two Ethnic Groups in Conflict.* Charlottesville: University Press of Virginia.

———— 1985. "The Need to Have Enemies and Allies: A Developmental Approach." *Political Psychology.* 6(2): 219–247.

Volney, C.F. 1788. *Travels Through Syria and Egypt in the Years 1783, 1784 and 1785.* London: G.G.J. and J. Robinson.

Waines, David. 1976. "Civil War in Lebanon: The Anatomy of a Crisis." *International Perspectives* (January–February): 14–20.

Walzer, Michael. 1991. "The Idea of Civil Society." *Dissent* (Spring): 293–304.

Wills, Garry. 1990. "The Politics of Grievance" *New York Review of Books.* July 19

Williams, Robin. 1981. "Legitimate and Illegitimate Uses of Violence." In Gaylin, Macklin and Powledge, eds. *Violence and the Politics of Research.* New York: Plenum: 23–45.

Wilson, K. B. 1992. "Cults of Violence and Counter-Violence in Mozambique." *Journal of Southern African Studies* 18(3) (September): 527–82

Winslow, Charles. 1996. *Lebanon: War and Politics in a Fragmented Society.* London: Routledge.

Wirth, Louis. 1938. "Urbanism as a Way of Life." Reprinted in Richard Sennett, *Classic Essays on the Culture of Cities,* New York: Prentice Hall, 1969.

Wolf, E. R. 1971. "On Peasant Rebellions." In Teodor Shanin, ed., *Peasants and Peasant Societies.* Harmondsworth: Penguin.

Wriston, Walter. 1992. *Twilight of Sovereignty.* New York: Scribner's.

Yahya, Maha. 1993. "Reconstituting Space: The Aberration of the Urban in Beirut." In Samir Khalaf and Philip S. Khoury, eds. *Recovering Beirut.* Leiden: E. J. Brill: 128–66.

Yamak, L. Z. 1966. "Party Politics in the Lebanese Political System." In L. Binder, ed. *Politics in Lebanon.* New York: Wiley: 143–66.

Yamin, Muhsin. 1999. "Al-Orfilian: Photographers of Tripoli and their Pioneer Lenses." *Al-Nahar Supplement.* Beirut, January 9: 16–17

Yaniv, Avner. 1987. *Dilemmas of Security Politics, Strategy and the Israeli Experience in Lebanon.* New York and Oxford: Oxford University Press.

Yazbak, Yusuf, ed. 1955. *Awraq Lubnaniyyah,* 3 volumes. Beirut: n.p.

Zamir, Meir. 1982. "Politics and Violence in Lebanon." *The Jerusalem quarterly* no. 25. (Fall): 3–26.

————. 1985. *The Formation of Modern Lebanon.* Ithaca: Cornell University Press.

Zur, O. 1987 "The Psychohistory of Warfare: The Co-Evolution of Culture-Psyche and Enemy." *Journal of Peace Research* 24(2) 125–34.

Zureik, Elia. 1997. *Palestinian Refugees and the Peace Process.* Beirut: Institute of Palestine Studies.

Index